Concise Guide
to Legal Research
and Writing

ASPEN COLLEGE SERIES

Concise Guide to Legal Research and Writing

Second Edition

Deborah E. Bouchoux, Esq.
Georgetown University
Washington, D.C.

Printed in the United States of America.

1 2 3 4 5 6 7 8 9 0

ISBN 978-1-4548-2051-2

Library of Congress Cataloging-in-Publication Data

Bouchoux, Deborah E., 1950- author.
  Concise guide to legal research and writing / Deborah E. Bouchoux, Esq.,
Georgetown University, Washington, D.C.—Second edition.
    pages cm.—(Aspen college series)
  Includes bibliographical references and index.
  ISBN 978-1-4548-2051-2 (alk. paper)—ISBN 1-4548-2051-9 (alk. paper) 1.
Legal research--United States. 2. Legal composition. I. Title.
  KF240.B678 2014
  340.072'073--dc23
                                          2013038728

About Wolters Kluwer Law & Business

Wolters Kluwer Law & Business is a leading global provider of intelligent information and digital solutions for legal and business professionals in key specialty areas, and respected educational resources for professors and law students. Wolters Kluwer Law & Business connects legal and business professionals as well as those in the education market with timely, specialized authoritative content and information-enabled solutions to support success through productivity, accuracy and mobility.

Serving customers worldwide, Wolters Kluwer Law & Business products include those under the Aspen Publishers, CCH, Kluwer Law International, Loislaw, ftwilliam.com and MediRegs family of products.

CCH products have been a trusted resource since 1913, and are highly regarded resources for legal, securities, antitrust and trade regulation, government contracting, banking, pension, payroll, employment and labor, and healthcare reimbursement and compliance professionals.

Aspen Publishers products provide essential information to attorneys, business professionals and law students. Written by preeminent authorities, the product line offers analytical and practical information in a range of specialty practice areas from securities law and intellectual property to mergers and acquisitions and pension/benefits. Aspen's trusted legal education resources provide professors and students with high-quality, up-to-date and effective resources for successful instruction and study in all areas of the law.

Kluwer Law International products provide the global business community with reliable international legal information in English. Legal practitioners, corporate counsel and business executives around the world rely on Kluwer Law journals, looseleafs, books, and electronic products for comprehensive information in many areas of international legal practice.

Loislaw is a comprehensive online legal research product providing legal content to law firm practitioners of various specializations. Loislaw provides attorneys with the ability to quickly and efficiently find the necessary legal information they need, when and where they need it, by facilitating access to primary law as well as state-specific law, records, forms and treatises.

ftwilliam.com offers employee benefits professionals the highest quality plan documents (retirement, welfare and non-qualified) and government forms (5500/PBGC, 1099 and IRS) software at highly competitive prices.

MediRegs products provide integrated health care compliance content and software solutions for professionals in healthcare, higher education and life sciences, including professionals in accounting, law and consulting.

Wolters Kluwer Law & Business, a division of Wolters Kluwer, is headquartered in New York. Wolters Kluwer is a market-leading global information services company focused on professionals.

To the Kenney Clan

Summary of Contents

Contents   *xi*
Preface   *xxix*
Acknowledgments   *xxxv*

Section I Legal Research: Primary Authorities   **1**

Chapter 1   Finding the Law and Introduction to Legal Research   3
Chapter 2   The Federal and State Court Systems   19
Chapter 3   Statutory Law   39
Chapter 4   Case Law and Judicial Opinions   61
Chapter 5   Locating Cases Through Digests and Annotated Law
             Reports   95

Section II Legal Research: Secondary Authorities and Special Research Issues   **117**

Chapter 6   Secondary Authorities   119
Chapter 7   Special Research Issues   157

Section III Legal Research: Using Electronic and Computer Resources   **191**

Chapter 8   The Digital Library: Lexis, Westlaw, and
             Non-Print Research Tools   193
Chapter 9   E-Research: Legal Research Using the Internet   229

Section IV Legal Research: Citing and Validating the Authorities 249

Chapter 10   Legal Citation Form   251
Chapter 11   Updating and Validating Your Research   283

Section V Putting It Together: An Overview of the Research Process 307

Chapter 12   Overview of the Research Process   309

Section VI Legal Writing: Putting Your Research to Work 325

Chapter 13   The Basics of Legal Writing   327
Chapter 14   Strategies for Effective Writing   341
Chapter 15   Legal Correspondence   359
Chapter 16   Legal Memoranda   373
Chapter 17   Legal Briefs   387
Chapter 18   Proofreading and Document Design   401

Appendix A   Sample Legal Memorandum   415
Appendix B   Sample Brief for Court   423
Glossary   429
Index   443

Contents

Preface   *xxix*
Acknowledgments   *xxxv*

Section I
Legal Research:
Primary Authorities   1

Chapter 1   Finding the Law and Introduction to Legal Research   3

Chapter Overview   3
A.   The Importance of Legal Research   3
B.   The Ethical Duty to Research Accurately   4
C.   Law Libraries   4
     1.   Types of Law Libraries   4
     2.   Arrangement of Law Libraries   5
D.   Sources of Law in the United States   6
     1.   Cases and Our Common Law Tradition   6
     2.   Constitutions   7
     3.   Statutes   7
     4.   Administrative Regulations   8
     5.   Executive Branch   8
E.   Legal Systems of Other Countries   8
F.   Legal System of the United States   9
G.   Law Book Publishing   10
H.   Non-Print Research Media   12

I.   Change in Our Legal System   12
J.   Identifying the Holding in a Case   14
K.   How the Legal Research Process Works: A Research Scenario   14
L.   Case Citation Form   16
     Internet Resources   16
     Research Assignment   18
     Internet Assignment   18

Chapter 2   The Federal and State Court Systems   19

Chapter Overview   19
A.   Federalism   19
B.   Jurisdiction   20
     1.   Introduction   20
     2.   Federal Question Jurisdiction   20
     3.   Diversity Jurisdiction   20
     4.   Concurrent Jurisdiction   21
     5.   Exclusive Jurisdiction   22
C.   Ground Rules for Cases   22
D.   The Federal Court Structure   22
     1.   Introduction   22
     2.   United States District Courts   23
     3.   United States Courts of Appeal   26
     4.   United States Supreme Court   28
     5.   Specialized Courts   32
E.   State Courts   33
F.   Citation Form   35
     Internet Resources   35
     Research Assignment   37
     Internet Assignment   37

Chapter 3   Statutory Law   39

Chapter Overview   39
A.   Federal Legislation   39
     1.   Enactment of Federal Statutes   39
     2.   Classification of Federal Statutes   40
     3.   Publication of Federal Statutes   41
          a.   *United States Statutes at Large*   41
          b.   *United States Code*   41
          c.   Annotated Versions of the *United States Code*   43
          d.   Use of U.S.C., U.S.C.A., and U.S.C.S.   48

4. Research Techniques	48
a. Descriptive Word Approach	49
b. Title or Topic Approach	49
c. Popular Name Approach	49
5. United States Constitution	51
B. State Legislation	53
1. Introduction	53
2. Publication and Codification of State Statutes	53
3. Research Techniques	54
C. Rules of Procedure and Court Rules	55
1. Introduction	55
2. Federal Rules of Procedure	55
3. Federal Court Rules	56
4. State Rules of Procedure and Court Rules	56
D. Uniform and Model Laws	56
E. Statutory Research Overview	57
F. Citation Form	58
Internet Resources	58
Research Assignment	59
Internet Assignment	60

Chapter 4   Case Law and Judicial Opinions   61

Chapter Overview	61
A. Selective Publication of Cases	61
1. Standards for Publishing Cases	61
2. The Controversy Surrounding Unpublished Opinions	62
B. Elements of a Case	63
1. Case Name	63
2. Docket Number and Deciding Court	63
3. Date of Decision	67
4. Case Summary or Synopsis or Background	67
5. Headnotes	67
6. Names of Counsel	67
7. Opinion	67
8. Decision	69
C. Publication of Cases	69
1. Official and Unofficial Publication	69
2. Series of Case Reports	70
3. Advance Sheets	70
D. Publication of State Cases	70
1. West's *National Reporter System*	70
2. Citation Form	73
3. Discontinuation of Some Official Reports	74

E. Publication of Federal Cases   74
    1. United States Supreme Court Cases   74
    2. United States Courts of Appeal Cases   75
    3. United States District Court Cases   75
    4. Cases Interpreting Federal Rules   76
F. Star Paging   76
G. Specialized *National Reporter System* Sets   78
H. Features of West's *National Reporter System*   80
    1. Table of Cases Reported   80
    2. Tables of Statutes and Rules   80
    3. Table of Words and Phrases   82
    4. List of Judges   82
    5. Key Number System   82
I. Finding Parallel Citations   82
J. Briefing Cases   83
    1. Introduction and Purpose of Case Briefs   83
    2. Elements of Case Briefs   85
K. Citation Form   90
    Internet Resources   91
    Case Brief Assignment   92
    Research Assignment   92
    Internet Assignment   93

Chapter 5 Locating Cases Through Digests and Annotated Law Reports 95

Chapter Overview   95
A. Using Digests to Locate Cases   95
    1. Introduction   95
    2. West's *American Digest System*   96
    3. Organization of the *American Digest System*   96
    4. Locating a Topic and Key Number   97
        a. Descriptive Word Approach   98
        b. Topic Approach   98
        c. Table of Cases Approach   100
        d. "Case on Point" Approach   100
    5. Using Your Topic and Key Number to Find Cases   100
    6. Other West Digests   102
    7. Common Features of West's Digests   104
        a. Uniform Classification   104
        b. Descriptive Word Indexes   104
        c. Table of Cases   104
        d. Words and Phrases Volumes   105
        e. Supplementation   105
        f. Integrated Cross-Referencing   105

8.	Other Digests	106
B.	*American Law Reports*	107
1.	Introduction	107
2.	A.L.R. Organization	107
3.	Features of A.L.R.	108
4.	Finding A.L.R. Annotations	109
a.	Index or Descriptive Word Approach	109
b.	Digest Approach	109
c.	Miscellaneous Approaches	109
5.	Updating A.L.R. Annotations	112
a.	Updating Older A.L.R. Annotations	112
b.	Updating Newer A.L.R. Annotations	112
C.	Citation Form	112
	Internet Resources	113
	Research Assignment	114
	Internet Assignment	115

Section II
Legal Research: Secondary Authorities and Special Research Issues   117

Chapter 6   Secondary Authorities   119

	Chapter Overview	119
A.	Encyclopedias	119
1.	Introduction	120
2.	General or National Encyclopedias	120
a.	C.J.S.	120
b.	Am. Jur. 2d	120
c.	Features Common to C.J.S. and Am. Jur. 2d	121
d.	Research Strategies for Using National Encyclopedias	123
e.	The Am. Jur. Total Client-Service Library	123
3.	Local or State Encyclopedias	124
a.	Introduction	124
b.	Features Common to State Encyclopedias	124
c.	Research Strategies for Using State Encyclopedias	126
4.	Special Subject Encyclopedias	126
5.	Summary of Encyclopedias	126
B.	Legal Periodicals	127
1.	Introduction	127
2.	Law School Publications	127

3. Bar Association Publications 128
4. Specialized Publications 128
5. Legal Newspapers and Newsletters 130
6. How to Locate Periodical Articles 130
   a. Print Indexes 130
   b. Other Indexes 131
   c. Electronic Finding Aids 131
C. Texts and Treatises 134
   1. Introduction 134
   2. Common Features of Treatises 136
   3. Research Strategies for Using Treatises 136
D. Restatements 137
   1. Introduction 137
   2. Arrangement of Restatements 137
   3. Research Strategies for Using Restatements 138
E. Miscellaneous Secondary Authorities 138
   1. Attorneys General Opinions 138
   2. *Words and Phrases* 140
   3. Legal Dictionaries and Thesauri 140
   4. Legal Directories 141
      a. Introduction 141
      b. *Martindale-Hubbell Law Directory* 141
   5. Form Books 143
   6. Uniform Laws 144
   7. Looseleaf Services 145
   8. Jury Instructions 145
F. Summary of Secondary Authorities 146
G. Citation Form 151
   Internet Resources 152
   Research Assignment 153
   Internet Assignment 155

Chapter 7   Special Research Issues   157

Chapter Overview 157
A. Legislative History 157
   1. Introduction to Federal Legislative History Research 157
   2. Documents Used in Compiling a Federal Legislative History 158
   3. The Process of Compiling a Federal Legislative History: Three Approaches 159
      a. Using Conventional Print Sources to Compile a Legislative History 159
      b. Using Electronic Sources and the Internet to Compile a Legislative History 160
      c. Using Compiled Legislative Histories 161

4. Alternative Methods of Obtaining Legislative
   History for Federal Statutes 161
5. State Legislative Histories 163
   a. The Process of Compiling a State Legislative
      History 163
   b. Alternate Methods of Obtaining Legislative
      History for State Statutes 164
6. Tracking Pending Legislation 165
B. Executive Materials 166
   1. Proclamations 166
   2. Executive Orders 166
C. Administrative Law 167
   1. Introduction 167
   2. Publication of Federal Administrative Law 167
   3. Research Techniques for Administrative Law 168
      a. C.F.R. Indexes 168
      b. *Code of Federal Regulations Annotated* 169
      c. *Federal Register Index* 169
   4. Updating C.F.R. Regulations 169
      a. Step One: Review the *List of C.F.R.*
         Sections Affected 169
      b. Step Two: Review C.F.R. Parts Affected 169
   5. Electronic and Online Methods of Administrative
      Law Research 173
   6. Agency Decisions 173
   7. Federal Cases Reviewing Agency Decisions 174
   8. State Administrative Law 175
D. International Law 177
   1. Introduction 177
   2. Sources of International Law 177
   3. Overview of International Law Research Procedure 177
   4. Basic Texts and Sources 178
   5. Treaties 179
      a. Introduction 179
      b. Sources for Treaties 179
      c. Determining the Current Status of Treaties 180
      d. Interpreting Treaties 181
   6. International Tribunals 181
E. Municipal Law 182
   1. Introduction and Terminology 182
   2. Municipal Research Materials and Procedure 183
   3. Interpretation of Municipal Ordinances 183
   4. Municipal Research on the Internet 183
F. Citation Form 184
   Internet Resources 186
   Research Assignment 187
   Internet Assignment 189

Section III
Legal Research: Using
Electronic and Computer
Resources   191

Chapter 8   The Digital Library:
Lexis, Westlaw, and
Non-Print Research Tools   193

Chapter Overview   193
A.   Introduction to Computer-Assisted Legal Research   193
     1.   Lexis and Westlaw   193
     2.   Getting Started Using Lexis or Westlaw   195
     3.   Boolean Searching   195
     4.   Plain English Searching   197
B.   Lexis   198
     1.   Getting Started   198
     2.   Constructing a Search   200
          a.   Boolean Searching   200
          b.   Plain English Searching   201
          c.   Easy Search   201
          d.   Display of Search Results   202
     3.   Specialized Searches   202
          a.   Searching for Statutes and Constitutions   202
          b.   Searching for Cases   203
          c.   Searching for Administrative and Legislative
               Materials   203
          d.   Searching for Law Reviews and Journals   203
          e.   Searching for Secondary Authorities   204
     4.   Shepardizing   204
     5.   Other Lexis Features   204
     6.   Lexis Advance   205
     7.   Quick Review of Lexis   207
C.   Westlaw   207
     1.   Getting Started   207
     2.   Constructing a Search   209
          a.   Boolean Searching   209
          b.   Plain English Searching   210
          c.   Database Wizard   210
          d.   Display of Search Results   211
     3.   Specialized Searches   212
          a.   Searching for Statutes and Constitutions   212
          b.   Searching for Cases   212

    c. Searching for Administrative and Legislative Materials 212

    d. Searching for Law Reviews and Journals 213

    e. Searching for Secondary Authorities 213

  4. KeyCiting 213

  5. Other Westlaw Features 213

  6. WestlawNext 215

  7. Quick Review of Westlaw Classic 217

D. Final Pointers on Computer-Assisted Legal Research 218

  1. When to Use Lexis or Westlaw 218

  2. Limitations of Computer-Assisted Legal Research 219

E. Other Competitors in Electronic Research 219

F. Non-Print Research Tools 221

  1. Microforms 221

    a. Types of Microforms 221

    b. Summary of Microforms 222

  2. Sound Recordings 222

  3. CD-ROMs, DVDs, and eBooks 222

G. Citation Form 223

  Internet Resources 223

  Research Assignment for Lexis 224

  Research Assignment for Westlaw 225

  Research Assignment for LoislawConnect 227

  Internet Assignment 228

Chapter 9   E-Research: Legal Research Using the Internet   229

Chapter Overview 229

A. Introduction 229

B. Conducting Legal Research Online 231

  1. Getting Started 231

  2. Using a Good Start Page 231

  3. Strategies and Tips for Internet Legal Research 234

  4. Assessing the Credibility of Websites 235

C. Best Internet Legal Research Sites 237

  1. Top Sites for Locating Cases 237

  2. Top Three Sites for Locating Statutes 237

  3. Top Three Sites for Government Materials 238

  4. Top Three Sites for Locating Forms 238

  5. Best Specialty Sites 238

  6. Top Three Non-Legal Sites 241

  7. Tech Trends: Blogs, Apps, and More 241

D. Cautionary Notes on Internet Legal Research 243

E. Citation Form 245

  Internet Assignment 247

Section IV
Legal Research: Citing and
Validating the Authorities   249

Chapter 10   Legal Citation Form   251

Chapter Overview   251
A. Introduction to Citation Form   251
B. Citation Manuals   252
C. *The Bluebook*   252
    1. Introduction   252
    2. Typeface Conventions   254
D. *Bluebook* Citation Rules and Examples for Primary
    Authorities   255
    1. Cases   256
        a. Introduction   256
        b. Case Names   256
        c. Citation Form for State Court Cases   258
        d. Citation Form for Federal Cases   259
        e. Subsequent and Prior History   260
        f. Spacing in Citations   260
    2. Statutes   260
        a. Federal Statutes   260
        b. State Statutes   261
        c. Notes on Citing Statutes   261
    3. Court and Other Rules   261
    4. Constitutions   261
    5. Administrative Regulations   262
E. *Bluebook* Citation Form for Secondary Authorities   262
    1. A.L.R. Annotations   262
    2. Encyclopedias   262
    3. Periodicals   262
    4. Texts and Treatises   263
    5. Restatements   263
    6. Attorneys General Opinions   263
    7. Dictionaries   263
    8. Uniform Laws   263
    9. Looseleaf Services   263
F. *ALWD* Citation Rules and Examples for Primary Authorities   264
    1. Cases   264
        a. Introduction   264
        b. Federal Cases   265
        c. State Cases   265
        d. Subsequent and Prior History   265
        e. Spacing in Citations   266

	2.	Statutes	266
		a. Federal Statutes	266
		b. State Statutes	266
	3.	Court and Other Rules	266
	4.	Constitutions	267
	5.	Administrative Regulations	267
G.		*ALWD* Rules and Examples for Secondary Authorities	267
	1.	A.L.R. Annotations	267
	2.	Encyclopedias	267
	3.	Periodical Materials	267
	4.	Texts and Treatises	267
	5.	Restatements	268
	6.	Attorneys General Opinion	268
	7.	Dictionaries	268
	8.	Uniform Laws	268
	9.	Looseleaf Services	268
H.		Special Citation Issues (*Bluebook* and *ALWD*)	269
	1.	Introduction	269
	2.	Punctuation	269
	3.	Quotations	270
		a. Introduction to Pinpoints	270
		b. Indicating Quotations in Text	271
		c. Altering Quotations and Using Ellipses	271
	4.	Citation Signals	271
	5.	Short-Form Citations	272
		a. Use of *Id.*	272
		b. Use of *Supra*	273
		c. Short Forms for Cases	273
		d. Short Forms for Statutes	274
	6.	Neutral Citation Format	274
	7.	Capitalization Rules	275
	8.	Electronic Sources	276
	9.	Lexis and Westlaw Assistance for Citation Form	277
		Internet Resources	278
		Citation Form Assignment	279
		Memorandum Assignment	280
		Internet Assignment	281

Chapter 11   Updating and Validating Your Research   283

		Chapter Overview	283
A.		Using *Shepard's* in Print Form to Shepardize Cases	283
	1.	Introduction	283
	2.	Locating *Shepard's* References to Your Case	284
	3.	Analysis of *Shepard's* References	284
		a. Abbreviations	284

b. History References   286
c. Treatment References   286
4. Arrangement of Later Case References   286
5. References to Headnotes   287
6. References to Sources Other Than Cases   287
7. FAQs: Using *Shepard's* and Analyzing Negative Letters   288
B. Using *Shepard's* in Print Form to Shepardize Other Authorities   290
1. Sheparding Statutes, Constitutions, and
Administrative Regulations   290
2. Sheparding Other Authorities   291
C. Electronic Updating of Legal Authorities   291
1. Introduction to Electronic Updating   291
2. Sheparding Online   291
a. How to Shepardize Cases Online Using Lexis   291
b. Features of *Shepard's* Online   293
c. Sheparding Statutes and Regulations Online   294
d. Other *Shepard's* Products   294
3. KeyCite   295
a. How to KeyCite Cases Using Westlaw   295
b. Features of KeyCite   295
c. KeyCiting Statutes and Regulations   297
d. Other West Products   298
4. Comparing Sheparding Online with KeyCiting   298
5. Other Electronic Citator Services   299
6. Summary   300
Internet Resources   301
Research Assignment Using Print Volumes of *Shepard's*   302
Research Assignment Using *Shepard's* on Lexis   302
Research Assignment Using KeyCite on Westlaw   303
Research Assignment Comparing Sheparding Online
with KeyCiting   304
Internet Assignment   304

Section V
Putting It Together: An
Overview of the Research
Process   307

Chapter 12   Overview of the
Research Process   309

Chapter Overview   309
A. How to Begin   309

1.	Introduction	309
2.	Thinking Things Through	310
3.	Narrowing Down the Possibilities	310
B.	Tackling the Project	312
C.	Working with the Authorities	315
1.	Note-Taking	315
2.	Staying Focused	316
D.	When to Stop	316
1.	Practical Considerations	317
2.	Complex Projects	317
3.	Quick Questions	318
4.	Established Issues	318
5.	Newly Emerging Issues	318
6.	Issues of First Impression	319
7.	How Many Authorities Are Enough?	319
8.	Ten Tips for Effective Legal Research	321
	Internet Resources	322
	Research Assignment	323
	Internet Assignment	323

Section VI
Legal Writing: Putting Your Research to Work 325

Chapter 13   The Basics of Legal Writing 327

	Chapter Overview	327
A.	Grammar	327
1.	Introduction	327
2.	Subject-Verb Agreement	327
a.	Multiple Word Subjects and Indefinite Pronouns	328
b.	Collective Nouns	328
c.	Intervening Words	329
d.	Prepositional Phrases	329
3.	Run-on Sentences	329
4.	Modifiers	330
5.	Split Infinitives	330
6.	Dangling Participles	330
7.	Pronouns	331
a.	Personal Pronouns	331
b.	Using the Pronouns That, Which, and It	331
c.	Gender-Linked Pronouns	332

B.	Spelling	332
C.	Punctuation	333
	1. Introduction	333
	2. Commas	334
	3. Apostrophes	334
	4. Quotation Marks	336
	5. Hyphens	336
	Internet Resources	337
	Assignment	338
	Internet Assignment	339

Chapter 14   Strategies for Effective Writing   341

	Chapter Overview	341
A.	Introduction	341
B.	Precision	342
	1. Word Choice	342
	2. Vague Words	344
	3. Word Connotation	345
C.	Clarity	345
	1. Elegant Variation	345
	2. Negatives	345
	3. Word Order	346
D.	Readability	346
	1. Prefer the Active Voice	347
	2. Use Lists	347
	3. Avoid Nominalizations	348
	4. Avoid Legal Jargon	348
	5. Keep Subjects and Verbs in Proximity	349
E.	Brevity	350
	1. Omit Needless Words	350
	2. Avoid Redundancy	350
F.	Drafting Techniques	351
	1. Getting Started	351
	2. Finishing on Time	351
	3. Using a Word Processor	352
G.	Electronic Communications	352
	1. Phones and Voice Mail	353
	2. Communication by Facsimile	353
	3. E-mail	353
	4. Text Messaging	354
	Internet Resources	355
	Assignment	356
	Internet Assignment	357

Chapter 15   Legal Correspondence   359

Chapter Overview   359
A.   Letterwriting   359
     1.   Introduction   359
          a.   Who Will Be Reading This Letter?   360
          b.   What Will This Letter Say?   360
     2.   The Elements of Letters   360
     3.   Format Considerations for Letters   361
     4.   Types of Letters   362
          a.   General Correspondence   362
          b.   Demand Letters   363
          c.   Opinion Letters   366
B.   Conclusion   369
     Internet Resources   370
     Assignment   371
     Internet Assignment   371

Chapter 16   Legal Memoranda   373

Chapter Overview   373
A.   Objectivity of Legal Memoranda   373
B.   Format of Legal Memoranda   374
     1.   Heading   374
     2.   Issue(s) or Question(s) Presented   374
     3.   Brief Answer(s)   375
     4.   Statement of Facts   376
     5.   Applicable Statutes (Optional)   377
     6.   Analysis or Discussion   377
     7.   Conclusion   381
C.   A Blueprint for Preparing a Memorandum   382
     Internet Resources   384
     Legal Memorandum Assignment   385
     Internet Assignment   385

Chapter 17   Legal Briefs   387

Chapter Overview   387
A.   Introduction   387
B.   Five Tips for Effective Briefs   388
     1.   Be Persuasive   388
     2.   Be Concise   388
     3.   Use a Thesis Statement   389
     4.   Be Honest   389

5. Know the Rules   390
C. Trial Court Briefs   390
    1. Introduction   390
    2. Elements of a Trial Court Brief   391
        a. Caption   391
        b. Introductory Statement   391
        c. Statement of Facts   391
        d. Argument   392
        e. Conclusion   393
        f. Signature and Date   393
        g. Certificates of Service and Compliance   393
        h. Exhibits   393
        i. Order   393
D. Appellate Briefs   394
E. Ten Pointers for Effective Brief Writing   396
    Internet Resources   397
    Court Brief Assignment   398
    Table of Authorities Assignment   398
    Internet Assignment   399

Chapter 18   Proofreading and Document Design   401

Chapter Overview   401
A. Reviewing and Revising: Stage One   401
B. Reviewing and Revising: Stage Two   403
    1. Needless Words and Phrases   403
    2. Legalese   403
    3. Passive Voice   403
C. Proofreading   403
D. Proofreading Projects by Others   406
E. Proofreaders' Marks   406
F. Document Design   406
    1. Paper   408
    2. Typeface   408
    3. Type Size   409
    4. Length of Document   409
    5. Headings   410
    6. Quotations and Lists   411
G. The Final Review   411

H. Conclusion   411
    Internet Resources   412
    Assignment   413
    Internet Assignment   413

    Appendix: A Sample Legal Memorandum   *415*
    Appendix: B Sample Brief for Court   *423*

    Glossary   *429*
    Index   *443*

Preface

Introduction

Legal research. Legal research is likely the most "hands on" subject you will take in the course of your legal education. Although numerous books discuss research methods and techniques, there is no substitute for actually performing the task of legal research. Thus, you will learn the most about legal research only by *doing* legal research.

Today's legal research projects are simultaneously easier and more difficult than they were years ago. They are easier because there are numerous sources for researchers to consult (including conventional print sources, the computerized legal research systems such as Lexis and Westlaw, and the Internet), and they are more difficult for the same reasons. There are so many sources to consult that deciding where to begin and what resources to use calls for careful analysis of the quality of sources and the economics of a research project so you can obtain the best answer to a legal question in the most efficient manner and at the lowest cost to the client.

To that end, library assignments are placed at the conclusion of each chapter so you can see and use the books discussed in each chapter. Similarly, each chapter includes an Internet Assignment, requiring you to locate information pertinent to the chapter by accessing well-known Internet sites.

Performing legal research can be both frustrating and gratifying. It can be frustrating because there is often no one perfect answer and because there are no established guidelines on how much research to do and when to stop. On the other hand, legal research is gratifying because you will be engaged in a task that requires you to *do* something and one in which you will be rewarded by finding the right case, statute, or other authority.

View legal research as an exciting treasure hunt—a search for the best authorities to answer a question or legal issue. In this sense, the task of using and exploring the law library, Lexis or Westlaw, or the Internet for answers to legal issues or questions should be a welcome relief from the assignments of other classes, which may be passive in nature and involve copious amounts of reading. Take the time to explore the books by reviewing the foreword, table of contents, and index found in each volume. Familiarize yourself with all of the features of the books or electronic resources you use, and you will simplify your legal research.

Consider researching with other students if you are comfortable doing so. Often you will learn a great deal by comparing notes with others who may be able to share successful strategies for effectively using various resources or finding the answers to research problems. Naturally, sharing ideas and tips for research techniques should not be viewed as an excuse not to do the work yourself or a license to use answers discussed by others. In other words, you should research with other students (if you find it useful to do so), but you should never share or copy answers from others. Not only is this practice dishonest, but it will prevent you from effectively learning the skill of legal research. Ultimately, an employer is not interested in how many "points" you obtained on a class exercise or what grade you obtained in a class, but in whether you can be depended upon to research an issue competently.

Legal writing. The legal profession rests on communication and requires its professionals not only to know the law but also to write about it. Legal writing takes many forms. Some documents, such as internal office memoranda, are intended to explain the law to the reader. Other documents, such as court briefs, are intended to persuade the reader. No matter what the form of the document, however, it must be accurate, clearly presented, readable, and concise.

The good news is that good legal writing is simply good writing. It should not differ greatly from other forms of writing. On the other hand, there are some quirks to legal writing that deserve special attention. Legal writing is more formal than other forms of writing. For example, the use of contractions is rare, and the use of the personal pronouns *I*, *we*, and *our* is uncommon (because the focus of most legal documents is on the client's position, not on the writer's opinions).

The writing chapters in this text are designed to be a thorough guide that legal writers can use to answer not only the "big" writing questions (such as determining the elements of a court brief) but the many "small" questions that continually occur during the writing process (such as when a comma precedes the words *and* and *but* and when a writer should indent quotations).

Writing is a skill that you can master by repeated practice. If you are inexperienced at writing, keep practicing. Enjoy writing and understand that your writing not only says something about the topic you discuss but also something about you. Make sure your finished project is understood by the reader and reflects well on you.

Structure of the Text

You will be expected "to hit the ground running" when you get a job, yet there is often a significant gap between what is learned in the classroom and the way to apply this knowledge in the real world of a law office environment. *Concise Guide to Legal Research and Writing* is meant to bridge this gap by combining a thorough grounding in legal research with a pragmatic approach to the types of legal research and writing assignments you will find in the "real world."

The text is divided into six main sections: The first section begins with a review of the American legal system and discusses the primary authorities used in legal research (namely, cases, constitutions, and statutes that are binding on courts); the second section covers the secondary sources used in legal research that are used to comment upon, explain, and help you locate the primary sources; the third section focuses on computer-assisted legal research using Lexis, Westlaw, and the Internet; the fourth section covers citation form for the authorities previously introduced and how to ensure that these sources are still "good law"; the fifth section provides an overview of the legal research process, discussing how to begin and end research projects; and the sixth section covers legal writing so you can put your research to work.

Each chapter and section builds on the previous one. For example, once you read Chapter 2's discussion of the federal and state court structure, you will be ready to understand Chapter 3's discussion on reading cases that interpret statutes, paying special attention to cases from higher courts. Similarly, once you read Chapter 4 and understand the elements of cases and how they are published, you will be ready for the discussion in Chapter 5 about how to locate cases using digests. The chapters on writing begin with the mechanics of writing: grammar, punctuation, and spelling. Once a writer has mastered or reviewed these basics, the writer will be ready to address the characteristics of effective legal writing and how to prepare various legal documents.

Features of the Text

The text includes a number of features to enhance learning. Each chapter includes the following features:

- **Chapter Overview.** Each chapter begins with a preview of the material that will be presented in the chapter.
- **Key Terms.** The key terms and concepts used in the chapter are presented in italics and are defined in the Glossary at the end of the text.
- **Practice Tips.** Most chapters include one or more pragmatic practice tips, linking the material in the chapter to "real-world" experience.
- **Ethics Alerts.** Most chapters include an ethics note or comment relating to the material discussed in the chapter.
- **Help Lines.** Nearly all chapters include at least one "go to" reference source, giving a telephone number or website to call or refer to for additional information on the material discussed in the chapter.
- **Internet Resources:** At the conclusion of each chapter, websites are given where you can locate additional information on

the topics covered in the chapter. Although every effort has been made to refer to useful websites, those sites can change both their content and addresses without notice. References to websites are not endorsements of those sites.

- **Research Assignments.** Each chapter includes questions requiring you to use the sets of books or other resources discussed in that chapter. You should never have to use a book or set of books that have not been discussed in the chapter you have read or a preceding chapter.
- **Internet Assignments.** Each chapter includes a series of practical questions that require readers to locate information pertinent to the chapter by accessing well-known legal or general-usage Internet sites.
- **Citation Form.** Each chapter demonstrates citation form for the resources discussed in that chapter, in both *Bluebook* and *ALWD* form, in a simple chart format, showing that in many instances the citation form in *The Bluebook* and in *ALWD* are the same. All citations in *Bluebook* form are displayed in the format used by practitioners, not in the "large and small cap" format used for law review articles and journals. When only one citation is given in the text, it is given in *Bluebook* form. Citations comply with *The Bluebook: A Uniform System of Citation* (Columbia Law Review Ass'n et al. eds., 19th ed. 2010) and ALWD & Darby Dickerson, *ALWD Citation Manual* (4th ed., Aspen Publishers 2010).

Each chapter also includes charts, graphs, sample forms, and other instructional aids, as needed. For example, Chapter 4 includes a chart showing commonly used abbreviations for legal resources, Chapter 8 includes a chart comparing the terms and connectors used by Lexis and Westlaw, and Chapter 11 includes a Frequently Asked Questions section on Shepardizing.

This second edition of the text provides several new features, including the following:

- Chapter 3 (Statutory Law) includes a discussion of new Title 51 (National and Commercial Space Programs) added to the U.S. Code and a discussion of a new website Congress.gov, the successor to THOMAS, used for finding legislative materials.
- Chapter 6 (Secondary Authorities) revamps the discussion of legal periodicals and journals with additional emphasis on the use of electronic finding aids to locate pertinent articles.
- Chapter 7 (Special Research Issues) includes a revised section on conducting legislative history research, with particular emphasis on using public domain websites to construct a legislative history.
- Chapter 8 (The Digital Library) explains the following new features in computer-assisted legal research:

- Lexis's new research platform, Lexis Advance, which mimics the ease of "Google"-like searching.
- Lexis Advance's combined searching of Lexis content and the Internet using Lexis Web.
- Lexis Communities, which provide free access to blogs, podcasts, and more.
- West's new, easy-to-use, and intuitive platform WestlawNext, which allows searching similar to "Google"-type searching and its useful features, including Citation Preferences, for assistance with citation form.
- Information on new entrants into the field of computer-assisted legal research, including Fastcase, Casemaker, and Bloomberg Law.
- Information on new law-related Apps and eBooks.
- Chapter 10 (Citation Form) includes new information on citation form, including the offering of *The Bluebook* as an App and the use of WestlawNext for assistance on citation form.
- Chapter 14 (Effective Writing) provides enhanced information on electronic communications such as e-mailing and text messaging.
- All new Discussion Questions and Internet Legal Research Assignments.

Additionally, new Practice Tips, websites, and sample documents are included as needed, such as a Practice Tip in Chapter 18 on the use of Style Sheets in editing and proofreading. Reflecting the continuing and dramatic effect of the Internet on legal research and the ever-increasing accessibility of resources in cyberspace, new websites and blog sites are provided, and links for web-based tutorials are given when applicable. Chapter 12 (which provides an overview of the legal research process) includes a full range of open-ended research questions, requiring readers to use and apply all skills learned in previous chapters to obtain answers to these research questions.

Textbook Resources

Instructor resources to accompany this text include a comprehensive Instructor's Manual, Test Bank, and PowerPoint slides. All of these resources are available for download at the companion website for this text, at www.aspenparalegal.com/bouchoux_concise. This text also comes packaged with four months of prepaid access to LoislawConnect's online legal research database at http://www.loislawschool.com.

Final Thoughts

When you begin reading this book, most of you will be unfamiliar with cases, statutes, constitutions, or the numerous other legal authorities. As you advance in class and complete the assignments in the text, you will readily be able to measure your progress. When you complete this text and your legal research and writing class, you will have gained thorough mastery of both legal research and writing techniques to ensure you can locate the legal authorities you need and then use them to make your legal writings accurate, clear, readable, and concise.

Deborah E. Bouchoux, Esq.

Fall 2013

Acknowledgments

I would like to express my sincere appreciation to the many individuals who contributed to the development of this text. First, as always, I would like to thank Susan M. Sullivan, Director at the University of San Diego Paralegal Program. Sue gave me my first teaching position many years ago, and I value and respect her many contributions to the legal profession.

Many thanks also to the various reviewers who reviewed the manuscript on behalf of the publisher. Their comments and advice were instructive and insightful. Throughout the more than 20 years I have taught legal research, I have received valuable comments and feedback from my students, who have offered their comments and insight regarding methods of teaching and productive legal research assignments.

Finally, my sincere appreciation to the following individuals at Aspen Publishers: Betsy Kenny, Developmental Editor, and David Herzig, Associate Publisher, College Market, who suggested this text and worked with me on its development. Thank you also to Christine Hannan, Managing Editor, Legal Education. A special thank you to Carol McGeehan, Publisher, and Richard Mixter, Director, Digital Development. Finally, thank you to Sylvia Rebert, Project Manager, and her team at Progressive Publishing Alternatives. All members of the Aspen Publishers team offered encouragement and support throughout the writing and production phases of this text. Their thoughtful comments and suggestions were much appreciated and greatly contributed to the text.

I would also like to acknowledge the following who permitted me to reproduce copyrighted material for this text.

Chapter 3: Statutory Law

Figure 3-2: Reprinted with permission of Thomson Reuters from Title 35 of U.S.C.A.

Figure 3-4: Reprinted with permission of Thomson Reuters from General Index to U.S.C.A.

Figure 3-5: Reprinted with permission of Thomson Reuters from U.S.C.A. Popular Name Table.

Figure 3-6: Va. Code Ann. § 18.2-256. Reprinted with permission of Thomson Reuters.

Chapter 4: Case Law and Judicial Opinions

Figure 4-1: Reprinted with permission of Thomson Reuters from 595 S.E.2d 697.

Figure 4-4: Reprinted with permission from 33 L. Ed. 2d 238, 263 from LexisNexis.

Figure 4-5: Reprinted with permission of Thomson Reuters from 32 F.3d XVII and L.

Chapter 5: Locating Cases Though Digests and Annotated Law Reports

Figure 5-2: Reprinted with permission of Thomson Reuters from *Descriptive Word Index to Ninth Decennial Digest, Part 2.*

Figure 5-3: Reprinted with permission of Thomson Reuters from 29 *Ninth Decennial Digest, Part 2.*

Figure 5-4: Reprinted with permission of Thomson Reuters from 29 *Ninth Decennial Digest, Part 2.*

Figure 5-5: Reprinted with permission of Thomson Reuters from *American Law Reports.*

Figure 5-6: Reprinted with permission of Thomson Reuters from Index to *American Law Reports.*

Chapter 6: Secondary Authorities

Figure 6-1: Reprinted with permission of Thomson Reuters from 25 Am. Jur. 2d.

Figure 6-3: Reprinted with permission of the publisher, California Western Law Review, Vol. 44, Number 1, Fall 2007, copyright © 2007.

Figure 6-4: *Index to Legal Periodicals and Books*, volume 43, page 22 (Ipswich, MA: H. W. Wilson, a division of EBSCO Information Services, 2004.) Reproduced by permission of the publisher.

Figure 6-5: Reprinted with permission of Thomson Reuters from *McCarthy on Trademarks and Unfair Competition* § 11:32.

Figure 6-7: Restatement, Second, Contracts, copyright © 1981 by the American Law Institute. Reproduced with permission. All rights reserved.

Figure 6-8: *Virginia Forms* Form 9-1002, by Frank J. Gallo, reprinted with the permission of LexisNexis.

Chapter 8: The Digital Library: LexisNexis, Westlaw, and Non-Print Research Tools

Figure 8-2: Reprinted with the permission of LexisNexis.

Figure 8-3: Reprinted with the permission of LexisNexis.

Figure 8-4: Reprinted with permission of LexisNexis.

Figure 8-5: Reprinted with permission of LexisNexis.

Figure 8-6: Reprinted with permission of Thomson Reuters

Figure 8-7: Reprinted with permission of Thomson Reuters.

Figure 8-8: Reprinted with permission of Thomson Reuters.

Figure 8-9: Reprinted with permission of Thomson Reuters.

Chapter 9: E-Research: Legal Research Using the Internet

Figure 9-1: Reprinted with permission from FindLaw, a Thomson Reuters company.

Figure 9-2: Reprinted with permission from Justia.

Chapter 11: Updating and Validating Your Authorities
Figure 11-1: Reprinted with the permission of LexisNexis.
Figure 11-3: Reprinted with the permission of LexisNexis.
Figure 11-4: Reprinted with permission from Thomson Reuters.

No copyright is claimed in any material owned by the United States Government, including material shown in Figures 2-3, 7-1, 7-2, 7-3, or 9-3.

Legal
Research

Primary Authorities

Finding the Law and Introduction to Legal Research

Chapter Overview

This chapter discusses the role of legal professionals in legal research, the ethical duty to perform research competently, types of law libraries and their uses, and the sources of law in the United States. The chapter also examines the classification of law books as either primary or secondary sources. Finally, there is a brief introduction to the major law book publishers.

A. The Importance of Legal Research

Legal professionals are expected to perform the task of legal research competently and cost effectively. Performing legal research today is both easier and more difficult than it was just a generation ago. It is easier because many materials are available through electronic sources and the Internet, making it quick and easy to find statutes, cases, and other legal authorities. At the same time, it is more difficult because these new media make so many sources accessible that tracking down the right authority can seem like finding a needle in a haystack.

Today's legal researchers are expected to know how and when to use conventional print sources, the computer-assisted research services Lexis and Westlaw, and the Internet to find the best answer to a research question as quickly and effectively as possible.

B. The Ethical Duty to Research Accurately

Perhaps the most fundamental aspect of the attorney–client relationship is the client's absolute trust and confidence in the attorney's competence. In fact, Rule 1.1 of the American Bar Association's Model Rules of Professional Conduct requires that attorneys provide competent representation, meaning the legal knowledge, skill, thoroughness, and preparation necessary for the representation.

Although it is important to *know* the law, particularly in a field in which you may intend to specialize, it is even more important to be able to *find* the law. In this sense, proficiency in legal research is the foundation for a successful legal career. Your employer will not be as interested in your final grade in any specific class as much as your ability to find accurate answers to questions relating to topics, even though you may not have been exposed to those topics in school.

In fact, the duty to perform accurate legal research has been addressed in a number of cases. For example, *People v. Ledesma*, 729 P.2d 839, 871 (Cal. 1987), held that an attorney's first duty is to investigate the facts of a client's case and to research the law applicable to those facts. Moreover, the failure to research adequately may lead to liability for legal malpractice. In *Smith v. Lewis*, 530 P.2d 589 (Cal. 1975), *overruled on other grounds*, 544 P.2d 561 (Cal. 1976), the California Supreme Court affirmed a lower court decision requiring an attorney to pay $100,000 to a former client because the attorney's research was inadequate. In sum, you will be expected to perform competent legal research not only because your employer will insist on it but also because ethical standards demand it.

C. Law Libraries

1. Types of Law Libraries

As noted in the preface to this text, legal research is a "hands-on" skill, requiring you to know how to use a law library. Your first task, therefore, is to locate a law library that you may use. There are approximately 3,600 law libraries in the United States. Following is a list of the most common types of law libraries:

• **Law School Libraries.** All accredited law schools have their own law libraries, most of which will have tens of thousands of volumes in print and nonprint forms. Many law school libraries are open only to their students. In a newer trend, many law libraries offer research tutorials and guides on their websites.

- **Federal Depository Libraries.** More than 1,250 libraries throughout the nation have been designated as *Federal Depository Libraries*, meaning that certain U.S. government publications, such as statutes and cases, will be sent to the library for access by the public. In many instances, local public libraries, law school libraries, or university libraries are designated as federal depositories. The location of the depository library nearest you can be found at http://www.gpoaccess.gov/libraries.html.
- **Local Law Libraries.** Often, a county or city will maintain a law library (typically near a courthouse), and these are usually open to the public. The American Association of Law Libraries provides a list of state, county, and court law libraries at http://www.aallnet.org/sections/sccll/membership/Member-Libraries.html.
- **Courthouse Law Libraries.** Many courts, both federal and state, maintain their own law libraries. Some law libraries are open to the public while others restrict access to courthouse personnel, attorneys, and their paralegals.
- **Law Firm Libraries.** Almost every law firm will maintain a law library. Large law firms maintain extensive collections. These law libraries are available for use only by employees of the firm.

To find a law library, consult a telephone book or use a general Internet search engine such as Google and call law schools, courthouses, and county offices in your area to determine library policy on use.

Additionally, law libraries exist in computer databases such as those offered by Lexis or Westlaw. In fact, these computer-assisted legal research services offer far more resources than most legal professionals could afford to maintain on their own. Finally, law libraries now exist in cyberspace with vast collections of legal materials available for free "24/7." These virtual law libraries afford quick and easy access to a significant number of legal resources, as discussed in detail in Chapter 9. See "Internet Resources" at the end of this chapter for a list of some websites that provide research guides and tutorials.

2. *Arrangement of Law Libraries*

There is no one standard arrangement for law libraries. Each law library is arranged according to the needs of its patrons. Spend an hour browsing the shelves and familiarizing yourself with the law library's arrangement, organization, and collections. The law library's website may also offer a "virtual" tour.

Few law libraries offer a conventional print card catalog (identical in its alphabetical arrangement to the card catalogs you may have been introduced to in grade school) to help you locate the books you need. The more modern approach is the online catalog or OPAC (online public access catalog). Simply type in or "enter" the title, author, or subject matter you desire in the search box displayed on the screen, and you will then be given the "call number." The shelves or *stacks* in the law library are clearly marked, and locating a book is merely a matter of matching up the call number provided by the card or online catalog with the appropriate stack label.

Ethics Alert

Library Courtesy

Assume that everyone who uses the law library is as busy as you are. Observe standard library etiquette by reshelving properly every book you use (unless the law library has a preshelving area for books that are to be reshelved). Do not deface books by turning pages down or marking in them. Do not resort to unfair conduct by hiding or intentionally misplacing books. There is no excuse for such overzealous tactics that not only impede learning but also reflect poorly on one who is joining the legal profession.

Practice Tip

Legal Abbreviations

In the beginning of your legal career, you may become confused by the numerous abbreviations used for legal books, case reports, and journals. To determine the meaning of abbreviations such as "Ala." for *Alabama Reports* or "C.J.S." for *Corpus Juris Secundum*, check Appendix A in *Black's Law Dictionary* (9th ed. 2009), which provides an extensive list of abbreviations commonly used in law. Additionally, be patient. Within just a few weeks you will probably know about 90 percent of all of the abbreviations you are likely to encounter. See Chapter 4 for a list of some other common legal abbreviations.

Law libraries are non-circulating libraries, meaning that few materials may be checked out by patrons. Your law library may offer other services, such as allowing you to reserve a room for group projects or to hold materials in a carrel.

D. Sources of Law in the United States

1. Cases and Our Common Law Tradition

The American legal system is part of what is referred to as the "common law" tradition. *Common law* is defined in part by *Black's Law Dictionary*

313 (9th ed. 2009) as that body of law that derived from judicial decisions rather than from statutes or constitutions.

In early English cases, people training to be lawyers began "taking notes" on what occurred during trials. When judges were called upon to decide cases, they then began referring to these written reports of earlier cases and following the prior cases in similar situations. The English referred to this system as the "common law" because it was applied equally throughout England and replaced a less uniform system of law.

This concept of following previous cases, or precedents, is called *stare decisis*, which is a Latin phrase meaning "to stand by things decided." Broadly, the doctrine of stare decisis means that once courts have announced a principle of law, they will follow it in future cases that are substantially similar. It is this doctrine of stare decisis that serves to protect litigants from inexperienced or biased judges. Moreover, stare decisis encourages stability in our judicial system because it promotes uniform and predictable rulings.

Under this system of precedent following, "the law" was thus found in the written decisions of the judges, and these decisions served as precedents that were followed in later cases involving substantially similar issues. Thus, the first source of law in the United States is judge-made case law.

2. *Constitutions*

A second source of law in the United States is constitutions. A *constitution* sets forth the fundamental law for a nation or a state. It is the document that provides the principles relating to organization and regulation of a federal or state government. We have a United States Constitution, our supreme law of the land (and which establishes the framework for our government by creating the legislative branch, the presidency, and the judiciary), and each state has its own individual constitution.

3. *Statutes*

A *statute*, or law, is defined by *Black's Law Dictionary* 1542 (9th ed. 2009) as "a law passed by a legislative body." In the United States, legislatures did not become particularly active in enacting statutes until the early to mid-1800s, when our economy began changing from a very rural one to a more urban one. This major change in American society was coupled with a tremendous population growth, and it became clear that rather than having a system in which disputes were decided on a case-by-case basis, which was slow and cumbersome at best, enacting broader laws that would provide rules to govern public behavior would best serve the needs of a growing society.

4. *Administrative Regulations*

A fourth source of law in the United States is found in the vast number of *administrative rules* or *regulations* promulgated by federal and state agencies such as the Food and Drug Administration or the Iowa Labor Services Division.

The agencies play a unique role in our legal system because they function quasi-legislatively and quasi-judicially. You may recall from basic history classes that our government is divided into three branches: the legislative branch, which makes laws; the judicial branch, which interprets laws; and the executive branch, which enforces laws. Each exercises its own powers, and, by a system usually called "checks and balances," each functions separately from the others.

The agencies, on the other hand, perform two functions: They act like a legislature by promulgating rules and regulations that bind us; and they act like a judiciary by hearing disputes and rendering decisions.

5. *Executive Branch*

Although the primary function of the federal executive branch is to enforce the law, it serves as a source of law itself in three ways. First, treaties are entered into by the executive branch with the advice and consent of the U.S. Senate. Second, the President, our chief executive, can issue executive orders to regulate and direct federal agencies and officials. State governors may also issue executive orders. Third, the executive branch exerts influence on the law through policies on enforcing laws. For example, if federal laws relating to possession of small amounts of drugs are rarely enforced, the effect is as if the law does not exist, despite the fact that a statute clearly prohibits such acts. Nevertheless, although such an approach by the executive branch influences the law as well as societal behavior, such influence on the law is indirect and remote. In the event the government prosecutes an individual for violation of a previously unenforced law, the individual usually may not raise the previous laxity as a defense.

E. Legal Systems of Other Countries

Although every country has its own system of law, most systems are classified as either being part of the common law tradition, described previously, or part of the civil law tradition. *Civil law* systems developed from Roman law, which followed a comprehensive set of codes. In general, civil law countries place much heavier reliance on their collections of statutes than on their much smaller collections of cases. China, France, Germany, Italy, Japan, Mexico, the Russian Federation, South Korea, Spain, and many of the countries of Latin and South America and Africa are civil law countries. Typically, English-speaking countries or those that are prior British Commonwealth colonies are part of the common law system (and are greatly dependent on cases used as precedents), whereas non-English-speaking countries are usually part of the civil law system (which is greatly dependent on codes or statutes). In practice, however, even in many countries with systems based on civil law, case law still plays a significant role. Table T.2 of *The Bluebook* identifies more than 40 foreign countries as either common law or civil law countries.

F. Legal System of the United States

Although the United States adheres to a uniform common law tradition, there is no one single legal system in this country. Federal laws are enacted by the U.S. Congress, and cases are decided by the federal courts. Moreover, unless an area of the law has been preempted by the U.S. Constitution or the federal government, each state is free to enact laws as well as to decide cases dealing with state or local concerns.

Thus, there is a tremendous body of legal literature on the shelves of law libraries: federal cases and statutes; state cases and statutes; federal and state administrative regulations; and numerous other texts and journals that explain the law.

All of the great mass of legal authorities can be classified as primary or secondary authority. *Primary authorities* are official pronouncements of the law by the executive branch (treaties and executive orders), legislative branch (constitutions, statutes, and administrative regulations and decisions), and judicial branch (cases).

If a legal authority does not fall within one of the previously mentioned categories, it is a secondary authority. In general, the *secondary authorities* provide comment, discussion, and explanation of the primary authorities, and, equally important, they help researchers locate the primary authorities. Secondary authorities include legal encyclopedias, law review articles written about various legal topics, and books or other treatises dealing with legal issues.

It is critical to understand thoroughly the differences between primary and secondary authorities because only primary authorities are binding on a court, agency, or tribunal. Thus, if an argument relies on or cites a case, constitution, statute, or administrative regulation that is relevant to the legal issue, it *must* be followed. The secondary authorities, on the other hand, are persuasive only and need not be followed. See Figure 1-1 for a chart showing primary and secondary authorities and other legal research tools.

In addition to the various authorities previously discussed, there are other books in the law library that are in the nature of practical guides or finding tools. These include books such as digests, which help locate cases (see Chapter 5); form books, which provide forms for various legal documents such as wills and contracts (see Chapter 6); and sets of books (and their electronic counterparts) that help you update the authorities you rely upon in any legal writing (see Chapter 11).

Figure 1-1
Primary and Secondary Authorities

Primary Authorities (binding)

Authorities	*Source*
Cases (state and federal)	Judiciary
Statutes and Constitutions (state and federal)	Legislature
Administrative regulations (state and federal)	Administrative agencies
Executive orders (federal and state) and treaties (federal only)	Executive branch

Secondary Authorities (persuasive)

A.L.R. Annotations
Encyclopedias
Legal periodicals
Texts and treatises
Restatements
Dictionaries

Finding Tools

Digests

Updating Tools

Shepard's Citations (in print and on Lexis)
KeyCite (on Westlaw)

G.   Law Book Publishing

There is a tremendous amount of publication of legal authorities, both primary and secondary, that occurs each year. You cannot be expected to know all of the law contained in the published authorities; however, you can be reasonably expected to be able to locate and use these legal authorities. That is the goal of legal research.

The actual publication of these authorities is conducted by only a handful of publishing companies, including the following, which are among the best-known legal publishers:

- **Thomson Reuters Westlaw ("West").** Although West, headquartered in Minnesota, is actually owned by Thomson Reuters Westlaw, a global information company, in the United States it retains its identification as "West." Founded in 1872, West publishes cases, statutes, secondary authorities, and provides Westlaw, the computer-assisted legal research system. West also owns FindLaw (http://www.findlaw.com), a leader in free online legal information. For simplicity, this text will generally use "West" when referring to print products and "Westlaw" to refer to the computer-assisted legal research system.
- **LexisNexis Legal & Professional ("Lexis").** Lexis is a division of Reed Elsevier, Inc. and competes head-on with West in the publication of many legal sources, including statutes. Lexis also provides its self-named computer-assisted legal research system. Through a series of recent acquisitions, Lexis has combined other publishers, including Matthew Bender, The Michie Company, Shepard's, and Martindale-Hubbell. You will likely notice some differences in the presentation of Lexis's name on its various publications. For simplicity, this text will generally use "Lexis" to refer both to the company's print publications and its electronic research service.
- **Wolters Kluwer.** Headquartered in the Netherlands, Wolters Kluwer includes a number of other "brands," including Aspen Publishers and CCH Incorporated. Wolters Kluwer's computer-assisted legal research system is called LoislawConnect and is of particular benefit to sole practitioners and smaller law offices.

One of the common features shared by the primary sources (cases, constitutions, statutes, and regulations) as they are initially published is that they are arranged in chronological order. Thus, a set of case reports may include a case related to a will, followed by one related to burglary, followed by one relating to a contract dispute. Similarly, during any given session, a legislature will enact laws relating to motor vehicles, regulation of utilities, and licensing of real estate salespeople. The initial publication of these statutes is in the order in which they were enacted rather than according to subject matter.

This type of organization makes research difficult. If you were asked to locate cases dealing with contracts, you would find that they have not been brought together in one specific set of books but rather may be scattered over several hundred volumes of cases. It is clear then that a method of obtaining access to these primary authorities is needed, and in general, the secondary authorities and digests will assist in locating the primary authorities. For example, a secondary source such as a legal encyclopedia will describe and explain contract law and will then direct you to cases that are primary or binding authorities relating to this area of the law. These cases, when cited in a legal argument, under the doctrine of stare decisis, must be followed by a court, whereas the encyclopedia discussion is persuasive only and need not be followed by a court.

H. Non-Print Research Media

Until fairly recently, almost all legal research was performed using conventional print volumes in law libraries. With the advent of computer-assisted legal research (see Chapter 8) and Internet legal research (see Chapter 9), legal professionals use a variety of media to get the right answers to their research questions and are no longer tied to the law library.

Good researchers must be adept at both methods of performing legal research: using conventional print sources and using newer technology sources such as Lexis and Westlaw (the computer-assisted research systems) and the Internet. These newer technologies allow legal professionals to perform research at their desks and on the road.

Some methods are more efficient and cost-effective than others. For example, if you need general background information about an area of the law, consider browsing an encyclopedia or treatise in print form. If you need information about a new or evolving area of law, computer-assisted legal research will likely provide the most current information. Today's researchers need to be flexible in using all methods of legal research in case materials are unavailable: Books can disappear from library shelves and networks can crash.

Successful legal researchers thus combine research media to obtain information for clients. Knowing which media to use requires an analysis of many factors, including the complexity of your task, the costs involved, and time constraints. Many research instructors urge students first to become familiar with the conventional print tools before becoming too wedded to computer-assisted or Internet legal research. Strong skills in conventional legal research provide a good foundation for using Lexis, Westlaw, and the Internet more effectively. Thus, this text will fully examine the conventional print research tools before discussing technologies such as computer-assisted and Internet legal research.

I. Change in Our Legal System

Although stare decisis promotes stability, fairness, and uniformity in our legal system, blind adherence to established precedents in the face of changing societal views and mores may result in injustice. For example, in 1896, the U.S. Supreme Court held that "separate but equal" public facilities for blacks and whites were lawful. *Plessy v. Ferguson*, 163 U.S. 537 (1896). This precedent served to justify segregation for more than 50 years. In 1954, however, in *Brown v. Board of Education*, 347 U.S. 483, 495 (1954), the Supreme Court overruled its earlier decision and held that segregation solely according to race in public schools violated the U.S. Constitution. A strict adherence to stare decisis would have precluded a second look at this issue and would have resulted in continued racial segregation.

Thus, it is clear that as society changes, the law must also change. A balance must be struck between society's need for stability in its legal system and the need for flexibility and change when precedents have outlived their usefulness or result in injustice. Change in established legal precedent comes about by rulings of higher courts, which then bind lower courts in that judicial system or hierarchy. Thus, because *Brown v. Board of Education* was decided by the U.S. Supreme Court, it can only be overruled by the U.S. Supreme Court. Nevertheless, a lower court might try to evade a binding precedent by striving to show that precedent is not applicable or that the facts in the case before it are distinguishable from the facts in the previously decided case. This flexibility in reasoning produces a rich, complex, and sometimes contradictory body of American case law.

Thus, stare decisis means more than following settled cases: It means following settled cases that are factually similar and legally relevant to the case or problem you are researching. Such a factually similar and legally relevant case from a court equivalent to or higher than the court that will hear your particular case is said to be *on point* or "on all fours" with your case. The goal of legal research is to locate cases on point with your particular problem. Such cases are binding upon and must be followed by the court hearing your case.

In the event you cannot locate cases on point in your judicial hierarchy (possibly because your case presents a novel issue not yet considered in your jurisdiction), expand your search for cases on point to other jurisdictions. For example, if Ohio has no precedents on a particular issue, expand your search to another state. The Ohio court, however, is not bound to follow cases from other jurisdictions, although it may be persuaded to do so. See Figure 1-2.

Change in our legal system can occur not only as a result of judges expanding or overruling precedents found in cases, but also through enactment, repeal, or amendment of a statute by a legislature or even through judicial interpretation of a statute. Although a court cannot change the plain meaning of a statute, it is free to interpret the statute or to declare it unconstitutional. Thus, even when you locate a statute that appears directly to address your research problem, you cannot stop researching. You must read the cases that have interpreted the statute, because it is the judicial interpretation of a statute rather than the statute's naked language that is binding under the doctrine of stare decisis.

Figure 1-2
Stare Decisis and Our Judicial Hierarchy

- Primary law consists of cases, constitutions, statutes, treaties, executive orders, and administrative regulations. All other legal authorities are secondary.
- Primary law from your state or jurisdiction is binding within your state or jurisdiction.
- Primary law from another state or jurisdiction is persuasive only in your state or jurisdiction.

- If your state or jurisdiction adopts the law or position of another state or jurisdiction, then that position is now binding within your judicial hierarchy.
- Secondary sources (no matter where they originate) are persuasive only.
- Higher courts in any given judicial hierarchy bind lower courts in that hierarchy.
- Higher courts can depart from a previously announced rule of law if there are compelling and important reasons for doing so.
- Cases from the United States Supreme Court are binding on all courts in the United States.

J.   Identifying the Holding in a Case

Although analysis of cases will be discussed in great detail in Chapter 4, you should be aware that under the concept of stare decisis, only the actual rule of law announced in a case is binding; that is, only the holding of the case is authoritative. The holding is referred to as *ratio decidendi* or "the reason for deciding." Other remarks or judicial comments in the case are often referred to as *dicta*, meaning remarks "in passing." Dictum in a case is persuasive only.

In many instances, distinguishing the holding from the dictum is easily done. Often, a court announces its holding by using extremely specific introductory language, such as the following: "Therefore, we hold that . . . ." On other occasions, finding the holding requires more persistence and probing.

You will shortly discover that some cases are difficult to read and use archaic and outmoded language. Do not become discouraged by this. Reading cases takes a great deal of experience and patience. You will find that the more cases you read, the more skillful you will become at locating the holding, distinguishing dicta from the holding, and understanding the relevance of the case for the future.

K.   How the Legal Research Process Works: A Research Scenario

Just as it is nearly impossible to put together a puzzle without first seeing a picture of the finished product, it is difficult to understand the process of legal research before actually performing a legal research project. To understand what you will be able to do when you have completed your research class, consider the following scenario, which is typical of the type of task a researcher often encounters.

Ann was recently hired by a law firm and asked by her supervising attorney to do some legal research. The attorney met with a client, Grace, whose husband, Phil, died two years ago. Grace is the mother of a ten-year-old boy. The son spends occasional time with Phil's parents. Grace is remarrying, and although Phil's parents, the grandparents, are kind and loving, Grace has decided that it would be better to limit any visits by her son with Phil's parents so that she can begin her new marriage and start her new family. Phil's parents have told Grace that they will go to court to seek visitation. The attorney wants Ann to find out how the courts in the state handle grandparent visitation.

After getting the assignment, Ann returned to her office to begin the research process. First, she thought about the places she might need to look to find an answer to this question. Because Ann was unfamiliar with family law, she realized that she would need to learn a bit more about grandparent visitation in general so that she would have the background to understand the materials she would be reading as she worked on this research assignment. Ann thus reviewed some introductory information in a legal encyclopedia (Chapter 6) to "get her feet wet." Next, she looked to see if her state had any statutes (Chapter 3) that addressed this issue. After reading the statutes, Ann realized that she needed a better understanding of the meaning of some of the language in the statute, so she looked up some court cases (Chapter 4) that interpreted the statute. One case in particular was relevant to this question, so she used a digest (Chapter 5) to find other cases that dealt with the same issue. She then reviewed a set of books on family law in general and read the chapters relating to grandparent visitation (Chapter 6). Ann also decided to use Lexis or Westlaw to locate the most current information and other specialized articles or texts on grandparent visitation (Chapter 8). Next, she made sure that the statutes and cases were still in effect and had not been modified or overturned (Chapter 11). Finally, Ann wrote her attorney a memorandum describing what she had found out from her research (Chapter 16), being careful to use correct citation form (Chapter 10).

Ann's approach to her research problem is only one way that the problem could be solved; another researcher might well approach the problem differently, but both would reach the same conclusion.

It is thus important for researchers to understand thoroughly all of the legal research resources that are available, so that when a project is received, it can be completed efficiently and correctly. Moreover, researchers need to understand the American legal system and court structures (Chapters 2 and 4) so that cases can be put into context and researchers can understand which authorities are binding. You may wish to read Chapter 12, "Overview of the Research Process," for additional information and practical guidelines on beginning and ending your research projects.

Legal research is not so much about following a predicable formula as it is about understanding how the numerous resources fit together so that researchers can make intelligent decisions about performing legal research. Thus, the next chapters will afford you an in-depth understanding of the available resources so that you will know how and where to look for answers, allowing you to fulfill your ethical duties to perform research accurately and efficiently to help clients with their legal problems.

L.   Case Citation Form

Although case citation will be discussed in much more depth in Chapter 10, the sooner you begin examining the books in which our cases are published and reading those cases, the more confident you will become about your ability to research effectively.

All cases follow the same basic citation form: You will be given the case name, the volume number of the set in which the case is published, the name of the set in which the case appears, the page on which it begins, and the year it was decided (and the deciding court, if not apparent from the name of the set). For example, in reading the citation to the United States Supreme Court case *Brown v. Board of Education*, 347 U.S. 483 (1954), you can readily see the following:

- The case name is *Brown v. Board of Education*;
- It is located in volume 347;
- It is found in a set of books entitled *United States Reports*;
- It begins on page 483 of volume 347; and
- It was decided in 1954.

Although this text shows case names, book titles, and other materials in italics, underlining or underscoring is also acceptable according to the two major citation manuals, *The Bluebook: A Uniform System of Citation* (Columbia Law Review Ass'n et al. eds., 19th ed. 2010) ("*The Bluebook*") and ALWD & Darby Dickerson, *ALWD Citation Manual* (4th ed., Aspen Publishers 2010) ("*ALWD*").

As discussed in Chapter 10, although *The Bluebook* is the standard reference tool for citation form, *ALWD* has gained in popularity due to its common-sense rules and user-friendly format. The citation example given previously complies with both *Bluebook* and *ALWD* rules. There are additional citation systems as well and variation among practitioners, so check with your firm or office to determine if there is a preference.

Internet Resources

http://www.lexisnexis.com	Information about Lexis products and services.
http://store.westlaw.com	Information about West products and services.
http://www.hg.org/publishers.html	HG.org's website, offering links to legal publishers.
http://www.law.cornell.edu	Cornell Law School's Legal Information Institute provides access to our Constitution, cases, statutes, and much more.

(continued)

Internet Resources *(Continued)*

http://www.loc.gov/law/guide	Guide to Law Online, prepared by the U.S. Law Library of Congress, Public Services Division, providing an annotated guide to sources of information and law available online and links to useful and reliable sites for legal information.
http://www.bc.edu/schools/law/ library/research/researchguides .html	Boston College Law Library's legal research guides and videos.
http://www.law.georgetown.edu/ library	Georgetown University Law Library's legal research tutorials and guides. Select "Research Guides."
http://libguides.law.ucla.edu	UCLA School of Law provides excellent research guides.

Research Assignment

1. a. Give the name of the case located at 551 U.S. 393 (2007).
   b. Who argued the case for the petitioners?
2. a. Give the name of the case located at 549 U.S. 102 (2007).
   b. Who delivered the opinion of the Court?
   c. Who dissented in this case?
3. a. Give the name of the case located at 540 U.S. 443 (2004)
   b. Who delivered the opinion of the Court?
   c. Was the lower court's ruling affirmed or reversed?
4. a. Give the name of the case located at 529 U.S. 362 (2000).
   b. Give the date the case was argued.
   c. Give the date the case was decided.
   d. In brief, what general subject matter or topic does this case discuss?
   e. Locate a case in this volume in which the defendant's name is *Shanklin* and give its citation.
   f. What part did Justice Breyer take in this case?

Internet Assignment

1. Access the website for the National Center for State Courts at http://www.ncsc.org and locate information about Florida's Supreme Court.
   a. Who is the Chief Justice of the Florida Supreme Court?
   b. Review Florida's State Court Structure Chart. How many District Courts of Appeal are there in Florida?
2. Access the site http://www.gpo.gov and locate information about the Federal Depository Library Program. Identify the library in Duluth, Minnesota that is a federal depository library.
3. Access Cornell University Law School's site at http://www .law.cornell.edu/wex. Briefly, what is the definition of "stare decisis"?
4. Access UCLA School of Law's Research Guides. Select "Legal Research" and then select "UCLA School of Law Legal Research and Writing Guide." Locate the Research Checklist. What are the first and last tasks in a research project?
5. Access the website for the American Bar Association and review the Model Rules of Professional Conduct. Specifically, review the Comment to Rule 1.1. May a lawyer and a client agree that the scope of representation may be limited for the matters for which the lawyer is responsible?

The Federal
and State
Court Systems

Chapter Overview

This chapter provides an overview of the federal and state court systems. To perform research tasks, you should understand these court structures so that when you are confronted with a research assignment or a case citation, you will readily understand the hierarchy of cases within a given court structure, giving greater emphasis to cases from higher courts than to cases from federal trial courts (called the United States District Courts) or lower state courts.

A. Federalism

At the time the nation was founded and to resolve conflict among the framers of the Constitution, a compromise was reached: For those delegates opposed to a strong national government, the principle developed that the national government could exercise only those powers specifically enumerated in the Constitution, including borrowing money, collecting taxes, declaring war, and making any other laws "necessary and proper" for carrying out these delegated powers. As can be readily seen, these specifically enumerated powers are extremely important and gave the emerging federal government wide powers. To appease the delegates in favor of states' rights, the Constitution was immediately modified by the addition of ten amendments, known collectively as the Bill of Rights, which were designed to protect individual and state liberties. The Tenth Amendment, in particular, was enacted to reassure those in favor of states' rights. Known as the "reserve clause," the Tenth Amendment provides that any powers not expressly given to the national government are reserved to the individual states (or to the people).

The result of the historic Constitutional Convention is our "living law"—a unique system referred to as *federalism* in which the states have formed a union by granting the federal government power over national affairs while the states retain their independent existence and power over local matters.

B.　Jurisdiction

1.　Introduction

The Constitution created the framework for our federal government by establishing the legislative branch, the presidency, and the judiciary. Moreover, the Constitution set forth the types of cases that could be heard by federal courts.

The *jurisdiction* (or power to act) of the federal courts does not extend to every kind of case or controversy, but instead only to certain types of matters. You will learn a great deal more about this topic in your litigation or civil procedure classes, but a brief explanation is in order here for you to understand fully why some research projects will be researched through the exclusive use of federal law, and others will be researched through the exclusive review of the law of a particular state.

There are two types of cases that are resolved by federal courts: those based on federal question jurisdiction and those based on diversity jurisdiction.

2.　Federal Question Jurisdiction

Federal courts may decide cases that involve a *federal question*; that is, any case arising under the United States Constitution, a United States (or federal) law, or any treaty to which the United States is a party. Cases arising under the Constitution thus include cases alleging racial, sexual, or age discrimination; cases involving freedom of speech; cases involving a defendant's right to a fair trial; cases involving federal crimes such as kidnapping or terrorism; and any other actions pertaining to a federal law or the Constitution. Additionally, the Supreme Court may decide controversies between states.

3.　Diversity Jurisdiction

The other category of cases handled by federal courts, those based on *diversity jurisdiction*, is determined not by the issue or subject matter itself (as are federal question cases) but by the status of the parties to the action. Imagine you are a New York resident on vacation in Utah, where you become involved in an automobile accident with a Utah resident. You may have some concern as to whether a court in Utah would treat you, an outsider, the same as it would treat its own citizens, particularly in a locality in which the residents elect their judges.

To ensure that litigants are treated fairly and to eliminate any bias against an out-of-state litigant, the federal courts may resolve cases based on the diversity of the parties; that is, in general, federal courts may hear cases in civil actions between citizens of different states. Note, however, that diversity jurisdiction is conditioned upon satisfying another key element: The amount in controversy must exceed $75,000, exclusive of interest and court costs. There is no monetary jurisdictional limit for cases instituted in federal court based on federal questions.

Diversity must be complete; all plaintiffs must be citizens of different states from all defendants (although there are some exceptions for class actions). A federal court in a diversity case will apply the state law of the state in which it is located. Finally, federal courts do not exercise jurisdiction in domestic relations or probate matters, even if other diversity requirements are satisfied. Thus, federal courts do not probate wills or issue divorce decrees.

See Figure 2-1 for a chart of federal jurisdiction.

Figure 2-1
Federal Jurisdiction

Federal jurisdiction may be based upon the following:

- **Federal question:** Any case arising under the U.S. Constitution or any federal law or treaty (28 U.S.C. § 1331 (2006)); or
- **Diversity:** Generally, cases in which all plaintiffs are from different states from all defendants and in which the matter in controversy exceeds $75,000 (28 U.S.C. § 1332 (2006)).

Additionally, cases originally filed in state court may be removed to a federal court, as follows:

- **Removal:** If a case is originally filed by a plaintiff in state court and federal jurisdiction exists, the case may be *removed* to federal court by the defendant (28 U.S.C. § 1441 (2006)).
- **Remand:** If it appears at any time before final judgment that a case was improperly removed because the district court lacked subject matter jurisdiction, it must be remanded or returned to the state court (28 U.S.C. § 1447 (2006)).

4. *Concurrent Jurisdiction*

If a case may be brought in more than one court, jurisdiction is said to be *concurrent*. For example, racial discrimination is a violation of both California state law and federal law. Thus, a victim of racial discrimination in California may initiate an action either in California state court or in federal court. Matters of trial tactics and strategy often dictate in which court the action will be brought. For example, a plaintiff may wish to proceed in a federal court because it is not as crowded with cases as the local state court. Moreover, any diversity jurisdiction case (regardless of the amount of money involved) may be brought in a state court rather than a federal court.

5. *Exclusive Jurisdiction*

Some matters are handled exclusively by federal courts and are never the subject of concurrent jurisdiction. For example, all maritime cases and all copyright infringement cases must be brought in federal court. Generally, statutes govern which cases are subject to *exclusive jurisdiction*.

C.   Ground Rules for Cases

Even if a federal question or diversity exists, there still remain some ground rules that must be satisfied before a federal court will hear a case. Although the following discussion relates primarily to federal cases, these ground rules must usually be satisfied for cases brought in state courts as well.

   In large part, these ground rules are rooted in Article III of the Constitution, which establishes the jurisdiction of federal courts and restricts federal courts to resolving "cases" and "controversies." There are three ground rules. First, with very few exceptions, federal courts will not consider issues that are "moot" or already resolved. Parties before the court must be involved in an existing, present controversy. Second, a close corollary to this first ground rule is that federal courts will not render advisory opinions, even if asked by the President. The federal courts are constitutionally bound to resolve actual ongoing disputes, not to give advice. Finally, a plaintiff must have personally suffered some actual or threatened legal injury; that is, the plaintiff must be adversely affected by some conduct or threatened conduct of the defendant and cannot base a claim on the rights or interests of some other persons. This requirement is referred to as *standing*, and it ensures that parties before the court have a personal stake in the outcome of the controversy.

D.   The Federal Court Structure

1. *Introduction*

Article III, Section 1 of the Constitution created the federal court system. This section provides in part that "the judicial power of the United

States shall be vested in one Supreme Court, and in such inferior courts as Congress may from time to time ordain and establish." Thus, only the existence of the Supreme Court was assured. It was left up to Congress to determine its composition and to create any other federal courts. In fact, the first Congress created the federal court structure that still exists today. Although the numbers of courts and judges have increased, the basic structure of our federal court system remains as it was in 1789: district courts, intermediate courts of appeal, and one United States Supreme Court. Judges appointed to these courts (and to the United States Court of International Trade) are often referred to as *Article III judges.*

There are three levels of courts in the federal system. Starting with the lowest courts, they are the district courts, the courts of appeal, and the United States Supreme Court. All judges in the federal court system are nominated by the President and confirmed by the United States Senate.

2. *United States District Courts*

The *district courts* are the trial courts in our federal system. At present, there are 94 district courts scattered throughout the 50 states, the District of Columbia, and the territories and possessions of the United States. There is at least one district court in each state, and the more populous states, namely, California, New York, and Texas, have four district courts within their territorial borders. Other less populous states, such as Alaska and Utah, each have only one district court (although they may have divisions in other parts of the state to allow easy access for litigants). Although Congress has the authority to create new district courts, it has not done so since 1971. See Figure 2-2 for a list of the district courts.

Help Line

Federal Court Websites and Opinions

All federal courts maintain websites, all of which can be accessed through a site entitled U.S. Courts at http://www.uscourts.gov. This site provides a map of the federal courts of appeal; direct linking to the websites for all federal courts; and access to opinions and to the federal rules of civil procedure, criminal procedure, and evidence.

Figure 2-2
United States District Courts and Courts of Appeal

Alabama	11th Cir.	**Idaho**	9th Cir.
M.D. Ala.		D. Idaho	
N.D. Ala.			
S.D. Ala.		**Illinois**	7th Cir.
		C.D. Ill.	
Alaska	9th Cir.	N.D. Ill.	
D. Alaska		S.D. Ill.	
Arizona	9th Cir.	**Indiana**	7th Cir.
D. Ariz.		N.D. Ind.	
		S.D. Ind.	
Arkansas	8th Cir.		
E.D. Ark.		**Iowa**	8th Cir.
W.D. Ark.		N.D. Iowa	
		S.D. Iowa	
California	9th Cir.		
C.D. Cal.		**Kansas**	10th Cir.
E.D. Cal.		D. Kan.	
N.D. Cal.			
S.D. Cal.		**Kentucky**	6th Cir.
		E.D. Ky.	
Colorado	10th Cir.	W.D. Ky.	
D. Colo.			
		Louisiana	5th Cir.
Connecticut	2d Cir.	E.D. La.	
D. Conn.		M.D. La.	
		W.D. La.	
Delaware	3d Cir.		
D. Del.		**Maine**	1st Cir.
		D. Me.	
District of	D.C. Cir.		
Columbia		**Maryland**	4th Cir.
D.D.C.		D. Md.	
Florida	11th Cir.	**Massachusetts**	1st Cir.
M.D. Fla.		D. Mass.	
N.D. Fla.			
S.D. Fla.		**Michigan**	6th Cir.
		E.D. Mich.	
Georgia	11th Cir.	W.D. Mich.	
M.D. Ga.			
N.D. Ga.		**Minnesota**	8th Cir.
S.D. Ga.		D. Minn.	
Hawaii	9th Cir.		
D. Haw.			

Figure 2-2 *(Continued)*

Mississippi N.D. Miss. S.D. Miss.	5th Cir.	**Oregon** D. Or.	9th Cir.
Missouri E.D. Mo. W.D. Mo.	8th Cir.	**Pennsylvania** E.D. Pa. M.D. Pa. W.D. Pa.	3d Cir.
Montana D. Mont.	9th Cir.	**Rhode Island** D.R.I.	1st Cir.
Nebraska D. Neb.	8th Cir.	**South Carolina** D.S.C.	4th Cir.
Nevada D. Nev.	9th Cir.	**South Dakota** D.S.D.	8th Cir.
New Hampshire D.N.H.	1st Cir.	**Tennessee** E.D. Tenn. M.D. Tenn. W.D. Tenn.	6th Cir.
New Jersey D.N.J.	3d Cir.	**Texas** E.D. Tex. N.D. Tex. S.D. Tex. W.D. Tex.	5th Cir.
New Mexico D.N.M.	10th Cir.		
New York E.D.N.Y. N.D.N.Y. S.D.N.Y. W.D.N.Y.	2d Cir.	**Utah** D. Utah	10th Cir.
		Vermont D. Vt.	2d Cir.
North Carolina E.D.N.C. M.D.N.C. W.D.N.C.	4th Cir.	**Virginia** E.D. Va. W.D. Va.	4th Cir.
North Dakota D.N.D.	8th Cir.	**Washington** E.D. Wash. W.D. Wash.	9th Cir.
Ohio N.D. Ohio S.D. Ohio	6th Cir.	**West Virginia** N.D. W. Va. S.D. W. Va.	4th Cir.
Oklahoma E.D. Okla. N.D. Okla. W.D. Okla.	10th Cir.		

Figure 2-2 (Continued)

Wisconsin E.D. Wis. W.D. Wis.	7th Cir.	**N. Mariana Islands** D.N. Mar. I.	9th Cir.
Wyoming D. Wyo.	10th Cir.	**Puerto Rico** D.P.R.	1st Cir.
Miscellaneous **Canal Zone** D.C.Z. (abolished 1982)	5th Cir.	**Virgin Islands** D.V.I.	3d Cir.
Guam D. Guam	9th Cir.	**U.S. Court of Appeals for the Federal Circuit**	Fed. Cir.
		U.S. Court of Federal Claims	Fed. Cl.

These district courts have jurisdiction over a wide variety of cases. In any given day, a district court judge may hear cases involving a bank robbery, a civil rights question, or a patent infringement case. Bankruptcy courts are also considered units of our district courts with judges appointed by the courts of appeal for 14-year terms. Each district includes a United States Bankruptcy Court.

The number of judges assigned to a particular district court will vary depending upon the number of cases the court is called upon to adjudicate. The district court judges, who are paid more than $170,000 annually, usually sit individually; that is, they hear cases and render decisions by themselves rather than as a panel or group as the United States Supreme Court justices sit.

The vast majority of all federal cases end at the district court level; only approximately 14 percent of these federal cases are appealed. In 2011, nearly 290,000 civil cases were commenced in the various district courts.

3.   United States Courts of Appeal

The 13 United States Courts of Appeal, sometimes called the *circuit courts*, are the intermediate courts in our federal system. The theory of our judicial system is that a litigant should have a trial in one court before one judge and a right to an appeal in another court before a different judge or judges.

It is critical to remember the difference between the district courts, which are trial courts that hear evidence, listen to witnesses testify, and render decisions, and the courts of appeal, whose primary function is to review cases from these district courts. The courts of appeal do not retry a case. They merely review the record and the briefs of counsel to determine

Figure 2-3

The Thirteen Federal Judicial Circuits (See 28 U.S.C.A § 41 (2006))

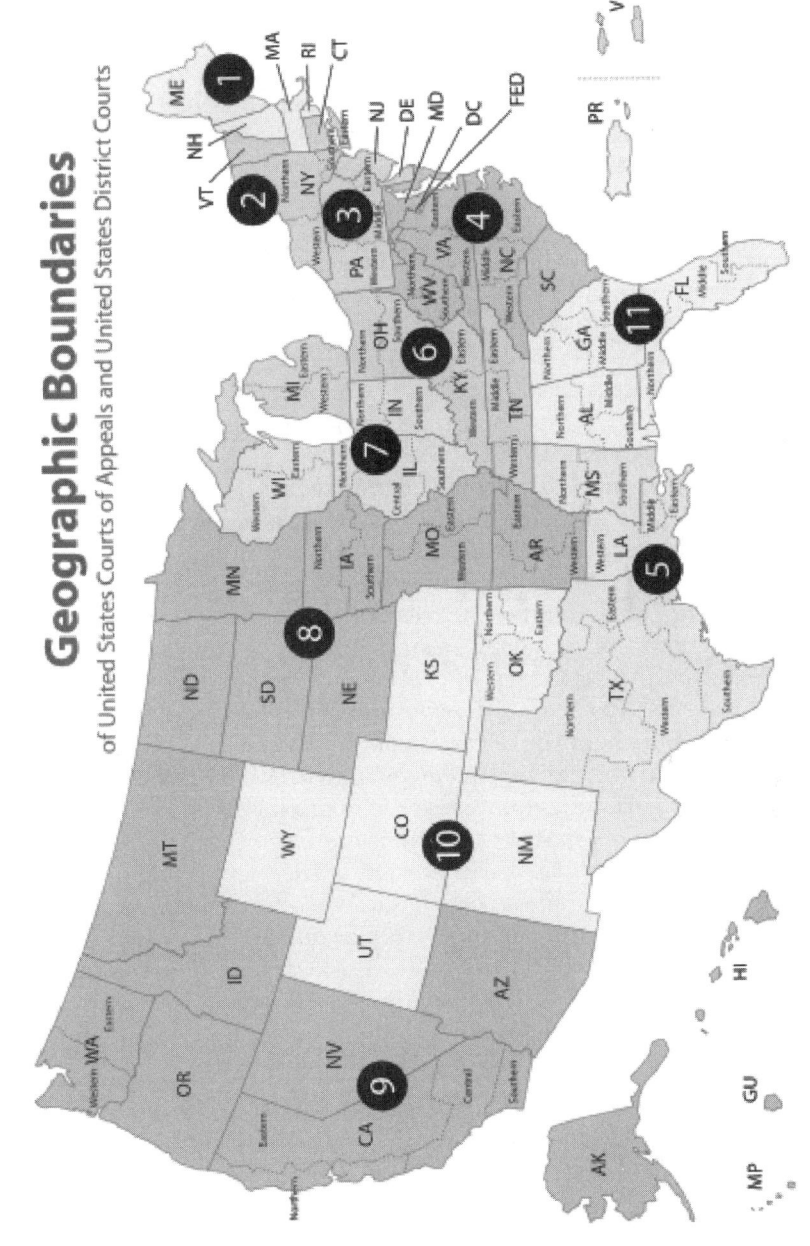

Geographic Boundaries
of United States Courts of Appeals and United States District Courts

if a prejudicial error of law was made in the district court below. A second important function of the United States Courts of Appeal is to review and enforce decisions from federal administrative agencies such as the FCC or NLRB.

The United States is divided into 12 geographical regions called "circuits," and there is a court of appeal in each of these circuits (including one for the District of Columbia circuit). Additionally, there is a Court of Appeals for the Federal Circuit, located in Washington, D.C., which has nationwide jurisdiction and handles specialized cases, such as patent and international trade cases. Figure 2-3 shows the grouping of states that make up each circuit. It is not critical to know which states or district courts fall within the boundaries of which circuits. A map of the circuit courts is readily available at http://www.uscourts.gov. You should, however, know which circuit covers the state in which you will be working and that 11 of the 13 circuits are assigned a number and will have several states (and their district courts) within their boundaries. For example, the Ninth Circuit covers California and most of the western states. Thus, if a trial occurs in the Northern District of California, the appeal is filed in the Ninth Circuit Court of Appeals.

Each of the intermediate circuit courts of appeal is free to make its own decisions independent of what the other circuits have held; in practice, however, the circuit courts are often guided by decisions from other courts. Decisions from the U.S. Supreme Court often resolve conflicts among the circuits. Congress has the authority to create additional circuits, but it has not done so since 1981.

Each of the courts of appeal has at least six judges and as many as 29 judges assigned to it, depending on the caseload for the circuit. The judges usually hear the appeals from the district courts as a panel of three judges, although they may sit *en banc*, with all judges present. These federal judges earn an annual salary of approximately $184,000. The United States Courts of Appeal typically issue more than 30,000 opinions each year (although only about 15 percent of them are published).

For the vast majority of litigants, these intermediate courts of appeal represent the last opportunity to prevail. As you will see, the popular notion that everyone has access to the Supreme Court is unfounded; for most litigants, the court of appeals is the last chance to win, because one who wishes to appeal a case to the U.S. Supreme Court is largely dependent on the Court's discretion in accepting the case for review.

4. United States Supreme Court

The United States Supreme Court consists of eight associate justices and one chief justice. Although the chief justice draws a higher salary than the associate justices (roughly $223,000 to their annual salaries of $213,000) and has prestige and certain authority by virtue of seniority, the chief justice's vote counts equally with that of any associate justice. Nevertheless, as the presiding officer of the Supreme Court, he or she is responsible for leadership of the federal judicial system. Upon the death or resignation of a chief justice, the President may either appoint one of the eight existing associate justices to the position of chief justice or appoint an "outsider" as chief justice.

As are all approximately 870 judges in the federal system, the Supreme Court justices are nominated by the President and hold office "during good behavior." This means they are not subject to mandatory retirement and may sit as federal judges until they die or voluntarily retire. Although federal judges may be impeached by Congress, this drastic remedy is seldom used, and only a few have actually been removed through impeachment.

In addition to their primary activities of hearing cases and writing opinions, each justice is assigned to one of the federal judicial circuits for the purpose of handling special and emergency matters such as stays of execution and injunctions. Because there are 13 federal courts of appeal and only nine Supreme Court justices, some justices are assigned to more than one circuit. Assignment to the circuits is made annually by the chief justice.

By federal law, the term of the Court commences on the first Monday in October, and the term typically ends at the end of June nine months later. In recent years, the Court has been reducing its docket. During the 1980s, the Court routinely decided roughly 150 cases each term. In its 2012–2013 term, the Court decided only 78 merits cases in total and issued 73 signed opinions.

By the authority of the Constitution, the U.S. Supreme Court has the jurisdiction to act not only as an appellate or reviewing court but also in very limited instances (usually disputes between two states) can act as a court of original jurisdiction or trial court. The Court usually hears fewer than five original jurisdiction cases per term (and heard none in its 2012-2013 term). See Figure 2-4 for a chart showing the jurisdiction of the Supreme Court.

Figure 2-4
Jurisdiction of United States Supreme Court

I. Original Jurisdiction (28 U.S.C. § 1251 (2006))
  A. Controversies between two or more states (exclusive jurisdiction)
  B. Actions in which ambassadors or other public ministers, consuls, or vice-consuls of foreign states are parties (non-exclusive jurisdiction)
  C. Controversies between the United States and a state (non-exclusive jurisdiction)
  D. Actions by a state against the citizens of another state (non-exclusive jurisdiction)
II. Appellate Jurisdiction (28 U.S.C. §§ 1253, 1254, 1257 (2006))
  A. Cases from federal courts
    1. United States District Courts (special statutes allow direct appeals as well as appeals from three-judge district courts granting or denying injunctive relief to be directly appealed to the United States Supreme Court)

2. United States Courts of Appeal
    (a) Certiorari
    (b) Certification (granted only in exceptional cases)
B. Cases from highest state courts that present a federal question (reviewed by writ of certiorari)

Although a few cases, such as some cases under the Interstate Commerce Act, are directly appealable from the district courts to the U.S. Supreme Court, the vast majority of federal cases that the Supreme Court reviews proceed to the Court in the expected "stair step" fashion: trial in the district court, an intermediate appeal to the appropriate circuit court, and a final appeal to the U.S. Supreme Court.

The most widely used means to gain access to the U.S. Supreme Court from the lower circuit courts of appeal is the writ of certiorari. *Certiorari* is a Latin word meaning "to be more fully informed." A litigant who has lost an appeal in the intermediate circuit court will file a document with the Supreme Court called a Petition for Writ of Certiorari, setting forth the basis for appeal. The Supreme Court will either grant the petition and direct the lower court to send its records and files to the Supreme Court or deny the petition, meaning that the lower court decision will stand. Issuance of the writ, or "granting cert," is discretionary with the Supreme Court; a litigant does not have an absolute right to have the Supreme Court review a case.

Approximately 8,000 petitions for certiorari are filed with the United States Supreme Court each year, and the justices typically grant cert in fewer than 100 of these cases. Full signed opinions are issued in approximately 70 cases, and the remaining cases are disposed of without oral argument or formal written opinions.

There are no clearly articulated or published criteria followed by the justices in determining which petitions will be deemed "cert worthy." Court rules provide that certiorari will be granted if there are "compelling" reasons for doing so. Sup. Ct. R. 10. In general, however, a review of the cases accepted by the Supreme Court reveals some common elements: If the lower courts are in conflict on a certain issue and the circuit courts of appeal are issuing contradictory opinions, the Supreme Court often grants certiorari so that it can resolve such a conflict; or if a case is of general importance, the Court may grant certiorari.

Denial of the writ of certiorari is not to be viewed as an endorsement by the Court of a lower court's holding, but rather its determination that for reasons of judicial economy not every case can be heard. Once a petition for certiorari has been granted, the attorneys or parties submit their written arguments, called briefs, which are then filed with the Court and made public. Oral arguments are then scheduled, after which the justices meet in conference to decide the case. A preliminary vote is taken to determine the Court's disposition of the case. The justice who is the most senior in the majority group then assigns the opinion to be drafted by another justice or may decide to author the opinion himself or herself. While one justice is drafting the majority opinion, others may be writing separate dissents or concurring opinions (see Chapter 4). Drafting the majority opinion may take weeks or even months. When the opinion is complete, it is circulated to the justices for comments and then released to the public and authorized for printing in the *United States Reports*, the official publication of the Court's work.

Although most cases arrive at the Court from the various United States courts of appeal by means of the writ of certiorari, there is one other means by which cases from these lower federal courts may be reviewed by the Supreme Court: certification. Certification is a rarely used process by which a court of appeals (rather than the parties) refers a question to the Supreme Court and asks for instructions.

Cases from the state courts may be appealed to the United States Supreme Court from the highest court in a state if and only if a federal question is involved. Even then the Court may, in its discretion, refuse to grant certiorari, thus rendering the state court decision final. See Figure 2-5 for a diagram of our federal court structure.

Figure 2-5
Structure of Federal Court System

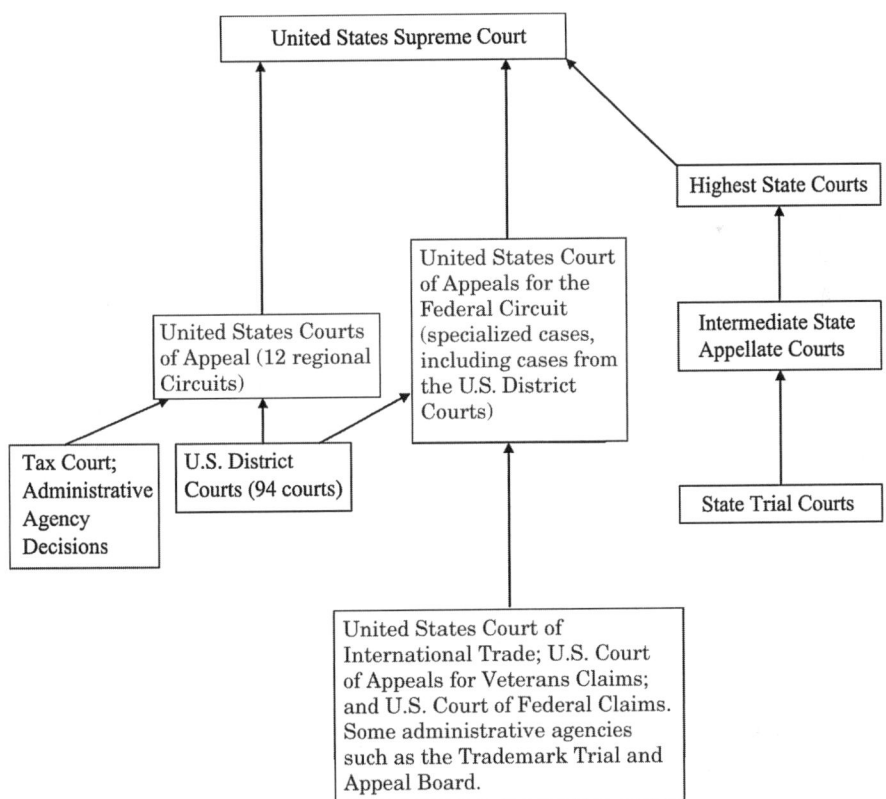

United States Supreme Court Trivia

- The present composition of nine justices on the Supreme Court has existed since 1869. At its beginning, the Court had only six justices. At one time, it had ten justices.
- A 2010 national survey by FindLaw disclosed that nearly two-thirds of Americans cannot name any members of the United States Supreme Court. Only 1 percent can name all nine Justices.
- Since the late 1800s, as the justices take their seats on the bench and at the beginning of the case conferences at which they meet and review cases, each justice formally shakes hands with each of the other justices. This handshake serves as a visible reminder that although the justices may offer differing views of the law, they are united in their purpose of interpreting the U.S. Constitution.
- On rainy days, the early justices would enliven case conferences with wine. On other days, even if the sun were shining, Chief Justice John Marshall would order wine anyway, saying, "Our jurisdiction is so vast that it must be raining somewhere."

---

5.   *Specialized Courts*

In addition to the district courts, the intermediate circuit courts of appeal, and the United States Supreme Court, certain specialized courts exist in the federal judicial system to determine particular issues, such as the United States Tax Court, which issues decisions in tax matters, and the United States Court of Federal Claims, which considers private claims seeking monetary damages from the United States government. Other specialized courts include the United States Court of Appeals for Veterans Claims (which reviews determinations regarding matters pertaining to veterans of the armed services, such as disability determinations) and the United States Court of International Trade (which handles civil actions arising out of customs and international trade laws).

Most of these specialized courts are referred to as *legislative courts*, as distinguished from the United States Court of International Trade, the district courts, intermediate courts of appeal, and Supreme Court, which are referred to as *constitutional courts* or "Article III courts" because they exist under Article III of the Constitution.

Ethics Alert

Court Rules

You must comply with all court rules when submitting any document to a court. Failure to follow local court rules may result in the court's refusal of your document, which could lead to liability for legal malpractice. Nearly all courts post their rules on their websites. See Table T.1.3 of *The Bluebook* or Appendix 2 of *ALWD* for identification of each state's judicial website.

E. State Courts

In addition to the federal court structure discussed above, each of the 50 states and the District of Columbia has its own arrangement for its court system. Although the names of these courts vary from state to state, the general organization is the same: A trial is held in one court and the losing party will usually have the right to at least one appeal in an appellate court.

Minnesota's court system is typical of many states and is shown in Figure 2-6. Note that in some states, trials involving lesser amounts of money and misdemeanors are held in courts called municipal courts or district courts, whereas trials involving greater amounts of money and felonies are held in the superior courts or circuit courts. In Minnesota, intermediate appeals are heard by the court of appeals, with the Minnesota Supreme Court serving as the court of last resort.

Although the majority of states have a two-tier appellate system, in 11 jurisdictions (Delaware, District of Columbia, Maine, Montana, Nevada, New Hampshire, Rhode Island, South Dakota, Vermont, West Virginia, and Wyoming) there is no intermediate court of appeal, and dissatisfied litigants proceed directly from the trial court, usually called the *court of first resort*, to the *court of last resort* in the state, usually called the supreme court in most states. The U.S. Supreme Court is also referred to as a court of last resort.

In 48 jurisdictions, the highest state court is called the supreme court, supreme judicial court, or supreme court of appeals. Maryland and the District of Columbia, however, call their highest courts the court of appeals. New York also calls its highest court the court of appeals and calls one of the courts below it, which handles felonies, marriage dissolutions, and miscellaneous civil actions, the supreme court, which can cause some confusion.

Figure 2-6
Minnesota Court Structure
(with intermediate appellate court)

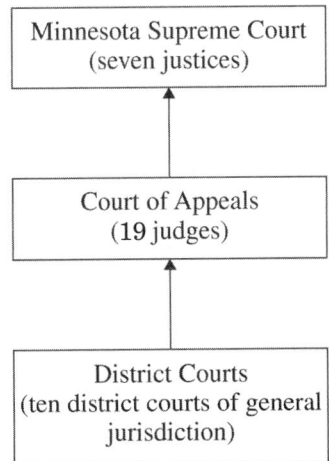

Practice Tip

Reading Citations

Gain as much information from citations as you can. When you see the word "App." in a case citation, immediately think to yourself that the case is likely *not* from the state's highest court, but rather from its intermediate court of appeals. Similarly, the absence of the word "App." from a state court case citation is typically a signal that the case is a strong one and is from your state's court of last resort.

Decisions by the highest courts in all states are rendered by odd-numbered panels of justices who function in a collective fashion. Diagrams of the structures of all state courts can be found at the website of the National Center for State Courts at http://www.ncsc.org.

As of 2012, the median annual salary for justices on the highest state courts is approximately $147,000. The median salary for state trial court judges is approximately $132,000. Note that all of these salaries are approximately the same as the starting salaries paid to new attorneys in the nation's largest law firms, where annual salaries range from $125,000 to $160,000.

Although all judges in the federal system are nominated by the President and are confirmed by the United States Senate, there is great variation among the states with regard to the selection of state court judges. The majority of states use a merit selection method (somewhat similar to the federal presidential appointment method), in which the governor appoints a judge from a list of nominees provided to him or her by a judicial nominating commission. Other states elect their judges either by vote of the state legislature or the general population for specific terms.

Practice Tip

State Court Names

Review Table T.1.3 of *The Bluebook* or Appendix 1 of *ALWD* to learn about your state courts. Both *The Bluebook* and *ALWD* identify the formal names of the courts in each state, identifying higher state courts first and then lower state courts.

F. Citation Form

	Bluebook (for practitioners)	ALWD
Federal Cases		
• United States Supreme Court	• *Ewing v. California,* 538 U.S. 11 (2003).	• *Ewing v. California,* 538 U.S. 11 (2003). *ALWD* permits parallel citations.
• United States Courts of Appeal	• *Bailey v. Talbert,* 585 F.2d 968 (8th Cir. 1989).	• *Bailey v. Talbert,* 585 F.2d 968 (8th Cir. 1989).
• United States District Court	• *Peters v. May,* 697 F. Supp. 101 (S.D. Cal. 1988).	• *Peters v. May,* 697 F. Supp. 101 (S.D. Cal. 1988).
State Cases		
• When parallel citations are not required	• *Janson v. Keyser,* 415 N.E.2d 891 (Mass. 1976).	• *Janson v. Keyser,* 415 N.E.2d 891 (Mass. 1976).
• When parallel citations are required by court rules	• *Janson v. Keyser,* 204 Mass. 617, 415 N.E.2d 891 (1976).	• *Janson v. Keyser,* 204 Mass. 617, 415 N.E.2d 891 (1976).

Internet Resources

http://www.uscourts.gov	Official listing of all federal courts with direct links to district courts, circuit courts of appeal, and United States Supreme Court.
http://www.fjc.gov	Federal Judicial Center, the education and research agency for the federal courts.
http://www.supremecourt.gov	Website of U.S. Supreme Court with general information about the Court and access to opinions.
http://www.justia.com	Select "State Laws" or "State Courts" and then the desired state for access to each state's courts, statutes, and cases.

(continued)

Internet Resources *(Continued)*

http://www.ncsc.org	National Center for State Courts, offering diagrams for each state's court structure and statistics about state court caseloads.
http://www.usa.gov	USA.gov, the federal government's official Web portal with links to all units of the federal judicial branch and a vast array of excellent information about the federal government (formerly called "FirstGov").
http://www.law.cornell.edu	Cornell University Law School's site, providing access to decisions of the U.S. Supreme Court and other federal and state courts.

Research Assignment

1. Use volume 552 of the *United States Reports*.
   a. Give the name of the case in this volume in which the defendant's name is *Siebert* and give the citation for the case.
   b. Who was acting as the U.S. Attorney General at the time this case was decided?
   c. During the period of time covered by this volume, which U.S. Supreme Court Justice was assigned or allotted to the Ninth Circuit?
   d. Locate a case in this volume in which the plaintiff's name is *LaRue*. Briefly, what issue did this case address?

2. Locate and review the case *In re TFT-LCD (Flat Panel) Antitrust Litigation*, 785 F. Supp. 2d 835 (N.D. Cal. 2011). Which party has the burden of establishing jurisdiction?

3. Locate and review the case published at 631 F.3d 537.
   a. In which circuit was this case decided?
   b. Review the portion of the case relating to diversity jurisdiction. What did the court state about the failure of complete diversity in a case?

Internet Assignment

1. Access the site U.S. Courts and answer the following questions:
   a. What is the address for the U.S. District Court for the Northern District Court in Tallahassee, Florida?
   b. In what city is the main office for the District Court of Oregon?
   c. Federal Judge Kelly would like to make a speech for a candidate for U.S. Senate in his state. Review the Code of Conduct for U.S. Judges and determine whether this is permissible. What Canon governs your answer?

2. Access the site for the National Center for State Courts and locate the "Court Structure Charts."
   a. How many justices sit on the Michigan Supreme Court?
   b. If you wish to bring an action in Virginia for breach of contract for $12,000, in which court would you initiate the action?

3. Access the website for the United States Supreme Court.
   a. Review the biographies of the Justices. Which president appointed Justice Alito to the Court?
   b. Review the "Frequently Asked Questions" relating to the Justices. Why do the Justices wear black robes?
   c. Review Rule 10 of the Rules of the Supreme Court. Is review on a writ of certiorari a matter of right?
4. Access Cornell University's Legal Information Institute. Locate Title 28 of the United States Code. How many Justices constitute a quorum for the U.S. Supreme Court? What statute governs your answer?

Statutory Law

Chapter Overview

Recall from Chapter 1 that courts are free to interpret statutes. This chapter focuses on statutory law because the logical progression many researchers follow when given a task is to first determine whether a statute relates to the issue. If so, they begin by reading the statute itself and then reviewing the cases and other sources that interpret it. Thus, this chapter discusses the enactment, publication, and codification of federal and state statutes and the research techniques that enable you to find statutes.

A. Federal Legislation

1. Enactment of Federal Statutes

The chief function of the U.S. Congress is its lawmaking task. Congress is a *bicameral* (two-chamber) legislature and consists of 100 members of the Senate (two from each state, regardless of state population) and 435 members of the House of Representatives (based on population of the state).

The framers of the Constitution anticipated that most legislation would originate in the House, and this is the case (although certain types of legislation can be introduced in the Senate). Legislation can be proposed by anyone, including members of Congress, executive departments of the federal government, and private individuals (who transmit their proposals to their representatives), but it is always introduced by a member of Congress.

Following are the steps in the enactment of legislation. Assume the legislation is originating in the House:

• **Introduction in House.** The *bill* (a proposed law) is introduced by its sponsor, who gives it to the Clerk of the House. The Clerk assigns a legislative number to the bill, with "H.R." used for bills originating in the House and "S." used for bills introduced in the Senate. The bill is printed by the Government Printing Office and distributed to each member of the House.

• **Assignment to Committee.** The bill is assigned to one of 20 permanent or standing House committees by the Speaker of the House so that it can be studied. The committee studies the bill, holds hearings, and will take one of three actions: It will release the bill with a recommendation to pass it (called "reporting it out"); revise the bill and release it; or set it aside (called "tabling" the bill).

• **House Rules Committee Action.** The bill is now placed on a calendar of bills awaiting action and scheduled for debate on the floor of the House.

• **Voting.** The bill now proceeds to the floor of the House for voting. If the bill passes by a simple majority (218 votes of 435), it moves to the Senate.

• **Introduction in Senate.** The bill is introduced in the Senate.

• **Assignment to Committee.** The bill is then assigned to one of the Senate's 16 permanent or standing committees. The committee studies the bill and either releases it (with or without modification) or tables it (just as occurred in the House).

• **Voting.** Once released, the bill proceeds to the Senate floor for debate and consideration. A simple majority (51 of 100) is required to pass the bill.

• **Signature by President.** If the bill passed by the Senate is identical to the one passed by the House, it goes to the President for signature.

• **Conference Committee Action.** If the House and Senate versions of the bill differ in any respect, the bill moves to a *conference committee*, composed of members of the House and Senate. The conference committee works out any differences between the two bill versions. The revised bill is then sent to both the House and the Senate for final approval.

• **Signature by President.** The final bill is sent to the President for signature. The President has ten days to sign or veto the bill. If the President vetoes the bill, it can still become a law if two thirds of the House and two thirds of the Senate approve it. When the President signs the bill, it is then called a *law* or a *statute*.

2. *Classification of Federal Statutes*

Federal statutes are classified as public or private and as permanent or temporary.

• **Public law.** A *public law* is one that affects the public generally, such as a bankruptcy or tax law.

• **Private law.** A *private law* is one that affects only one person or a small group of persons, granting them some special benefit not afforded to the public at large. Most private laws are those dealing with immigration or naturalization.

• **Permanent law.** A *permanent law* remains in effect until it is expressly repealed.

• **Temporary law.** A *temporary law* has limiting language in the statute itself, such as the following: "This law shall have no force or effect after May 31, 2013."

3. *Publication of Federal Statutes*

a. *United States Statutes at Large*

As each federal law is passed by Congress, it is published by the United States Government Printing Office as a pamphlet or sheet of paper, referred to as a *slip law*. At the end of each congressional session, these slips are taken together and are published in a hardback set of volumes called *United States Statutes at Large*.

The laws in *United States Statutes at Large* appear in chronological order—namely, in the way in which they were passed by Congress—rather than by topic, making the slip laws extremely difficult to research. Moreover, there is no one master index to this set, and laws relating to the same topic are scattered throughout several volumes. Thus, *United States Statutes at Large* serves more as a historical overview of Congress's work than as a viable research tool.

Practice Tip

Early Access to Federal Statutes

To obtain the exact wording of a federal statute without waiting for *United States Statutes at Large* to be published (which can take one year), consult the following:

• **Slip Laws.** The slips themselves are usually available in the more than 1,200 federal depository libraries (see Chapter 1).
• *United States Code Congressional and Administrative News* **("USCCAN").** This monthly West publication provides the text of public laws passed during the previous month.
• **Congressional Representatives.** Contact your congressional representative to ask for the complete text of a recently enacted law.
• **Lexis and Westlaw.** The computerized legal research systems provide access to recently enacted federal statutes.
• **Congress.gov.** One of the best websites for legislative information is Congress.gov (the successor to THOMAS and now in its beta stage), provided by the Library of Congress to make federal legislation available to the public. Access http://beta.congress.gov (see Figure 9-3). Searching may be done by key word or bill number.

---

b. *United States Code*

Because the organization and lack of indexing of *United States Statutes at Large* make using the set so difficult, it became readily apparent to researchers that a set of books should be developed to eliminate these barriers to efficient research. The process of developing a set of books that compiles currently valid laws on the same subject together with any amendments to those laws is referred to as *codification*, and the result is a *code*.

The current codification of *United States Statutes at Large* that legal professionals use to find federal statutes is called the *United States Code* (U.S.C.). The set U.S.C. arranges all federal laws by topic or subject matter into 51 largely alphabetically arranged categories, called *titles* (see Figure 3-1). Note that Title 51 was added in 2010. At the time of the writing of this text, proposals are pending to add four additional titles. See Office of the Law Revision Counsel (http://uscode.house.gov) for information.

Figure 3-1
Titles of United States Code

1. General Provisions
2. The Congress
3. The President
4. Flag and Seal, Seat of Government, and the States
5. Government Organization and Employees
6. Surety Bonds
7. Agriculture
8. Aliens and Nationality
9. Arbitration
10. Armed Forces
11. Bankruptcy
12. Banks and Banking
13. Census
14. Coast Guard
15. Commerce and Trade
16. Conservation
17. Copyrights
18. Crimes and Criminal Procedure
19. Customs Duties
20. Education
21. Food and Drugs
22. Foreign Relations and Intercourse
23. Highways
24. Hospitals and Asylums
25. Indians
26. Internal Revenue Code
27. Intoxicating Liquors
28. Judiciary and Judicial Procedure
29. Labor
30. Mineral Lands and Mining
31. Money and Finance
32. National Guard
33. Navigation and Navigable Waters
34. Navy (see Title 10, Armed Forces)
35. Patents
36. Patriotic Societies and Observances
37. Pay and Allowances of the Uniformed Services
38. Veterans' Benefits
39. Postal Service
40. Public Buildings, Property, and Works
41. Public Contracts
42. The Public Health and Welfare
43. Public Lands
44. Public Printing and Documents
45. Railroads
46. Shipping
47. Telegraphs, Telephones, and Radiotelegraphs
48. Territories and Insular Possessions
49. Transportation
50. War and National Defense
51. National and Commercial Space Programs (added 2010)

For example, Title 11 includes all federal bankruptcy laws, and Title 29 contains all labor laws. Within the titles, statutes are further divided into sections. Citations to federal statutes in U.S.C. appear as follows:

42	U.S.C.	§	1390	(2006)
Title	*Set*	*Abbr. for section*	*Section no.*	*Year of code*

It is not important to know what subject each of the 51 titles refers to. It is sufficient to understand that there are, in fact, 51 groups or titles of federal statutes, that they are arranged largely alphabetically, and that these titles are permanently established, meaning, for example, that any federal statute relating to labor will always be found in Title 29.

The *United States Code* is *official*, a term meaning that its publication is approved by the government. A new edition of the *United States Code* is published every six years (although there is often delay in publishing new editions). The Federal Digital System or "FDsys" offers authenticated government documents, including the United States Code. Access http://www.gpo.gov/fdsys and browse the federal statutes by title. FDsys is the successor to "GPO Access."

c. Annotated Versions of the *United States Code*

Although the *United States Code* (U.S.C.) is an efficiently organized set of federal statutes, it has one glaring drawback from the perspective of legal researchers: It includes the exact language of our federal statutes, but it does not send researchers to cases that might interpret those statutes. Under the concept of stare decisis, discussed in Chapter 1, it is not the naked statutory language that controls a given situation but a court's interpretation of that statute. Thus, because U.S.C. simply recites the exact text of a federal statute without providing any comment regarding the law or any reference to any cases that may have interpreted the law, two private publishers, Lexis and West, have separately assumed the task of providing this critical information to legal professionals. Because the publication of their sets is not government approved, these publications are referred to as *unofficial*. Note that the terms "official" and "unofficial" relate to whether the publication of a set is government approved or not. The terms do not relate to the accuracy or credibility of a set. The text of a statute will be the same whether it is published in the official set, U.S.C., or in one of the unofficial sets, namely, U.S.C.A. or U.S.C.S. Both U.S.C.A. and U.S.C.S. are referred to as *annotated* codes, meaning that they include "notes" referring readers to cases interpreting statutes.

You will see from the following discussion that the two sets are highly similar. Generally, researchers will use one set rather than another, based on habit and convenience.

(1)   United States Code Annotated
and United States Code Service

West's set is called *United States Code Annotated* (U.S.C.A.); Lexis's set is *United States Code Service* (U.S.C.S.). Both are divided into the same 51 titles as U.S.C. and both include a multi-volume general index at the end of the set. The value of these sets is found not in their providing the language of federal statutes—U.S.C. provides that. Rather, these unofficial sets are valuable because of the helpful "extra" features they provide, which are nearly identical. These features are shown in Figure 3-2 and include the following (note that the names of these features vary slightly in U.S.C.A. and U.S.C.S.):

• **Historical and Statutory Notes.** Historical notes provide an overview of the history of a statute, including the Public Law number, the effective date of the statute, its citation to *United States Statutes at Large*, and an indication of the date(s) on which certain parts or subsections were amended, added, or deleted.

• **Cross-References.** Following the historical notes, you will be directed to other federal statutes that may help you understand this federal statute.

• **Library References.** Library references (called "Research Guide" in U.S.C.S.) direct you to other sources in the law library (including form books, practice manuals, texts and treatises, encyclopedias, and law review articles) that deal with the topic covered by the statute.

• **Annotations.** The annotations (called "Notes of Decisions" in U.S.C.A. and "Interpretive Notes and Decisions" in U.S.C.S.) are the most valuable part of U.S.C.A. and U.S.C.S. because they will direct you to cases that have interpreted the statute you have just read. You will be given a one-sentence description of the case and then its citation. You can then decide whether to read the case in full. Both U.S.C.A. and U.S.C.S. organize these annotations for you by topic or issue, making it easy for you to select the right cases to read.

(2)   *Pocket Parts and Updating*

Because federal statutes are amended so frequently, U.S.C.A. and U.S.C.S. are kept current by the most typical method of updating legal volumes: annual cumulative pocket parts. A slit or "pocket" has been created in the back cover of each hardback volume of U.S.C.A. and U.S.C.S. During each year, West and Lexis mail small, softcover pamphlets called *pocket parts* to law firms and law libraries. These pocket parts slide into the slits in the back of each hardback volume of U.S.C.A. and U.S.C.S. and provide current information about the statutes in that volume, including amendments to the statute and references or annotations to cases decided since the hardback volumes were placed on the library shelves. The pocket parts or supplements are cumulative, meaning that if a hardback volume is issued in 2009, the 2013 pocket part or supplement will include all changes and updates since 2009. The numbering of statutes in

Figure 3-2
Sample Pages from U.S.C.A.

Gibson-Stewart Co., D.C.Ohio 1961, 202 F.Supp. 6.

There can be no recovery for period before a defendant is expressly notified by patentee that it is infringing a particular patent. International Nickel Co. v. Ford Motor Co., D.C.N.Y.1958, 166 F.Supp. 551.

In patent infringement action, accounting period was properly commenced on date when written infringement notice was given to infringer rather than on date of patent grant. Mathey v. United Shoe Machinery Corporation, D.C.Mass.1944, 54 F.Supp. 694.

In patent infringement suit, where evidence showed that defendant corporation's employee, whom plaintiff told that defendant would be held liable if it infringed patent, had no authority to receive such notice and communicate it to defendant, and there was no proof of defendant's manufacture or sale of infringing machine after actual notice of infringement in letter to defendant from plaintiff's attorney, plaintiff was not entitled to accounting for profits or damages. Federal Machine & Welder Co. v. Mesta Mach. Co., D.C.Pa. 1939, 27 F.Supp. 747, reversed on other grounds 110 F.2d 479.

The filing of bill of complaint and service thereof on defendant in patent infringement suit did not of itself constitute such a compli-

ance with this section as to entitle plaintiff to an accounting for infringement by defendant occurring pendente lite. Hazeltine Corporation v. Radio Corporation of America, D.C. N.Y.1937, 20 F.Supp. 668.

37. Injunction

This section, limiting damages in patent infringement suit, pertains only to damages and does not preclude grant of injunctive relief. Eversharp, Inc. v. Fisher Pen Co., D.C.Ill.1961, 204 F.Supp. 649.

Where infringement of patent had not interfered with patentee's business, patentee was not entitled to any damages but infringer would be enjoined from making article and selling same. Metal Stamping Co. of Greenville v. General Mfg. Co., D.C.Tex.1957, 149 F.Supp. 508.

Defendant's motion for preliminary injunction restraining plaintiff from sending notices of infringement to defendant's customers and from threatening or starting suit against defendant's customers would be denied, where there was nothing in moving papers to justify conclusion that such letters were sent out in bad faith or otherwise than as notices of infringement as provided for in this section. Glatt v. Notion Accessories, D.C.N.Y.1954, 129 F.Supp. 297.

---

§ 288. Action for infringement of a patent containing an invalid claim

Whenever, without deceptive intention, a claim of a patent is invalid, an action may be maintained for the infringement of a claim of the patent which may be valid. The patentee shall recover no costs unless a disclaimer of the invalid claim has been entered at the Patent and Trademark Office before the commencement of the suit.

— Text of Statute

(July 19, 1952, c. 950, § 1, 66 Stat. 813; Jan. 2, 1975, Pub.L. 93–596, § 1, 88 Stat. 1949.)

Historical and Revision Notes

Reviser's Note. Based on Title 35, U.S.C., 1946 ed., § 71 (R.S. 4922 [derived from Act July 8, 1870, c. 230, § 60, 16 Stat. 207]).

The necessity for a disclaimer to recover on valid claims is eliminated. See section 253.

Language is changed.

1975 Amendment. Pub.L. 93–596 substituted "Patent and Trademark Office" for "Patent Office".

Effective Date of 1975 Amendment. Amendment by Pub.L. 93–596 effective Jan. 2, 1975, see section 4 of Pub.L. 93–596, set out as a note under section 1111 of Title 15, Commerce and Trade.

Legislative History. For legislative history and purpose of Pub.L. 93–596, see 1974 U.S. Code Cong. and Adm.News, p. 7113.

— Historical and Statutory Notes

Figure 3-2 *(Continued)*

CH. 29 INFRINGEMENT—INVALID CLAIMS   35 § 288
                                                              Note 2

**Cross
References**

Cross References

Costs as excluded from judgment in infringement action unless disclaimer was filed in Patent
   and Trademark Office prior to commencement of action, see section 1928 of Title 28,
   Judiciary and Judicial Procedure.
Filing fee, see section 41 of this title.
Infringement of patent, see section 271 of this title.
Right to disclaim and requisites and effect of disclaimer, see section 253 of this title.

Federal Rules

Effect of rule 54 on former section 71 of this title, see note by Advisory Committee under said
   rule 54, Federal Rules of Civil Procedure, Title 28, Judiciary and Judicial Procedure.
Judgment and costs, see rule 54, Federal Rules of Civil Procedure, Title 28.
One form of action, see rule 2, Federal Rules of Civil Procedure, Title 28.

Code of Federal Regulations

Disclaimer, see 37 CFR 1.321, set out in the Appendix.

**Library
References**

Library References

Patents ⊛⊐226 et seq.   C.J.S. Patents § 282.

Notes of Decisions

**Index to
Numbered
Annotations**

Abandonment of claims 5
Appellate costs 18
Burden of proof 14
Combination claims 6
Compliance with section 3
Construction with other laws 1
Costs
    Generally 17
    Appellate costs 18
    Partial success 19
Deception 10
Dismissal 22
Failure to file disclaimer
    Generally 7
    Unreasonable neglect or delay 8
Fraud or deception 10
Material and substantial parts 4
Partial success, costs 19
Persons entitled to sue 12
Pleadings 13
Prerequisites to action 11
Purpose 2
Questions of fact 16
Res judicata 20
Scope of
    Determination 15
    Review 21
Substantial parts 4
Unreasonable neglect or delay, failure to file
    disclaimer 8
Validation 9

1. Construction with other laws

This section should be construed in connection with former section 65 [now 253] of this

title. Sessions v. Romadka, Wis.1892, 12
S.Ct. 799, 145 U.S. 29, 36 L.Ed. 609.

This section, construed in connection with
former section 65 [now 253] of this title, gives
no authority for amending a patent by means
of a disclaimer. Hailes v. Albany Stove Co.,
N.Y.1887, 8 S.Ct. 262, 123 U.S. 582, 31
L.Ed. 284.

Where certain claims were not put in issue
by either party in action for infringement, any
determination as to the validity would have
been error and would have violated rights
reserved to patentee by section 253 of this
title and this section, which were enacted to
mitigate earlier rule under which patent was
held void if any claims thereof were found to
be invalid. Chemical Const. Corp. v. Jones
& Laughlin Steel Corp., C.A.Pa.1962, 311
F.2d 367.

**Anno-
tations**

Section 253 of this title providing for filing
of disclaimers of claims in patent and this
section providing for actions for infringement
of patents which include unpatentable claims,
should be read together. Del Riccio v.
Photochart, 1954, 268 P.2d 814, 124 C.A.2d
301.

2. Purpose

Object of this section is to legalize and
uphold suits brought on such patents as are
mentioned in former section 65 [now 253] of
this title, to the extent that the patentees are
entitled to claim the inventions therein pat-
ented. Hailes v. Albany Stove Co., N.Y.
1887, 8 S.Ct. 262, 265, 123 U.S. 582, 31
L.Ed. 284. See, also, General Electric Co. v.

587

the pocket parts is identical to that in the hardback volumes. Eventually, if a book becomes worn out, the publisher will replace that single volume. On occasion, a softcover book, called a *supplement*, is placed on the shelf next to a hardbound volume to update it.

There are few invariable or inflexible rules in legal research, but one of them is that you must always consult a pocket part (or supplement) if the volume you are using is updated by one.

The publishers of U.S.C.A. and U.S.C.S. also publish additional pamphlets to help researchers update statutes before the publication of next year's pocket part. Therefore, after you check the pocket part (published yearly) when using West's U.S.C.A., check West's Statutory Supplements (published monthly) to determine if more recent changes have occurred. When using Lexis's U.S.C.S., check its pamphlets called *Cumulative Later Case and Statutory Service* (published three times annually) and its monthly pamphlet called *U.S.C.S. Advance*. Of course, Lexis and Westlaw (the computerized legal research systems) provide "one-stop" immediate updating and offer hyperlinks to relevant cases, making statutory research using Lexis and Westlaw easy and effective.

Finally, you may be able to do some updating using the following online sources:

- Office of the Law Revision Counsel (http://uscode.house.gov) lists the sections of the *United States Code* affected by recently enacted laws. Select "Classification Tables."
- FDsys (http://www.gpo.gov/fdsys) the Federal Digital System (the successor to GPO Access), attempts to ensure that its online references to the *United States Code* are always current.

See Figure 3-3 for a chart showing how to update research of federal statutes.

Figure 3-3
Updating Federal Statutory Research

U.S.C.	U.S.C.A.	U.S.C.S.
Read statute in main hardbound volume.	Read statute in main hardbound volume.	Read statute in main hardbound volume.
Check annual hardbound supplements.	Check annual pocket part or softcover supplements.	Check annual pocket part or softcover supplements.
Check slip laws or USCCAN.	Check U.S.C.A.'s Statutory Supplements.	Check U.S.C.S.'s *Cumulative Later Case and Statutory Service* and its *Advance* pamphlets.
	Check slip laws or USCCAN.	Check slip laws or USCCAN.

Figure 3-3 *(Continued)*

U.S.C.	U.S.C.A.	U.S.C.S.
Check FDsys at http://www.gpo.gov/fdsys or the website http://uscode.house.gov.	Check FDsys at http://www.gpo.gov/fdsys or the website http://uscode.house.gov.	Check FDsys at http://www.gpo.gov/fdsys or the website http://uscode.house.gov.

d. Use of U.S.C., U.S.C.A., and U.S.C.S.

Researchers often wonder which set they should use when researching federal statutes. Here are some tips:

• Use U.S.C. only when you need the exact wording of a federal statute and do not need references to cases or other authorities interpreting the statute. Many researchers use U.S.C. only infrequently.

• Use either U.S.C.A. or U.S.C.S. when you are interested in researching the history of a statute, finding other sources in the law library that discuss that statute, and, most important, locating judicial decisions that have interpreted the statute. Remember that in most respects, U.S.C.A. and U.S.C.S. are *competitive* sets, meaning they are essentially the same. The choice of which set you ultimately use will likely depend on habit or convenience. Some researchers prefer an integrated approach to all legal research and will consistently use all West publications when possible, whereas others prefer to use Lexis's sets. Only in the most detailed research project should you consult both sets. Ordinarily, one set will be sufficient for nearly all of your research needs, and most law firms, corporations, and agencies purchase one set or the other, but not both.

Ethics Alert

How to Use the Annotations

Never fully rely on or quote from the one-sentence annotations or descriptions of cases provided by U.S.C.A., U.S.C.S., or any other annotated set. It is not possible to convey complex case analysis in one sentence. They are not the law but rather very brief summaries of the law that are prepared by commercial publishers, not courts, solely for the convenience of readers.

---

4. *Research Techniques*

Researchers generally use one of the three following techniques to find statutes:

a. Descriptive Word Approach

Both U.S.C.A. and U.S.C.S. have a multi-volume general index, which is arranged alphabetically and is usually located after Title 51, the last title in both sets. These softcover general indices are replaced and updated every year. When you are assigned a legal research problem, think of key words and phrases that describe this problem, and then look up these words or phrases in the general index of either U.S.C.A. or U.S.C.S., which will then direct you to the appropriate title and section you need. This technique, usually called the *descriptive word approach* or *index method*, is the simplest and most reliable way to locate federal statutes.

U.S.C.A. and U.S.C.S. will direct you to the appropriate statute by listing the title first and then identifying the specific statute section, as follows:

Citizenship, **8 § 1409**

You are thus directed to Title 8, Section 1409. See Figure 3-4 for a sample page from U.S.C.A. General Index.

This descriptive word approach (sometimes called the "index method" because you use the general index to find statutes) is usually the easiest and most efficient way to locate a statute, particularly for beginning researchers.

b. Title or Topic Approach

You may become so familiar with the organization of U.S.C.A. or U.S.C.S. that when given a research problem you can bypass the general index and go directly to the appropriate title. This is the *title* or *topic approach*. For example, if you know that a patent statute is in Title 35, you can retrieve the appropriate volume and look at the table of contents for Title 35 at the beginning of Title 35, or go directly to the index for all of the patent statutes found at the end of the title. You will then review the statutes and annotations.

This title/topic approach is best employed by researchers who are sufficiently familiar with U.S.C.A. and U.S.C.S. so they can confidently select the one relevant title of the 51 titles available and review the statutes therein.

c. Popular Name Approach

Many of our federal statutes are known by a popular name—either that of the sponsors of the legislation (for example, the Sarbanes-Oxley Act of 2002) or that given the legislation by the public or media (for example, the AMBER Alert Act). If you are asked to locate one of these statutes, you can easily do so in either U.S.C.A. or U.S.C.S. by using the *popular name approach*.

Figure 3-4
Sample Page from U.S.C.A. General Index

TRADE SECRETS—Cont'd
Steel and aluminum energy conservation, 15 § 5104
Technical Study Group on Cigarette and Little Cigar Fire Safety, 15 § 2054 nt
Trade agreements, 19 § 2155
United States Court of International Trade, 28 § 2641
Water Pollution, this index

TRADE SHOWS
Exports and imports, regulation and control of, Peoples Republic of China, goods for, license applications, approval, national security controls, 50 App. § 2404
Income Tax, this index
Secretary of Commerce, authority, 15 § 4724
Small businesses, definitions, authority of Secretary of Commerce, 15 § 4724
United States business, definitions, authority of Secretary of Commerce, 15 § 4724

TRADE UNIONS
Labor Organizations, generally, this index

TRADE ZONE
Foreign Trade Zones, generally, this index

TRADEMARK ACT
Generally, 15 § 1051 et seq.

TRADEMARK AMENDMENTS ACT OF 1999
See Popular Name Table

TRADEMARK CLARIFICATION ACT OF 1984
See Popular Name Table

TRADEMARK COUNTERFEITING ACT OF 1984
See Popular Name Table

TRADEMARK LAW REVISION ACT OF 1988
See Popular Name Table

TRADEMARK REMEDY CLARIFICATION ACT
See Popular Name Table

TRADEMARK TRIAL AND APPEAL BOARD
Appeal to,
Board from a decision of examiner, 15 § 1070
United States Court of Appeals for the Federal Circuit on Board's decision, 15 § 1071
Composition, 15 § 1067
Determination of respective rights of registration, 15 § 1067
Election of remedies on dissatisfaction with Board's decision, 15 § 1071
Fee on appeal to Board from examiner's decision, 15 § 1070
Hearing on application for cancellation of registration on supplemental register, 15 § 1092

TRADEMARK TRIAL AND APPEAL BOARD —Cont'd
Notice to registrant of application for cancellation of registration on supplemental register, 15 § 1092
Number of members to hear cases, 15 § 1067
Reference to board of application for cancellation of registration on supplemental register, 15 § 1092
United States Court of Appeals for the Federal Circuit, jurisdiction of appeals from decisions, 28 § 1295

TRADEMARKS AND TRADE NAMES
Generally, 15 § 1051 et seq.
Abandonment, 15 §§ 1062, 1127
Defense, infringement suit, 15 § 1115
Definitions, 15 § 1127
Foreign countries, 15 § 1141c
Time for petitioning to cancel registration, 15 § 1064
Acknowledgments, 15 § 1061
Assignment, 15 § 1060
Actions and proceedings, 15 § 1114 et seq.
Civil action, against persons using deceptive conduct, false or misleading descriptions in attempts to deceive, 15 § 1125
Cyberpiracy, 15 §§ 1125, 1129
False designations of origin, false descriptions and dilution, 15 § 1125
Foreign register mark or name, 15 § 1126
Infringement, generally, post
Pending actions not affected by repeal of laws, 15 § 1051 nt
Postal emergency, relief as to filing date of trade-mark application or registration, 35 § 111 nt
United States Olympic Committee, 36 § 220506
Waiver or election by adverse party, civil actions, dissatisfaction with decision of Commissioner or Trademark Trial and Appeal Board, 15 § 1071
Adjustment, fees, filing, application, 15 § 1113, 1113 nt
Advertisements,
Certification mark, 15 § 1064
Destruction of infringing trademark, 15 § 1118
Injunction against presenting advertising matter containing trademark, 15 § 1114
Affidavits,
Duration, affixing specimen or facsimile, 15 § 1058
Foreign countries, 15 § 1141k
Obtain incontestable right to use mark, 15 § 1065
Use of trademarks, 15 § 1058
Appeals to court by registrant who has filed, dissatisfaction with decisions of Commissioner or Trademark Trial and Appeal Board, 15 § 1071
Agent for service of process, foreign countries, 15 §§ 1141h, 1141k
Alien property, divestment, 50 App. § 43

Reference to other part of U.S.C.A. Index

Reference to 15 U.S.C.A. § 1051

Both U.S.C.A. and U.S.C.S. include a volume or volumes titled *Popular Name Table*, which lists in alphabetical order federal laws known by their popular names. Simply look up the law you are interested in, and you will be directed to the appropriate title and section. See Figure 3-5 for a sample page from U.S.C.A.'s Popular Name Table.

Finally, if you have only a public law number (such as Pub. L. No. 112-114) or a reference to the statute from *United States Statutes at Large* (such as 117 Stat. 660), both U.S.C.A. and U.S.C.S. have separate volumes marked "Tables," which convert a public law number or a *United States Statutes at Large* citation into a citation to U.S.C.A. or U.S.C.S.

Practice Tip

Infra *and* Supra

When using indices for almost any set of law books, you may encounter the words *infra* (meaning "below") and *supra* (meaning "above"). These are signal terms that direct you to other pages within the index. For example, if you look up the word "tenant" in an index, you may see the instruction "See landlord, *supra*," meaning that you should look at the entries listed under the word "landlord" given previously in the index. The instruction "See tenant, *infra*," directs you to look at entries given later in the index.

---

5. *United States Constitution*

Although the United States Constitution is not one of the 51 titles of the *United States Code*, nevertheless, both U.S.C.A. and U.S.C.S. contain volumes for the Constitution. When conducting constitutional research in U.S.C.A. or U.S.C.S., you will be provided with the text of the pertinent constitutional provision and then, by the use of annotations, you will be referred to cases that interpret it. The three primary research techniques described above should also be used when you research a constitutional law issue.

Help Line

Personal Research Assistance

If you have any difficulty performing statutory research using Lexis or Westlaw, you may call either Lexis (800-897-7922) or West (800-733-2889) to receive personal assistance from reference attorneys.

Figure 3-5
Sample Page from U.S.C.A. Popular Name Table

973   POPULAR NAME TABLE

San Carlos Apache Tribe Water Rights Settlement Act of 1992
Pub.L. 102–575, Title XXXVII, Oct. 30, 1992, 106 Stat. 4740 (25 §§ 390, 390 note; 43 §§ 1524, 1524 note)
Pub.L. 103–263, § 2(a), May 31, 1994, 108 Stat. 708
Pub.L. 103–435, § 13, Nov. 2, 1994, 108 Stat. 4572 (25 §§ 390 note)
Pub.L. 104–91, Title II, § 202(a), Jan. 6, 1996, 110 Stat. 14 (25 § 390 note)
Pub.L. 104–261, § 3, Oct. 9, 1996, 110 Stat. 3176 (25 § 390 note)
Pub.L. 105–18, Title II, § 5003, June 12, 1997, 111 Stat. 181 (25 § 390 note)

San Carlos Indian Irrigation Project Divestiture Act of 1991
Pub.L. 102–231, Dec. 12, 1991, 105 Stat. 1722
Pub.L. 102–497, § 6, Oct. 24, 1992, 106 Stat. 3256

San Carlos Mineral Strip Act of 1990
Pub.L. 101–447, Oct. 22, 1990, 104 Stat. 1047

San Domingo Resolution
Jan. 12, 1871, No. 7, 16 Stat. 591

San Francisco Maritime National Historical Park Act of 1988
Short title, see 16 USCA § 410nn note
Pub.L. 100–348, June 27, 1988, 102 Stat. 654 (16 §§ 410nn, 410nn note, 410nn–1 to 410nn–4, 460bb–3)
Pub.L. 103–437, § 6(d)(11), Nov. 2, 1994, 108 Stat. 4584 (16 §§ 410nn, 410nn–2)

San Gabriel River Watershed Study Act
Pub.L. 108–42, July 1, 2003, 117 Stat. 840

San Juan Basin Wilderness Protection Act of 1984
Pub.L. 98–603, Oct. 30, 1984, 98 Stat. 3155 (16 § 1132 note; 25 § 640d–10)
Pub.L. 101–556, § 6, Nov. 15, 1990, 104 Stat. 2764

Referecnce to 43 U.S.C.A. § 1785

Pub.L. 104–333, Div. I, Title X, Subtitle C, § 1022(b) to (e), Nov. 12, 1996, 110 Stat. 4211 to 4213 (16 § 1132 note; (43 § 1785))
Pub.L. 106–176, Title I, § 124, Mar. 10, 2000, 114 Stat. 30 (43 § 1785)

San Juan Island National Historical Park Act
Pub.L. 89–565, Sept. 9, 1966, 80 Stat. 737 (16 §§ 282–282c)

San Luis Rey Indian Water Rights Settlement Act
Pub.L. 100–675, Title I, Nov. 17, 1988, 102 Stat. 4000
Pub.L. 102–154, Title I, § 117, Nov. 13, 1991, 105 Stat. 1012
Pub.L. 106–377, § 1(b) [Title II, § 211], Oct. 27, 2000, 114 Stat. 1441, 1441A–70

Sand Creek Massacre National Historic Site Establishment Act of 2000
Pub.L. 106–465, Nov. 7, 2000, 114 Stat. 2019 (16 § 461 note)

Sand Creek Massacre National Historic Site Study Act of 1998
Pub.L. 105–243, Oct. 6, 1998, 112 Stat. 1579

Sanitary Food Transportation Act of 1990
Pub.L. 101–500, Nov. 3, 1990, 104 Stat. 1213 (49 § 521; 49 App. §§ 1814, 2501 note, 2801, 2801 notes, 2802 to 2812)
Pub.L. 103–272, § 7(b), July 5, 1994, 108 Stat. 1398 (49 App. §§ 1814, 2501 note, 2801 to 2812)
Pub.L. 103–429, § 8(15), Oct. 31, 1994, 108 Stat. 4391 (49 App. §§ 2501 note, 2801 note)

Santa Fe Indian School Act
See, also, Omnibus Indian Advancement Act
Pub.L. 106–568, Title VIII, Subtitle B (§§ 821 to 824), Dec. 27, 2000, 114 Stat. 2921

Santa Monica Mountains National Recreation Area Boundary Adjustment Act
Short title, see 16 USCA § 1 note
Pub.L. 107–236, Oct. 9, 2002, 116 Stat. 1483 (16 §§ 1 note, 460kk)

Santa Rosa and San Jacinto Mountains National Monument Act of 2000
Pub.L. 106–351, Oct. 24, 2000, 114 Stat. 1362 (16 § 431 note)
Pub.L. 106–434, § 2, Nov. 6, 2000, 114 Stat. 1912 (16 § 431 note)

Santini-Burton Act
Pub.L. 96–586, Dec. 23, 1980, 94 Stat. 3381 (16 §§ 461 note, 467, 467a, 467a–1)

B.   State Legislation

1. *Introduction*

The process of enacting and publishing legislation at the state level is substantially similar to the process described previously for the federal level. Just as the U.S. Congress is divided into two chambers—the House of Representatives and the Senate—each state (except for Nebraska) has a legislature divided into two chambers. The names given to the two chambers, however, will vary from state to state.

Similar to the process of enacting federal law, much of the work in enacting state law is done by committees. When a final version of a bill is agreed upon, it will be sent to the governor of the state for signature, at which time it is now a "law" or "statute" rather than a bill. The website of the National Conference of State Legislatures (http://www.ncsl.org) provides direct links to each state's legislative home page.

2. *Publication and Codification of State Statutes*

State statutes initially appear in slip form and are then compiled in sets of books generally called *session laws*. The session laws are analogous to *United States Statutes at Large* in that they contain laws, but due to their chronological arrangement, they are not particularly helpful to researchers. Thus, the states have codified their session laws to bring together all the current laws on the same subject and eliminate repealed laws. These state codifications may be called "codes," "compilations," "revisions," or "consolidations" depending on the state. Most states have annotated codes, meaning that after you are given the wording of the pertinent statute, you will be directed to cases that interpret the statute.

Although the publication of each state's statutes will vary somewhat, and the publication may be unofficial or official, most state codes share the following features:

- The state's constitution is usually included in the state's code;
- The statutes will be organized by subject matter so that all of the corporations statutes are grouped together, all of the probate statutes are grouped together, and so forth;
- There will be a general index to the entire set, and often, each title (such as "Probate") begins or ends with its own index;
- The statutes are kept current by annual cumulative pocket parts or supplements;
- Annotations will be provided to direct you to cases interpreting the statutes, typically through the use of a one-sentence summary of the case and the case citation, similar to the organization of U.S.C.A. and U.S.C.S. annotations;

- "Extra" features, such as historical notes and library references, will be provided to assist you in interpreting the statute; and
- Conversion tables are provided in each volume so that if a state statute has been repealed or renumbered, you will be informed of the repealing or provided with the new section number. See Figure 3-6 for a sample page showing a state statute.

3. *Research Techniques*

The same techniques used to locate federal statutes are used to locate state statutes. They are as follows:

• **Descriptive Word Approach.** This method requires you to determine which words or phrases relate to the issue you are researching and then locate those words or phrases in the general index, which will then direct you to the pertinent statute.

• **Title/Topic Approach.** This technique may be used when you have become so familiar with your state code that you bypass the general index and immediately locate the particular title or section that deals with the research problem.

• **Popular Name Approach.** This method of locating statutes is used in those instances in which a state statute is known by a popular name, such as the "Megan's Law" in your state. Look up the name of the statute in the alphabetically arranged general index.

Figure 3-6
Sample Page from Code of Virginia

Text of state statute and historical notes

§ 18.2-256. **Conspiracy.** — Any person who conspires to commit any offense defined in this article or in the Drug Control Act (§ 54.1-3400 et seq.) is punishable by imprisonment or fine or both which may not be less than the minimum punishment nor exceed the maximum punishment prescribed for the offense, the commission of which was the object of the conspiracy. (Code 1950, § 54-524.104; 1970, c. 650; 1972, c. 798; 1975, cc. 14, 15; 1978, c. 130.)

Cross references. — As to exception of offenses defined in this chapter from the provisions of the general statute governing conspiracy to commit felony, see § 18.2-22 (d).

Law Review. — For survey of Virginia criminal law for the year 1972-1973, see 59 Va. L. Rev. 1458 (1973).

Annotation

A single agreement can form the basis for multiple violations of this section. Otherwise, criminals would be encouraged to plot a number of drug-related crimes simultaneously, because only one conspiracy would exist. This could not have been the intention of the General Assembly. Wooten v. Commonwealth, 235 Va. 89, 368 S.E.2d 693 (1988).

Conspiring with police officer and officer's informant. — An accused may not be convicted under this section for conspiring to distribute cocaine with a police officer and the officer's confidential informant. Fortune v. Commonwealth, 12 Va. App. 643, 406 S.E.2d 47 (1991).

Evidence of acts of co-conspirators. — Where the Commonwealth's evidence established a prima facie case of conspiracy, the trial court did not err in admitting evidence of acts of co-conspirators in furtherance of that conspiracy. Barber v. Commonwealth, 5 Va. App. 172, 360 S.E.2d 888 (1987).

Evidence of another conspiracy was properly admitted to prove defendant's intent and to show that both conspiracies were part of a common scheme or plan. Barber v. Commonwealth, 5 Va. App. 172, 360 S.E.2d 888 (1987).

Evidence that defendants constructively possessed cocaine was probative of the object of the conspiracy. Hodge v. Commonwealth, 7 Va. App. 351, 374 S.E.2d 76 (1988).

Finally, there is no single set of books that will provide you with all of the laws for all 50 states. Such a set would be unwieldy, expensive, and generally not very useful, because researchers in one state are usually not interested in the statutes of another state.

C. Rules of Procedure and Court Rules

1. Introduction

To promote efficient operation, courts are empowered to enact certain rules relating to various court procedures and administrative matters, such as when papers must be filed and the format of papers presented to the court. In addition to rules relating to such administrative matters, there are rules relating to more substantive matters, such as rules of evidence and rules of civil and criminal procedure. Although many rules are not statutes or laws, they are binding on those practicing before the court, and thus they are discussed here.

In civil actions, all federal district courts follow the Federal Rules of Civil Procedure (FRCP), which provide rules on pleadings, motions, discovery, and civil trials. In addition, the district courts may make their own local rules governing practice in their courts.

Similarly, nearly all states have modeled their own civil procedural rules after the FRCP, and in addition, have local or court rules governing practice before the courts. For simplicity, this discussion will refer to the more significant rules (such as the FRCP) as *rules of procedure* and the more local rules, which generally govern less substantive matters (for example, the format of documents), as *court rules*.

2. Federal Rules of Procedure

The FRCP became effective in 1938 and govern the conduct of all civil litigation in the United States District Courts. The FRCP govern all trial-related matters, from the commencement of an action to motions and discovery practice to the trial itself. The FRCP can be found in both U.S.C.A. and U.S.C.S. and can be located by any of the standard research techniques used for locating statutes: the descriptive word approach, the topic approach, or the popular name approach. Once you review the rule, scan the annotations, and then select cases to read that have interpreted the rule.

Appellate practice in the federal courts of appeal is governed by the Federal Rules of Appellate Procedure. Matters of evidence are governed by the Federal Rules of Evidence, and matters relating to criminal procedure are governed by the Federal Rules of Criminal Procedure. All of the major federal rules (the Federal Rules of Civil Procedure, Federal Rules of Criminal Procedure, Federal Rules of Appellate Procedure, and Federal Rules of Evidence) are available through the U.S. Courts website at http://www.uscourts.gov/RulesandPolicies/rules.aspx.

Several sets of books are useful in interpreting the federal rules, such as *Federal Rules Service, 3d* and *Moore's Federal Practice*, which include the text of the federal rules and direct you to cases interpreting the rules.

3. *Federal Court Rules*

In addition to the substantive federal procedural rules that govern practice in our nation's federal courts, the lower federal courts themselves are free to enact their own more local rules of court. Often these rules are administrative and relate to matters such as the maximum length of a brief or citation form.

With 94 district courts and 13 circuits, determining the specific rules for each court can be a daunting task. All of these rules are now available on the Internet through www.uscourts.gov/RulesandPolicies/rules.aspx. Finally, the rules for the U.S. Supreme Court are posted on its website at http://www.supremecourt.gov.

4. *State Rules of Procedure and Court Rules*

To promote efficiency in litigation, states have also adopted rules of procedure and rules of court. Most states now publish their rules on their websites. Failure to follow the local rules regarding even such seemingly minor matters as the type size to be used may result in rejection of documents and pleadings. If your pleading is rejected for nonconformance with local rules and the time limit for filing the pleading expires before you can submit an acceptable pleading, the client's rights may be jeopardized, and your firm may be subject to a claim of legal malpractice.

To obtain a copy of the local rules, contact the clerk of the court and arrange to purchase a set of the rules. Alternatively, access FindLaw at http://lp.findlaw.com, which will link you to many local court rules for each state. Review Table T.1.3 of *The Bluebook* or Appendix 2 of *ALWD* for a reference to each state's judicial website (which usually provides the court's rules).

D. Uniform and Model Laws

Uniform laws are those drafted for topics of the law in which uniformity is desirable and practical. For example, a set of laws relating to the formation, operation, and dissolution of partnerships, called the Uniform Partnership Act, has been adopted in some form by nearly all United States jurisdictions. Once adopted in a state, a uniform law is then a state statute like any other and can be located using any of the research techniques discussed previously. Many states, however, often make changes and modifications to the uniform laws, resulting in laws that are highly similar from state to state but that are not perfectly uniform across the nation. Uniform laws and model acts (designed to promote reform) are discussed further in Chapter 6.

E. Statutory Research Overview

When you are undecided whether to begin a project by examining federal or state statutes, keep in mind that some matters are exclusively presumed to be federal in nature. For example, patent law is the exclusive province of the federal government, which eliminates the confusion that would result if each state issued its own patents. On the other hand, states have the power to enact laws relating to local concerns, such as residency laws for obtaining a divorce. If you are uncertain whether an area of law is governed by federal or state law, examine the federal statutes first, and then proceed to examine your state statutes if the topic is not covered by federal statute.

Following are some tips to help you research statutes more efficiently:

- Quickly review the entire scope of the statutes governing your topic. Generally, terms used in the act are first defined. Definitions are usually followed by the rules announced in the statute and then by penalties for violations of the statute.
- Assume that each word in the statute is there for a purpose and that the words are to be given their plain meaning.
- Examine the cases that discuss the statute to determine how courts have interpreted the statute. Remember that it is the province of our courts to apply and interpret statutes and even strike down statutes as unconstitutional.

Finally, although the rules and regulations of administrative agencies such as the Food and Drug Administration or the Securities and Exchange Commission are as binding as statutes (in that violations can be punished, usually by fines), administrative law is discussed in Chapter 7 because it is somewhat of a "specialized" field of research and not commonly performed by most legal professionals.

F. Citation Form

	Bluebook (for practitioners)	ALWD
Federal Statutes	• 11 U.S.C. § 1327(a) (2006). • 11 U.S.C.A. § 1327(a) (West 2004). • 11 U.S.C.S. § 1327(a) (LexisNexis 2009).	• 11 U.S.C. § 1327(a) (2006). • 11 U.S.C.A. § 1327(a) (West 2004). • 11 U.S.C.S. § 1327(a) (Lexis 2009).
State Statutes (Citation form may vary between *Bluebook* Table T.1.3 and *ALWD* Appendix 1.)	• Ind. Code Ann. § 14-11-2-2 (West 1998). • Wash. Rev. Code § 8.04 (1997).	• Ind. Code Ann. § 14-11-2-2 (West 1998). • Wash. Rev. Code § 8.04 (1997).
Court Rules	• Fed. R. Civ. P. 12(b). • Cal. R. Ct. 3.54	• Fed. R. Civ. P. 12(b). • Cal. R. Ct. 3.54

Internet Resources

http://beta.congress.gov	Congress.gov contains the full text of pending bills, key legislation, committee and congressional information, and additional information.
http://www.gpo.gov/fdsys	FDsys, the United States Government Printing Office site, offers access to bills, public and private laws, and the authenticated *United States Code*.
http://uscode.house/gov	The Law Revision Counsel provides information about and searching of the *United States Code*.
http://www.uscourts.gov	U.S. Courts provides direct links to all federal courts and federal rules.
http://www.law.cornell.edu	Cornell University Law School's site offers easy access to federal and state statutes and federal and state court rules.
http://www.justia.com	Justia is a general legal site, allowing researchers to find statutes, court rules, and a wide variety of other legal materials.

Research Assignment

1. What title of the United States Code relates to National Commercial and Space Programs?
2. Use U.S.C.A. and cite the title and section that govern the following:
   a. The banning of harmful medical devices.
   b. The motto "In God We Trust."
3. Use either U.S.C.A. or U.S.C.S. and cite the title and section that govern the following:
   a. The term of office of the advisory board of the National Institute on Deafness and Other Communication Disorders.
   b. Using dogs to detect explosives at airports.
4. Use the popular name tables as directed and cite the title and section for the following:
   a. Use U.S.C.A. and give the citation for the short title of the Do-Not-Call Improvement Act of 2007.
   b. Use U.S.C.S. and give the citation for the short title of the STOP Act.
   c. Use either U.S.C.A. or U.S.C.S. and give the citation for the Comstock Act.
5. Use U.S.C.A. How is the word "boxer" defined?
6. Use either U.S.C.A. or U.S.C.S. Give the citation for the statute that provides the definition of "armor piercing ammunition."
7. Use the U.S.C.A. volumes for the Constitution. Answer the following questions and cite the best case to support your answer. Give case names only.
   a. Under the Fourth Amendment Plain View Doctrine, if an inspector was in a legitimate position to view tennis shoes, may the shoes be seized without a warrant?
   b. Under the Eighth Amendment (Prison Sentences), is imposition of a mandatory life sentence on a defendant convicted of carjacking pursuant to federal three strikes laws grossly disproportionate to the offense so as to violate the Eighth Amendment?
8. Use U.S.C.A.
   a. Under 7 U.S.C.A. § 2132, does "exhibitor" include a circus? Answer the question and give the name of the case that supports your answer.
   b. What 1996 law review article are you directed to in order to better understand this statute?
   c. Give the public law designation for the 2013 amendments to this statute.
   d. To which C.F.R. provision are you directed?
9. Use U.S.C.S. What is the sentence of imprisonment if one is convicted of violating 18 U.S.C.S. § 473?

Internet Assignment

1. Access Congress.gov. Locate H.R. 41 introduced in the 113th Congress.
   a. What is the name of this legislation?
   b. What is its Public Law number?
2. Access Congress.gov. Select "Members." Who are the current senators from Florida?
3. Access Congress.gov. Locate H.R. 530 introduced in the 108th Congress.
   a. What is the title of this legislation?
   b. What was the purpose of this legislation?
   c. What is its Private Law number?
4. Access the website of the National Conference of State Legislatures. Select "Legislatures & Elections" and then "Origin/Procedures/Facilities." Review the information on full-time and part-time legislatures.
   a. Identify the "Red" legislatures.
   b. Briefly, what does it mean to say that a legislature has been categorized as a "Red" legislature?
5. Access FDsys. Select the U.S. Code for the most current year. Locate 15 U.S.C. § 12.
   a. What is the "legend" or note in the blue banner at the top of the page?
   b. What is the short title of this legislation?
6. Access the Rules for the U.S. Court of Appeals for the District of Columbia. Review Circuit Rule 28 (in particular, review the "Contents of Briefs: Additional Requirements" information).
   a. What does an asterisk placed next to an authority listed in a table of authorities mean?
   b. May the word *"passim"* be used?

Case Law and Judicial Opinions

Chapter Overview

This chapter discusses judicial opinions and provides you with an understanding of the publication of cases, the elements of a typical court case, and the types of opinions written by judges. The chapter also discusses West's *National Reporter System,* a comprehensive series of case reporters, which publishes both federal and state court cases. Finally, the process of analyzing and briefing cases is addressed.

A. Selective Publication of Cases

1. *Standards for Publishing Cases*

Not all cases are published or "reported." In general, and with the exception of some trial cases from our federal courts and a few from some state courts, trial court decisions are not usually published. If you consider the overwhelming number of routine assault and battery cases or cases relating to the possession of narcotics, you can readily see why trial court decisions are not usually published. Many of these cases add little to our body of precedents. Generally, only the decisions of the courts of last resort in a jurisdiction are published in full. For example, all of the decisions of the U.S. Supreme Court and the California Supreme Court are published in full, but not all decisions of the lower federal courts and lower California courts are. In fact, in 2011, only about 15 percent of cases from the U.S. Courts of Appeal were published.

In many instances, the courts themselves decide whether a case merits publication. Many courts publish only cases that establish a new rule of law, address an apparent conflict of authority, or involve a legal issue of continuing public interest. *See, e.g.,* Cal. R. Ct. 8.1105. In general, only appellate court cases that advance legal theory are published. Publishing every case decided in the United States this year would not be of any great value to researchers and would simply result in needless publication. Thus, a certain amount of "weeding out" or selectivity occurs in the publication of cases.

2.   *The Controversy Surrounding Unpublished Opinions*

As discussed previously, generally a court decides which cases to publish by certifying them for publication after determining that the cases meet the court's standards for publication. In recent years, however, the issue whether legal professionals may cite cases that have *not* been designated for publication has sparked a great deal of controversy.

Remember that "unpublished" does not mean "unavailable"; it simply means that the case will not be printed in a conventional hardbound book. As courts have published their opinions on their own websites and released them to Lexis and Westlaw, the online legal research systems, the public has been able to access these otherwise *unpublished* or *unreported decisions,* and attorneys and litigants have wanted to refer to, cite to, and rely upon these unpublished decisions to support their arguments and their clients' positions. Moreover, in 2001, West created the *Federal Appendix,* a set that prints the unpublished federal courts of appeal decisions, making these unpublished cases even more readily available to researchers. Finally, pursuant to the E-Government Act of 2002, 44 U.S.C. § 3601 (2006), all federal appellate courts must provide access over the Internet to all of their written opinions, regardless of whether such opinions are to be published. Thus, researchers were able to locate and access these "unpublished" cases through numerous means and demanded the right to cite to them in their briefs.

Yet, many courts retained "no citation" rules, meaning that unless the case had been designated by the court for publication, it could not be cited in court briefs and other documents. The issue was settled on December 1, 2006, when the Federal Rules of Appellate Procedure were amended to permit citation in briefs of cases that have been designated as "not for publication." Fed. R. App. P. 32.1. However, it was left up to the individual circuits to decide what effect or precedential value these unpublished opinions would have. For example, Rule 36-3 for the Ninth Circuit Court of Appeals provides that except in limited situations, unpublished decisions are not binding precedent.

State courts also differ in their treatment of unpublished decisions, with about one half of the states allowing citation of unpublished decisions, although most of these agree that these unpublished decisions are not binding precedent under the doctrine of stare decisis. Others, such as California, strictly prohibit courts and parties from citing or relying upon opinions not certified for publication except in very limited circumstances. Cal. R. Ct. 8.1115.

You may wonder whether you have an obligation to locate and cite to one of these numerous unpublished authorities if it supports a client's position. At present there is no legal obligation to locate authorities that may be persuasive only; thus, failure to cite to such unpublished opinions would likely not constitute malpractice.

B. Elements of a Case

Cases that are published or reported typically contain the following elements (see Figure 4-1).

1. *Case Name*

The name or title of a case identifies the parties involved in the action and also provides additional information about the nature of the proceeding. There are several types of case names, including the following:

- *Smith v. Jones.* A case name with a "v." in its title indicates an adversarial proceeding.
- *In re Smith.* The phrase "in re" means "regarding" or "in the matter of." This case name usually designates a case that is not adversarial in nature, such as a bankruptcy proceeding or probate matter involving only one party. Additionally, "in re" is used to designate civil cases involving multiple claims that are transferred to one federal court for coordinated and consistent handling, such as the case *In re Vitamins Antitrust Litigation.*
- *State v. Smith* (or *United States v. Smith).* This case name generally indicates a criminal proceeding, initiated by the state or federal government on behalf of its citizens, all of whom are injured by a crime.
- *In re Alison A.* Case names that provide only a party's first name or initials (such as *In re A.S.)* are typically used to designate matters involving minors.
- *Ex rel. Smith.* The phrase "ex rel." is short for "ex relatione," meaning "upon relation or information." Such a case name indicates a legal proceeding initiated by an attorney general or some other state or governmental official on behalf of a governmental entity but at the instigation of a private party who has an interest in the matter.

2. *Docket Number and Deciding Court*

Immediately beneath the case name you will be given the docket number of the case, which is a number used by the court to identify the case as it progresses through the court system. Following the docket number, the deciding court is usually identified.

Figure 4-1
Sample of a Published Case

Case Name

STATE of North Carolina

v.

John BOYD.

Docket Number

No. COA03–37.

Deciding Court

Court of Appeals of North Carolina.

Date of Decision

Jan. 6, 2004.

Background: Defendant was convicted in the Superior Court, Mecklenburg County, J. Gentry Caudill, J., of conspiracy to sell a controlled substance and was acquitted of sale of a controlled substance, contributing to the delinquency of a minor, and employing and using a minor to commit a controlled substance offense. He appealed conviction and sentence.

Holdings: The Court of Appeals, Wynn, J., held that:

Case Summary or Synopsis

(1) even if issue had been properly preserved for appeal, evidence was sufficient to sustain denial of defendant's motion to dismiss charge of conspiracy to sell a controlled substance, and

(2) defendant's acquittals did not preclude trial court from considering sentencing aggravating factor that defendant involved a person under 16 in commission of conspiracy.

Affirmed.

1. Criminal Law ⬳1044.2(2)

Headnote

Defense counsel, who did not avail himself of his opportunity to move to dismiss conspiracy charge at the close of State's evidence, could not renew nonexistent motion at close of all evidence, as was required to attack on appeal sufficiency of evidence supporting conviction for conspiracy to sell a controlled substance. Rules App.Proc., Rule 10(b)(3).

2. Conspiracy ⬳47(12)

Even if issue had been properly preserved for appeal, evidence was sufficient to sustain denial of defendant's motion to dismiss charge of conspiracy to sell a controlled substance; evidence showed defendant approached undercover police officers in response to juvenile's call, that officer told defendant he wanted to find some cocaine, that defendant told officer to pull his car over and wait while he went down the street to get "it," that defendant and juvenile crossed street, and that juvenile returned and handed officer clear plastic bag containing a rock of crack cocaine, which officer paid for with a marked twenty dollar bill.

3. Sentencing and Punishment ⬳98

Fact that defendant was acquitted of contributing to the delinquency of a minor and employing and using a minor to commit a controlled substance offense did not preclude trial court from considering the sentencing aggravating factor that defendant involved a person under 16 in the commission of conspiracy to sell a controlled substance. West's N.C.G.S.A. § 15A–1340.16(d)(13); § 15A–1340.4(a) (Repealed).

Appeal by Defendant from judgment entered 13 August 2002 by Judge J. Gentry Caudill in Superior Court, Mecklenburg County. Heard in the Court of Appeals 28 October 2003.

Assistant Attorney General Martin T. McCracken, for the State.

Robert W. Ewing, Winston-Salem, for the Defendant.

Names of Counsel

WYNN, Judge.

Author of Opinion

From his conviction for Conspiracy to Sell a Controlled Substance, Defendant, John Boyd, argues on appeal that the trial court erred by failing to grant his motion to dismiss, and considering as an aggravating sentencing factor that he involved a person under 16 years of age in the commission of a crime. We find no error in Defendant's trial.

At trial, the State's evidence tended to show that on 25 October 2001, while conducting undercover drug buys, Charlotte Police Officers Eric Duft and Susan O'Donohue stopped two juveniles in the Colony Acres Drive neighborhood and asked for some "hard" or "rock"—slang terms for the drug crack cocaine. In response, Quintine Hamp-

Figure 4-1 *(Continued)*

ton, one of the youths, pointed across the street and yelled for "J.B." to come over to the car. Responding to Hampton, Defendant approached the officers' car. Officer Duft reiterated his desire to find some "hard," but before discussing the drug request, Defendant asked the officers whether they were police. Officer Duft denied being a police officer and assured Defendant he "just wanted to get hooked up." Apparently satisfied, Defendant told Officer Duft to pull his car over and wait while he went down the street to get "it."

The officers then observed Hampton and Defendant cross Colony Acres Drive before losing sight of them. After two or three minutes, Hampton returned alone and handed Officer Duft a clear plastic bag containing a rock of crack cocaine. Officer Duft paid Hampton with a marked twenty dollar bill. Thereafter, Defendant and Hampton were arrested separately.

After estimating that he had conducted approximately 200–300 similar undercover drug buy stings, Officer Duft testified that "it is common for more than one person to be involved in the [drug] transaction" and sometimes, "they will use a younger person to sell them [because] [t]here is less consequences for a juvenile than there is for an adult." The arresting officer testified that, when Defendant was apprehended, "He stated to me; and I, quote, 'I did not sell shit. All I did was get a piece of the rock.'" At the close of the State's evidence, defense counsel did not "care to be heard" on the conspiracy charge, but did move to dismiss all remaining charges; the motions were denied.

In his defense, Defendant denied the statement attributed to him by the arresting officer. Rather, Defendant testified that he was walking towards Hampton to warn him that Officers Duft and O'Donohue were police officers. When Defendant "couldn't catch [Hampton's] bicycle" he turned around to go home. Defendant maintained "I don't have nothing to do with it."

Ultimately, the jury convicted Defendant of Conspiracy to Sell a Controlled Substance but acquitted him of the remaining charges of Sale of a Controlled Substance, Contributing to the Delinquency of a Minor [1], and Employing and Using a Minor to Commit a Controlled Substance Offense.[2] The trial judge found one aggravating factor (that Defendant involved a person under the age of 16 in the commission of the offense) outweighed mitigating factors (that Defendant had a support system in the community and was gainfully employed) and sentenced Defendant in the aggravated range of 18 to 22 months imprisonment. Defendant appealed.

[1] Defendant first argues the trial court erred by denying his motion to dismiss the charge of Conspiracy to Sell a Controlled Substance. For procedural reasons, we disagree.

N.C.R.App. P. 10(b)(3) provides that "a defendant in a criminal case may not assign as error the insufficiency of the evidence to prove the crime charged unless he moves to dismiss the action...." The rules further provide that by presenting evidence after the close of the State's case, a defendant waives any previous motion to dismiss, and in order to preserve an insufficiency of the evidence argument for appeal, defendant must renew his motion to dismiss at the close of all evidence.

[2] At the close of the State's case, the trial judge in the instant case asked defense counsel whether he cared to make "any motions for the defendant?" Defense counsel responded:

Yes, Your Honor. I think, taking the evidence in the light most favorable to the state, their strongest case seems to be for conspiracy. And so, I don't care to be heard on that ... I'll ask you to dismiss the sale, at the close of evidence.

---

1. N.C.G.S. § 14.316.1: "to knowingly or willfully cause, encourage or aid any juvenile within the jurisdiction of the court to be in a place or condition, or to commit an act whereby the juvenile could be adjudicated delinquent, undisciplined, abused or neglected."

2. N.C.G.S. § 90–95.4: "to hire or intentionally use a minor to violate G.S. § 90–95(a)(1)."

Figure 4-1 *(Continued)*

STATE v. BOYD   N. C.   **699**
Cite as 595 S.E.2d 697 (N.C.App. 2004)

At the close of all evidence, Defense counsel renewed prior motions to dismiss: "We would rest and renew our motions to dismiss; and, re-adopt our arguments, special as they relate to the sale, conspiracy, contributing to the delinquency of a minor; and, the engaging a minor in drug trafficking." By that statement, defense counsel renewed his argument that he "didn't care to be heard" on the conspiracy charge because "their strongest evidence seems to be for conspiracy." Defense counsel did not avail himself of his opportunity to move to dismiss the conspiracy charge at the close of the State's evidence, and thus, he could not renew a nonexistent motion at the close of all evidence. Accordingly, we are precluded from reviewing the merits of Defendant's argument. *See State v. Stocks,* 319 N.C. 437, 439, 355 S.E.2d 492, 492 (1987) (holding that "a defendant who fails to make a motion to dismiss at the close of all the evidence may not attack on appeal the sufficiency of the evidence at trial."). We note, however, that even if this issue had been properly preserved for appeal, the evidence in the record sustains the trial court's denial of Defendant's motion to dismiss this charge.

[3] Defendant next argues that because Hampton's age was an element of the crimes for which he was acquitted, Contributing to the Delinquency of a Minor and Employing and Using a Minor to Commit a Controlled Substance Offense, the trial court erred by considering the sentencing aggravating factor that he "involved a person under 16 in the commission of a crime." We disagree.

In North Carolina, a trial court may consider any aggravating factors it finds proved by the preponderance of the evidence that are reasonably related to the purposes of sentencing. N.C.G.S. § 15A–1340l.4(a). N.C.G.S § 15A–1340.16(d)(13) allows a court to aggravate a defendant's sentence from the presumptive range when "defendant involve[s] a person under the age of 16 in the commission of the crime."

In *State v. Marley,* 321 N.C. 415, 424, 364 S.E.2d 133, 138 (1988), our Supreme Court stated that "once a defendant has been acquitted of a crime he has been set free or judicially discharged from an accusation; released from ... a charge or suspicion of guilt." Therefore, our Supreme Court held "to allow the trial court to use at sentencing an essential element of a greater offense as an aggravating factor, when the presumption of innocence is not, at trial, overcome as to this element, is fundamentally inconsistent with the presumption of innocence itself." In *Marley,* the defendant had been tried for first degree murder upon the theory of premeditation and deliberation. The jury found the defendant guilty of second degree murder. Thus, one can infer from the jury's verdict in *Marley* that the jury determined there was insufficient evidence of premeditation and deliberation.

In this case, it cannot be inferred from the jury's acquittal of Defendant on the contributing to the delinquency of a juvenile and employing and intentionally using a minor to commit a controlled substance offense charges that it found there was insufficient evidence to conclude beyond a reasonable doubt that Hampton was a minor. Indeed, the parties in this case stipulated Hampton was thirteen years old. Unlike Marley, where the difference between first degree murder and second degree murder was the jury "decided that there [was] not sufficient evidence to conclude beyond a reasonable doubt that defendant premeditated and deliberated the killing," *Marley,* 321 N.C. at 424, 364 S.E.2d at 138, in this case, we are unable to explain rationale behind the jury's verdict. Thus, by convicting Defendant of conspiracy to sell a controlled substance, the jury concluded that Johnny Boyd and Quintinie Hampton were conspirators. Therefore, we uphold the trial court's consideration as an aggravating sentencing factor that Defendant involved a person under the age of 16 in the commission of a crime.

No error. ▬▬▬▬▬▬▬▬▬▬▬▬▬ Decision

Judges TIMMONS–GOODSON and ELMORE concur.

3. *Date of Decision*

The date the case was decided by the court will be given. If two dates are given, one will be identified as the date the case was argued, and the other will be the date the case was decided. For citation purposes, the critical date is the date of decision.

4. *Case Summary or Synopsis or Background*

Before you are given the actual opinion of the court, you will be provided with a brief paragraph summarizing the nature and background of the case, a description of the parties, a summary of what occurred in the court below, and an overview of this court's decision. This summary is typically prepared by the legal publishing companies (usually West), not by the court. This case summary serves as a quick preview of the case, but it can never be quoted from or relied on as authority because it was not prepared by the court.

5. *Headnotes*

Before the actual opinion of the court, you will be provided with short paragraphs, each of which is assigned a number and a title, such as **"4. Damages."** These are called *headnotes*. Each point of law discussed in the case is assigned a headnote. Thus, if the case discusses six points of law, there will be six headnotes. The headnotes provide a condensed snapshot of the case and reduce the time you might spend reading a case that is irrelevant to you. Headnotes may be thought of as the table of contents to your case. Because the headnotes are typically prepared by publishers and not judges, you cannot rely on them or quote from them, although they are excellent overviews of the issues in the case to follow. Headnotes in West reporters also include a pictorial diagram of a key, a topic name, and a number. This Key Number System is a method of finding other cases on the same topic and is discussed in detail in Chapter 5.

6. *Names of Counsel*

The names of the attorneys who represented the parties in the case are provided so that you can make contact with them. Although you can readily obtain copies of the briefs and papers filed in a court case from the court itself, discussing the case with the attorney involved may be of value to you.

7. *Opinion*

The beginning of the opinion of the court is almost always marked by an identification of the author of the opinion. This is a signal that everything

that follows is the court's opinion. Some sets of case reports include introductory summaries before the case begins. For example, the set *United
States Reports,* which publishes decisions of the U.S. Supreme Court,
includes a *Syllabus* before most opinions, which is a summary of the
decision to follow. The *Syllabus* is prepared by the Court's Reporter of
Decisions, who is responsible for editing and publishing cases. Similarly,
some older sets of case reports and some of the unofficial sets include
summaries of the arguments advanced by each party or summaries of the
opinion to follow. Make sure you understand the difference between these
useful editorial enhancements and the actual opinion. Only the court's
opinion is binding; summaries or syllabi are helpful overviews of the case
to follow, but they are usually prepared by a court official or a private
publisher, and you may not quote from them or rely on them.

Most opinions begin with a recital of the facts of the case. There are
various types of opinions:

- *Majority opinions* are those written by a member of the majority
after the court has reached its decision. The holding of the majority is the
law and serves as binding authority.
- *Plurality opinions* are those lacking sufficient votes by appellate
judges to constitute a majority; separate opinions are written by members
of the majority and no single opinion receives the support of a majority of
the judges hearing the case. Plurality opinions are usually said to establish no precedent for future cases.
- *Concurring opinions* are opinions written by justices who agree
with the actual result reached in a case (for example, that the case should
be affirmed) but disagree with the reasoning of the majority opinion.
Concurring opinions are persuasive and not binding.
- *Dissenting opinions* are those written by members of the minority.
They are persuasive only.
- *Per curiam opinions* are opinions of the whole court in which no
specific author is identified. These "unsigned" opinions tend to be short
and usually (although not always) relate to issues that the court deems
noncontroversial.
- *Memorandum opinions* report routine decisions. They provide a holding or result but little, if any, reasoning therefor. A memorandum decision
may state only, "For the reasons given by the court below, we also affirm."

Ethics Alert

Reliance on Non-Majority Opinions

**Whenever you cite a case in a document, the reader will assume
that you are relying on the majority opinion. If you are relying
on anything other than the majority opinion, such as a dissent,
concurring, or plurality opinion, you must inform the reader by
indicating such, as follows: *Circuit City Stores, Inc. v. Adams,* 532
U.S. 105, 125 (2001) (Stevens, J., dissenting).**

8. *Decision*

The final element in a case is the actual decision reached by the court. The final decision may be to affirm or uphold the determination of the lower court, to reverse or overturn the determination reached below, or to remand or return the case to the lower court for further action consistent with the court's findings. Although strictly speaking, the word *decision* refers only to the final disposition of a case, in many instances and in common usage, the words "opinion," "judgment," "decision," "case," and "holding" are often used interchangeably.

C. Publication of Cases

1. *Official and Unofficial Publication*

The books in which cases are published are referred to as *reports* or *reporters* and each one has its own abbreviation, such as "P." for *Pacific Reporter*. If cases are published pursuant to some statutory directive or court rule, the set of books in which they are collected is referred to as an *official report*. Cases published without this type of governmental approval are collected in sets of books called *unofficial reporters*. The terms "official" and "unofficial" have nothing to do with accuracy or quality—the terms relate solely to the method of publication. The fact that many cases are published both officially and unofficially means that researchers have a choice as to what set of books to use to locate a case. As discussed previously, statutes are also published officially and unofficially. It is also important to understand the difference between official and unofficial sets because in many instances case citation rules require one form of citation over another or may require that a writer provide both citations, giving the official citation first.

For example, consider the following citation: *Jones v. Smith*, 236 Va. 109, 402 S.E.2d 16 (1995). Citations to cases always include the same elements: the name of the case; a reference to the volume number, name of the set, and page number on which the case begins; the date of decision; and the deciding court, if not apparent from the name of the set. Thus, the citation given above informs the reader that the case named *Jones versus Smith* can be located in volume 236 of a set of books called *Virginia Reports* at page 109 and the same case can also be located in volume 402 of a set of books called *South Eastern Reporter, Second Series*, at page 16. The case was decided in 1995. The two citations are called *parallel citations*, and the first one given above is the official citation, and the second one is the unofficial citation. The case opinion itself will be exactly the same in both sets because what the judge has said in issuing the opinion is "etched in stone." What will vary will be type size, quality of paper, and some "extra" features provided by the respective publishers, such as the headnotes and case summary or synopsis. Note that when citing cases, writers should also provide not only the page on which the case begins but also the page in the case where the specific material can be found. These "pinpoint" citations are discussed in Chapter 10.

2. *Series of Case Reports*

You may have noticed that some of the case reports on the shelves are marked, for example, *Pacific Reporter,* while others indicate *Pacific Reporter, 2d Series* on their spines. The switch to a new series by a publisher merely indicates newer cases. You do not need to know which years are covered by which series. It is sufficient to know, for example, that any case in *Federal Reporter, 3d Series* is newer than any case published in *Federal Reporter, 2d Series,* and so forth.

3. *Advance Sheets*

Cases are first published in slip form and then published in *advance sheets,* which are temporary softcover publications that appear a few weeks after release of the court's opinion and are published to provide rapid access to cases. Eventually, after several months, the cases will be published in hardback volumes, and the softcover advance sheets will be discarded. The permanent volumes will share the identical volume number and pagination as the earlier advance sheets, providing reliability in quoting from cases in the advance sheets. In sum, there are three stages in case publication: slip form, advance sheets, and then hardback volumes.

D. Publication of State Cases

1. *West's* National Reporter System

In 1879, West created and published the *North Western Reporter* to publish decisions from the northwestern region of the United States. In many instances, these cases were already being published officially. Thus, for example, a Minnesota case would appear both officially in the *Minnesota Reports* and unofficially in West's *North Western Reporter.* Practitioners became so enthusiastic about the various features offered by West's *North Western Reporter* and its groupings of cases from neighboring states that West followed it by creating reporters for other geographical regions of the United States.

West's sets of books that collect state and federal cases are collectively referred to as the *National Reporter System.* Practitioners often refer to these as the *regional reporters.* In these sets of books, all of which are unofficial, West publishes all of the cases released by courts for publication, as well as adding thousands of cases not released for official publication and those that were reported as memorandum decisions. Within the *National Reporter System* there are various units or sets of case books. The states that compose each unit of the *National Reporter System* can be seen in Figure 4-2.

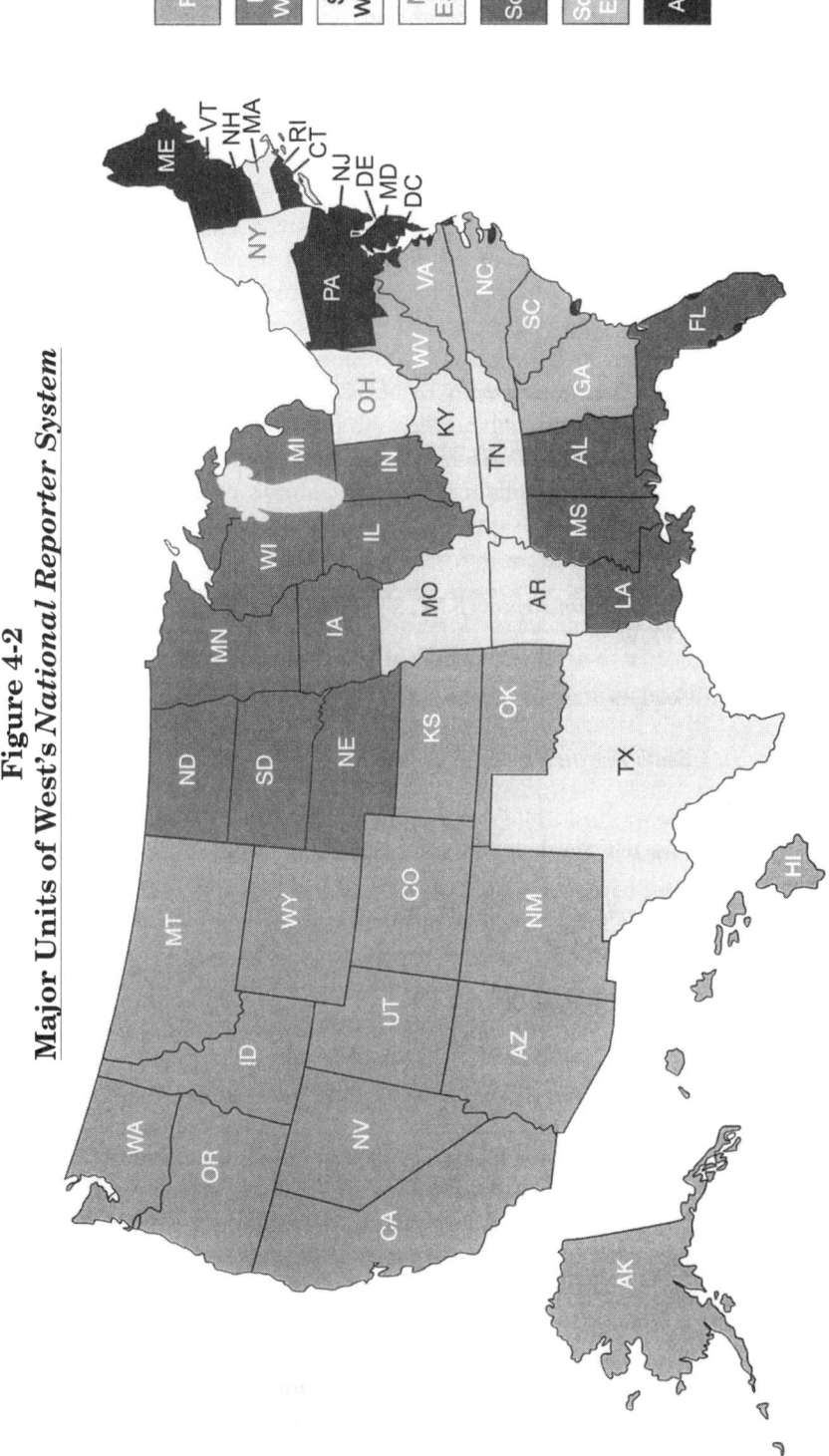

Figure 4-2
Major Units of West's *National Reporter System*

Figure 4-2
Major Units of West's *National Reporter System*

Name of Case Reporter and Abbreviation	Courts Covered
North Western Reporter N.W., N.W.2d	State courts in Iowa*, Michigan, Minnesota*, Nebraska, North Dakota*, South Dakota*, Wisconsin
Pacific Reporter P., P.2d, P.3d	State courts in Alaska*, Arizona, California, Colorado*, Hawaii, Idaho, Kansas, Montana, Nevada, New Mexico, Oklahoma*, Oregon, Utah*, Washington, Wyoming*
North Eastern Reporter N.E., N.E.2d	State court cases in Illinois, Indiana*, Massachusetts, New York, Ohio
Atlantic Reporter A., A.2d, A.3d	State court cases in Connecticut, Delaware*, Maine*, Maryland, New Hampshire, New Jersey, Pennsylvania, Rhode Island*, Vermont, Washington, D.C.*
South Western Reporter S.W., S.W.2d, S.W.3d	State court cases in Arkansas*, Kentucky*, Missouri*, Tennessee*, Texas*
Southern Reporter So., So. 2d, So. 3d	State court cases in Alabama*, Florida*, Louisiana*, Mississippi*
South Eastern Reporter S.E., S.E.2d	State court cases in Georgia, North Carolina, South Carolina, Virginia, West Virginia
New York Supplement N.Y.S., N.Y.S.2d	Cases from various New York state courts
California Reporter Cal. Rptr., Cal. Rptr. 2d, Cal. Rptr. 3d	Cases from the California Supreme Court, California Court of Appeal, and Appellate Departments of the California Superior Courts
Illinois Decisions Ill. Dec.	Cases from the Illinois Supreme Court and Illinois Appellate Court
Supreme Court Reporter S. Ct.	Cases from U.S. Supreme Court
Federal Reporter F., F.2d, F.3d	Cases from U.S. Courts of Appeal
Federal Supplement F. Supp., F. Supp. 2d	Cases from U.S. District Courts
Federal Rules Decisions F.R.D.	Cases interpreting federal rules of civil procedure, criminal procedure, and evidence (and some articles)

---

*State no longer publishes official versions of its cases.

It is not important to memorize or know which state is published or covered in which unit. It is sufficient if you understand the general structure of West's *National Reporter System*: It is a set of books, published unofficially, which reports many cases already published officially by many states themselves. You should know, however, which unit covers the state in which you will be working.

After West created the regional reporters to report decisions from groups of neighboring states, it created specialized sets for three states because of the volume of litigation in those states: *California Reporter, Illinois Decisions,* and the *New York Supplement.* Thus, there may be three parallel citations to a California case, as follows:

Powers v. City of Richmond, 10 Cal. 4th 85, 893 P.2d 1160, 40 Cal. Rptr. 2d 839 (1995).

This citation shows that the *Powers* case can be located in three separate sets of books. The opinion issued by the court in *Powers* will be the same no matter which of the three sets you select to locate the case. What will differ, however, may be the color of the covers, the typeface, and the editorial enhancements, such as headnotes and the case summary or synopsis.

One of the advantages of the *National Reporter System* units lies in its groupings of states. A law firm in Ohio that purchases the official *Ohio State Reports* will acquire a set of books that contains cases only from Ohio. If that firm purchases the *North Eastern Reporter,* however, it acquires a set of books that contains decisions not only from Ohio but also from Illinois, Indiana, Massachusetts, and New York. This allows legal professionals to review decisions from other neighboring states, which might be helpful if a case of first impression arises in Ohio.

2. *Citation Form*

Although citation form will be covered in depth in Chapter 10, at this point you should know one importance of distinguishing an official citation from an unofficial one. Many courts require that citations to state court cases include a citation to the official state report followed by a parallel citation to West's regional reporter. Thus, you will need to know the major units in West's *National Reporter System* so that when you are confronted with a case citation such as *Deyo v. Deyo,* 474 Mich. 952, 707 N.W.2d 339 (2005), you will know that because the *North Western Reporter* is one of West's *National Reporter System* unofficial units, the citation to it should follow the official *Michigan Reports* citation. Under *The Bluebook* and *ALWD* (unless local rules require otherwise), the citation would include only the West regional reporter and not the official citation, as follows: *Deyo v. Deyo,* 707 N.W.2d 339 (Mich. 2005).

```
┌──────────────────────── Practice Tip ────────────────────────┐
│                                                               │
│  Citations in Case Reports                                    │
│                                                               │
│  The citations that appear in published cases are often not in│
│  correct Bluebook or ALWD form. For space reasons, publishers │
│  often take shortcuts in citing cases and other authorities.  │
│  Rely on The Bluebook or ALWD when citing legal authorities   │
│  and not the way the citations look in the books themselves or│
│  on Lexis or Westlaw screens.                                 │
│                                                               │
└───────────────────────────────────────────────────────────────┘
```

3.   Discontinuation of Some Official Reports

Because of the popularity of West's *National Reporter System,* about 20 states (generally, smaller states) stopped publishing their cases officially. In those states, you will be able to locate cases only in West's respective regional reporter, and there will be only one citation for any case decided after the state stopped publishing officially. Figure 4-2, Table T.1.3 of *The Bluebook,* and Appendix 1 of *ALWD* identify which states have ceased official publication.

E.   Publication of Federal Cases

1.   United States Supreme Court Cases

United States Supreme Court cases are published in the following three sets of books: *United States Reports* (the official set), *Supreme Court Reporter* (West's unofficial set), and *United States Supreme Court Reports, Lawyers' Edition* (Lexis's unofficial set, commonly called *Lawyers' Edition*).

Thus, there are at least three parallel citations for all U.S. Supreme Court cases, and you can locate the 1986 case *Batson v. Kentucky* in three locations: 476 U.S. 79, 106 S. Ct. 1712, and 90 L. Ed. 2d 69. In the event of any conflict in versions of the cases reported in these volumes, the version of a case found in the official *United States Reports* governs.

For rapid access to U.S. Supreme Court cases, use one of the following sources:

- *United States Law Week,* a weekly journal;
- The Supreme Court's website at http://www.supremecourt.gov; or
- Lexis or Westlaw.

The Court's website and Lexis and Westlaw usually have the full text of a U.S. Supreme Court case within hours after the decision is released.

2. *United States Courts of Appeal Cases*

The set of books that publishes cases from the intermediate courts of appeal (for example, First Circuit, Second Circuit, and so forth) is the *Federal Reporter* (abbreviated "F.") and the *Federal Reporter, Second Series* and *Third Series* (abbreviated as "F.2d" and "F.3d"). Although the primary function of the *Federal Reporter* is to publish decisions from the U.S. Courts of Appeal, it has published cases from various other courts as well (see Figure 4-3).

This set of reporters is unofficial and is yet another of the units in West's *National Reporter System*. In fact, the *Federal Reporter* is the *only* set that reports decisions from these intermediate courts of appeal. Thus, there are no parallel citations for cases from these courts of appeal.

In 2001, West created a new set of books, the *Federal Appendix*, which reports opinions from all federal courts of appeal that are not selected for publication in the *Federal Reporter*. Each case begins with the statement, "This case was not selected for publication in the *Federal Reporter*." Remember to research whether you may cite to (and the effect of) such an "unpublished" case in documents submitted to any court.

3. *United States District Court Cases*

The beginning of this chapter noted that trial court decisions are not usually published. An exception to this general rules lies in the *Federal Supplement* and *Federal Supplement, Second Series* (abbreviated as "F. Supp." and "F. Supp. 2d"), created in 1932 by West and which publish decisions from the United States District Courts, our federal trial courts. Although the *Federal Supplement* and *Federal Supplement, Second Series* publish decisions from some other courts as well (see Figure 4-3), their key function is to report decisions from these U.S. District Courts. The *Federal Supplement* and *Federal Supplement, Second Series* are the primary sets of books that publish U.S. District Court cases. Thus, there are no parallel citations for cases from these courts.

Figure 4-3
Coverage of the *Federal Reporter* and *Federal Supplement*

Date	*Federal Reporter* (F., F.2d, and F.3d)
1880-1912	U.S. Circuit Courts
1911-1913	Commerce Court of the United States (abolished in 1932)
1880-1932	U.S. District Courts (after 1932, cases reported in *Federal Supplement* and *Federal Supplement, Second Series*)

Figure 4-3 *(Continued)*

Date	*Federal Reporter* (F., F.2d, and F.3d)
1930-1932, 1960-1982	U.S. Court of Federal Claims
1891-Date	U.S. Courts of Appeal
1929-1982	U.S. Court of Customs and Patent Appeals
1943-1961	U.S. Emergency Court of Appeals
1972-1993	Temporary Emergency Court of Appeals

Date	*Federal Supplement* and *Federal Supplement, Second Series* (F. Supp. and F. Supp. 2d)
1932-1960	U.S. Court of Federal Claims
1932-Date	U.S. District Courts
1956-Date	U.S. Court of International Trade (previously named U.S. Customs Court)
1968-Date	Judicial Panel on Multidistrict Litigation
1973-1996	Special Court, Regional Rail Reorganization Act (abolished in 1996)

4. *Cases Interpreting Federal Rules*

Yet another unit in West's *National Reporter System,* the *Federal Rules Decisions* set, publishes cases that have not been published in F. Supp. or F. Supp. 2d that interpret and construe the Federal Rules of Civil Procedure, Federal Rules of Criminal Procedure, Federal Rules of Evidence, Federal Rules of Appellate Procedure, and other rules. Articles that provide comment on the federal rules are also included.

All of the sets of books discussed in this section which publish decisions from our federal courts publish the cases first in advance sheets, which are later replaced by permanent, hardbound volumes.

F. Star Paging

Citation form will be thoroughly discussed in Chapter 10, but for now it is sufficient if you are aware that many state rules require that citation to state cases include all parallel citations. The rule for U.S. Supreme Court cases is far different. *The Bluebook* requires that for these cases, you are to cite only to the official *United States Reports.* The *ALWD* rule is substantially similar.

Obviously, therefore, the publishers at West and Lexis were in a dilemma. It would be extremely difficult for these publishers to attempt to market their sets of books (*Supreme Court Reporter* and *United States Supreme Court Reports, Lawyers' Edition,* respectively) because no matter how wonderful the sets might be, law firms and other users would be highly unlikely to purchase a set of case books that could not be cited or quoted.

The publishers at West and Lexis thus developed a technique of continually indicating throughout their sets which volume and page a reader would be on if that reader were using the official *United States Reports*. This technique of indicating page breaks in the official set is called *star paging* because the early method of indicating when a new page began was through the use of a star or asterisk (*). West now uses an inverted "T," as shown in Figure 4-4, and Lexis now uses boldface print, as in **[516 US 14]**, to indicate the page breaks.

Practice Tip

Common Legal Abbreviations

Newcomers to the legal profession are often bewildered by the numerous odd abbreviations found in law books. With just a little time and effort, you will be able to understand and translate the quirky abbreviations you see. *Black's Law Dictionary* (9th ed. 2009) includes a table of abbreviations, and both *The Bluebook* and *ALWD* are helpful in interpreting legal abbreviations. Following are some of the more common abbreviations you will encounter:

A.	Atlantic	Super.	Superior
P.	Pacific (or Procedure)	D. or Dist.	District
S.E.	South Eastern		
S.W.	South Western	C.D.	Central District
N.E.	North Eastern	E.D.	Eastern District
N.W.	North Western	M.D.	Middle District
S. or So.	Southern	N.D.	Northern District
F. or Fed.	Federal	S.D.	Southern District
R.	Rule, Rules	W.D.	Western District
Supp.	Supplement	J.	Judge, Justice (or Journal)
App.	Appellate (or Appeal)		
		JJ.	Judges, Justices
Div.	Division	A.J.	Associate Judge, Associate Justice
Ch.	Chapter or Chancery		
Cl.	Claims	C.J.	Chief Judge, Chief Justice
Cir.	Circuit		
Civ.	Civil	P.J.	Presiding Judge
Crim.	Criminal	L.	Law
Ct.	Court		

Star paging thus allows you to read a U.S. Supreme Court case in one of the unofficial sets and yet know what page you would be on if you were holding the official *United States Reports*. Figure 4-4 shows a sample page illustrating star paging. Star paging is also found in some other West sets, including the *California Reporter* and the *New York Supplement*, directing you to pagination for the official California and New York reports. Star paging is also used by Lexis and Westlaw so that as you review a case on your computer screen, you can determine (through the use of brightly colored numbers) the page you would be reviewing if you were holding a hardbound volume of case reports.

G. Specialized *National Reporter System* Sets

Additional sets of books that are also a part of West's *National Reporter System* series publish very specialized cases. They include the following:

- **West's *Military Justice Reporter*.** This set publishes decisions from the United States Court of Appeals for the Armed Forces and the military courts of criminal appeals and their predecessors.
- **West's *Veterans Appeals Reporter*.** This set publishes cases decided by the United States Court of Appeals for Veterans Claims, created in 1988, and previously named the United States Court of Veterans Appeals.
- **West's *Bankruptcy Reporter*.** The *Bankruptcy Reporter* publishes cases decided by U.S. Bankruptcy Courts and all federal courts dealing with bankruptcy matters.
- **West's *Federal Claims Reporter*.** This set publishes decisions from the United States Court of Federal Claims. Cases include tax refund suits, government contract disputes, environment and natural resource disputes, and civilian and military pay questions.
- *Federal Cases*. Until 1880, when West began publishing cases from the lower federal courts, there was no one comprehensive set of books that reported decisions from these courts. Although several sets existed, none were adequate. Therefore, in 1880, West collected all of these lower federal court cases together and republished them, in alphabetical order, in a set of books titled *Federal Cases*. Because *Federal Cases* covers much older cases, it is rarely used and is often available only at larger law libraries.
- **State Specific Sets.** For the convenience of practitioners, West also publishes case reporters for about 30 individual states. For example, the *Minnesota Reporter* includes decisions from Minnesota state courts that are published in the *North Western Reporter* (but omits cases from other states covered by the *North Western Reporter*, such as Michigan cases). These separate sets offer ease of use to practitioners and include helpful features such as Key Number references, headnotes, and other editorial enhancements. These specialized sets have various names, such as *Alaska Reporter*, *Georgia Cases*, and *Kentucky Decisions*.

Figure 4-4
Sample Page from Lexis's *Lawyers' Edition*,
Second Series Showing "Star Paging"

UNITED STATES v BYRUM 263

Parallel Citations
for Case

408 US 125, 33 L Ed 2d 238, 92 S Ct 2382

I note also that Northern Trust rests on a conceptual framework now rejected in modern law. The case is the elder sibling of May v Heiner, 281 US 238, 74 L Ed 826, 50 S Ct 286, 67 ALR 1244 (1930), a three-page 1930 decision which quotes Northern Trust, at length. May in effect held that under § 402 (c) a settlor may be considered to have fully alienated property from himself even if he retains the very substantial string of the right to income from the property so long as he survives. The logic of May v Heiner is the logic of Northern Trust. As one authority has written:

"When retention of a life estate was not taxable under the rule of May v Heiner, it followed that mere retention of a right to designate the persons to receive the income during the life of the settlor was not taxable . . . ." 1 J. Beveridge, Law of Federal Estate Taxation § 8.06, p. 324 (1956).

Star Paging (The
date "1956" appears on
page 164 of volume 408
of the United States
Reports, and the words
"that logic" appear
on page 165 of that
volume.)

[408 US 165]

That logic no longer survives. When three Supreme Court per curiams affirmed May on March 2, 1931, and thus indicated that this view would not be confined to its facts, the Treasury Department, on the next morning, wrote Congress imploring it to promptly and finally reject the Court's lenient view of the Estate Tax system. Congress responded by enacting the predecessor § 2036 (a) (2) that very day. The President signed the law that evening. Thus the holding of May and the underlying approach of Northern Trust has no present

life. I note further that though Congress has refused to permit pre-1931 trusts to be liable to a rule other than that of May, in 1949 this Court itself came to the conclusion that May was wrong, and effected "a complete rejection" of its reasoning. Commissioner v Estate of Church, 335 US 632,[12] 645, 93 L Ed 288, 299, 69 S Ct 322 (1949).

I seriously doubt that one could confidently rely on Reinecke v Northern Trust when Byrum drafted his trust agreement in 1958. This Court is certainly not bound by its logic, in 1972. I do not mean any disrespect, but as Mr. Justice Cardozo said about another case, Northern Trust is a decision "as mouldy as the grave from which counsel . . . brought it forth to face the light of a new age." B. Cardozo, The Growth of the Law, in Selected Writings 244 (M. Hall ed 1947).

2. The majority argues that there were several lower court cases decided after the enactment of § 2036 (a) (2)

[408 US 166]

upon which Byrum was entitled to rely, and it is quite true that cases exist holding that a settlor's retention of the power to invest the assets of a trust does not by itself render the trust taxable under § 2036 (a) (2). But the majority's emphasis on these cases as a proper foundation for Byrum's reliance is doubly wrong. First, it could not have evaded Byrum's attention and should not escape the majority that all cited prior cases —save King (the tax court case written four years *after* Byrum

12. In considering this and its companion case, Estate of Spiegel v Commissioner, 335 US 701, 93 L Ed 330, 69 S Ct 301 (1949), the Court in effect invited argument on whether Northern Trust itself should be overruled. Journal of the Supreme Court, O. T., 1947, pp 296–297. Though the Court held for the government without having to reach this issue, I note that in the 23 years since Church and Spiegel an opinion of this Court has not once cited, much less relied upon, Northern Trust. Mr. Justice Reed, dissenting in Church and concurring in Spiegel, announced at the time that he thought these cases overruled Northern Trust.

Practice Tip

Google Scholar

A new feature introduced by Google is "Google Scholar," which allows free and easy searching of court opinions from federal and state courts. Access http://scholar.google.com and select the "Legal documents" button. Type in your case name, citation, or search terms in plain English and you will be directed to cases relating to your topic. You may also explore related cases and cases that have cited your case.

H. Features of West's *National Reporter System*

The case reporters in West's *National Reporter System* offer a number of useful editorial features that aid and simplify legal research. These features are found in both the advance sheets and the permanent hardbound volumes (except as noted) and are as follows:

1. *Table of Cases Reported*

There will be at least one alphabetical table of cases in each reporter volume. For example, each volume of the *Supreme Court Reporter* includes a complete alphabetical list of all of the cases in that volume. This feature is useful if you know the approximate date of a Supreme Court case and need to examine a few volumes of the set to locate a case or if you mistakenly transpose numbers in a citation. Cases can be found by using either the plaintiff's or defendant's name (see Figure 4-5).

Some sets of books have two tables of cases. For instance, any volume in the *Pacific Reporter* will contain one complete alphabetical list of the cases in that volume as well as an alphabetized list of the cases arranged by state, so that the Alaska cases are separately alphabetized, the Arizona cases are separately alphabetized, and so on.

2. *Tables of Statutes and Rules*

The table of statutes will direct you to cases in a volume that have interpreted any statutes or constitutional provisions. Thus, if you are interested in whether any recent cases have interpreted Cal. Evid. Code § 225 (West 2000), you can consult the table of statutes in a volume of the *California Reporter,* and you will be directed to any page in the volume that interprets that statute (see Figure 4-5). Similarly, there are tables listing federal rules of civil and criminal procedure and so forth that are

Figure 4-5
Sample Pages from *Federal Reporter, 3d Series* Showing
Table of Cases and Table of Statutes

CASES REPORTED

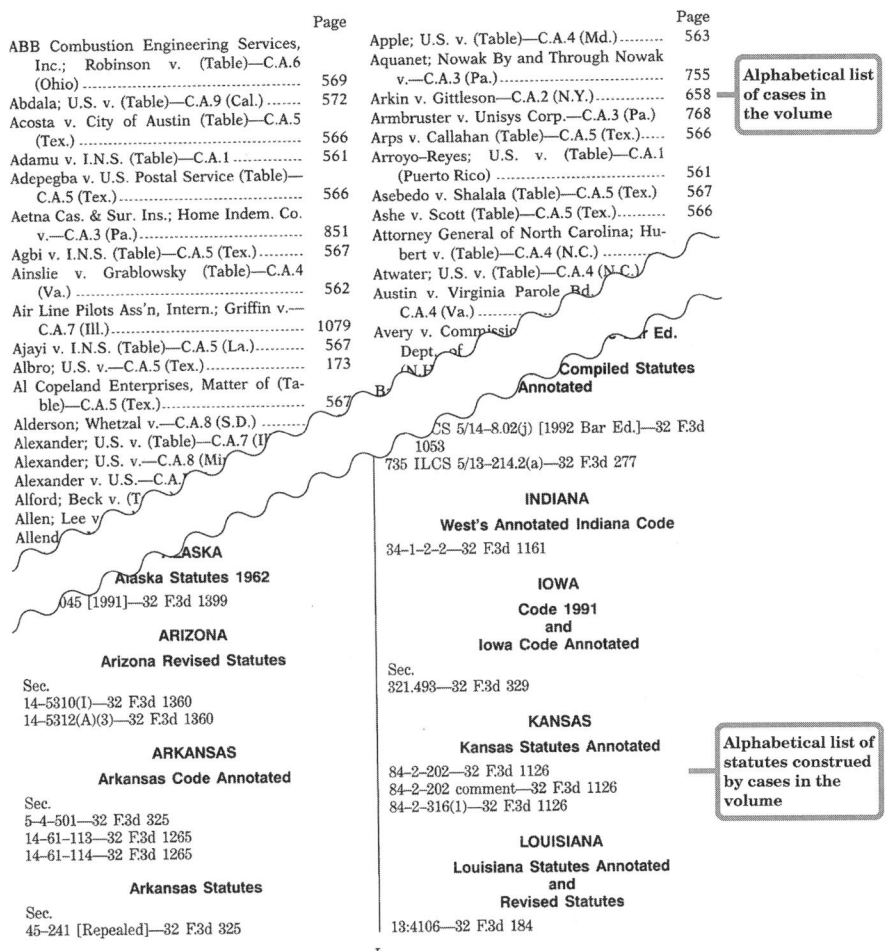

Page

ABB Combustion Engineering Services, Inc.; Robinson v. (Table)—C.A.6 (Ohio) 569
Abdala; U.S. v. (Table)—C.A.9 (Cal.) 572
Acosta v. City of Austin (Table)—C.A.5 (Tex.) 566
Adamu v. I.N.S. (Table)—C.A.1 561
Adepegba v. U.S. Postal Service (Table)— C.A.5 (Tex.) 566
Aetna Cas. & Sur. Ins.; Home Indem. Co. v.—C.A.3 (Pa.) 851
Agbi v. I.N.S. (Table)—C.A.5 (Tex.) 567
Ainslie v. Grablowsky (Table)—C.A.4 (Va.) 562
Air Line Pilots Ass'n, Intern.; Griffin v.— C.A.7 (Ill.) 1079
Ajayi v. I.N.S. (Table)—C.A.5 (La.) 567
Albro; U.S. v.—C.A.5 (Tex.) 173
Al Copeland Enterprises, Matter of (Table)—C.A.5 (Tex.) 567
Alderson; Whetzal v.—C.A.8 (S.D.) ....
Alexander; U.S. v. (Table)—C.A.7 (I
Alexander; U.S. v.—C.A.8 (Mi
Alexander v. U.S.—C.A.
Alford; Beck v. (T
Allen; Lee v
Allend

Page

Apple; U.S. v. (Table)—C.A.4 (Md.) 563
Aquanet; Nowak By and Through Nowak v.—C.A.3 (Pa.) 755
Arkin v. Gittleson—C.A.2 (N.Y.) 658
Armbruster v. Unisys Corp.—C.A.3 (Pa.) 768
Arps v. Callahan (Table)—C.A.5 (Tex.) 566
Arroyo–Reyes; U.S. v. (Table)—C.A.1 (Puerto Rico) 561
Asebedo v. Shalala (Table)—C.A.5 (Tex.) 567
Ashe v. Scott (Table)—C.A.5 (Tex.) 566
Attorney General of North Carolina; Hubert v. (Table)—C.A.4 (N.C.) ....
Atwater; U.S. v. (Table)—C.A.4 (N.C.)
Austin v. Virginia Parole Bd.
C.A.4 (Va.) ....
Avery v. Commissi
Dept. of

Alphabetical list of cases in the volume

ALASKA

Alaska Statutes 1962

045 [1991]—32 F.3d 1399

ARIZONA

Arizona Revised Statutes

Sec.
14–5310(I)—32 F.3d 1360
14–5312(A)(3)—32 F.3d 1360

ARKANSAS

Arkansas Code Annotated

Sec.
5–4–501—32 F.3d 325
14–61–113—32 F.3d 1265
14–61–114—32 F.3d 1265

Arkansas Statutes

Sec.
45–241 [Repealed]—32 F.3d 325

Ed.

Compiled Statutes Annotated

CS 5/14–8.02(j) [1992 Bar Ed.]—32 F.3d 1053
735 ILCS 5/13–214.2(a)—32 F.3d 277

INDIANA

West's Annotated Indiana Code

34–1–2–2—32 F.3d 1161

IOWA

Code 1991
and
Iowa Code Annotated

Sec.
321.493—32 F.3d 329

KANSAS

Kansas Statutes Annotated

84–2–202—32 F.3d 1126
84–2–202 comment—32 F.3d 1126
84–2–316(1)—32 F.3d 1126

LOUISIANA

Louisiana Statutes Annotated
and
Revised Statutes

13:4106—32 F.3d 184

Alphabetical list of statutes construed by cases in the volume

L

construed by any cases in a particular volume. Some sets include separate tables for statutes and rules, some sets combine the two into one table, and newer sets no longer include this feature.

3. *Table of Words and Phrases*

This table alphabetically lists words and phrases that have been interpreted or defined by any cases in a volume. For example, you can consult the Table of Words and Phrases and determine if the word "negligence" has been construed by any cases in a volume, and you will be directed to the specific page in a volume on which the word is interpreted. This feature is not found in all volumes or sets.

4. *List of Judges*

This feature (found only in the hardbound volumes of the *National Reporter System*) allows you to identify judges sitting on the courts covered by that particular volume.

5. *Key Number System*

West's Key Number System will be described in the next chapter; for the present, it is sufficient to know that all of the books in the *National Reporter System* are participants in the Key Number System, West's integrated research system that helps you find cases discussing similar points of law.

I. Finding Parallel Citations

On occasion, you may have one parallel citation and need the other(s). This could be because citation rules require all parallel cites or because the volume you need is missing from the law library shelf, and you must obtain the parallel citation to locate the case you need. There are several techniques you can use to find a parallel citation:

• **Cross-References.** Many cases provide all parallel citations. For example, if you open a volume of *California Reports* to the case you need, at the top of each page, in the *running head*, you are given all parallel citations for this case. Lexis and Westlaw screens also provide parallel citations.

• *National Reporter Blue Book* **and State** *Blue and White Books.* West's *National Reporter Blue Book* gives you tables converting official citations to unofficial regional citations. Similarly, about one half of the states have state *Blue and White Books,* which provide conversion tables with parallel citations. Unfortunately, West recently discontinued publishing all of these sets, and no further updates to the sets are being produced.

• ***Shepard's Citations*** **and KeyCite.** As you will learn in Chapter 11, when you Shepardize or KeyCite either an official or an unofficial citation, you are given the parallel citation.

• **State Digests.** West has published sets of books called "digests" for each state except Delaware, Nevada, and Utah. These digests (discussed in Chapter 5) contain tables of cases that provide parallel citations.

J. Briefing Cases

1. Introduction and Purpose of Case Briefs

The importance of cases in our common law system has already been discussed. You will also recall that in our legal system it is not sufficient merely to read a statute assuming that it will provide the answer to a question or problem because it is the task of our courts to interpret statutory language. Thus, reading, interpreting, and analyzing cases are of critical importance to all legal professionals.

Few people find it natural to read cases. The language used by courts is often archaic, and the style of writing can make it difficult to comprehend the court's writing. Moreover, the topics discussed in cases are often complex. The most common technique used to impose some order or structure on the confusing world of case law is case briefing. A *case brief* or *brief* is a short, written summary and analysis of a case.

It is common for law students to brief cases so that in the event they are called on in class to discuss a case, they will have a convenient summary to use. Moreover, practicing attorneys often desire to have cases briefed so they may save time by reading the briefs first and then, based upon their initial reading, analyze only selected cases in full. In some instances, months can go by between hearings in court, or new professionals may join the legal team. The case briefs for a matter handled by the team should be sufficiently readable and useful that new team members can be immediately brought "up to speed" by reviewing the briefs. Do not confuse the word "brief" in this context (meaning a summary of the key elements of case) with the written argument an attorney submits to a court, which is also called a "brief."

One of the best reasons for briefing cases is to learn how to focus on the important parts of the case in order to obtain a thorough understanding of the case and its reasoning. Although you may be tempted to view case briefing as busywork and may believe you can understand a case by simply reading it through, research has shown that people tend to read quickly and see words in groupings. Briefing a case will force you to slow down and concentrate on the critical aspects of the case.

Preparing a case brief requires you to tear the case apart and rebuild it in a structure that helps you and others understand it. In a sense, you are taking notes on the cases you read, and just as explaining a difficult concept to another helps you understand it better, preparing a case brief will help clarify your comprehension of the case. Thus, case briefing is a first step in learning how to write legal memoranda and court documents. Consider using the abbreviations shown in Figure 4-6.

The first briefs you prepare may be nearly as long as the case itself because it takes practice to learn to recognize the essential elements of a case. Initially, every part of the case will seem critical to you. With time, however, you will develop skill at briefing and will be able to produce a concise case brief. Ideally, your brief should be one typed page, although longer and more complex cases may require a longer brief.

Figure 4-6
Note-Taking Abbreviations

To be efficient, you need to develop a system of abbreviations for taking notes on the job or when briefing cases. Although there are some common legal and general symbols, any symbol or abbreviation will be satisfactory so long as you understand it.

Common Legal Abbreviations and Symbols

Π	plaintiff
Δ	defendant
§	section
K	contract
Atty	attorney
Cert	certiorari
Dep	deposition, deponent
J, J'ment	judgment
JNOV	judgment notwithstanding the verdict
Re:	regarding
SJ	summary judgment
S/F	statute of frauds
S/L	statute of limitations
v., vs.	versus, as opposed to, against

There is no one perfect form for a case brief. If no form is given to you, use a style that best suits your purpose and helps you understand the case and its significance as a precedent for the research problem on which you are working. Read through a case at least once before you begin to brief it so you will have a general idea as to the nature of the issues involved and how the court resolved these issues. See Figure 4-7 for some reading strategies.

It may take you several readings of a case to understand it thoroughly. You may need to take notes and prepare a diagram or flowchart showing the path the case followed in reaching this court and the relationship of the parties to each other.

2. *Elements of Case Briefs*

The most common elements to be included in a case brief are the following:

- **Case Name.** Give the case name following *Bluebook* or *ALWD* rules.
- **Citations.** All parallel citations should be included, as well as the year of decision. These citations will enable you to retrieve the case later if you need to locate it. Use correct citation form.
- **Procedural History.** A *procedural history* describes how the case got to this court and how this court resolves the case. It will be significant whether the prior decision is a trial court decision or an appellate court decision. Briefly identify the parties, describe the nature of the action, the relief sought, and defenses raised. Then state what the court(s) below held and the final disposition by this reviewing court. In many instances, the procedural history or background can be summed up in one or two sentences.

> *Example:* The case was appealed by the defendant employer after a trial court awarded monetary damages to the plaintiff employee for sexual harassment. The Florida District Court of Appeals affirmed the decision of the trial court.

Practice Tip

Determining Procedural History

Westlaw has added a new feature called "Graphical History" to allow you to view the procedural background of cases. When you access a case on Westlaw, click on "Direct History (Graphical View)," which will be displayed on the screen. You will be given a flowchart, showing the path a case has followed through the courts, allowing you to visually grasp a case's procedural history. Although Lexis does not show the procedural history of a case in a flowchart format, it includes a brief description of a case's subsequent and prior history when a case is displayed on the screen.

Figure 4-7
Case Reading Strategies

Consider the following strategies to help you better understand the cases you read and to help prepare case briefs.

- During your first reading, review the headnotes and the case. Focus on who the parties are and what relief they wanted from the court. Ask, "What is the plaintiff's gripe?" and "What is the defendant's defense?"

Figure 4-7 *(Continued)*

- Figure out what happened at the court(s) below, and then determine what this reviewing court's decision is. Knowing the court's decision in advance will help you make sense of the case when you read it more thoroughly.
- Look for clues. Watch for language in the court's opinion such as "It is critical to note that," "although we have previously held that," and other signals that what follows such expressions is important.

- **Statement of Facts.** A case brief should include a concise summary of the facts of the case. You need not include all facts but rather only the significant facts relied on by the court in reaching its decision. Facts that affect the outcome of a case are called *relevant* or *material facts*. The facts are more readable if they are presented in a narrative rather than outline or "bullet" format. Discuss facts in the past tense. A chronological presentation of the facts is usually the most helpful to the reader. Tell the story in plain English. If certain facts are disputed, indicate such. Some individuals prefer to place the statement of facts after the case name and citations (and before the procedural history). Providing the statement of facts first may aid comprehension of a case's procedural history (especially if the procedural history is complex).
- **Issue(s).** You must formulate the question(s) or issue(s) being decided by this court. Focus on what the parties asked the court to determine. In some instances, courts will specifically state the issues being addressed, using language such as, "The issue we must decide is whether . . . ." In other instances, the issues are not expressly provided, and you will have to formulate the issue being decided. Phrase the issue so that it has some relevance to the case at hand. Thus, rather than stating the issue in a broad fashion, such as "What is an assault?," state the issue so it incorporates some of the relevant facts of the case, such as "Does a conditional threat constitute an assault?" Keep your issues or questions to one sentence in length.

If you have trouble formulating the issue, locate the rule that the court announces and then convert this into question form.

> *Example of rule:* The goodwill of a celebrity is a marital asset that can be evaluated and distributed in a divorce.

> *Example of issue:* Is a celebrity's goodwill acquired during a marriage a property asset that can be evaluated and distributed in a divorce?

In any event, the issue should be phrased so that it can be answered "yes" or "no." If there are several issues, number each one. Do not number a single issue.

There are three ways issues can be phrased: a direct question, the "whether" format, or the "under" format. A direct question might ask, "Is pointing an unloaded gun at a person an assault?" The "whether" format would phrase the same question as follows: "Whether pointing an unloaded gun at a person is an assault." The "under" format would result in the following phrasing: "Under California law, is pointing an unloaded gun at a person an assault?" Generally, any of these formats is acceptable, although some attorneys dislike the "whether" form of issue because it produces a fragment rather than a complete sentence. Pick one format and use it for all of your issues.

   • **Answer(s)** or **Holding(s).** Provide an answer(s) to the question(s) you phrased. Rather than merely stating "yes" or "no," phrase the answer in a complete sentence and incorporate some of the reasons for the answer.

> *Example:* A conditional threat does not constitute an assault because a condition negates a threat so that the hearer is in no danger of immediate harm.

If you have set forth three issues, you will need three separate answers. Each answer should be no more than two or three sentences in length. Do not include formal citations.

   • **Reasoning.** The reasoning is the most important part of a brief. This is the section in which you discuss *why* the court reached the conclusions it did. Were prior cases relied upon? Did the court adopt a new rule of law? Fully discuss the reasons why the court reached its decision and the thought process by which it arrived at this decision. Make sure you apply the court's reasoning to the facts of your case. Re-read your questions and then ensure that the reasoning section is directly responsive to the questions you framed. Citations may be included in this section but are often not necessary. Use your own words in summarizing and explaining the court's reasoning rather than overquoting from the case. This will help ensure that you understand the rationale for the court's decision. Don't be concerned that there will be some repetition in your case brief. As you have seen, the brief answer or holding nearly parrots the language of the issue. The same or similar language will then reappear as part of your reasoning section. A case brief is not meant to be a thrilling work of literature. It is meant to help you develop your analytical skills and provide a convenient summary of a case.

   • **Decision.** Include the actual disposition of this case, such as "The Idaho Supreme Court affirmed the decision of the Court of Appeals."

   No matter what their format, good case briefs share the following elements:

   • They use complete sentences.
   • They do not overquote from the opinion.
   • They do not include unnecessary or distracting citations.
   • They do not include the writer's personal opinions.
   • They are brief, ideally one page in length.

See Figure 4-8 for a sample case brief, briefing *State v. Boyd*, the case shown as Figure 4-1.

Figure 4-8
Sample Case Brief

State v. Boyd,
595 S.E.2d 697 (N.C. Ct. App. 2004)

Procedural History

Defendant Boyd was convicted of conspiracy to sell a controlled substance but acquitted of the crimes of sale of a controlled substance, contributing to the delinquency of a minor, and employing and using a minor to commit a controlled substance offense. He appealed his conviction and sentence. The Court of Appeals affirmed.

Statement of Facts

Defendant was convicted of conspiracy to sell crack cocaine. The evidence at trial showed that Defendant supplied the cocaine to a minor, Hampton, who actually conducted the sale to undercover police officers. At the close of the State's evidence, Defendant's attorney did not move to dismiss the conspiracy charge but did move to dismiss all other charges. Counsel renewed all motions at the conclusion of all evidence. The motions were denied. The jury convicted Defendant of the conspiracy charge and acquitted him of the remaining charges. In sentencing the Defendant, the trial judge found as an aggravating factor that Defendant involved a person under the age of 16 in the commission of a crime.

Issues

1. May Defendant appeal his conspiracy conviction if he did not make a motion to dismiss the conspiracy charge at trial?
2. If Defendant is acquitted of certain charges relating to a minor, may the minor's age be considered as an aggravating sentencing factor when Defendant is sentenced for conspiring with a minor to sell a controlled substance?

Answers

1. No. On appeal, a Defendant may not attack the sufficiency of evidence at trial unless he makes a motion to dismiss such evidence at trial.
2. Yes. A trial court may consider any aggravating factors that it finds proved by a preponderance of evidence that are reasonably related to the purposes of sentencing.

Reasoning

North Carolina's rules of appellate procedure provide that to preserve an issue for appeal, a defendant must make a motion to dismiss the action at trial. Because Defendant's counsel moved to dismiss all charges against Defendant *except* the conspiracy charge at the close of the State's case, at the close of all evidence, he could not renew a nonexistent motion. Thus, the appellate court was precluded from reviewing the merits of Defendant's argument.

If a defendant is acquitted of a crime, it cannot be used as an aggravating sentencing factor. In this case, Defendant was convicted of conspiracy to sell a controlled substance; thus, Defendant and Hampton were conspirators. Moreover, the parties expressly stipulated that Hampton was a minor. Thus, the trial court could consider Hampton's age as an aggravating sentencing factor when sentencing Defendant on the conspiracy count.

Decision

The Court of Appeals affirmed the conviction and sentence.

The preceding brief follows a very standard format. A more thorough brief would include the name of the author of the majority opinion, a reference to how many justices were in the majority and how many dissented (for example, 2-1), a summary of any dissenting and concurring opinions, a summary of each party's contentions, and a final section including your comments and criticism of the case. In most instances, such a thorough brief is not needed, and the format shown above should suffice for most purposes.

Help Line

Briefing Cases

Westlaw provides an interesting and informative article titled *How to Write a Brief* by attorney Dana L. Blatt on its website at http://lawschool.westlaw.com/highcourt/HowToBrief.doc. The article includes tips and pointers on writing various types of briefs and includes sample briefs as well.

After you have gained experience in case briefing, you may be able to use a technique some experts refer to as *Technicolor briefing,* in which you use colored pens and highlighters to mark sections of cases as you read them. You will photocopy or print the cases you need to brief and annotate the critical sections in the margins. For example, use "F" to mark the facts section, "I" to mark the issue the court is deciding, and so forth. In law school, this technique is usually called *book briefing* because you brief the cases in your casebooks by these notes rather than preparing a separate brief.

K.   Citation Form

	Bluebook (for practitioners)	ALWD
United States Supreme Court Cases	*Roe v. Wade*, 410 U.S. 113 (1973).	*Roe v. Wade*, 410 U.S. 113 (1973). (Parallel citations are permitted but disfavored.)
United States Courts of Appeal Cases	*Scorteanu v. INS*, 339 F.3d 407 (6th Cir. 2003).	*Scorteanu v. INS*, 339 F.3d 407 (6th Cir. 2003).
United States District Court Cases	*Trent Partners v. Digital Corp.*, 120 F. Supp. 2d 84 (D. Mass. 1999).	*Trent Partners v. Digital Corp.*, 120 F. Supp. 2d 84 (D. Mass. 1999).
State Court Cases (when parallel citations are required)	*Graniteville Co. v. Williams*, 209 N.C. 112, 39 S.E.2d 202 (1946).	*Graniteville Co. v. Williams*, 209 N.C. 112, 39 S.E.2d 202 (1946).
State Court Cases (when parallel citations are not required)	*Graniteville Co. v. Williams*, 39 S.E.2d 202 (N.C. 1946).	*Graniteville Co. v. Williams*, 39 S.E.2d 202 (N.C. 1946).

Practice Tip

Formulating Issues in Case Briefs

To gain experience in formulating issues for case briefs and other court documents, review the briefs filed with the U.S. Supreme Court and examine the "Questions Presented." The Supreme Court requires all petitions for writs of certiorari and all petitioners' merits briefs to set forth the questions the Court is asked to review. Examine these questions to sharpen your skills at writing your own issue statements. The briefs may be accessed through the Court's website at http://www.supremecourt.gov. Select "Merits Briefs."

Internet Resources

http://www.uscourts.gov	U.S. Courts provides links to federal courts and information about the federal court system.
http://www.supremecourt.gov	The website of the U.S. Supreme Court provides information about the Court, its docket, Court rules, and access to its opinions and to briefs filed with the Court.
http://scholar.google.com	Google Scholar offers free and easy access to federal and state court cases. Search by case name or topic.
http://www.washlaw.edu	Washburn University School of Law's site offers links to federal and state cases as well as links to numerous excellent law-related sites.
http://lp.findlaw.com	FindLaw, one of the best known legal sites, provides easy access to federal and state cases as well as to a wide variety of other law-related information and links to other sites.
http://www.lawschool.westlaw.com	Westlaw's site for law students offers a guide to briefing cases. Select "User Guides" and then "Briefing Cases" or access the site at http://lawschool. westlaw.com/highcourt/ HowToBrief.doc.

Case Brief Assignment

Prepare a brief of the case *Heirs of Goza v. Estate of Potts*, 374 S.W.3d 132 (Ark. Ct. App. 2010).

Research Assignment

1. Give the name of the case located at 231 P.3d 289 and give its parallel citations.
2. Review volume 805 N.W.2d.
   a. What case in this volume construes the term "manifest injustice"?
   b. Review the case. Generally, what does the term mean?
3. Review volume 326 S.W.3d.
   a. Give the name of the case located at 326 S.W.3d 538.
   b. Review the case synopsis or background. Describe the procedural background of the case.
   c. What topic name and key number have been assigned to headnote 1?
   d. Look up the topic name and key number in the Key Number Digest in the back of the volume. To which case are you directed?
4. Use the *Atlantic Reporter*.
   a. Give the name of the case located at 33 A.3d 205.
   b. Give the parallel citation for the case.
   c. What does headnote 8 of the case discuss?
5. Review 948 N.E.2d.
   a. Give the citation to an Illinois case in this volume in which the plaintiff's name is *Tully*.
   b. Locate the case. How many headnotes are in this case?
6. Briefly state the holding in the case located at 908 So. 2d 360 (Fla. 2005).
7. Use the *Federal Reporter*.
   a. What is the name of the case located at 892 F.2d 763?
   b. Who or what is the named defendant?
8. Use the *Federal Supplement*.
   a. Give the name of the case located at 799 F. Supp. 2d 599.
   b. What type of case or action is this case?
9. Use the *Federal Appendix*.
   a. What is the name of the case located at 437 F. App'x 13?
   b. What words or instructions are given before the case name?

10. Locate the case at 549 U.S. 150 (2006).
    a. In what capacity did the author of the opinion act?
    b. Briefly describe the nature of this case.
11. Locate the case at 124 S. Ct. 885. How does page 426 of the parallel *United States Reports* begin?
12. Locate the case at 154 L. Ed. 2d 208. How does page 110 of the parallel *United States Reports* begin?
13. Locate the case at 18 A.3d in which the defendant's name is *Emmanuel*.
    a. Give the case name and citation.
    b. What kind of decision is this?
    c. Who was the Chief Justice of the Delaware Supreme Court during the period of time covered by this volume?
    d. What case in this volume construes the phrase "res judicata"? On which page is this phrase discussed?

Internet Assignment

1. Access the U.S. Supreme Court website and locate "Opinions."
    a. Select "2011 Term Opinions of the Court" and review the case with the docket number 11—1184.
        i. What is the name of this case?
        ii. What type of opinion was issued in this case?
        iii. In which volume of the *United States Reports* will it by published?
    b. Select "2012 Term In-Chambers Opinions" and review the case with the docket number 12A644.
        i. What is the name of this case?
        ii. Identify the Justice with whom this case was filed and in what capacity it was filed.
        iii. What relief was sought? Was the relief sought granted?
2. Access the U.S. Supreme Court website and review the Justice's Year-End Report on the Federal Judiciary for 2012. What was the percentage decrease in cases filed in the U.S. Supreme Court in its 2011 Term?
3. Access the site Washlaw (Washburn University School of Law). Select "Texas" and review decisions of the Eighth District Court of Appeals. Locate the case with the docket number 08-1-00295-CV.
    a. What is the name of this case?
    b. Briefly, describe the nature of this case.
    c. What was the decision?

4. Locate a case in the U.S. Court of Appeals for the Second Circuit (posted on May 31, 2013), in which Oprah Winfrey is a defendant. Review this case. Briefly, describe the nature of this case.
5. Access Google Scholar and search for cases relating to the permissibility of prayers offered at high school graduations.
   a. What is the first case to which you are directed?
   b. How many cases have cited this case?
   c. Give all parallel citations for this case.
   d. Briefly, were the prayers offered in this case constitutionally permissible?

Locating Cases Through Digests and Annotated Law Reports

Chapter Overview

This chapter completes the discussion of the primary authorities previously introduced (statutes, constitutions, and cases) by explaining the use of digests, which serve as casefinders. Additionally, you will be introduced to annotated law reports, which can "speed up" the research process and provide you with an exhaustive treatment of an area of the law. Digests and annotated law reports help you find cases on point.

A. Using Digests to Locate Cases

1. Introduction

Although you know that you can locate cases by using a citation or annotated codes (which send you to cases interpreting statutes), some cases have not been interpreted by statutes and thus cannot be found through the use of annotated codes such as U.S.C.A. or U.S.C.S. One way to find cases is through the use of sets of books called *digests*. Digests serve as comprehensive casefinders. They arrange cases by subject matter so that, for example, all of the battery cases are brought together and all of the venue cases are brought together. These digests do not reprint in full all of the battery or venue cases, however, but rather print a brief one-sentence summary or "digest" of each battery or venue case and then provide you with a citation so you can determine whether to retrieve and read the case. In this way, digests serve as guideposts, which help direct you to the specific cases you need so you can research as effectively as possible. Because the digests are written by publishers (primarily West) and are mere summaries of cases, the digest entries cannot be quoted from or relied upon as precedent. The cases the digests direct you to, however, will serve as binding authority.

2.   *West's* American Digest System

Although there are several varieties of digests, all of them function in a similar manner. Most are published by West, which realized shortly after it introduced its *National Reporter System* that legal professionals needed a method of finding the cases published therein. The most comprehensive digest set published by West is called the *American Digest System*. Once you understand how to use this digest set, you will be able to use all other West digests because they are all organized in the same manner.

The *American Digest System* is an amazingly thorough set of books that aims at citing and digesting every reported case so you can readily locate *all* cases on a given area of law, such as deeds, fraud, or wills.

Almost all West publications show pictures of keys, which inform the reader that the set is a participant in the West digest system, sometimes called the *Key Number System*.

3.   *Organization of the* American Digest System

West has categorized all of American case law into various topics. In fact, West has created more than 400 topic names for areas of law (for example, Corporations, Negligence, and Trespass) and has assigned various numbers, called *Key Numbers*, to these areas of law. As an editor at West receives a case from a court, the editor reads the case, divides it into separate issues of law, each of which is represented by a headnote number, and then assigns each of the headnotes one of West's more than 400 topic names and a Key Number (which includes an image of a key and a number). If the case discusses four areas of law, it will have four headnotes. If the case discusses 12 areas of law, it will have 12 headnotes. These headnotes are the brief paragraphs that precede the opinion of the court in a published case. Each headnote is thus given a consecutive number, a topic name (for example, Covenants, Insurance) based on the area of law the headnote deals with, and a Key Number. For example, West might assign the topic name and Key Number **Landlord & Tenant 166** to a case dealing with injury to a tenant's property in leased premises. Every time thereafter that any portion of a case reported in the *National Reporter System* discusses injury to a tenant's property in leased premises, West will create a headnote for the case and assign it the topic name and Key Number **Landlord & Tenant 166.** If a headnote deals with more than one topic, West might assign more than one topic name and Key Number. A list of West's more than 400 topic names is available at http://static.legalsolutions.thomsonreuters.com/product_files/westlaw/wlawdoc/wlres/keynmb06.pdf. See Figure 4-1 for depictions of keys, topic names, and Key Numbers in a published case.

West then gathers all of the headnotes into the *American Digest System*, allowing researchers to readily find numerous cases from all over the country that deal with the same issue. The *American Digest System* consists of sets of books that each cover ten-year periods called *Decennials*. Thus, the *Tenth Decennial (Parts 1* and *2)* covers the time period 1986-1996, the *Ninth Decennial* (*Parts 1* and *2*) covers the time period 1976-1986, and so forth, back to the *First Decennial*, which covers the time period 1897-1906. Note that West has also created a set of books called the *Century Digest* to cover the time period 1658-1897 (the date coverage of the *First Decennial* commences). It is unlikely that you will use the *Century Digest* very often, if ever, as it digests cases that are very old. Figure 5-1 shows the time period covered by each of the *Decennials*.

As you can see, starting in 1976, West began issuing the *Decennials* in two five-year parts (and recently began issuing Decennials in three parts). This change was brought about by the explosion in case law.

General Digest is the name of the set of books currently in use that updates the most recent Decennial set.

It is not necessary to memorize the time periods covered by each *Decennial* unit. It is sufficient to understand the general structure of the *Decennial* units: Each *Decennial* covers approximately a ten-year period, and each *Decennial* will contain all of the headnotes from all of the units of the *National Reporter System* for its particular ten-year period.

4. *Locating a Topic and Key Number*

Assume you are asked to research whether a tenant may recover damages from her landlord when the tenant's valuable rug is ruined by rain caused by a leak in the roof at the leased premises. Further assume that you need to find cases from all over the United States on this issue. There are four strategies you can use to locate a topic and Key Number that you can then use to find on-point cases.

Figure 5-1
Coverage of Decennial Units

Century Digest (uses a different classification scheme than other *Decennial* units)	1658-1897
First Decennial	1897-1906
Second Decennial	1907-1916
Third Decennial	1916-1926
Fourth Decennial	1926-1936
Fifth Decennial	1936-1946
Sixth Decennial	1946-1956
Seventh Decennial	1956-1966
Eighth Decennial	1966-1976
Ninth Decennial, Part 1	1976-1981
Ninth Decennial, Part 2	1981-1986
Tenth Decennial, Part 1	1986-1991
Tenth Decennial, Part 2	1991-1996
Eleventh Decennial, Part 1	1996-2001
Eleventh Decennial, Part 2	2001-2004
Eleventh Decennial, Part 3	2004-2007
Twelfth Decennial, Part 1	2008-2010
General Digest, 12th Series	2004-Date

a. Descriptive Word Approach

Each of the *Decennial* units includes volumes titled "Descriptive Word Index" and which are usually placed at the end of the respective *Decennial* set. Use the Descriptive Word Index exactly as you do the indexes for U.S.C.A. and U.S.C.S. as described in Chapter 3. Think of words and phrases that describe the problem you are researching (for example, landlord or tenant) and then look up these words in any Descriptive Word Index. You will be given your topic name (**Landlord & Tenant**) and your Key Number (**166**).

If you have difficulty thinking of words to use, think of synonyms (renter), antonyms (owner), defenses a party might assert (waiver), or the cause of action a plaintiff might assert (breach of contract). These should assist you in thinking of words to look up in the index. Just as you have seen with the indexes for U.S.C.A. and U.S.C.S., the Descriptive Word Indexes in the *American Digest System* are very "forgiving." Many topics are indexed under more than one entry, making it easy for you to locate the all-important topic name and Key Number.

When starting a research problem, use the Descriptive Word Index to one of the newer digest units, such as the current *General Digest* or the *Twelfth Decennial Digest, Part 1*. If you cannot locate a topic name and a Key Number in these digests (perhaps because no cases discussed your particular legal issue during the time period covered by the digests), try the *Eleventh Decennial Digest*, and so forth.

The descriptive word method is the easiest and most reliable way of locating a topic name and a Key Number, and this should be the approach you use until you have become thoroughly familiar with West's *Key Number System*. See Figure 5-2 for a sample page from the Descriptive Word Index to the *Ninth Decennial Digest, Part 2*, which demonstrates how to locate a topic name and Key Number through the descriptive word approach.

b. Topic Approach

Recall that in locating statutes, the topic approach calls for you to bypass the general index at the end of a set of statutes, and go directly to the appropriate title and begin examining the statutes. The topic approach for locating a topic name and a Key Number is exactly the same. Thus, if you were using the topic approach for the landlord–tenant problem described previously, you would bypass the Descriptive Word Index and go immediately to the "L" volume of a *Decennial* unit such as the *Twelfth Decennial Digest, Part 1*, and look up the phrase "Landlord and Tenant." Prior to the digest listing of the headnotes (**Landlord & Tenant 1, Landlord & Tenant 2,** and so on), you will be given an overview of the coverage of this topic, Landlord & Tenant, much like a book's table of contents. You can then scan the entries to determine the appropriate Key Number and proceed to look up and examine the headnotes listed or digested under Landlord & Tenant. See Figure 5-3 for a sample page from the *Ninth*

Figure 5-2
Sample Page from Descriptive Word Index

43-9th D Pt 2—77

LANDLORD   Guide Word

LANDLORD AND TENANT—Cont'd
GUIDE dogs, waiver of pet restriction inapplicable to dog neither trained nor used as guide dog. **Land & Ten 134(1)**
HABITABILITY. **Land & Ten 125**
Implied warranty—
   Coextensive with Residential Rental Agreements Act. **Land & Ten 125(1)**
HEALTH regulations, see this index **Health and Environment**
HEAT, see this index **Heat**
HEAT violation, notice as condition precedent to prosecution. **Health & E 39**
HOLDING over—
Damages—
   Landlord's proper measure of damages for tenant's willful holdover. **Land & Ten 144**
Estoppel, effect on. **Land & Ten 62(4)**
Extension by. **Land & Ten 90**
Month to month tenancy. **Land & Ten 115(3)**
Renewal by. **Land & Ten 90**
Rent, amount while holding over. **Land & Ten 200.9**
Sufficiency to create new tenancy. **Land & Ten 90(4)**
Tenancy at sufferance, creation by. **Land & Ten 119(2)**
Tenancy at will, creation by. **Land & Ten 118(4)**
Year-to-year tenancy. **Land & Ten 114(3)**
HOMESTEAD, see this index **Homestead**
HOMICIDE conviction arising from death of tenant's guest—
Due process guarantees. **Const Law 258(3)**
HOTELS—
Duties owed to renter's patrons—
   Providing guard for coat rack. **Inn 11(3)**
HUNTING rights. **Land & Ten 134(3)**
HUSBAND and wife—
Lease of community property. **Hus & W 267(3)**
Administration of community. **Hus & W 276(6)**
Separate property of wife, see this index **Separate Estate of Wife**
ICE and snow—
Generally, see this index **Ice and Snow**
ILLUSORY tenancy—
Effect—
   Protecting against speculative profiteering by tenants of rent controlled apartment. **Land & Ten 278.4(6)**
   Summary proceedings to dispossess, right to maintain. **Land & Ten 298(1)**
ILLUSORY tenants—
Entering into sublease in order to evade rent stabilization requirements. **Land & Ten 200.16**
IMPLIED contracts, see this index **Implied Contracts**
IMPLIED covenants. **Land & Ten 45**
IMPLIED tenancy, see this index **Implied Tenancy**
IMPROVEMENTS. **Land & Ten 150–161**
Actions. **Land & Ten 159**
Claims for. **Land & Ten 223(7)**

LANDLORD AND TENANT—Cont'd
IMPROVEMENTS—Cont'd
Compensation. **Land & Ten 157(6–8)**
Damages for failure to make. **Land & Ten 223(6)**
Lien. **Land & Ten 157(10)**
Ownership in general. **Land & Ten 157(2)**
Reimbursing tenant for repair of boiler made at request of tenant. **Impl & C C 40**
Remedy for failure to make. **Land & Ten 159**
Removal. **Land & Ten 157(4)**
INCOME tax, see this index **Income Tax**
INCUMBRANCES. **Land & Ten 145–149**
Reasonable rent, incumbrances as factor in determining. **Land & Ten 200.25**
INDEMNITY against liability for negligence. **Indem 8.1(2)**
INDORSEMENT, extension or renewal on lease. **Land & Ten 89**
INFANT'S property, lease of. **Infants 44**
INJUNCTION—
Assessing tenants nonrefundable rental fees. **Inj 136(2)**
Communication by tenant by signs or notices—
   Free speech. **Const Law 90.1(1)**
Covenants as to use of leased premises. **Inj 62(2)**
Disturbance of possession of tenant. **Land & Ten 132(2)**
Preliminary injunction, tenant's consent to sale of building's air rights. **Inj 136(2)**
Summary proceedings. **Land & Ten 299**
Unlawful detainer, action for. **Land & Ten 290½**
Violation of laws relating to suspension of right of reentry and recovery of possession by landlord. **Land & Ten 278.16**

    nd & Ten 55(4)

INJURIES—
    d & Ten 139(4)
Dangerous or defective condition. **Land & Ten 162–170**
Mobile home parks, see this index **Trailer Parks or Camps**
Employees of tenant. **Land & Ten 165, 169(5)**
Patrons of lessee—
Liability of lessee. **Land & Ten 167(8)**
Premises. **Land & Ten 140–142**
   Eviction. **Land & Ten 176**

Property of tenant. **Land & Ten 166**

    trance of trespassers and vandals. **Land & Ten 166(6)**
Property of third persons. **Land & Ten 167(9)**
Reversion. **Land & Ten 55**
Scalding of cleaning woman when steam pipe burst—
Liability of tenant. **Land & Ten 167(2)**
Tenants or occupants. **Land & Ten 164**
INNKEEPERS—
See this index **Innkeepers**

LANDLORD AND TENANT—Cont'd
INNKEEPERS—Cont'd
Membership in metropolitan hotel industry stabilization association. **Inn 2**
INSANE persons, see this index **Mental Health**
INSOLVENCY, termination of lease. **Land & Ten 101½**
INSURANCE—
Covenants to insure. **Land & Ten 156**
Insurable interest. **Insurance 115(4)**
Landlord's liability insurance—
Risks and causes of loss. **Insurance 435.34**
   Nature and cause of injury or damage. **Insurance 435.35**
Lessee's good-faith efforts to obtain—
   Preventing cancellation of lease. **Land & Ten 103(1)**
Right to proceeds. **Insurance 580(4)**
INTERFERENCE with—
Possession of tenant. **Land & Ten 131–133**
Relationship. **Land & Ten 19**
Use of premises. **Land & Ten 134(4), 172(2)**
INTERVENTION, see this index **Intervention**
INTOXICATING liquors, see this index **Intoxicating Liquors**
INTRUDER—
Lessor's liability for lessee's injuries inflicted by. **Land & Ten 164(1)**
INVALIDITY as affecting action for unlawful detainer. **Land & Ten 290(4)**
JOINT tenants, implied tenancy between. **Land & Ten 8**
JUDGMENT—
Conclusiveness. **Judgm 684**
Recovery of possession, action for. **Land & Ten 285(6)**
Summary proceedings for possession, post
Unlawful detainer, action for. **Land & Ten 291(17)**
JURISDICTION, see this index **Jurisdiction**

Justices of the Peace
KEY to leased premises, see this index **Keys**
KNOWLEDGE of defects affecting liability for injuries. **Land & Ten 164(6, 7), 165, 166(10)**
LACHES, affecting rescission of lease. **Land & Ten 34(4)**
LANDLORD'S title, estoppel dependent on. **Land & Ten 62(2)**
LARCENY of property from landlord or tenant, see this index **Larceny**
LEASES. **Land & Ten 20–49**

Bankruptcy proceedings. **Bankr 3086–3088**
Farm lease. **Land & Ten 322**
Female tenant's right to possession of apartment though not married to signing tenant—
Civil R 11.5
   Land & Ten 43
Nonassignment clauses—
Restraints on alienation, policy against. **Perp 6(17)**
Protection leases—
Nature of. **Mines 56**

Subtopic Heading

Topic Name and Key Number

Decennial Digest, Part 2, showing a partial list of Key Numbers within the topic **Landlord & Tenant.**

Because West's *American Digest System* has more than 400 topics, the topic method of locating topic names and Key Numbers should be used only after you have become thoroughly familiar with West's Key Number classification system.

c.   Table of Cases Approach

As an alternative research approach to the descriptive word approach, if you know the name of a case, you can look it up in an alphabetically arranged Table of Cases (which accompanies all newer *Decennial* units), and you will be given the citation(s) to the case and a list of the topics and Key Numbers under which it has been digested or classified.

d.   "Case on Point" Approach

If you have already located a case on point, its headnotes will display applicable topic names and Key Numbers. If one of these headnotes is relevant to your research, you can then use that headnote to locate other similar cases by looking up your topic name and Key Number in the various units of the *Decennial Digest System*. For example, if you decide that the topic name and Key Number **Sentencing and Punishment 98** (see Figure 4-1) is critical to your research, you can simply look up this topic and Key Number in the various units of the *Decennial Digest System* to obtain similar and newer cases. Alternatively, you can sign onto Westlaw and search for other cases classified to your topic name and Key Number.

5.   *Using Your Topic and Key Number to Find Cases*

Once you have obtained a topic name and a Key Number, such as **Landlord & Tenant 166,** you merely look this up in the various units of the *American Digest System* and you will unlock the door to cases from 1658 until last month, all of which relate to injuries to a tenant's property.

Because the *Decennials* are arranged alphabetically, you simply retrieve the "L" volume in any of the *Decennial* units and look up **"Landlord & Tenant 166."** Topics are arranged in alphabetical order, and Key Numbers within those topics are given in numerical order, making it as easy to use the *Decennials* as it is to use a dictionary. At this point, West will do more than merely list or digest the case headnotes in a haphazard fashion. West has carefully arranged the entries, first giving you federal cases and then state court cases (arranged alphabetically). Consider browsing adjacent Key Numbers to determine if another Key

Figure 5-3
Sample Page from *Ninth Decennial Digest, Part 2*

LANDLORD & TENANT ◄ Topic name

VII. PREMISES, AND ENJOYMENT AND USE THEREOF.—Cont'd

(D) REPAIRS, INSURANCE, AND IMPROVEMENTS.

☞150. Right and duty to make repairs in general.
    (1). In general.
    (2). Duty to rebuild on destruction of property.
    (3). Landlord's right of entry to make repairs.
    (4). Rights of subtenants.
    (5). Right of tenant to repair at landlord's cost.
151. Statutory provisions.
152. Covenants and agreements as to repairs and alterations.
    (1). In general.
    (2). Consideration for agreement.
    (3). Construction and operation of covenants in general.
    (4). Nature of repairs included in covenant or agreement.
    (5). Duty to rebuild on destruction of property.
    (6). Right of landlord to notice that repairs are necessary.
    (7). Agreement by landlord to pay for repairs.
    (8). Rights and liabilities of assignees and subtenants.
    (9). Waiver of claims under or stipulations in covenant or agreement.
    (10). Right of tenant to repair and recover cost.
    (11). Alterations by tenant.
153. Mode of making repairs.
154. Remedies for failure to make repairs and alterations.
    (1). Nature and form of remedy.
    (2). Right of action and defenses.
    (3). Pleading and evidence.
    (4). Damages.
    (5). Trial.
155. Maintenance of boundaries and fences.
156. Covenants and agreements as to insurance.
157. Improvements by tenant and covenants therefor.
    (1). Covenant by lessee to make improvements.
    (2). Ownership of improvements in general.
    (4). Right to remove and agreements for removal of improvements.
    (5). Forfeiture or waiver of right to remove improvements.
    (6). Right to compensation in general.
    (7). Covenants and agreements to pay for improvements.
    (8). Liabilities of successors of lessor.
    (9). Mode of termination of tenancy as affecting right to compensation.
    (10). Lien for value of improvements.
    (11). Determination of compensation.
    (12). Actions for compensation.
158. Improvements by landlord and covenants therefor.
159. Remedies for failure to make improvements.
    (1). Actions for breach of tenant's covenant to make improvements.
    (2). Actions for breach of landlord's covenant to make improvements.
160. Condition of premises at termination of tenancy.
    (1). In general.
    (2). Covenants and agreements as to condition of premises on termination of tenancy.

    (3). Duty of tenant to rebuild or replace personal property.
    (4). Actions for breach of covenant.
161. Personal property on premises at termination of tenancy.
    (1). Rights and liabilities as to property on premises in general.
    (2). Care of property left on premises by outgoing tenant.
    (3). Actions to recover property or value.

(E) INJURIES FROM DANGEROUS OR DEFECTIVE CONDITION.

☞162. Nature and extent of landlord's duty to tenant.
163. Mutual duties of tenants of different portions of same premises.
164. Injuries to tenants or occupants.
    (1). Injuries due to defective or dangerous condition of premises in general.
    (2). Injuries due to failure to repair.
    (3). Injuries due to negligence in making repairs.
    (4). Injuries due to unlighted passageways.
    (5). Liability for injuries to subtenant.
    (6). Liability of landlord as dependent on knowledge of defects.
    (7). Notice to or knowledge of tenant as to defects.
165. Injuries to employé of tenant.
    (1). Injuries due to defective or dangerous condition of premises in general.
    (2). Injuries due to failure to repair.
    (3). Injuries due to unlighted passageway.
    (4). Liability of landlord as dependent on knowledge of defects.
    (5). Failure to guard dangerous places.
    (6). Operation or condition of elevators.
    (7). Notice to or knowledge of tenant as to de-

166. Injuries to property of tenant on premises.
    (1). Nature and extent of the duties of landlord and tenant respectively.
    (2). Injuries due to defective condition of premises in general.
    (3). Injuries due to failure to repair.
    (4). Injuries due to negligence in making repairs.
    (5). Injuries due to defective water pipes or drains.
    (6). Injuries due to negligent acts of landlord.
    (7). Injuries due to negligence of third persons in general.
    (9). Injuries due to negligence of cotenant.
    (10). Liability of landlord as dependent on knowledge or notice of defects.

Outline of topics and key numbers listed under "Landlord & Tenant"

    (1). Duties of landlord and tenant to third persons.
    (2). Injuries due to defective or dangerous condition of premises in general.
    (3). Injuries due to failure to repair.
    (4). Failure to light or guard dangerous places.
    (5). Injuries due to openings, defects, or obstructions in walks or streets.
    (6). Injuries caused by fall of snow or ice from roof.
    (7). Injuries due to the negligence of tenant.

Number may be helpful. See Figure 5-4 for a sample page from the *Ninth Decennial Digest, Part 2*, showing the organization of cases.

In looking up your topic name and Key Number in the *Decennial* units, you should start with the more recent *Decennial* units. If you cannot find the cases you need, proceed to examine earlier *Decennial* units.

Practice Tip

Knowing Your Topic and Key Number

You need both a topic name and your Key Number to identify the issue you are researching. Consider getting into a cab and asking to be taken to "address 1530." This is as meaningless to the driver as if you asked to be taken to "Main Street." You need a street name and a number—just the way you need both a topic name and a Key Number, as in Landlord & Tenant 166.

---

6. Other West Digests

The *American Digest System* is most useful when conducting comprehensive research, because it covers all federal and state cases to the present time. If you do not need to conduct such thorough research, West has created several specialized digests that will assist you in locating cases from a specific jurisdiction, region, or state, all of which are organized identically to the *American Digest System*. In fact, many law libraries now only carry the specialized digests for their state or region. The following specialized digests are kept up to date by annual cumulative pocket parts.

• **United States Supreme Court Digest.** This digest provides headnotes and references only to U.S. Supreme Court cases.

• **Federal Practice Digests.** West has created several digests that serve as casefinders for cases from the federal courts. Each digest covers a specific time period similar to the manner in which the *Decennials* each cover a ten-year period:

Federal Digest:	Federal Courts (1754-1938)
Modern Federal Practice Digest:	Federal Courts (1939-1961)
West's Federal Practice Digest 2d:	Federal Courts (1961-1975)
West's Federal Practice Digest 3d:	Federal Courts (1975-1984)
West's Federal Practice Digest 4th:	Federal Courts (1984-2012)
West's Federal Practice Digest 5th:	Federal Courts (2003-Date)

Figure 5-4
Sample Page from *Ninth Decennial Digest, Part 2*, Showing Digests of Cases

⌘166   LANDLORD & TENANT   29 9th D Pt 2—956

⌘166. Injuries to property of tenant on premises.

Library references

C.J.S. Landlord and Tenant § 423 et seq.

⌘166(1). Nature and extent of the duties of landlord and tenant respectively.

Cal.App. 1 Dist. 1983. Where lessee of storage space was afforded option, by operator of space, of greater monthly payments under lease with insurance or of purchasing insurance elsewhere, and she was not subjected to an adhesive contract under which she had to accept exculpatory clause or forego lease, storage lease did not involve the public interest so as to render exculpatory clause in lease invalid under Civil Code section providing, inter alia, that all contracts which have as their object to exempt anyone from responsibility for his own fraud or willful injury to person or property of another are against policy of the law. West's Ann.Cal.Civ. Code § 1668.—Cregg v. Ministor Ventures, 196 Cal.Rptr. 724, 148 C.A.3d 1107.

Cal.Super. 1982. Apartment building owners and managers had no affirmative duty to secure parking facilities, which they never represented as being protected, merely because they had notice of previous instances of vandalism to parked cars and thus tenant could not recover from owners and managers for destruction by fire of tenant's automobile in building parking area.—Jubert v. Shalom Realty, 185 Cal.Rptr. 641, 135 C.A.3d Supp. 1.

D.C.App. 1983. Exculpatory clause in lease which purported to relieve landlord of liability for personal property damage caused by any source, including defective roofing and plumbing, was ineffective to bar recovery of damages from landlord inasmuch as clause amounted to waiver or modification of tenant's rights under implied warranty of habitability.—George Washington University v. Weintraub, 458 A.2d 43.

Kan. 1982. Landlord, having leased premises in their entirety to tenants, did not have control over portion of premises wherein fire started and had no duty to inspect same, and thus failure of landlord to inspect wiring and failure to discover and correct latent defect on premises could not, as a matter of law, constitute negligence.—Moore v. Muntzel, 642 P.2d 957, 231 Kan. 46.

There were no warranties flowing from landlord to tenants on which liability for fire damage could be predicated.—Id.

La.App. 4 Cir. 1982. Alleged failure of lessee to present evidence of negligence by ultimate building owner or lessor had no effect on her right to recover for loss of personal property destroyed in fire at apartment under statutes which base liability on status, either as owner or lessor, rather than on personal fault. LSA-C.C. arts. 2322, 2695.—Barnes v. Housing Authority of New Orleans, 423 So.2d 750.

Minn.App. 1984. Lease provision exculpating landlords from liability for water damage was not ambiguous, even though contract's reference to "premises" varyingly referred to entire building or to first floor and basement.—Fena v. Wickstrom, 348 N.W.2d 389.

N.Y.A.D. 1982. Where the tenant had notice that water would be turned off in building on a Friday and knew that water would be turned on before he reopened his shop on the following Monday, and where building owner did not have access to tenant's premises, it was tenant's responsibility to be particularly careful in closing all the faucets, and his failure to do so was proximate and sole cause of flooding.—Arthur Richards, Inc. v. 79 Fifth Ave. Co., 450 N.Y.S.2d 13, 88 A.D.2d 517, reversed 455 N.Y.S.2d 596, 57 N.Y.2d 824, 441 N.E.2d 1114.

Pa. 1986. Exculpatory clause in commercial lease agreement relieving lessor of liability for injury or damage to personal property in premises caused by fire in any part of building of which demised premises was a part, was valid and enforceable; the clause did not contravene any policy of the law, commercial lease related entirely to parties' own private affairs, there was no disparity in bargaining power between parties, and clause, as modified, spelled out intention of parties with particularity.—Princeton Sportswear Corp. v. H & M Associates, 507 A.2d 339, 510 Pa. 189, appeal after remand 517 A.2d 963, 358 Pa.Super. 325.

Pa.Super. 1984. Exculpatory clauses in lease were valid and enforceable where lease was commercial lease, there was no disparity in bargaining power between the parties, exculpatory clauses had been reviewed, negotiated and modified by both parties and their counsel, and clauses, as modified, evidenced clear and unambiguous intent to release landlords from liability for damages caused by fire when such fire was not the result of any negligence on landlords' part.—Princeton Sportswear Corp. v. H & M Associates, 484 A.2d 185, 335 Pa.Super. 381, reversed 507 A.2d 339, 510 Pa. 189, appeal after remand 517 A.2d 963, 358 Pa.Super. 325.

Landlords were not liable for damages tenant suffered as result of fire which damaged building's power center and thereby deprived tenant of heat, electricity and water, where under exculpatory clauses in lease, it was clear that landlords were not liable for any property damage caused by fire in any portion of the building of which demised premises was a part unless such fire was caused by landlords' negligence, power center constituted portion of building in which demised premises was a part, and lower court specifically found that landlords' conduct was not tortious.—Id.

⌘166(2). Injuries due to defective condition of premises in general.

C.A.La. 1983. Not every defect in leased premises will serve as a part for a claim of damages against lessor under Louisiana law; instead, vices and defects must be substantial and of such nature as are likely to cause injury to a reasonably prudent individual. LSA-C.C. art. 2695.—Volkswagen of America, Inc. v. Robertson, 713 F.2d 1151.

D.C.App. 1983. While landlords clearly bear burden of maintaining rented premises in compliance with housing code provisions, liability is not imposed upon landlords for losses arising from all conditions that violate the code.—George Washington University v. Weintraub, 458 A.2d 43.

Fla.App. 1 Dist. 1984. Lessee's complaint, which alleged making of the lease and lessor's covenant to keep the roof in good repair, the undertaking by lessor through services of a roofing contractor to keep the roof in good repair, a breach of that covenant by reason of the roof collapsing during course of repairs due either to defects in the structure or to overloading of the roof by the contractor, and resulting damages to lessee's property, was sufficient to state cause of action against lessor for breach of contract.—Cisu of Florida, Inc. for Use and Benefit of Aetna Cas. and Sur. Co. v. Porter, 457 So.2d 1118.

Ill.App. 1 Dist. 1985. Under common law, landlord is not liable for injury to property of tenant caused by defects in demised premises absent express warranty as to condition of premises or covenant to repair.—Wanland v. Beavers, 86 Ill.Dec. 130, 474 N.E.2d 1327, 130 Ill. App.3d 731.

Ill.App. 1982. Warranty of habitability implied in lease of building does not give rise to a cause of action for permanent injuries or proper-

ty damage.—Auburn v. Amoco Oil Co., 61 Ill. Dec. 939, 435 N.E.2d 780, 106 Ill.App.3d 60.

La.App. 1 Cir. 1986. Lessee and its property insurer were not required to show negligence on the part of the lessor in order to recover damages resulting from a fire caused by a defect in the premises. LSA-C.C. arts. 2322, 2695.—Great American Surplus Lines Ins. Co. v. Bass, 486 So.2d 789, writ denied 489 So.2d 245.

Even if lessee assumed responsibility for the electricity, lessor was liable for damages resulting from the destruction of the lessee's property due to a fire caused by a defect in the building's electrical system where there was no proof of negligence on the part of the lessee and where the lessor knew or should have known of the defect. LSA-R.S. 9:3221.—Id.

La.App. 3 Cir. 1985. Under LSA-C.C. art. 2695, lessor is liable to lessee for any losses sustained as result of "vice and defects" in premises, provided they did not arise as result of lessee's fault.—Freeman v. Thomas, 472 So.2d 326.

La.App. 3 Cir. 1984. Mere fact that common wall between premises leased for jewelry store purposes and adjacent premises was constructed of sheetrock and thus susceptible to breach by burglars did not render the condition a "vice" under statute so as to render owner lessor liable to lessees for damages arising out of the burglary. LSA-C.C. arts. 2322, 2703.—Hall v. Park Dell Terrace Partnership, 452 So.2d 342.

La.App. 4 Cir. 1985. Tenant's allegation that security services provided by landlord were inadequate did not provide basis for landlord's liability for arson damage, where all security services promised in lease were provided.—U.S. Fidelity and Guar. Ins. Co. v. Burns Intern. Sec. Services, Inc., 468 So.2d 662, writ denied 470 So.2d 882.

Implied warranty of fitness for intended use and freedom from defects, applicable to leased office building, did not extend to fire damage caused by arson, in light of provisions in lease waiving landlord's liability for damage caused by fire or unauthorized persons.—Id.

La.App. 4 Cir. 1984. Clause in lease clearly and unambiguously transferred liability of lessor to lessee for damage caused by leaks in roof, and thus lessor and its managing partner could not be held liable to lessee for damage which occurred when roof of premises failed under the burden of a heavy rainstorm.—St. Paul Fire & Marine Ins. Co. v. French Eighth, 457 So.2d 35, writ denied 462 So.2d 195 and Oreck v. French Eighth, 462 So.2d 195, reconsideration not considered 462 So.2d 1240, two cases.

La.App. 4 Cir. 1983. Tenants of building destroyed by fire were entitled to recover damages from landlord, despite fact that defect in leased premises was alleged not to have been in building in which tenants leased premises, but within the building, owned by same landlord, next door to tenants' building, unless landlord could exculpate himself. LSA-C.C. arts. 660, 2322.—Broome v. Gauthier, 443 So.2d 1127, writ denied 445 So.2d 449.

N.J.Super.A.D. 1982. Exculpatory clause in commercial lease which exempted landlord from liability for damage or injury resulting from carelessness or negligence or improper conduct of landlord or others, but did not exclude liability for damage flowing from defective design and construction of major structural aspects of building, did not immunize landlord from liability for water damage to tenant's computer equipment caused by defective design of roof.—Ultimate Computer Services, Inc. v. Biltmore Realty Co., Inc., 443 A.2d 723, 183 N.J.Super. 144, 30 A.L.R.4th 963.

Where exculpatory clause did not clearly express intention to exclude liability for injuries resulting from improper construction, landlord, in

For references to other topics, see Descriptive-Word Index

Note alphabetical arrangement of cases from states and arrangement from higher to lower courts within a state

• **Regional Digests.** West has created the following regional digests, which allow researchers to locate cases from a given region: *Atlantic Digest, North Western Digest, Pacific Digest,* and *South Eastern Digest.*

• **State Digests.** West publishes state-specific digests for 47 of the states (Delaware, Nevada, and Utah are excluded) and the District of Columbia, allowing researchers to locate cases from a given state when such is sufficient for their research purposes.

• **Other Specialized Digests.** West has created some specialized digests as well, such as the *Bankruptcy Digest, Military Justice Digest,* and the *Federal Immigration Law Digest* to cover specialized areas of the law.

7. *Common Features of West's Digests*

a. Uniform Classification

All of West's digests are classified to West's uniform topic name and *Key Number System.* Thus, once a legal issue is assigned the topic name and Key Number **Landlord & Tenant 166,** any later cases that deal with this issue will also be digested under **Landlord & Tenant 166,** whether they appear in a *Decennial* unit, the *Pacific Digest,* or the *Ohio Digest.*

b. Descriptive Word Indexes

All of West's digests include Descriptive Word Indexes arranged in similar fashion that provide you with topic names and Key Numbers, which you then look up in the pertinent digest volumes. The indexes use words describing facts, places, things, and legal principles taken from actual cases.

c. Table of Cases

All of the West digests contain a Table of Cases by plaintiff so you may look up a case by the plaintiff's name and obtain parallel citations and the topic names and Key Numbers under which it has been digested. More recent digests also include a Defendant–Plaintiff Table of Cases, listing the defendant's name first, or integrate the two tables into one complete listing of all cases.

```
┌──────────────── Practice Tip ────────────────┐

  *Using State and Regional Digests*

  Because West's classification scheme for its *Key Number System*
  is uniform throughout the system, the process of locating cases
  from a state or region is identical to that of locating cases using a
  *Decennial.*

  • Select the appropriate digest (for example, the *Atlantic Digest* or
    the *New York Digest*).
  • When researching, think small. Start with the smallest digest
    unit that will be helpful to you. For example, when researching
    Oregon law, start with the *Oregon Digest*. If it is not helpful, then
    review the *Pacific Digest*, and then the various Decennial units.
  • Use the Descriptive Word Index to the set to determine your
    topic name and Key Number.
  • Look up your topic name and Key Number in the appropriate
    volume in your digest set.
  • Examine the entries.
  • Update, as needed, using pocket parts or supplements, to find
    more recent cases.

└───────────────────────────────────────────────┘
```

d. Words and Phrases Volumes

The digest sets contain Words and Phrases volumes, which alphabetically list words and phrases that have been construed by cases. Thus, if
you look up the word "conspiracy" in the *Florida Digest, 2d*, you will be
given citations to the cases decided in Florida that define or interpret this
word.

e. Supplementation

Many of the digests (including the regional and state digests) are kept
current by annual cumulative pocket parts and supplemental pamphlets.
The *American Digest System*, of course, is supplemented by the *General
Digest*. If a pocket part or supplement exists, you must consult it to locate
more recent cases and to determine if any new topics have been added.

f. Integrated Cross-Referencing

Because West's *Key Number System* is a truly integrated research
approach, other West publications will give you topic names and Key
Numbers, allowing easy access into the system. For example, as you read
about an area of the law in West's encyclopedia *Corpus Juris Secundum*,

you will be given the appropriate topic names and Key Numbers so that you can use these to find additional cases. Finally, the *Key Number System* is also used in West's computerized legal research system Westlaw. Thus, this cross-referencing by West continually helps you find all cases on a similar point of law.

Ethics Alert

Using Digests

Digests are wonderful sources to find cases; however, you may not cite to them, and you must read the cases to which you are directed. Never quote from or rely on the digest or summary of a case; you must read the case itself and analyze it. Only then may you cite it as authority.

---

8. *Other Digests*

Although West is the largest publisher of digests and while its *Key Number System* provides easy access to all reported cases relating to a particular legal issue, it is not the only publisher of digests. The best known of the non-West digests is the *United States Supreme Court Digest, Lawyers' Edition*, published by Lexis. This digest uses its own classification scheme to direct readers to U.S. Supreme Court cases. Use either the descriptive word approach or table of cases approach to access this digest. Because this digest is published by Lexis, it provides references to other Lexis publications.

Are the Digests Relevant Today?

Although there is a tendency among beginning researchers to log on to Lexis and Westlaw whenever they need to find cases to solve a research problem, a number of experts believe that the print digests will always be needed. In fact, one review concluded "[a] print digest search followed by the application of relevant key numbers in Westlaw is a powerful and efficient combination." Judy Meadows & Kay Todd, *Our Question: Is the Use of Digests Changing?*, 13 Perspectives: Teaching Legal Res. and Writing 113, 115 (2005). Thus, don't make the mistake of thinking that using print digests is "old school"; they remain excellent case finders.

There are also a few state digests published by companies other than West. These non-West digests also use their own classification schemes. Nevertheless, the basic system is the same: The researcher identifies topics and uses these to find citations to relevant cases.

B. *American Law Reports*

1. *Introduction*

American Law Reports ("A.L.R.") is a West product that publishes selected appellate court cases from all over the nation as well as comprehensive and objective essays relating to the legal issues raised in those cases. A.L.R. combines features of primary sources (in that it publishes cases) with features of secondary sources (in that it publishes essays, called "articles" or "annotations") that explain and expand upon the issues raised by the cases published in A.L.R. West lawyer-editors review both state and federal appellate court decisions from all over the country and publish certain selected decisions that they believe are of widespread interest to legal professionals. In general, an A.L.R. annotation takes a very narrow topic and analyzes it in great depth.

The significance of A.L.R. does not lie in the fact that it publishes cases. Many sets of reporters do that; the true value of A.L.R. lies in its scholarly and comprehensive articles (the *annotations*), which comment upon each case A.L.R. elects to publish. In fact, West states that the annotations are the "most complete method to locate cases and understand [a] point of law."

If you are researching a certain area of the law and an A.L.R. annotation has been written on your topic, you should immediately retrieve the annotation and view it as "free research," as seldom, if ever, will you have the luxury of being able to devote as much time to an analysis of a legal topic as the A.L.R. legal scholars have in their annotations.

2. *A.L.R. Organization*

A.L.R. is published in eight series and consists of more than 800 volumes, whose coverage and updating is as follows:

Name of Set	Area of Coverage	Volumes and Years of Coverage	Method of Updating
A.L.R.	Federal and state cases	175 volumes; 1919-1948	*A.L.R. Blue Book of Supplemental Decisions*
A.L.R.2d	Federal and state cases	100 volumes; 1948-1965	*A.L.R. 2d Later Case Service*
A.L.R.3d	Federal and state cases	100 volumes; State cases: 1965-1980 Federal cases: 1965-1969	Pocket parts
A.L.R.4th	State cases	90 volumes; 1980-1991	Pocket parts

Name of Set	Area of Coverage	Volumes and Years of Coverage	Method of Updating
A.L.R.5th	State cases	120 volumes; 1992-2005	Pocket parts
A.L.R.6th	State cases	2005 to date	Pocket parts
A.L.R. Fed.	Federal cases	200 volumes; 1969-2005	Pocket parts
A.L.R. Fed. 2d	Federal cases	2005 to date	Pocket parts

3.   Features of A.L.R.

Following are features of A.L.R., although not all features are found in all sets.

- **Cases.** All of the volumes publish contemporary cases illustrating new developments or significant changes in the law. A citation to a case published in A.L.R. might appear as follows: *Epstein v. Brown*, 363 N.C. 372, 610 S.E.2d 816, 14 A.L.R.6th 741 (2005). Each volume currently publishes about eight to ten cases. Cases published in A.L.R. can be located by using digests, secondary authorities (see Chapter 6), or when one Shepardizes or KeyCites cases (see Chapter 11). A brief synopsis of the case is provided together with headnotes summarizing the issues in the case.
- **Annotations.** A complete research brief or annotation is provided, analyzing all case law relating to the selected case and its topics. Before 1992 (when A.L.R.5th was introduced), the lead case precedes the article or annotation; after this date, all cases are printed at the back of each volume. The annotations include the following features:
  - **Outline and Index.** An article outline is presented that shows how the annotation is organized so you can easily locate the sections of most interest to you. Similarly, an alphabetical index is presented, allowing you to quickly find the sections of the annotation that are most relevant to your research issue.
  - **Research References.** A.L.R. will direct you to additional sources relating to the topic under discussion, including law review articles, texts, and encyclopedias. Additionally, you will be given suggestions for drafting electronic search queries so you can find additional information on Lexis and Westlaw, the computerized research systems. Finally, you are directed to West topic names and Key Numbers to find other similar cases.
  - **Table of Cases, Laws, and Rules.** Because you may be interested in the way in which certain jurisdictions have treated the topic under discussion, A.L.R. provides a table showing you which sections in the annotation discuss cases and statutes from individual states and circuits.

- **Scope Note.** Each annotation begins with a section or note titled "Scope," which briefly describes the matters discussed in the annotation and then refers to related or earlier annotations discussing the topic that are now superseded.
- **Related Annotations.** This section directs you to other A.L.R. annotations that might be of interest.
- **Summary.** Each annotation begins with a concise and useful summary of the entire annotation, setting the stage for the extensive research brief to follow. Additionally, annotations often contain "practice pointers," which provide practical tips on how to handle a case dealing with the topic under discussion.

See Figure 5-5 for features of A.L.R.

4. *Finding A.L.R. Annotations*

a. Index or Descriptive Word Approach

A multi-volume alphabetical index called *A.L.R. Index* will direct you to annotations in all A.L.R. volumes. Using this index is similar to using any other—use the descriptive word approach and look up words or phrases that describe the problem you are researching, and you will be directed to the appropriate annotation. Be sure to check the pocket parts located in the back of each volume. See Figure 5-6 for a sample page from the *A.L.R. Index*.

West also provides a one-volume softcover index called *Quick Index*, which is easy to use and directs you to annotations in A.L.R.3d through A.L.R.6th. The *Quick Index* does not provide as much detail as the multi-volume *A.L.R. Index*, but it is a useful starting place for many research problems. A similar index, the *A.L.R. Federal Quick Index*, will direct you to annotations dealing with federal law collected in A.L.R. Fed. and A.L.R. Fed. 2d.

b. Digest Approach

The *A.L.R. Digest*, a 22-volume set, organizes the law into more than 700 topics, presented alphabetically. For example, if you look up the word "nuisance" in the *A.L.R. Digest*, you will be given brief summaries of the various annotations dealing with this topic. The Digest is kept current by annual pocket parts.

c. Miscellaneous Approaches

Many other sets of books refer to A.L.R. annotations. For example, the legal encyclopedia Am. Jur. 2d (discussed in Chapter 6) routinely directs readers to A.L.R. annotations. Similarly, when you update cases to make sure they are still good law by Shepardizing (using Lexis) or KeyCiting (using Westlaw), you will be informed whether the case has been published

Figure 5-5
Sample Page from A.L.R. Annotation
Showing Features of Annotations

Annotation

WHAT CONSTITUTES DEMISE OR BAREBOAT CHARTER OF VESSEL
IMPOSING ON CHARTERER LIABILITIES OF OWNER PRO
HAC VICE

Annotation analyzes issues raised by leading case

by

Jean F. Rydstrom, LL.B.

I. INTRODUCTION

§ 1.   Generally:
        [a] Scope, 547
        [b] Related matters, 547
§ 2.   Summary and comment:
        [a] Generally, 547
        [b] Practice pointers, 549

II. DEMISE OR BAREBOAT CHARTER IN GENERAL

§ 3.   Generally; construction, 551
§ 4.   Presumption against demise, 552
§ 5.   Characteristics; transfer of possession and control:
        [a] Generally, 553
        [b] Particular terms, 556
§ 6.   — Appointment of master and crew, 557
§ 7.   Effect; charterer as owner pro hac vice, 559
§ 8.   Operation of vessel on "lay" or "shares," 560

Annotation outline shows overall organization of annotation

Total Client-Service Library® References

Am Jur, Shipping 1st ed §§ 297–300, 326, 327, 335–337, 340
3 Am Jur Legal Forms 2d, Boats and Boating § 42:43
11 Am Jur Legal Forms, Shipping, Forms 11:1916 et seq.
ALR Digests, Shipping §§ 5, 7–8.5
US L Ed Digest, Shipping §§ 21, 24, 25
ALR Quick Index, Ships and Shipping
Federal Quick Index, Ships and Shipping

TCSL provides references to other helpful sources (not found in all volumes)

Consult POCKET PART in this volume for later cases and statutory changes

544

Figure 5-6
Sample Page from *A.L.R. Index*

NUISANCES—Cont'd

Lewdness, indecency, and obscenity —Cont'd
- porno shops or similar places disseminating obscene materials as nuisance, 58 ALR3d 1134

Life tenant's right of action for injury or damage to property, 49 ALR2d 1117

Lights and lighting, casting of light on another's premises as constituting nuisance, 5 ALR2d 705

Limitation of actions, when statute of limitations begins to run as to cause of action for nuisance based on air pollution, 19 ALR4th 456

Liquors, see group Intoxicating liquors in this topic

Litter and debris, what constitutes special injury that entitles private party to maintain action based on public nuisance—modern cases, 71 ALR4th 13

Livestock, see group Animals in this topic

Location, funeral home as private nuisance, 8 ALR4th 324

Loudspeakers
- bells, carillons, and the like as nuisance, 95 ALR3d 1268
- use of phonograph, loud-speaker, or other mechanical or electrical device for broadcasting music, advertising, or sales talk from business premises, as nuisance, 23 ALR2d 1289

Massage parlor as nuisance, 80 ALR3d 1020

Merry-go-round as nuisance, 75 ALR2d 803

Mines and Minerals (this index)

Minors, see group Children in this topic

Motel or hotel as nuisance, 24 ALR2d 571

Motion pictures
- drive-in theater as nuisance, 93 ALR2d 1171
- obscene motion pictures as nuisance, 50 ALR3d 969

Motor vehicles, see group Automobiles in this topic

Moving of buildings on highways as nuisance, 83 ALR2d 478

NUISANCES—Cont'd

Mufflers or similar noise-preventing devices on motor vehicles, aircraft, or boats, validity of public regulation requiring, 49 ALR2d 1202

Municipal corporations
- attractive nuisance doctrine, liability of municipality for injury to children by fire under, 27 ALR2d 1194
- dump, municipal liability for maintenance of public dump as nuisance, 52 ALR2d 1134
- rule of municipal immunity from liability for acts in performance of governmental functions as applicable to personal injury or death as result of, 56 ALR2d 1415
- swimming pools, public swimming pool as a nuisance, 49 ALR3d 652

Music and musicians
- bells, carillons, and the like as nuisance, 95 ALR3d 1268
- drive-in theater or other outdoor dramatic or musical entertainment as nuisance, 93 ALR2d 1171
- use of phonograph, loud-speaker, or other mechanical or electrical device for broadcasting music, advertising, or sales talk from business premises, as nuisance, 23 ALR2d 1289

Neighborhood, see group Residential area or neighborhood in this topic

Noise or sound
- air conditioning, existence of, and relief from, nuisance created by operation of air conditioning or ventilating equipment, 79 ALR3d 320
- bells, carillons, and the like as nuisance, 95 ALR3d 1268
- carwash as nuisance, 4 ALR4th 1308
- coalyard, noise caused by operation of, as nuisance, 8 ALR2d 419
- dogs, keeping of dogs as enjoinable nuisance, 11 ALR3d 1399
- electric generating plant or transformer station as nuisance, 4 ALR3d 902
- special injury, what constitutes special injury that entitles private party to maintain action based on public nuisance—modern cases, 71 ALR4th 13
- windmill as nuisance, 36 ALR4th 1159
- zoo as nuisance, 58 ALR3d 1126

in A.L.R. and whether any A.L.R. annotations mention your case. A.L.R. annotations are also available on Lexis and Westlaw.

5. *Updating A.L.R. Annotations*

You must always update any annotation you read to make sure that the annotation remains an accurate interpretation of the law and to find newer cases and annotations relating to the topic you have researched. The process of updating A.L.R. annotations varies, depending on how old the annotation is.

a. Updating Older A.L.R. Annotations

To update an annotation in A.L.R. (namely, one written between 1919 and 1948), use the *A.L.R. Blue Book of Supplemental Decisions*. To update an annotation in A.L.R.2d (namely, one written between 1948 and 1965), use the *A.L.R.2d Later Case Service*.

b. Updating Newer A.L.R. Annotations

To update any annotation in A.L.R.3d through A.L.R.6th, A.L.R. Fed., and A.L.R. Fed. 2d, check the pocket part in each volume, which will direct you to more recent annotations and more recent cases relating to the topic discussed by your annotation (see chart in Section B.2).

To update an annotation, you may also use the Annotation History Table in *A.L.R. Index*. This table will inform you whether the annotation you have been researching has been supplemented with new information or completely superseded by a newer annotation.

C. Citation Form

Digests are used solely to locate cases. You may never cite to them. You may, however, cite to an A.L.R. annotation.

	Bluebook *(for practitioners)*	*ALWD*
A.L.R. Annotation	Michael F. Alberti, Annotation, *Validity, Construction, and Application of State Right-to-Work Provisions*, 105 A.L.R.5th 243 (2003).	Michael F. Alberti, *Validity, Construction, and Application of State Right-to-Work Provisions*, 105 A.L.R.5th 243 (2003).

Help Line

Assistance with A.L.R. Annotations

Call A.L.R.'s Latest Case Service Hotline at 1-800-225-7488 to obtain the most recent information regarding annotations.

Practice Tip

Use of A.L.R. Annotations

You may cite to A.L.R. annotations in memos and court documents. Although the annotations are a secondary source, they are credible and well written. A better approach, however, is to allow the A.L.R. annotations to direct you to binding primary authorities that you then cite in your documents.

Internet Resources

http://www.law.georgetown.edu/library/research/tutorials/index.cfm	Georgetown University Law Library offers a number of tutorials to teach and explain legal research. Select "Secondary Sources" for a tutorial on A.L.R.
http://www.bu.edu/lawlibrary/research/guides/alr.html	Boston University offers several guides to legal research, including one for A.L.R.
http://www.tsulaw.edu/library/pathfinder/index.html	Thurgood Marshall School of Law offers research guides on numerous topics, including the use of digests and A.L.R.

Research Assignment

Unless otherwise directed, give case names only rather than full citations.

1. Use the Table of Cases for the *Eleventh Decennial Digest, Part 1*.
   a. Under which topic and key numbers is the case *In re Marriage of Handeland* digested?
   b. Give the citation to the case in which the defendant's name is *Lindbergh School District*.
2. Use the Descriptive Word Index to the *Tenth Decennial Digest, Part 2*.
   a. Which topic and key number discuss keeping animals as a nuisance?
   b. Look up this topic and key number in the *Tenth Decennial, Part 2*. Which 1991 Alabama case discusses this general topic?
   c. Which 1998 Alabama Court of Civil Appeals case updates this general topic?
3. Use the Descriptive Word Index to West's set *Federal Practice Digest, 4th Series*.
   a. Which topic and key number generally discuss searches of vessels?
   b. Review this topic and key number. Which 2008 case from the First Circuit Court of Appeals held that people on a vessel are afforded a lesser expectation of privacy than in their homes, obviating the usual Fourth Amendment requirements of a warrant?
   c. Review the case. Which headnote discusses this specific issue?
4. Use West's set *United States Supreme Court Digest*.
   a. What is the most recent case that interprets the term "necessary"?
   b. Give the citation to the case *Bilski v. Kappos*.
   c. Update the topic and key number you gave for Answer 3a above. Which 1974 case held that generally less stringent search standards are applicable to vehicles than to homes?
5. Use the *Pacific Digest*.
   a. Generally, what topic and key number discuss the right of an action for breach of marriage promise?
   b. Review this topic and key number. What 2002 Montana Supreme Court case discusses this topic?
   c. Use the Words and Phrases volumes for this set. What 2003 Kansas Court of Appeals case construes the term "invitee"?

6. Use the Table of Words and Phrases for West's *New York Digest, 4th Series*.
   a. What 1982 case interprets the meaning of the word "state officer"?
   b. Under what topic and key number is the case digested?
7. Use the A.L.R. Quick Index and answer the following questions.
   a. Which annotation deals with the liability of a doctor, psychiatrist, or psychologist for failure to take steps to prevent a patient's suicide?
   b. Review the annotation.
      i. Who is the author?
      ii. What Am. Jur. Proof of Facts, 3d reference are you directed to that relates to a psychotherapist's negligence in diagnosing and treating mental illness?
      iii. What is the most recent New York case that discusses the requirement that the patient's suicide be foreseeable?
8. Use the A.L.R. Federal Quick Index for A.L.R. Fed. and A.L.R. Fed. 2d.
   a. What annotation deals with the definition of a "miner" under the Black Lung Benefits Act?
   b. Review Section 16 of this annotation. What is the most recent case holding that employees of concerns that consume coal for a particular industrial purpose are not "miners" under the Federal Mine Safety and Health Act of 1977?

Internet Assignment

1. Access the website for the Thurgood Marshall School of Law Library at http://www.tsulaw.edu/library. Select "Legal Research Guides–Pathfinders" and review the materials on Digests.
   a. If you have a case on point, how do you find the correct digest topics and key numbers?
   b. How do you choose a correct digest if you aren't sure of the jurisdiction?
2. Access the website for Georgetown University's Law Library at http://www.law.georgetown.edu/library. Select "Research Guides."
   a. Review the information on Digests. What is a Key Number?
   b. Select the Research Guide for Secondary Sources and review the information relating to A.L.R. annotations. Why should you use an A.L.R. annotation?

3. Access the website for Thomson Reuters ("West") at http://legalsolutions.thomsonreuters.com/law-products. Search for the Pacific Digest, 2d (1978 to date). Review the information about this Digest.
   a. How is this Digest updated?
   b. What do the *Words and Phrases* volumes provide?
4. Access Zimmerman's Research Guide. If you find an A.L.R. annotation on the issue you are researching, what are your next steps?

Legal
Research

Secondary Authorities and Special Research Issues

Secondary Authorities

Chapter Overview

Section I of this text discussed the major primary legal authorities: statutes, constitutions, and cases. Administrative rules and regulations and treaties are discussed in Chapter 7. Nearly all other sources are secondary authorities. In general, the secondary sources serve to explain, summarize, analyze, and locate primary sources.

If you suspect that a legal question is addressed by a statute, you should begin your research in one of the annotated codes by locating the statute and then examining the case annotations following it to find cases that interpret the statute. Often, however, you may not know where to begin a research project. In these instances, many experts recommend that you start your research projects by using a secondary source.

The secondary authorities discussed in this chapter are those most frequently used: encyclopedias, legal periodicals, texts and treatises, the Restatements, and miscellaneous secondary authorities (including attorneys general opinions, legal dictionaries, form books, and jury instructions).

A. Encyclopedias

1. Introduction

Legal encyclopedias function in the same way as any other encyclopedia in that they discuss various topics. *Legal encyclopedias* thus explain legal subjects, in alphabetical order, from abandoned property to zoning. They are easy to use, and they serve as an excellent introduction to an area of the law. In addition to providing summaries of legal topics, encyclopedias direct you to cases through the use of footnotes. Generally, the narrative statements or summaries of legal topics will cover the top half of each page in the set, and the bottom half of each page will provide citations to legal authorities that support the narrative statements of the law.

The treatment of legal topics in encyclopedias is general and somewhat elementary. For this reason, encyclopedias are seldom cited in court documents such as briefs. They are rather most useful for giving you the background you need on a legal topic before reading cases. Moreover, they are *noncritical*, meaning that they explain the law as it *is* and do not provide critical comment or suggest what the law *should be*.

There are three types of encyclopedias: general or national sets, local sets, and special subject sets.

2. *General or National Encyclopedias*

A *general* or *national encyclopedia* is a set that aims at discussing all American law, civil and criminal, state and federal, substantive and procedural. There are two general or national encyclopedias: *Corpus Juris Secundum* (C.J.S.) and *American Jurisprudence 2d* (Am. Jur. 2d). Both are published by West. These sets are competitive, meaning that they are so similar that it cannot be said which is better; you should research in one or the other, not both. Your choice of which set to use will therefore be based largely on habit or convenience.

a. C.J.S.

As its name indicates (*Corpus Juris Secundum*, meaning "Body of Law Second"), C.J.S. was preceded by an earlier set, *Corpus Juris*, no longer in use. C.J.S. consists of more than 160 dark blue volumes and discusses more than 400 different areas of the law in alphabetical order, making it easy for you to locate discussions on topics such as Assault, Bail, or Contracts.

C.J.S. is an extremely thorough and comprehensive set. The text is articulately presented and easy to understand. The cases that support the narrative statements are arranged in the footnotes alphabetically by jurisdiction and state, so you can readily locate cases of most interest to you. Often, the "leading case" in an area of the law is summarized briefly for you.

Each topic (for example, Deeds) begins with a thorough outline to provide you with quick access to the most pertinent parts of the discussion. Because C.J.S. is a West publication, all cases are fully referenced to West's *Key Number System*.

b. Am. Jur. 2d

American Jurisprudence 2d (Am. Jur. 2d), the successor set to *American Jurisprudence*, consists of more than 100 green volumes and discusses more than 400 areas of law. Similar to the arrangement of C.J.S., Am. Jur. 2d arranges its topics (or "titles") alphabetically, enabling you to easily locate the discussion you need. Although C.J.S. historically has aimed at directing you to *all* cases that support any legal principle, Am. Jur. 2d has prided itself on "weeding out" redundant or obsolete cases.

Many of the features of Am. Jur. 2d are similar to those of C.J.S., namely, the narrative statements of the law are clearly and concisely presented, and each topic begins with a complete outline. See Figure 6-1 for a sample page from Am. Jur. 2d.

Am. Jur. 2d features two unique books in its encyclopedia system: the *Am. Jur. 2d Desk Book*, which serves as a legal almanac and the *Am. Jur 2d New Topic Service*, which is a binder that includes pamphlets on emerging areas of the law, such as Real Estate Time-Sharing.

c. Features Common to C.J.S. and Am. Jur. 2d

The following features are common to C.J.S. and Am. Jur. 2d:

- **Coverage.** Both sets discuss more than 400 topics of law, arranged alphabetically.
- **Table of Laws and Rules.** Although neither set includes exhaustive coverage of statutes (which would make the sets too voluminous), each does include a volume with a table that directs you to specific sections that discuss or cite federal statutes, rules, and the *Code of Federal Regulations*.
- **Text Treatment.** Both sets have similar narrative statements of the law and contain clear and straightforward discussions of the law. Thus, it cannot be said that one set is superior to the other.
- **Indexing.** Each set includes a multi-volume General Index (located after the last volume on the shelf), and each of the more than 400 topics begins with its own outline, allowing you to quickly locate sections of interest.
- **Scope Notes.** Each topic discussion in both sets begins with a *scope note* or paragraph, which briefly outlines what will be discussed in the topic and what subjects may be discussed elsewhere in the set.
- **Supporting References.** Both sets support their narrative discussions of the law with footnotes that provide citations to cases and other sources. Both sets participate in West's Key Number System, and both refer you to numerous other resources, including useful A.L.R. annotations.
- **Updating.** Both sets are updated by annual cumulative pocket parts that supplement the hardbound volumes (with pertinent new cases and statutory changes) and by replacement volumes, when needed.
- **New Media.** Both sets are available on Westlaw. Am. Jur. 2d is also available on Lexis and in CD-ROM form.

Figure 6-1
Sample Page from Am. Jur. 2d

§ 242   DRUGS AND CONTROLLED SUBSTANCES   25 Am Jur 2d

2. Conduct Related to Filling of Prescriptions [§§ 242-244]

§ 242. Generally

     A pharmacist has a duty to act with due ordinary care and diligence in the compounding and selling of drugs.[93] In this regard, a pharmacist owes his customers a duty to properly[94] and accurately[95] fill prescriptions. A pharmacist is required to assure that the drug prescribed is properly selected and measured.[96] Indeed, a pharmacist is held to a high standard of care in filling prescriptions[97] and dispensing prescription drugs,[98] and may be held liable in tort for any breach of his duty to properly fill prescriptions.[99] Generally, however, a pharmacist will not be held liable for correctly filling a prescription issued by a licensed physician.[1] In addition, a pharmacist who sells a generic drug as a substitute for the drug specifically prescribed, as authorized by statute and a physician's prescription, is not negligent for injuries resulting from an adverse side effect of a generic drug, unless the pharmacist knew that the generic drug is inferior or defective.[2]

§ 243. Mistakes in preparing, filling, or dispensing prescriptions; dispensing drug other than that prescribed

     Liability may be imposed on a pharmacists for negligently misfilling a prescription,[3] or negligently dispensing a drug other than that prescribed[4] or requested,[5] when a druggist negligently supplies a drug other than the drug

---

249. app den (Tenn) 1990 Tenn LEXIS 362.

93. Ferguson v Williams, 101 NC App 265, 399 SE2d 389, review den 328 NC 571, 403 SE2d 510; Dooley v Everett (Tenn App) 805 SW2d 380.

94. Adkins v Mong, 168 Mich App 726, 425 NW2d 151, app den 431 Mich 880.

95. Nichols v Central Merchandise, 16 Kan App 2d 65, 817 P2d 1131, review den 250 Kan 805; McKee v American Home Products Corp., 113 Wash 2d 701, 782 P2d 1045, CCH Prod Liab Rep ¶ 12399.

96. Murphy v E. R. Squibb & Sons, Inc., 40 Cal 3d 672, 221 Cal Rptr 447, 710 P2d 247, CCH Prod Liab Rep ¶ 10818.

97. Adkins v Mong, 168 Mich App 726, 425 NW2d 151, app den 431 Mich 880.

98. French Drug Co. v Jones (Miss) 367 So 2d 431, 3 ALR4th 259.

99. Adkins v Mong, 168 Mich App 726, 425 NW2d 151, app den 431 Mich 880.

1. Adkins v Mong, 168 Mich App 726, 425 NW2d 151, app den 431 Mich 880.
Forms: Answer—Denial of negligence—No breach of duty. 9 Am Jur Pl & Pr Forms (Rev), Drugs, Narcotics, and Poisons, Form 37.

2. Ullman v Grant, 114 Misc 2d 220, 450 NYS2d 955.

462

3. Boeck v Katz Drug Co., 155 Kan 656, 127 P2d 506.

Annotations: Druggist's civil liability for injuries sustained as result of negligence in incorrectly filling drug prescriptions, 3 ALR4th 270.

Forms: Complaint, petition, or declaration—Against pharmacy and pharmacist—Damages resulting from alteration of prescription by pharmacist. 9 Am Jur Pl & Pr Forms (Rev), Drugs, Narcotics, and Poisons, Form 31.1.

4. Stebbins v Concord Wrigley Drugs, Inc., 164 Mich App 204, 416 NW2d 381; Walgreen, Inc. v Knatt (Tex Civ App Beaumont) 506 SW2d 751.

Practice References: 18 Am Jur Proof of Facts 1, Medication Errors.

Forms: Complaint, petition, or declaration—Injuries sustained as result of negligence in filling drug prescription—Filling prescription with drug other than drug prescribed. 9 Am Jur Pl & Pr Forms (Rev), Drugs, Narcotics, and Poisons, Form 31.

     Complaint, petition, or declaration—Allegation—Harmful drug supplied in place of harmless drug ordered. 9 Am Jur Pl & Pr Forms (Rev), Drugs, Narcotics, and Poisons, Form 36.

5. Troppi v Scarf, 31 Mich App 240, 187 NW2d 511 (criticized on other grounds by Bushman v Burns Clinic Medical Center, 83 Mich App 453, 268 NW2d 683) and (criticized on other grounds by Rinard v Biczak, 177 Mich

---

Margin annotations:

Note aphhabetical arrangement of cases by state

Reference to A.L.R. annotation

Reference to forms

Reference to *Proof of Facts*

d. Research Strategies for Using National Encyclopedias

There are four techniques you may use to locate the discussion of an area of law in C.J.S. or Am. Jur. 2d.

- **Descriptive Word Approach.** To use the descriptive word approach, think of words or phrases that describe the issue you are researching. Look up these words in the General Index volumes for C.J.S. and Am. Jur. 2d, and you will be directed to the appropriate topic and section. Read the narrative, review the pocket part, and then select the cases and other resources that you will read in full.
- **Topic Approach.** Because the more than 400 topics discussed in C.J.S. and Am. Jur. 2d are arranged alphabetically, it is often possible to use the topic approach and successfully locate a discussion of the area of law in which you are interested. To use the topic approach, simply think of the area of law you are researching (for example, Fraud or Trusts) and then retrieve that volume from the shelf. Examine the outline of the topic, which will direct you to the appropriate section.
- **Table of Statutes Approach.** Use the Table of Laws and Rules volume for each set to look up specific statutes, administrative regulations, or rules in which you are interested. You will be directed to the appropriate volume, topic, and section.
- **Table of Cases Approach.** C.J.S. includes an alphabetical table of cases so you can readily locate a discussion of a case if you know its name. Am. Jur. 2d does not include a table of cases.

e. The Am. Jur. Total Client-Service Library

Lawyers Cooperative Publishing Company, the former publisher of Am. Jur. 2d, created a number of other sets of books, which it has referred to as the *Total Client-Service Library* (TCSL), which are now published by West. The books in TCSL are designed to be used with Am. Jur. 2d. Most relate to litigation and trial practice. All of the sets are kept current by the use of pocket parts, which provide new forms, checklists, or other pertinent material. To access these sets, use the descriptive word approach, and look up words that describe your issue in the General Index. You will then be directed to the appropriate volume and page. The four sets that make up TCSL are as follows:

- ***Am. Jur. Proof of Facts.*** This set of more than 130 volumes is designed to assist in the preparation for and proving of facts at trial (civil and criminal). Articles explain how to determine the facts essential to winning a case. *Proof of Facts* provides practical and expert information regarding trial preparation. Checklists, forms, strategy tips, and practice aids are provided.

- **Am. Jur. Trials.** This set of more than 120 volumes focuses on trial tactics and strategies. The articles in *Am. Jur. Trials* are written by experienced litigators and judges and provide a step-by-step guide to all aspects of litigation, from the initial client interview, through discovery, to trial and appeals. Checklists, forms, opening statements, and litigation aids and charts are all included. Following are examples of actual topics covered by *Am. Jur. Trials*: Pharmacist Malpractice; Stockbroker Liability Litigation; and Litigating Toxic Mold Cases.
- **Am. Jur. Pleading and Practice Forms Annotated.** This set of more than 70 volumes includes more than 43,000 forms for every stage of state and federal litigation, including forms for complaints, answers, interrogatories, motions, jury instructions, and orders. Practical checklists are included to remind you of items to include in various forms. This set is available on Westlaw, allowing researchers to download and edit the forms.
- **Am. Jur. Legal Forms 2d.** This set provides forms that are not litigation oriented. These documents are often used in connection with a client's personal or business needs, such as a will, trust, lease, or minutes of a corporate meeting. The set provides more than 20,000 such forms together with checklists, tips, and advice for preparing the forms and documents. The set's availability on Westlaw allows for easy downloading and editing of the forms.

3.   *Local or State Encyclopedias*

a.   Introduction

You have seen that C.J.S. and Am. Jur. 2d are general encyclopedias that provide a national overview of more than 400 areas of the law. It is highly likely, however, that you may not need such broad coverage of a topic and are interested only in the law for your particular state. In this instance, you should consult a *local encyclopedia* for your state, *if* one is published. Generally, encyclopedias are published only for the more populous states.

To determine if an encyclopedia exists for your state, check your law library's card catalog, ask a reference librarian, or simply look at the law library stacks devoted to the law of your state.

If your state does not have its own encyclopedia, use C.J.S. or Am. Jur. 2d, and research your state's law by locating cases in the footnotes from your state. See Figure 6-2 for a list of the local encyclopedias and their publishers.

b.   Features Common to State Encyclopedias

The following features are common to most state encyclopedias:

- **Coverage.** The discussion of the law presented will relate only to the law of a particular state, and the cases you will be directed to will be from that state and from federal courts interpreting that state's law.

Figure 6-2
List of Local Encyclopedias

Encyclopedias Published by West	*Encyclopedias Published by Lexis*
California Jurisprudence, Third	Illinois Jurisprudence
Florida Jurisprudence, Second	Michigan Law and Practice
Georgia Jurisprudence	Encyclopedia, Second
Illinois Law and Practice	Pennsylvania Law Encyclopedia
Indiana Law Encyclopedia	Tennessee Jurisprudence
Kentucky Jurisprudence (ceased	Michie's Jurisprudence of Virginia
in 2001)	and West Virginia
Maryland Law Encyclopedia	
Massachusetts Jurisprudence	
(ceased in 1998)	
Michigan Civil Jurisprudence	
Encyclopedia of Mississippi	
Law (successor to *Grant's*	
Summary of Mississippi Law)	
New York Jurisprudence,	
Second	
Ohio Jurisprudence, Third	
Summary of Pennsylvania	
Jurisprudence, Second	
South Carolina Jurisprudence	
Texas Jurisprudence, Third	

Practice Tip

Selecting Relevant Cases

As you read discussions of law in the encyclopedias, you may be presented with numerous case citations in the footnotes. There are some techniques you can use effectively to select cases when time or budget constraints prevent you from examining all cases:

- Select and read cases from your jurisdiction before reading those from other jurisdictions;
- Review newer cases before older cases; and
- Review cases from higher courts before those from lower courts.

• **Arrangement.** The various topics are arranged alphabetically. The narrative statements of the law are clearly presented, and you will be directed to cases and other authorities through the use of supporting footnotes.

- **Table of Cases.** Many local sets include tables that alphabetically list the cases cited in the set. If you know the name of a case, you can readily locate the discussion of it by using the Table of Cases.
- **Table of Statutes.** Many state encyclopedias contain a detailed table of statutes, which will direct you to a discussion of a statute in which you are interested. For example, if you are interested in Section 62 of the California Labor Code, simply look this up in the table of statutes in Cal. Jur. 3d and you will be directed to any sections in the set that discuss this statute.
- **Indexing.** Most state encyclopedias have a multi-volume general index. Additionally, many encyclopedias provide an individual index or outline of a topic just before the discussion of the topic begins.
- **Supplementation.** State encyclopedias are kept up to date by pocket parts and replacement volumes.

c.   Research Strategies for Using State Encyclopedias

The research techniques used to access the state encyclopedias are identical to the techniques used to access the national encyclopedias discussed previously, namely, the descriptive word approach, topic approach, table of statutes approach, and table of cases approach.

4.   Special Subject Encyclopedias

The encyclopedias previously discussed, C.J.S., Am. Jur. 2d, and the local encyclopedias, discuss hundreds of areas of the law. There are, however, a few encyclopedias, called *special subject encyclopedias*, which are devoted to just one area of the law. For example, West's *Encyclopedia of Employment Law* discusses all aspects of employment law. Check the card catalog at your law library to determine if an encyclopedia exists for a particular subject. Browse the stacks of the library devoted to the topic in which you are interested. Many of these "encyclopedias," however, are more accurately classified as treatises, discussed later in this chapter. Retrieve the index to the set, and use the descriptive word approach to access special subject encyclopedias.

5.   Summary of Encyclopedias

Encyclopedias provide excellent introductions to numerous areas of the law. You must remember, however, to read the primary sources you are directed to by the encyclopedias, because these mandatory authorities *must* be followed by courts, and the encyclopedias are merely persuasive authorities. In fact, although encyclopedias are excellent ways to "get your feet wet" and gain background information about a topic, you should not cite to them in a court document or research memorandum unless you can find no other relevant authority, because they are not sufficiently scholarly to serve as the sole support for an argument you advance.

B. Legal Periodicals

1. *Introduction*

Just as you might subscribe to a periodical publication such as *Sports Illustrated*, law firms and legal professionals subscribe to a variety of publications that are produced on a regular or periodic basis. All *legal periodicals* are secondary sources, although many of them, particularly the law school publications, are very well respected and scholarly. Typically, the legal periodicals direct you to primary authorities through the use of extensive footnotes. Periodicals serve many functions: Some provide extensive analyses of legal topics; some serve to keep practitioners current on recent developments in the law; some include articles that analyze how the law in a particular area should be changed; and others provide practical information relating to issues of interest to legal professionals.

There are four broad categories of legal periodicals: publications of law schools, publications of bar and other associations, specialized publications for those in the legal profession sharing similar interests, and legal newspapers and newsletters.

2. *Law School Publications*

Most law schools produce a periodical publication generally referred to as a *law review*, such as the *Harvard Law Review*, although some title their publications "journals," such as the *Yale Law Journal*. Because the law reviews are published so frequently (three or more times each year), they often provide current analysis of recent cases or legislation. Each issue includes its own table of contents.

The law reviews are edited by students who have been selected to write for the law review on the basis of academic distinction or writing skill. Law reviews provide scholarly analysis of legal topics and are routinely cited with approval by courts. They differ greatly from encyclopedias, which are noncritical in their approach and usually focus on merely explaining the law. Law reviews offer a critical approach and often advocate reform in the law.

A law review usually has several sections:

- **Articles.** *Articles* are usually scholarly monographs written by professors, judges, or practicing attorneys. Often exceeding 40 pages in length, an article examines a topic in depth.
- **Comments or Notes.** *Comments* or *Notes* are generally shorter pieces authored by students.
- **Case Comments/Recent Cases/Recent Developments.** This section is also authored by students and examines the effect of recent cases and new legislation.

• **Book Reviews.** Many law reviews contain a section that reviews books or texts relating to legal issues, such as a book written about antitrust law.

Almost all law schools publish one of these general types of law reviews, that is, a review containing articles on a variety of topics. In addition to these general law reviews, many schools also produce law reviews devoted to a specific area, such as international law or civil rights.

Law reviews are often arranged alphabetically in a law library, so that the *Akron Law Review* is followed by the *Alabama Law Review*, and so forth, making locating a law review easy and efficient.

See Figure 6-3 for a sample cover from a law review.

3. *Bar Association Publications*

Each state has a bar association. The dues paid to the association by its members fund various legal programs as well as the periodical publication of a journal for that state's members of the bar. Some bar associations publish monthly journals, but others publish less frequently. In addition, other legal associations publish periodicals. For example, the *ABA Journal* is a highly professional-looking publication that is sent to members of the American Bar Association each month. In a newer trend, many bar associations, such as the State Bar of California, provide their publications in electronic form only.

These publications usually offer a very practical approach to practicing law in a jurisdiction and feature articles on ethics, notices of changes to local court rules, human interest biographies of judges and attorneys, reviews of books and software of interest to legal professionals, and lists of attorneys who have been disciplined. The articles published in these bar association publications are far more practical in their approach than the academic articles published in law reviews.

Just as there are state bar associations, many local jurisdictions have city or county bar associations, such as the San Diego County Bar Association. These associations also produce periodical publications: Some are pamphlets, and others are informal newsletters or flyers. Generally, these publications are very practical and informal in approach. Job postings are often included.

Because bar associations tend to focus on practical guidelines for law practice, it is unlikely that you would conduct substantive research using these publications. It is far more likely that you will use these publications to keep you current on legal issues facing your jurisdiction.

4. *Specialized Publications*

Just as individuals who are interested in fashion might subscribe to *Vogue*, legal practitioners who have an interest in a specialized area of the law might subscribe to a specialized periodical, such as the *Bankruptcy Developments Journal* or the *Tax Adviser* to keep current with developments in these fields.

Figure 6-3
Sample Cover from Law Review

Fall 2007

Volume 44 Number 1

CALIFORNIA
WESTERN
LAW REVIEW

CALIFORNIA WESTERN
SCHOOL OF LAW | San Diego

ARTICLES

AMERICAN REPARATIONS THEORY AND PRACTICE AT THE
   CROSSROADS

*Eric K. Yamamoto,
Sandra Hye Yun Kim
& Abigail M. Holden*

XBRL AND THE SEC: HOW THE COMMISSION USES
   INTERACTIVE DATA TO INVESTIGATE ILLEGAL STOCK
   OPTIONS BACKDATING AND WHAT INTERACTIVE DATA
   MEANS FOR THE FUTURE OF FEDERAL SECURITIES LAW
   ENFORCEMENT

Susan M. Brunka

UNITED STATES V. FORT AND THE FUTURE OF WORK
   PRODUCT IN CRIMINAL DISCOVERY

Anne Shaver

"WHO ARE THOSE GUYS?": THE RESULTS OF A SURVEY
   STUDYING THE INFORMATION LITERACY OF INCOMING
   LAW STUDENTS

Ian Gallacher

OPPORTUNITY LOST: HOW LAW SCHOOL DISAPPOINTS LAW
   STUDENTS, THE PUBLIC, AND THE LEGAL PROFESSION

Jason M. Dolin

COMMENTS

POWERED BY GREASE: THE CASE FOR STRAIGHT VEGETABLE
   OIL IN THE NEW FUEL ECONOMY

Robert Scott Norman

A TANGLED SITUATION OF GENDER DISCRIMINATION:
   IN THE FACE OF AN INEFFECTIVE ANTIDISCRIMINATION
   RULE AND CHALLENGES FOR WOMEN IN LAW FIRMS—
   WHAT IS THE NEXT STEP TO PROMOTE GENDER
   DIVERSITY IN THE LEGAL PROFESSION?

Lea E. Delossantos

Similarly, many periodicals are published for individuals who may share common interests, such as the *National Black Law Journal* or the *Women's Rights Law Reporter*. These specialized journals vary in their approach, with some being more analytical and academic and others being more practical.

5. *Legal Newspapers and Newsletters*

In large cities such as New York and Los Angeles, you will find daily legal newspapers such as the *New York Law Journal* and the *Los Angeles and San Francisco Daily Journal*. These newspapers contain the text of recent court cases, cover legislative issues, and include articles of interest to legal professionals in that jurisdiction. They usually also include extensive classified advertisements and serve as a useful source of job announcements. Some legal newspapers do not restrict their coverage to any locality and are national in scope, such as the weekly *National Law Journal*.

In addition to legal newspapers, more than 2,000 legal and law-related newsletters are published in the United States. Some are one-page bulletins; others are multipage newsletters. Examples are *Jury Trials and Tribulations* (containing summaries of civil jury trials in Florida) and *Internet Litigation News* (reporting on cases relating to litigation about the Internet).

6. *How to Locate Periodical Articles*

Although each issue of any periodical will contain its own table of contents, the best way to locate an article in a periodical publication is to consult one of several published indexes that will direct you to articles published in periodicals. There are several well-known indexes you can use:

a. Print Indexes

Most law libraries provide indexes in print that direct researchers to articles published in journals and periodicals. The two best known print indexes are *Index to Legal Periodicals & Books* ("I.L.P.") and *Current Law Index*. Each set will direct you to about 1,000 legal periodicals and journals. The sets are initially published in monthly or quarterly softcover pamphlets that are later bound in hardbound volumes. They are usually located in the reference section of a law library. To locate periodical articles in either I.L.P. or *Current Law Index*, use one of the following methods:

• **Subject Approach.** Think of words that describe the topic you are interested in, such as bankruptcy or divorce. Look up these words in the alphabetically arranged index to be directed to published articles relating to this topic.

- **Author Approach.** If you happen to know that a certain author has written on a topic, you may look up the author's name to be directed to articles written by this individual.
- **Table of Cases Approach.** If you wish to read articles that have discussed certain cases, such as *Bush v. Gore*, you can look up this case name in either set's Table of Cases, and you will be directed to periodical articles written about this case.
- **Table of Statutes Approach.** If you are interested in whether any periodical articles have analyzed a particular statute, you can look up the statute in either set's Table of Statutes, which will direct you to pertinent articles.
- **Book Review Approach.** If you are looking for a review of a certain book, use the Book Review Index in each set to be directed to articles that have reviewed the book. See Figure 6-4 for a sample page from I.L.P.

b. Other Indexes

Although I.L.P. and *Current Law Index* are the most comprehensive indexes because they send you to hundreds of periodicals, there are several other indexes that may assist in your research efforts, including the following:

- *Index to Foreign Legal Periodicals.* This index will direct you to periodical articles from countries other than the United States and the British Commonwealth. Access is gained through an alphabetically arranged subject index (in English) or an index by author name.
- *Index to Periodical Articles Related to Law.* Remember that I.L.P. and *Current Law Index* will direct you only to legal publications. It is possible, however, that articles related to legal topics may appear in the popular press, such as *TIME* magazine or *Wired*. The *Index to Periodical Articles Related to Law* will direct you to such articles through its alphabetically arranged index.

c. Electronic Finding Aids

The major print indexes, I.L.P. and *Current Law Index*, are cumulated on a monthly, quarterly, and annual basis. Thus, you may need to check several pamphlets and bound volumes to find articles of interest to you. This is highly time consuming; therefore, nearly all researchers use electronic or online versions of these or other indexes.

Figure 6-4
Sample Page from *Index to Legal Periodicals & Books*

22   INDEX TO LEGAL PERIODICALS & BOOKS

Coal
The Phasing Constraint: Who May Request Relief and When?
J. O. Moreno. *Journal of Transportation Law, Logistics and Policy* v71 no4 p419-33 2004
Coalbed methane
Northern Plains Resource Council v. Fidelity Exploration and Development Co., 325 F.3d 1155 (9th Cir. 2003), cert. denied, 124 S. Ct. 434 (2003). *Environmental Law* v34 no3 p845-8 Summ 2004
Coastal zone
    New Zealand
Coastal Management and the Environmental Compensation Challenge. S. Turner. *New Zealand Journal of Environmental Law* v4 p181-200 2000
Coburn, David H.
Rail Construction Cases: Environmental and Other Issues. *Journal of Transportation Law, Logistics and Policy* v71 no4 p379-92 2004
Cochrane, Drew J.
Disability Law in Wisconsin Workplaces. *Wisconsin Lawyer* v77 no10 p8-10, 53-5 O 2004
Codes and codification
    History
Special Issue on Comparative Legal History. *The Journal of Legal History* v25 no2 p99-194 Ag 2004
Two Early Codes, the Ten Commandments and the Twelve Tables: Causes and Consequences. A. Watson. *The Journal of Legal History* v25 no2 p129-49 Ag 2004
    Canada
Of Codifications, the Uniform Trust Code and Quebec Trusts: Lessons for Common Law Canada? A. Grenon. *Estates Trusts & Pensions Journal* v23 no3 p237-65 Ag 2004
    China
Structures of Three Major Civil Code Projets in Today's China. G. Xu. *Tulane European and Civil Law Forum* v19 p37-56 2004
    European Union countries
European Code of Contract [Special Issue] *Edinburgh Law Review* v8 Special Issue p I-X, 1-89 2004
Explanatory Note [European Code of Contract: Special Issue] H. McGregor. *Edinburgh Law Review* v8 Special Issue p IX-X 2004
Introduction [European Code of Contract: Special Issue] J. A. D. H. Hope of Craighead. *Edinburgh Law Review* v8 Special Issue p I-VIII 2004
The Optional European Code on the Basis of the Acquis Communautaire—Starting Point and Trends. S. Grundmann. *European Law Journal* v10 no6 p698-711 N 2004
The Politics of a European Civil Code. M. W. Hesselink. *European Law Journal* v10 no6 p675-97 N 2004
    France
Thoughts from a Scottish Perspective on the Bicentenary of the French Civil Code. E. Clive. *Edinburgh Law Review* v8 no3 p415-20 S 2004
    Great Britain
Codification in England: The Need to Move from an Ideological to a Functional Approach—A Bridge too Far? E. Steiner. *Statute Law Review* v25 no3 p209-22 2004
    Louisiana
Interpretations of the Louisiana Civil Codes, 1808-1840: The Failure of the Preliminary Title. T. W. Tucker. *Tulane European and Civil Law Forum* v19 p57-182 2004
Mapping Society Through Law: Louisiana Civil Law Recodified. D. Gruning. *Tulane European and Civil Law Forum* v19 p1-36 2004
    Middle East
    History
Wrongs and Responsibility in Pre-Roman Law. D. Ibbetson. *The Journal of Legal History* v25 no2 p99-127 Ag 2004
    Québec (Province)
    German influences
Imported Books, Imported Ideas: Reading European Jurisprudence in Mid-Nineteenth-Century Quebec. E. H. Reiter. *Law and History Review* v22 no3 p445-92 Fall 2004
    History
Imported Books, Imported Ideas: Reading European Jurisprudence in Mid-Nineteenth-Century Quebec. E. H. Reiter. *Law and History Review* v22 no3 p445-92 Fall 2004
    Scotland
Thoughts from a Scottish Perspective on the Bicentenary of the French Civil Code. E. Clive. *Edinburgh Law Review* v8 no3 p415-20 S 2004
Codicils *See* Wills
Coerced treatment *See* Involuntary treatment
Cogeneration of electric power *See* Electricity
Cohabitation *See* Unmarried couples

Cohen, Adam I.
Rules 33 and 34: Defining E-documents and the Form of Production. Panel Discussion. *Fordham Law Review* v73 no1 p33-51 O 2004
Cohen, Elizabeth J.
The Meaning of 'Forever'. *American Bar Association Journal* v90 p28 N 2004
Cohen, Fred
Silence of the experts. *Trial* v40 no10 p20-2, 24-5, 27-9 O 2004
Cohen, Jerry
The new Massachusetts Business Corporation Act, chapter 127, Acts of 2003. *Massachusetts Law Review* v88 no4 p213-17 Spr 2004
Colb, Sherry F.
A World without Privacy: Why Property Does Not Define the Limits of the Right against Unreasonable Searches and Seizures. *Michigan Law Review* v102 no5 p889-903 Mr 2004

            Entry by author

Collateral estoppel
  See also
  Res judicata
The U.N. Convention on the Recognition and Enforcement of Foreign Arbitral Awards and Issue Preclusion: A Traditional Collateral Estoppel Determination. S. M. Sudol, student author. *University of Pittsburgh Law Review* v65 no4 p931-50 Summ 2004
Collecting societies (Copyright)
    European Union countries
Collective hysteria? A. Hobson. *Copyright World* no143 p15-17 S 2004
Collective bargaining
  See also
  Employee benefits
Promoting Labour Rights in International Financial Institutions and Trade Regimes. P. Barnacle. *Saskatchewan Law Review* v67 no2 p609-36 2004
    Canada
ILO Freedom of Association Principles as Basic Canadian Human Rights: Promises to Keep. K. Norman. *Saskatchewan Law Review* v67 no2 p591-608 2004
"Labour is Not a Commodity": The Supreme Court of Canada and the Freedom of Association. J. Fudge. *Saskatchewan Law Review* v67 no2 p425-52 2004
Collective security *See* International security
Collectivism
    Yugoslavia
The Fate of the Yugoslav Model: A Case Against Legal Conformity. K. Medjad. *The American Journal of Comparative Law* v52 no1 p287-319 Wint 2004
College admissions *See* Colleges and universities—Admission
College and university libraries
Exclusion or Efficient Pricing? The "Big Deal" Bundling of Academic Journals. A. S. Edlin, D. L. Rubinfeld. *Antitrust Law Journal* v72 no1 p119-57 2004
College athletics *See* College sports
College sports
With the First Pick in the 2004 NFL Draft, the San Diego Chargers Select . . . ?: A Rule of Reason Analysis of What the National Football League Should Have Argued in Regards to a Challenge of Its Special Draft Eligibility Rules under Section 1 of the Sherman Act. J. M. Ganderson, student author. *University of Miami Business Law Review* v12 no1/2 p1-33 Spr/Summer 2004

            Entry by topic

Colleges and universities
  See also
  Academic freedom
  College sports
  Colleges and universities—Finance
  Fraternities and sororities
  Law schools
Does the Tax Law Discriminate against the Majority of American Children?: The Downside of Our Progressive Rate Structure and Unbalanced Incentives for Higher Education. L. B. Snyder. *San Diego Law Review* v41 no3 p1311-35 Summ 2004
Dreaming of an Equal Future for Immigrant Children: Federal and State Initiatives to Improve Undocumented Students' Access to Postsecondary Education. A. Stevenson, student author. *Arizona Law Review* v46 no3 p551-80 Fall 2004
    Admission
Litigators and Communities Working Together: Grutter v. Bollinger and the New Civil Rights Movement. M. Massie. *Berkeley Women's Law Journal* v19 no2 p318-23 2004
    Finance
    Florida
Monetary and Regulatory Hobbling: The Acquisition of Real Property by Public Institutions of Higher Education in Florida. C. L. Zeiner. *University of Miami Business Law Review* v12 no1/2 p103-68 Spr/Summer 2004

- **Index to Legal Periodicals & Books.** The online version of I.L.P. is also called "Index to Legal Periodicals & Books." Researching using the online index is much easier than using the conventional print volumes because the online version is completely cumulative. Once you type in the appropriate search terms (topic, author name, and so on), you will be directed to all pertinent articles after 1982. This online index is a subscription service, meaning that a law library must subscribe to it and then typically only its members or students may access it.

- **Current Index to Legal Periodicals.** Many law schools and universities subscribe to Current Index to Legal Periodicals, which allows researchers to search for articles in nearly 600 legal publications. Researchers can customize the service so that, for example, they will be notified any time a new article is published in *Business Lawyer* or any time any journal publishes an article about copyright law. Current Index to Legal Periodicals is available in both print and electronic forms and provides the most up-to-date access to journals and articles.

- **LegalTrac.** LegalTrac is an online index to the articles found in the *Current Law Index* together with articles found in business and general interest periodicals. Many law libraries subscribe to LegalTrac, allowing you desktop computer access, so you can easily search for and locate articles since 1980 by subject matter, author name, and so forth.

- **HeinOnline.** Many law schools and universities subscribe to HeinOnline, which provides the full text of more than 1,600 periodicals. HeinOnline provides exact page images of law review articles so that all charts and graphs appear just as in their print counterparts. You may search by topic, author, or citation. Access is typically limited to students and other registered users.

- **Lexis and Westlaw.** Periodical articles are easily retrieved on both Lexis and Westlaw. You may locate articles by their citation or by key words. After you locate an article, you may then Shepardize it or KeyCite it to locate more recent articles and cases that cite your article.

- **University Law Review Project.** The University Law Review Project is a free service, available at http://www.lawreview.org, which offers links to hundreds of law reviews and periodicals. The site allows searching for journal articles by key words inserted into a search box. The site also offers direct linking to numerous law reviews by topic. Thus, if you select Family Law, you will be given a list of journals that discuss family law.

- **Law Review Websites.** Most law reviews now have their own websites and post their most recent issues. Some also post the full text of older articles. Use a general search engine to locate journals. For example, enter "Duke Law Journal" into Google's search box and you will be able to access all *Duke Law Journal* articles since 1950.

C.   Texts and Treatises

1.   *Introduction*

Texts written by legal scholars that focus on one topic of the law are referred to as *treatises*. Treatises comment on and analyze an area of the law. The authors may be academics or practicing attorneys, and the treatises vary a great deal in scope and depth. A treatise may be a one-volume work on a fairly narrow topic or a multi-volume work on a broader topic, such as the 27-volume set *Collier on Bankruptcy, 16th Edition*.

Treatises cover an area of the law in greater depth than encyclopedias. For example, if you were to read all of the C.J.S. treatment on Contracts, you would be presented with approximately 2,000 pages of material. If you were to review the well-known treatise *Williston on Contracts 4th*, you would be presented with more than 30 volumes and approximately 18,000 pages of material. Moreover, the commentary found in a treatise is typically more analytical than those found in encyclopedias. Encyclopedias are noncritical summaries of the law, meaning that the information you are given merely summarizes the law relating to that topic. Treatises, however, may be *critical* in the sense that they may criticize current case law and suggest a different approach than courts are currently taking.

One feature treatises share in common with encyclopedias, however, is that they serve as casefinders. The format of many treatises is similar to that of encyclopedias: Narrative discussions of the law are found on the top portion of each page with citation to cases and other authorities located through the use of supporting footnotes on the lower portion of each page.

Although treatises are secondary authorities and are therefore persuasive rather than binding authority, many treatises are highly regarded and are often cited with approval by courts. Thus, you may and should rely on them and quote from them in memoranda and briefs so long as you also have at least one "on point" primary authority to support your position. Following are some tips that suggest that a treatise is highly regarded: if the treatise is published in multiple editions (showing wide acceptance and use); if court decisions frequently cite a treatise; and if the author has produced other writings on this topic.

To determine whether a treatise exists for an area of the law, check your card catalog (whether conventional or online), which will direct you to the "stack" where the treatise is located; browse the shelves where the books relating to that area of law are maintained and skim the titles; or ask a reference librarian. See Figure 6-5 for a sample page from a treatise.

Figure 6-5
Sample Page from a Treatise

§ 11:32   Abbreviations

An abbreviation of a descriptive term which still conveys to the buyer the descriptive connotation of the original term will still be held to be descriptive. For example, the mark "B and B" for benedictine and brandy was held descriptive of the ingredients of the product.[1] Further, ALR was held merely descriptive and unregisterable in that members of the electrical industry equate ALR with "aluminum revised," used to describe aluminum wire meeting the revised and upgraded standards of the Underwriter's Laboratories.[2] Other abbreviations held to be descriptive include:

- B-100 was held descriptive of vitamins with 100 milligrams of vitamin B[3]
- V2 was held a descriptive grade designation for vitamin enriched 2 percent butterfat milk[4]
- the letter "O" was held to be descriptive of an orange flavored vodka[4.1]

[Section 11:32]

[1]Martell & Co. v. Societe Anonyme de La Benedictine, 116 F.2d 516, 48 U.S.P.Q. 116 (C.C.P.A. 1941). *See* Automatic Electric, Inc. v. North Electric Mfg. Co., 28 F.2d 979 (6th Cir. 1928); In re General Aniline & Films Corp., 136 U.S.P.Q. 306 (T.T.A.B. 1962); Foremost Dairies, Inc. v. Borden Co., 156 U.S.P.Q. 153 (T.T.A.B. 1967) (HOMO for homogenized milk); Calgon Corp. v. Hooker Chemical Corp., 151 U.S.P.Q. 359 (T.T.A.B. 1966); Spin Physics, Inc. v. Matsushita Electric Industrial Co., 168 U.S.P.Q. 605 (T.T.A.B. 1970) (HPF recognized abbreviation in the trade for "hot-pressed ferrite"). *See also* §§ 12:37-12:40 and 13:20.

[2]Southwire Co. v. Kaiser Aluminum & Chemical Corp., 196 U.S.P.Q. 566 (T.T.A.B. 1977). *See* CPP Ins. Agency, Inc. v. General Motors Corp., 212 U.S.P.Q. 257 (S.D. Cal. 1980) (CPP is recognizable acronym for descriptive term CONSUMER PROTECTION PLAN for supplemental auto repair insurance plan).

[3]Nature's Bounty, Inc. v. Basic Organics, 432 F. Supp. 546, 196 U.S.P.Q. 622 (E.D.N.Y. 1977). *Compare* Nature's Bounty, Inc. v. Super X Drugs Corp., 490 F. Supp. 50, 207 U.S.P.Q. 263 (E.D.N.Y. 1980) (KLB6 held neither generic nor descriptive of food supplement containing kelp, lecithin and vitamin B6).

[4]East Side Jersey Dairy, Inc. v. Jewel Cos., 197 U.S.P.Q. 535 (S.D. Ind. 1977).

[4.1]Star Industries, Inc. v. Bacardi & Co. Ltd. Corp., 71 U.S.P.Q.2d 1026, 2003 WL 23109750 (S.D. N.Y. 2003), aff'd, 412 F.3d 373, 75 U.S.P.Q.2d 1098 (2d Cir. 2005), petition for cert. filed (U.S. Dec. 13, 2005) (no secondary meaning was proven).

2. *Common Features of Treatises*

Treatises usually share the following features:

- **Format.** Treatises are essentially expert opinions on one topic of the law. The analysis of the law is presented in narrative form, and readers are usually directed to cases and other authorities through the use of footnotes.
- **Index.** An index to the treatise consisting of an alphabetical arrangement of the topics, words, and phrases discussed in the treatise will be located in the last volume of the set or as a separate index volume.
- **Table of Contents.** A table of contents is usually given in the front of each volume, showing how the discussion of this area of law is arranged by chapter.
- **Tables of Cases and Statutes.** Many treatises include a table of cases and a table of statutes so you may readily locate a discussion of a certain case or statute.
- **Appendices.** Many treatises include the entire text of statutes and regulations in an appendix at the end of the set.
- **Updating.** Most treatises are updated by the traditional method of updating law books: an annual cumulative pocket part (or a separate softcover supplement). Other treatises are in looseleaf binders, and the publisher will send replacement pages to provide new information.

3. *Research Strategies for Using Treatises*

To locate information of interest to you in a treatise, use the following standard research methods:

- **Descriptive Word Approach.** Select the word or phrase that describes your issue and look it up in the index, which will then direct you to the appropriate treatise volume and section. For example, if the index directs you to **4:12**, this is a signal for you to retrieve chapter 4 and review section 12.
- **Topic Approach.** Review the table of contents for the treatise (check the first volume) and scan the list of chapter titles and subsections, and proceed to the appropriate chapter.
- **Table of Cases/Table of Statutes Approach.** To locate a discussion of a particular case or statute, look up the case name or statute number in the table of cases or table of statutes, respectively, which will direct you to the pertinent chapter and section.
- **Other Approaches.** Researchers are often directed to treatises through other sources. For example, if you are reading a pertinent case on an issue and the case relies on a treatise, you should then examine the cited treatise. Similarly, other sources (encyclopedias, periodical articles, and library references found in U.S.C.A. and U.S.C.S.) may direct you to a treatise.

D. Restatements

1. *Introduction*

The *Restatements* are multi-volume sets of books on specific topics. They are a product of a group of legal scholars called the American Law Institute (ALI), which was formed in 1923 to restate United States case law in a clear and concise manner because the scholars believed case law was uncertain and complex. Individuals are selected for membership in ALI on the basis of their professional accomplishments and their commitment to improving the law.

Because the Restatements are a secondary source, courts are not required to adopt or follow the Restatement positions. Nevertheless, the Restatements have been cited in cases more than 180,000 times. Many legal experts believe the Restatements are the most highly regarded of all of the secondary authorities, and you may freely rely on them and cite to them in your research projects. Restatements do not exist for every area of law but only for selected topics. See Figure 6-6 for a chart of Restatements.

Figure 6-6
Chart of Restatements

Topic	*Current Series*
Agency	Third
Conflict of Laws	Second
Contracts	Second
Foreign Relations Law of the United States	Third
Judgments	Second
Law Governing Lawyers	Third
Property	Second and Third
Restitution and Unjust Enrichment	Third
Suretyship and Guaranty	Third
Torts	Second and Third
Trusts	Third
Unfair Competition	Third

2. *Arrangement of Restatements*

Each Restatement typically consists of two to six volumes. Each volume is arranged in chapters, and the chapters are then arranged in titles and numbered sections. Each section states a principle of the law in clear, straightforward language printed in bold typeface. These Restatement sections are followed by "Comments" that provide general analysis of the legal principle previously given and "Illustrations" that provide clearly written examples demonstrating the application of the principle. The Reporter's Notes then complete each section by providing general discussion and explanations, together with references to relevant cases. See Figure 6-7 for a sample page from Restatement (Second) of Contracts.

3. *Research Strategies for Using Restatements*

The easiest way to locate a pertinent Restatement provision is to use the descriptive word approach. Consult the alphabetically arranged index to your Restatement, which is usually found in the last volume of the Restatement set. Look up words or phrases that describe your research problem, and you will be directed to the appropriate section of the Restatement. Alternatively, you may be directed to a pertinent Restatement section in the course of your research; for example, a case you may be reading may refer to a Restatement section. You may also browse through your Restatement's table of contents. Finally, you may use the alphabetical Table of Cases (for newer Restatements) to be directed to Restatement sections that have discussed certain cases.

The Restatements are kept current through pocket parts and appendix volumes (which themselves contain pocket parts). The Restatements are available on Lexis and Westlaw.

E. Miscellaneous Secondary Authorities

Although the most frequently used secondary authorities are A.L.R. annotations, encyclopedias, periodicals, treatises, and Restatements, there are also numerous other secondary authorities that researchers often use. The following are the most commonly used of these other secondary authorities.

1. *Attorneys General Opinions*

The U.S. Attorney General (appointed by the President) is the chief legal officer for the federal government. Each of the 50 states and the District of Columbia also has an attorney general. The attorneys general issue written opinions on a variety of topics, including the interpretation of statutes and the duties of government agencies. These *attorneys general opinions* typically are written in response to questions by legislators, the executive branch, or other government officials.

Any large law library in your area will collect the opinions of the U.S. Attorney General and will also have the opinions of your state attorney

Figure 6-7
Sample Page from Restatement (Second) of Contracts

§ 145   CONTRACTS, SECOND   Ch. 5

Text
of
Restatement

§ 145.   Effect of Full Performance

Where the promises in a contract have been fully performed by all parties, the Statute of Frauds does not affect the legal relations of the parties.

Comment

Comment:

   a. Rationale. The Statute of Frauds renders certain contracts unenforceable by action or defense; it does not forbid the making or performance of such contracts, or authorize their rescission after full performance on both sides. After such full performance, neither party can maintain an action for restitution merely because the contract was unenforceable under the Statute. See § 141. The Statute has no further function to perform, and the legal relations of the parties are the same as if the contract had been enforceable. Compare § 147.

Illustrations

Illustrations:

   1.   A owes B a debt of $20,000. A's land, worth $10,000, is about to be sold on foreclosure under a mortgage held by C. B contracts to bid in the land and to deduct from A's debt to B $10,000 less the amount B pays. B bids in the land for $6,000. A's debt is reduced by $4,000.

   2.   At D's request S orally guarantees to C that D will pay a debt D owes to C. On D's failure to pay at maturity, S pays the debt. C's claim against D is discharged, and S has the same rights against D as if S's promise to C had been enforceable.

REPORTER'S NOTE

This Section is based on former § 219. See 3 Williston, Contracts § 528 (3d ed. 1960); 2 Corbin, Contracts § 285 (1950 & Supp. 1971).

   Comment a. Illustrations 1 and 2 are based on Illustrations 1 and 2 to former § 219. See Mapes v. Kalva Corp., 68 Ill. App.3d 362, 24 Ill. Dec. 944, 386 N.E.2d 148 (1979); Trimmer v. Short, 492 S.W.2d 179 (Mo. Ct. App. 1973); Scott v. Southern Coach & Body Co., 280 Ala. 670, 197 So.2d 775 (1967); cf. Rice v. Insurance & Bonds, Inc., 366 So.2d 85 (Fla. Dist. Ct. App. 1979).

§ 146.   Rights of Competing Transferees of Property

(1) Where a contract to transfer property or a transfer was unenforceable against the transferor under the Statute of Frauds but subsequently becomes enforce-

---

See Appendix for Court Citations and Cross References
366

general. Although attorneys general opinions are secondary authorities, because they are written by the chief legal advisor to the executive branch (whether federal or state) and are usually followed, they are highly persuasive, and you should feel free to cite them in your research projects.

Most sets of opinions of attorneys general will have an index, which you can access by using the descriptive word approach. It is more likely, however, that you will be directed to a pertinent attorney general opinion by another source you are using, such as U.S.C.A., U.S.C.S., or a state annotated code. Similarly, when you update a case by Shepardizing or KeyCiting it, you will be directed to attorneys general opinions that have mentioned your case. Finally, many opinions are now available on the Internet. Almost all states now offer their attorneys general opinions on their respective websites. Access the site of the Office of Legal Counsel at http://www.justice.gov/olc/opinions.htm to link to the U.S. Attorney General opinions or to the website of the National Association of Attorneys General at http://www.naag.org/current-attorneys-general.php to link to your state's attorneys general opinions.

2. Words and Phrases

West's 100-plus volume set *Words and Phrases* will direct you to cases that have interpreted words, terms, or phrases. Arranged alphabetically, the set is as easy to use as any dictionary. Once you look up the word or phrase in which you are interested, *Words and Phrases* will provide a brief summary of the cases that interpret your word and then give you the case citations. Be sure to review the pocket part in each volume to locate newer cases. Many students mistake *Words and Phrases* for a general index and thus overlook its value. Don't make that mistake.

3. *Legal Dictionaries and Thesauri*

A *legal dictionary* will give you the spelling, pronunciation, and meaning of a legal word or phrase such as "en banc" or "abatement." In many instances you will be directed to a case or secondary authority in which the word was defined. The best known of the legal dictionaries is *Black's Law Dictionary* (9th ed. 2009). *Black's* not only includes more than 45,000 definitions, but also provides a table of common legal abbreviations, definitions of legal maxims, and West Key Numbers. *Black's* differs from *Words and Phrases* in that the coverage of *Words and Phrases* is limited to words and phrases that have been defined in cases; *Black's* defines words whether they have been the subject of court interpretation or not.

A *legal thesaurus* provides synonyms and antonyms for legal words and terms. For example, if you wish to find another word for "abandon," a thesaurus will suggest "disclaim," "forfeit," and other terms. One of the best known of the legal thesauri is *Burton's Legal Thesaurus* by William C. Burton, which provides more than 8,000 terms, synonyms, and definitions. Dictionaries and thesauri are found in the reference section of your law library.

A recent trend is publication of glossaries of legal terms on the Internet. For example, the website Law.com offers a legal dictionary at http://dictionary.law.com. Although these online glossaries are not particularly comprehensive, they may be helpful in providing you with a quick understanding of a legal term or Latin phrase. Similarly, the *Wolters Kluwer Bouvier Law Dictionary* is available in abridged form as a free app from the iTunes store.

4. *Legal Directories*

a. **Introduction**

A *legal directory* is simply a list of lawyers. Some law directories, such as the highly regarded *Martindale-Hubbell Law Directory*, aim at listing all lawyers admitted to any jurisdiction. Other directories are more limited in scope and may list only those lawyers in a certain practice field, city, or locality. Law directories are usually kept in the reference section of a law library.

b. *Martindale-Hubbell Law Directory*

The best known law directory in the United States is *Martindale-Hubbell Law Directory*, in existence for more than a century. At present, most major United States law firms pay to be listed in *Martindale-Hubbell*. The set is published annually in hardbound volumes and is organized alphabetically by state. For example, Volume 1 covers the states Alabama, Alaska, Arizona, Arkansas, and California. Within each state listing, law firms and attorneys are identified alphabetically by city name and then by law firm or attorney name. Each firm that has an entry will list its attorneys and provide brief biographical information about them. Moreover, the firm's address, phone number, website, representative clients, and practice areas will be noted. By reviewing *Martindale-Hubbell*, you may be able to target your résumé to a law firm that focuses on a field of law in which you are interested. Legal professionals also use *Martindale-Hubbell* to refer clients to other firms if a conflict of interest arises or if a firm cannot represent a client.

Although the print set formerly included state digests (giving some of the laws from each state), since 2007, these state digests are no longer available. The set also includes two volumes titled *International Law Directory* that profile lawyers and law firms from more than 160 countries.

Nearly all of the attorney information found in the conventional print volumes of *Martindale-Hubbell* can also be located on the Internet at http://www.martindale.com. Searching is easily accomplished by lawyer name, firm name, location, or law school attended. Another excellent free legal directory on the Internet is provided by FindLaw, West's legal

Figure 6-8
Sample Page from Virginia Forms—Criminal Procedure

No. 9-1002. Order Allowing Attorney to Withdraw.

ORDER ALLOWING ATTORNEY TO WITHDRAW

This matter came on this ___ day of _____, 1998, to be heard on the motion of Hope N. Pray, counsel, for leave to withdraw as counsel of record for Daniel Dissatisfied.

Daniel Dissatisfied being present in person in court, the Court heard statements by counsel and defendant.

The Court finding there being good cause and it being proper so to do, it is hereby ORDERED that Hope N. Pray is relieved as counsel of record for Daniel Dissatisfied.

It is further ORDERED that the next attorney on the court-appointed list be assigned this case.

Enter: _____

Judge

Date: _____

I ask for this:

_____

Hope N. Pray

Seen and Agreed:

_____

Daniel Dissatisfied

Note: Rules of the Supreme Court of Virginia, Virginia Code of Professional Responsibility, DR 2-108 as to termination representation.

website at http://lawyers.findlaw.com. *Martindale-Hubbell* is available on Lexis; Westlaw offers its own legal directories.

5. *Form Books*

Much of a legal professional's time is spent drafting documents. Some documents are litigation related, such as complaints or answers, whereas others are transaction related, such as a partnership agreement. *Form books* help practitioners get a jump start on drafting these documents by providing sample forms. Most sets of form books are multi-volume sets with an alphabetically arranged index that allows you to use the descriptive word approach to locate desired forms. Most sets are annotated, meaning that you will be referred to cases that have approved or supported language used in the form. Moreover, many form books provide analysis and commentary on use of the forms and practical aids such as checklists, suggesting items to consider in drafting a certain type of document. See Figure 6-8 for a sample page from a form book. Although the form books themselves are practice aids, they include secondary authority references and commentary. Most form books are kept current by pocket parts.

In addition to the form books described previously as part of the Am. Jur. Total Client-Service Library (see Section A.2.e), some of the better known form books include the following:

- *Bender's Forms of Discovery.* This set, by publisher Matthew Bender (part of Lexis), provides forms related solely to discovery matters and includes forms for interrogatories, requests for production of documents, depositions, and other discovery devices for both federal and state practice.
- *Bender's Federal Practice Forms.* This multi-volume set provides litigation forms for use in federal practice, both civil and criminal.
- *Current Legal Forms with Tax Analysis.* This set by Jacob Rabkin and Mark H. Johnson is a 34-volume set of forms for every area of law practice (except criminal law and litigation).

Many publishers produce sets of form books devoted strictly to forms for use in one state. For example, a set commonly used in California for business or transactional matters is Matthew Bender's *California Legal Forms: Transaction Guide*. Treatises often provide forms as well. Finally, the Internet offers thousands of legal forms. As with many offerings on the Internet, however, it is unknown who authored the forms or whether they have been subjected to the rigorous review that accompanies print publications. Thus, they should be used with extreme caution, although they may serve as a useful starting place. Better forms may be found on a state's official website. For example, all states now provide comprehensive forms for organizing, maintaining, and dissolving business entities such as corporations. Similarly, many courts now offer free forms on their websites, and these are highly reliable.

Ethics Alert

Using Form Books and Metadata

Drafting a legal form requires more than finding a good form and then filling in the blanks. You are required to research the area of law and then modify any preprinted form to comply with the law. Use an annotated form book; it will direct you to primary authorities that endorse use of the language given in the form and provide additional critical references. Because the law changes frequently, using an outmoded form from one of your form files may be malpractice.

   In addition, documents created at law firms often contain *metadata*, or information describing the history, management, and tracking of an electronically created document. For example, if you change the name "Smith" in an older contract that you are now drafting for "Jones," metadata enables a reader to discover that the document was originally prepared for Smith. Metadata also reveals who received documents, comments and deletions made during the drafting process, sequences of changes, delays in sending a document, and other critical information. Many law firms now use sophisticated "scrubbing" programs to eliminate metadata and protect confidential client information. Check your law firm's policies and your ethics codes on metadata mining and scrubbing, and be scrupulous about maintaining confidential client information.

To locate form books, check the card catalog in your law library, browse the shelves, or consult your law librarian. When you locate a pertinent set, use the descriptive word approach to locate appropriate forms, and be sure to check any pocket parts.

6. *Uniform Laws*

A group of more than 300 practicing attorneys, judges, law professors, and other legal scholars form the National Conference of Commissioners on Uniform State Laws, which meets on an annual basis to draft proposed legislation on various areas of the law in which national uniformity is desirable. These proposed laws, called *uniform laws* or *uniform acts*, are then presented to the legislatures of the various states with the hope and expectation that the legislature will pass the Conference's version of the law. No uniform law is effective until a state legislature specifically enacts it. Some states will adopt the uniform act "as is." Other states may reject the act, and others may revise the act, adding certain provisions and omitting others. Thus, although the goal of the Conference is to produce a statute that will be uniform from state to state, the end result is a statute that nearly always has some variation from state to state. The Conference has approved more than 300 uniform laws; the best known is the Uniform Commercial Code (relating to commercial practices and sales), which has been adopted in whole or in part by every state.

The Conference and other organizations also draft proposed legislation known as *Model Acts*, which serve as a source to which states can look for guidance in drafting their own laws and which are seldom enacted in their entirety. Uniform laws, however, are intended to be adopted as written.

To locate the text of the uniform laws, use West's *Uniform Laws Annotated* (U.L.A.), which includes the text of all uniform laws (arranged by general subject matter), the comments of the drafters explaining the purpose of each uniform law, a list of the states that have adopted each particular uniform law, brief descriptions of how various states have modified the uniform law, and other resources. To locate specific uniform laws, you may scan the spines of the volumes or use the *Uniform Laws Annotated Directory of Acts*, a pamphlet that lists all uniform laws alphabetically and directs you to a uniform law's location in U.L.A. The text of all uniform laws is available on Westlaw and many are available on Lexis. Finally, the uniform laws are available on the Internet on the website of the Conference at http://www.uniformlaws.org. The text of uniform laws is given, along with a summary of each act and legislative facts about the adoption of an act in the various states.

Remember that uniform laws are secondary authorities, but once a uniform law is adopted by a state legislature, it becomes a primary authority like any other statute, and it can be located in your state's code. If another state has adopted the same uniform law, its interpretation of that law may be persuasive (but not binding) to a court interpreting your state's uniform law.

7. *Looseleaf Services*

Looseleaf services are sets of ringed binders with individual looseleaf sheets of paper, which are easily removed and replaced. The looseleaf services are a variety of treatise, and many are devoted to rules and regulations promulgated by our federal agencies, such as the service titled *Immigration Law Service, 2d*. The looseleaf services usually include primary authorities (such as cases, statutes, and administrative regulations) as well as secondary authorities (such as commentary and discussion of the topic and recent developments). Looseleaf services are discussed further in Chapter 7.

8. *Jury Instructions*

At the end of a trial, when a judge "charges" a jury by providing it with instructions for reaching a decision, the judge relies on form or pattern *jury instructions*, which are usually drafted by legal scholars or bar associations to make sure the instructions given to a jury are accurate and understandable. Many sets of jury instructions not only provide the actual text of an instruction but also follow it with analytical commentary. Both the commentary and the instructions themselves are excellent research tools. For example, if you needed to list the elements of a cause of action for breach of contract, a jury instruction will likely set them forth. Thus, jury instructions serve to provide a quick summary of the key elements of many areas of the law, including contracts, fraud, negligence, and so forth.

To locate jury instructions, check the card catalog at your law library. Nearly every state has its own sets of jury instructions for civil and criminal cases, and many states make them available on the Internet (use Table T.1.3 of *The Bluebook* to locate your state's judicial website). Similarly, many of the federal courts also post jury instructions on their websites. Use http://www.uscourts.gov to link to all federal courts. If there is no set of jury instructions specific to your state, consult *Am. Jur. Pleading and Practice Forms, Annotated*. For federal cases, consult *Modern Federal Jury Instructions*.

F.   Summary of Secondary Authorities

All of the sources discussed in this chapter are secondary authorities, meaning that although you may refer to these sources and cite them in memoranda and briefs, courts are not required to follow them. Although secondary authorities are often highly reputable, they remain persuasive at best and lack the force of the primary authorities of cases, constitutions, statutes, and administrative regulations.

Remember that some of the secondary authorities such as Restatements and law review articles are highly regarded and often cited, whereas others, such as encyclopedias, are viewed as elementary in approach and are seldom cited. One of the best indications of the strength of a secondary source is found in Rule 1.4(i) of *The Bluebook*, which provides a hierarchical order when string-citing numerous secondary authorities, listing the Restatements in the "first tier." *ALWD* Rule 45 is similar.

All of the secondary sources do an excellent job of providing commentary on the law and typically direct you to the primary authorities that you should rely on and cite in your memoranda and briefs. A summary of the secondary sources is provided in Figure 6-9.

Figure 6-9
Chart of Secondary Authorities

Secondary Authority	Overview	Identification of Sets	Supplementation	Research Techniques	Use Notes
A.L.R. Annotations	Thorough articles or "annotations" on various legal topics	Multi-volume sets	Annual cumulative pocket parts	Descriptive word approach	A.L.R. annotations are very well respected.
Encyclopedias	Alphabetically arranged narrative statements of hundreds of legal topics, supported by cases and other authorities in footnotes	National sets are C.J.S. and Am. Jur. 2d; about 15 states have their own local sets; some specialized sets exist	Annual cumulative pocket parts	Descriptive word approach; topic approach	Good introductory information but somewhat elementary in their approach.
Legal Periodicals	Publications produced on a periodic basis on a variety of topics	Law school publications; bar association publications; special interest publications; and newspapers	No supplementation	*Index to Legal Periodicals & Books; Current Law Index;* online indexes	Law reviews are often scholarly and well respected; other periodicals are more practical.

Figure 6-9 (*Continued*)

Secondary Authority	Overview	Identification of Sets	Supplementation	Research Techniques	Use Notes
Texts and Treatises	Texts written by scholars on one topic that analyze cases and statutes	Multi-volume sets include thorough and often critical analysis.	Annual cumulative pocket parts; new pages; or softcover supplements	Descriptive word approach; topic approach; table of cases or statutes approach	Many treatises are highly regarded.
Restatements	Statements of the law in clear language	Multi-volume sets on selected areas of the law, such as trusts	Appendix volumes and pocket parts	Descriptive word approach; topic approach	Restatements are highly authoritative.
Attorneys General Opinions	Written opinions by U.S. attorney general and state attorneys general on various topics	Multi-volume sets	No supplementation; each volume is complete	Descriptive word approach; references from other sources; online access	Attorneys general opinions are strongly persuasive and highly respected.
Words and Phrases	Set providing references to cases that have interpreted words or phrases	Multi-volume set	Annual pocket parts	Alphabetical approach	Useful in locating cases interpreting words or phrases.

Figure 6-9 (Continued)

Secondary Authority	Overview	Identification of Sets	Supplementation	Research Techniques	Use Notes
Dictionaries	Books providing definitions of legal words and phrases	One-volume alphabetical arrangements of words and phrases	No supplementation; each volume is complete	Alphabetical approach	Useful in determining meaning of a word or phrase.
Directories	Lists of lawyers	Usually multi-volume sets; *Martindale-Hubbell* provides lists of lawyers	New set or volume issued annually	Alphabetical approach by state, city, firm, and attorney's name	Used to locate attorneys and law firms.
Form Books	Sets of books with standard forms to help in drafting documents	Multi-volume sets of books	Pocket parts	Descriptive word approach; topic approach	Used primarily to assist in preparing documents; never cited.
Uniform Laws	Drafts of statutes proposed by legal scholars for certain areas of the law	Multi-volume set, *Uniform Laws Annotated*, containing text of uniform laws, commentary, references to other sources, etc.	Pocket parts and supplements	Use *Uniform Laws Annotated Directory of Acts* to locate a uniform law; available online	Cases interpreting a uniform law (even those from another state) may be highly persuasive in your state if your state has also adopted the uniform law.

Figure 6-9 (Continued)

Secondary Authority	Overview	Identification of Sets	Supplementation	Research Techniques	Use Notes
Looseleaf services	Type of treatise devoted to one area of law	Multi-volume sets of ringed binders	Replacement pages	Descriptive word approach	Services provide a thorough overview of an area of law.
Jury Instructions	Sets of books containing instructions for charging the jury in civil and criminal trials as well as commentary and annotations	One-volume or multi-volume sets specific to federal courts, one state, or general in nature	Pocket parts	Descriptive word approach	Useful in obtaining a "snapshot" of an area of the law, although seldom cited in research projects.

G. Citation Form

You will never cite to some of the secondary authorities discussed in this chapter, namely, *Words and Phrases*, legal directories, or form books. Other secondary sources are cited as follows:

	Bluebook (for practitioners)	*ALWD*
Encyclopedias	44 C.J.S. *Insurance* § 281 (2007). 38 Am. Jur. 2d *Guaranty* § 29 (2010).	44 C.J.S. *Insurance* § 281 (2007). 38 Am. Jur. 2d *Guaranty* § 29 (2010).
Periodicals	Sharon Dolovich, *State Punishment and Private Prisons*, 55 Duke L.J. 437 (2005).	Sharon Dolovich, *State Punishment and Private Prisons*, 55 Duke L.J. 437 (2005).
Treatises	3 J. Thomas McCarthy, *McCarthy on Trademarks and Unfair Competition* § 9:12 (4th ed. 1996).	J. Thomas McCarthy, *McCarthy on Trademarks and Unfair Competition* vol. 3, § 19:12 (4th ed., West 1996).
Restatements	Restatement (Second) of Contracts § 101 (1981).	*Restatement (Second) of Contracts* § 101 (1981).
United States Attorneys General Opinions—Office of Legal Counsel	Validity of Statutory Rollbacks, 33 Op. O.L.C. 123 (2009)	Validity of Statutory Rollbacks, 33 Op. Off. Leg. Counsel 123 (2009)
Dictionaries	*Black's Law Dictionary* 781 (9th ed. 2009).	*Black's Law Dictionary* 781 (Bryan A. Garner ed., 9th ed., West 2009).
Uniform Laws	Unif. P'ship Act § 103, 7B U.L.A. 119 (1997).	Unif. Partn. Act § 103, 7B U.L.A. 119 (1997).
Looseleaf Services	*In re Stevens Textiles Co.*, 4 Bankr. L. Rep. (CCH) ¶ 16,041 (Bankr. D.N.J. Mar. 10, 2003).	*In re Stevens Textiles Co.*, 4 Bankr. L. Rep. (CCH) ¶ 16,041 (Bankr. D.N.J. Mar. 10, 2003).
Jury Instructions	2 John S. Siffert, *Modern Federal Jury Instructions* § 12.04 (1984).	John S. Siffert, *Modern Federal Jury Instructions* vol. 2, § 12.04 (Lexis 1984).

Internet Resources ▰▰▰▰▰▰▰▰▰▰▰▰▰▰▰▰▰▰

http://libguides.law.harvard.edu	Harvard Law School offers a number of useful Research Guides that provide research tips for using encyclopedias, treatises, Restatements, and other secondary authorities.
http://www.law.georgetown.edu/ library/research/tutorials	Georgetown Law Center offers several tutorials for using secondary sources, including periodicals, encyclopedias, treatises, and other authorities.
http://www.lawreview.org	The University Law Review Project, a coalition of legal educators, provides links to hundreds of law reviews, legal periodicals, and newsletters. Search by topic or specific journal names.
http://www.ali.org	The website of the American Law Institute lists the Restatements in print and discusses Restatements in the drafting or revising process.
http://www.justice.gov/olc/ opinions.htm	The Department of Justice provides access to opinions of the Office of Legal Counsel. Search by year or topic.
http://www.naag.org	The National Association of Attorneys General provides direct links to each state's website for its attorney general, where opinions may be located.
http://dictionary.law.com	Law.com offers a law dictionary at its site.
http://www.martindale.com	Lexis offers a searchable directory of more than 1 million lawyers and law firms.
http://www.justia.com	Justia offers a wide variety of legal materials and forms. Select "Legal Forms."
http://www.allaboutforms.com	AllAboutForms offers hundreds of legal forms.
http://www.uniformlaws.org	The website of the National Conference of Commissioners on Uniform State Laws provides the text of all final uniform laws and information about and legislative status of uniform laws.

Research Assignment

1. Use Am. Jur. 2d.
   a. Which title and section generally deal with making statements impugning someone's integrity as libel?
   b. Review the section. What topics and key numbers relate to this area of law?
   c. Which 1984 Iowa case dealt with this issue? Give case name only.
2. Use the Am. Jur. 2d Table of Laws and Rules. Which topic and section of Am. Jur. 2d discuss 43 U.S.C.A. § 1336?
3. Use C.J.S.
   a. Use the Table of Cases. Under which topic and section is the case *Sieve v. Rosar* discussed?
   b. Which topic and section generally discuss the defense of duress to perjury?
   c. Read the section in part b. above. Does the fact that a person is testifying under judicial compulsion excuse perjury?
   d. To which A.L.R. annotation are you directed by the section in part b. above?
   e. Give a short summary of the definition of the word "conversion."
4. Use *Am. Jur. Proof of Facts (3d)*.
   a. Give the citation to an article relating to adverse reactions to the drug Doxepin.
   b. Locate the article. What does Section 25 of the article provide?
5. Use the *Index to Periodicals & Books* (volume 46, September 2006 to August 2007). Cite an article written by Paul Holland in 2006 relating to the *Miranda* case.
6. Locate the November 2012 article located at 111 (No. 2) Mich. L. Rev. 145.
   a. Give the title and author of the article.
   b. What type of information escrow is discussed on page 159?
7. Locate the treatise *Collier on Bankruptcy* (16th ed.).
   a. Which section generally discusses that the filing of a reorganization under Chapter 11 of the Bankruptcy Act operates as an automatic stay?
   b. Review the first section listed. Without the automatic stay, what would happen to the debtor's assets?
8. Locate the Restatement (Third) of Trusts.
   a. What section discusses a trustee's duty to act with skill in the administration of a trust?
   b. Review the general comments to this Restatement section. At what time is the trustee's conduct to be judged?

c. Review the cases interpreting this section. Which 2007 Massachusetts case held that if a trustee is a professional trustee, the fiduciary duty is higher than that imposed on a lay person? Give the case name only.

9. Use West's *Words and Phrases*. What is the most recent case that construes the meaning of the term "propensity"?

10. Use *Black's Law Dictionary* (9th ed. 2009).
    a. What is the definition of "meretricious relationship"?
    b. Review the definition. To which topic and key number are you directed?
    c. What does the legal maxim *ita lex scripta est* mean?

11. Use the current volumes of *Martindale-Hubbell Law Directory*.
    a. Jessica K. Hew is an attorney with the Winter Park, Florida law firm Burr & Forman LLP. Where and when did she receive her J.D. degree?
    b. An attorney named Susanne Schmidt is with the Kassel, Germany law firm Kubler. Where did she receive her law degree? What languages does she speak?
    c. Use the section entitled "Corporate Law Departments." Who is the Vice President and General Counsel for Chevron's Law Department?

12. Use *Am. Jur. Pleading and Practice Forms Annotated*.
    a. Which general form relates to a complaint for failure to deliver a mobile home at the time and place specified?
    b. Review this form. What does Paragraph Five allege?
    c. To which topic and key numbers are you directed?

13. Use *Uniform Laws Annotated* (West's Master Edition).
    a. Has Virginia adopted the Uniform Premarital Agreement Act?
    b. If your answer in part a. above is affirmative, give the citation to the Virginia statute.
    c. Review the Uniform Premarital Agreement Act. What is the general topic of section 3?
    d. Review Section 3. Generally, may a premarital agreement limit spousal support?
    e. In what way did South Dakota change the official text of subsection (a)(4)?

14. Use West's *Federal Jury Practice and Instructions, Civil and Criminal* (6th ed.), authored by O'Malley, Grenig, and Lee.
    a. What instruction is used to instruct a jury on the elements of age discrimination as employment discrimination?
    b. Review the instruction. What is the first element of a plaintiff's claim?

Internet Assignment

1. Access and review Georgetown University Law Library's tutorial on Secondary Sources at http://www.law.georgetown.edu/library/research/tutorials/index.cfm. When should you use a secondary source for legal research?

2. Access the University Law Review Project at http://www.law-review.org. Select "Entertainment and Sports Law." Select the *Columbia University Journal of Law and the Arts* and access Volume 36, Issue No. 2.
   a. Who authored the article "Downstream Alternation of Copyrighted Works in a World of Licensed, Digital Distribution"?
   b. Review the Introduction to the article. In what year did digital music sales subscriptions exceed physical sales for the first time in history?

3. Access the Washington and Lee Law School study on the most cited legal periodicals at http://lawlib.wlu.edu/LJ/index.aspx. Sort the table by "Combined Score" and "Journal Cites" and review the information for 2012.
   a. What were the two most cited law reviews?
   b. What law review is listed tenth?
   c. How many times was the *Harvard Law Review* cited?

4. Access the website of the American Law Institute at http://www.ali.org.
   a. Review "Projects." Briefly, what is the main difference between Restatements and Principles?
   b. Select "Publications" and then select "Contracts." Review the information for Restatement Second, Contracts. In which volume is information about the formation of contracts and consideration discussed?
   c. Select "Publications" and review the FAQs. May you cite a draft of a current project?

5. Access the website of the Department of Justice Office of Legal Counsel at http://www.justice.gov/olc. Review the Opinions for 2012.
   a. Which Memorandum Opinion was posted on May 29, 2012?
   b. Who requested the Opinion?
   c. What conclusion was reached whether the fact that a patient who has reviewed child pornography may give reason to suspect that a child has suffered an incident of child abuse?

6. Access Law.com's legal dictionary. Briefly, give the definition of "harmless error."

7. Access the website "U.S. Courts" at http://www.uscourts.gov. Select "Forms & Fees." Access Civil Form JS 044.
   a. What does Section II require?
   b. How would you request a jury trial?

8. Access the website for Florida State Courts at http://www.flcourts.org. Select "Family Law Forms." Select the form an adult would use to change his or her name. What information is required in Section 12?

9. Access the website Martindale.com. An attorney named Scott Metzger practices law in California. Where did Mr. Metzger attend law school?

10. Access the website of the National Conference of Commissioners on Uniform States Laws. Review the Uniform Limited Liability Company Act (Revised). May a person contribute a promissory note as a form of contribution to a limited liability company? What section governs your answer?

11. Access the website for the U.S. Court of Appeals for the Fifth Circuit's Library System at http://www.lb5.uscourts.gov. Select "Jury Instructions." Review the most recent Civil Jury Instructions for cases brought under the Americans with Disabilities Act in which the plaintiff alleges that the employer failed to accommodate the plaintiff's disability. What must the plaintiff prove to succeed in such a case?

Special Research Issues

Chapter Overview

Most legal research problems can be solved by examining and analyzing the conventional primary and secondary authorities. There are, however, a few types of legal research tasks that lie outside those usual approaches and that involve sources arranged and published differently from other sources. Some are primary authorities (executive orders, administrative regulations, treaties, and municipal ordinances, and any cases interpreting the same) and others are secondary sources (legislative histories, some executive materials, and commentary on any topic). This chapter examines these special research issues and provides basic information on legislative histories, executive materials, administrative law, international law, and municipal law research.

A. Legislative History

1. Introduction to Federal Legislative History Research

If a statute you are researching is unclear, adverse to the position you wish to advocate, or lacks cases interpreting it, you may wish to examine the various documents that reflect the activity of the legislature that enacted the statute to help you determine the intent of the legislature. This process is referred to as preparing or compiling a *legislative history*.

Although a well-constructed argument relating to a legislative history may be helpful to a court, a court is not required to adopt an interpretation of a statute based on the legislature's intent in enacting the law. In fact, many courts dislike legislative history arguments and will examine the legislative history of a statute only if the meaning of a statute is not clear or "plain" from a reading of it.

Alternatively, you may be monitoring a piece of legislation as it progresses in order to better assist clients or your employer. You may wish to review Chapter 3, which discusses the process by which legislation is enacted.

Review the following guides, available on the Internet, for background on legislative histories, the process of compiling one, and links to other sources:

- Carol D. Davis, *Tracking Current Federal Legislation and Regulations: A Guide to Basic Sources*, http://www.fas.org/sgp/crs/98-461.pdf (last updated Jan. 2005).
- Richard J. McKinney & Ellen A. Sweet, Law Librarians' Society of Washington, D.C., Inc., *Federal Legislative History Research: A Practitioner's Guide to Compiling the Documents and Sifting for Legislative Intent*, http://www.llsdc.org/federal-legislative-history-guide.
- Law Librarians' Soc'y of Washington, D.C., Inc., *Legislative Sourcebook*, http://www.llsdc.org/sourcebook (last updated Jan. 7, 2013).

2.   *Documents Used in Compiling a Federal Legislative History*

The documents that you might analyze in compiling a legislative history are as follows:

- **Bill Versions.** By examining the various versions of a bill as it passed through Congress, you may be able to draw some inferences about Congress's intent. Additionally, the bill may include a preamble or introductory section explaining its intent and purpose.
- **Transcripts of Committee Hearings.** When individuals testify before congressional committees, their testimony is recorded and transcribed in booklet form. Many courts view this testimony with skepticism because although some of those testifying are neutral parties, others are well-paid lobbyists.
- **Committee Reports and Prints.** After the committee concludes its hearings, it will issue a report with its recommendations and its reasons therefor. Committee reports are viewed as considerably more credible than transcripts of committee hearings. Committee prints consist of reports and studies prepared by consultants or staff members.
- **Debates.** If debate is held on a bill, the remarks of the speakers are published in the *Congressional Record*, a publication prepared for each day that Congress is in session. These remarks may reflect the intent of the legislature when it enacted a statute.

3. *The Process of Compiling a Federal Legislative History: Three Approaches*

There are three approaches you may take in compiling a legislative history: You may gather the materials in conventional print format; you may use electronic sources (both free and subscription services); or you may be able to locate a prepackaged or compiled legislative history.

a. Using Conventional Print Sources to Compile a Legislative History

Researchers often struggle in compiling a legislative history because the documents are diverse and are seldom located together. This is often true because a statute may have been enacted one year and then amended on several occasions thereafter, and you may need to compile a legislative history for each version of the statute. There are two steps you can take to gather the documents you need.

(1) *Step One: Locating a Public Law Number*

After you read a statute, you will be given historical notes about the enactment of a statute. For example, immediately following a statute in U.S.C.A., you will see the following information:

Jan. 2, 1975, Pub. L. 93-596, § 1, Oct. 22, 1999, 88 Stat. 1949. (See Figure 3-2.)

Thus, U.S.C.A. gives you the public law number of your statute (namely, Public Law 93rd Congress, 596th law), the date of its enactment, and its citation in *United States Statutes at Large*. For newer statutes, West also refers you to its publication *United States Code Congressional and Administrative News* (USCCAN), a monthly pamphlet that includes public laws, legislative history for selected bills, some committee reports, presidential signing statements, and other material. Once you have a public law number, you can access USCCAN and many other sources.

(2) *Step Two: Using a Public Law Number to Obtain Legislative Documents*

• **Using USCCAN.** Once you have a public law number, access USCCAN's Table of Legislative History (called Table 4) and look up your public law number. Table 4 will give you the original bill number (for example, H.R. 289), references to committee reports to examine, and dates of any debates. USCCAN also provides you with official committee reports, conference reports, statements by legislative leaders, and presidential signing statements. Read these materials to determine legislative intent.

• **Using *Congressional Information Service*.** *Congressional Information Service* (CIS), previously part of the Lexis family but now owned by ProQuest LLC, is published in three bound volumes for each year. Many experts consider CIS the most thorough and useful source for compiling a legislative history. Each CIS yearly set includes a comprehensive index, allowing you to access documents through several methods: by subject matter (for example, social security); by name of any witness who testified at committee hearings; and by bill number. The CIS Index will then direct you to the appropriate pages in its Annual Abstracts volume, which contains summaries or "abstracts" of the bill as introduced, the testimony at committee hearings, the committee reports, and the dates of debate, so you can read the debates in the *Congressional Record*. Review these Abstracts to determine which documents you should examine in full. Additionally, you can use CIS's annual volume, titled *CIS Annual Legislative Histories*, arranged by public law number. By looking up your public law number, you will be directed to a brief summary of the law and references to the documents you need (including House and Senate Reports, committee hearing transcripts, and debates).

b. Using Electronic Sources and the Internet to Compile a Legislative History

Using Lexis, Westlaw, THOMAS (Congress's database) and its successor, Congress.gov, or FDsys, you can usually find the documents you need by searching by bill number or key words and then linking to the pertinent documents.

• **Lexis.** After logging on to Lexis, select the database or "Library" called "Legislation & Politics" and then select "U.S. Congress." You can search by Congress number (such as the 113th Congress), bill number, public law number, topic of the legislation, and so forth. You will then be linked to the full text of the bill, selected hearing transcripts, committee reports, and the *Congressional Record*. You may also select "Legislative Histories" for full "prepackaged" legislative histories for selected statutes (usually those of widespread public interest, such as the Americans with Disabilities Act). If you know the citation to a bill number or other document, use "Get a Document" to retrieve the document.
• **Westlaw.** Westlaw also offers compiled, full legislative histories for some statutes of public interest, such as the USA Patriot Act. After you log on, select the pertinent database. For example, the database Legislative History (enter "LH") allows searching for legislative history documents for any federal law.
• **ProQuest Congressional.** ProQuest Congressional (the successor to LexisNexis Congressional) is the electronic version of CIS, discussed previously. This database provides links to a vast array of legislative history materials. Your law library or law firm may subscribe to this fee-based service.

• **THOMAS and Congress.gov.** Unlike Lexis, Westlaw, and ProQuest Congressional, which are fee-based services, THOMAS (http:// thomas.loc.gov) is a free service provided by the Library of Congress. THOMAS (named for Thomas Jefferson) offers a wealth of information, including historical documents such as the Constitution, House and Senate directories, committee schedules, and links to other legislative agencies. More important, THOMAS offers easy access to many documents of legislative history. When you access THOMAS you may search by key words (for example, "Patent Reform Act"), bill number (for example, 112-31), or public law number. You will then be given access to the exact text of the bill or public law, a summary of it, and its status (such as when it was introduced or referred to a committee). Once you locate the bill you are interested in, you will be directed by hyperlinks to committee reports, the *Congressional Record* (since 1989), and other documents. As noted in Chapter 3, THOMAS is being replaced by a new site, Congress .gov (located at http://beta.congress.gov), which at the time of the writing of this text is in its test or "beta" phase and does not yet include all of the information contained in THOMAS. Eventually, all of the information on THOMAS will be included on the Congress.gov site. (See Figure 9-3.) Until then, however, you may need to conduct legislative history research using both sites, particularly if you are interested in reviewing committee reports, debates, and so forth.

• **FDsys.** The Government Printing Office offers numerous official publications through its comprehensive website called Federal Digital System or FDsys, located at http://www.gpo.gov/fdsys. FDsys, the successor to GPO Access, offers bills, calendars, committee prints, transcripts of select committee hearings, committee reports, the *Congressional Record*, and other documents. Coverage dates vary, but most documents are available since about 1990. You may search by particular congressional session (for example, looking at documents from the 112th Congress), by key words (for example, searching for "affordable health care"), or by citation (for example, searching for "Public Law 112-109"). Documents provided on FDsys are verified as "authentic," meaning they may be cited as if a conventional source (*Bluebook* R. 18).

c. Using Compiled Legislative Histories

A *compiled legislative history* is a "prepackaged" legislative history, namely, one that has already been compiled for the statute in which you are interested. Generally, compiled legislative histories exist for legislation that is well known or of public importance. USCCAN, Lexis, and Westlaw all offer several compiled legislative histories, especially for significant legislation. About 25 legislative histories are available for well-known legislation, such as the USA Patriot Act, by the Law Librarians' Society of Washington, D.C., at http://www.llsdc.org/sourcebook.

4. *Alternative Methods of Obtaining Legislative History for Federal Statutes*

Because compiling a legislative history can be difficult and usually requires either locating numerous sets of books or linking to numerous websites, and because there may not be a compiled or prepackaged legislative history for your statute, there are some alternative approaches you might use for legislative history research.

• **Commercial Services.** There are several commercial companies that will assist you in obtaining documents or in monitoring legislation. Check your local phone book or local legal directory to obtain information about private companies that will obtain government documents for you for a fee. Following are two well-known companies:

- StateNet, a leader in the field of providing legislative information, will provide legislative materials for Congress and all 50 states. The telephone number is (800) 726-4566, and its website is http://www.statenet.com.
- Legislative Intent Service will obtain either federal or state legislative histories. Call (800) 666-1917 or visit http://www.legintent .com.

• **Reference Assistance.** Law librarians are well aware of the complex nature of gathering the documents needed to compile a legislative history and will not be surprised if you ask for help. Some law libraries provide worksheets for you to use that provide a step-by-step approach for compiling a legislative history.

• **Congressional Assistance.** Members of Congress employ office staff and assistants whose job it is to respond to requests for information by constituents. Call the office of your congressional representative and ask for copies of the bill, the committee reports, or other pertinent materials. Check the House and Senate rosters in Congress.gov to locate your representative.

• **Law Reviews and Annotations.** A law review article or A.L.R. annotation may provide a thorough analysis of a statute you are researching and already may have examined the bill, committee hearing transcripts, committee reports, and debates. To determine if an article or annotation discusses your statute, Shepardize or KeyCite it (see Chapter 11).

• **Westlaw's Graphical Statutes.** One of the easiest ways to locate and compile a legislative history is to use Westlaw's product Graphical Statutes. When you view a statute on the Westlaw screen, select "Graphical Statutes," which will show you the evolution of your statute in an easy-to-read flowchart and allow you to link to previous versions of the statute, conference reports, the *Congressional Record*, and other pertinent legislative materials. Graphical Statutes is available for all federal statutes (since 1996) and for selected states, including California, New York, Texas, and other larger jurisdictions. This feature allows nearly instantaneous location of legislative history documents.

┌───┐

━━━━━━━━━━━━━━━━━━ **Practice Tip** ━━━━━━━━━━━━━━━━━━

Legislative History Research in Three Easy Steps

There are many places for you to locate the documents that make up a legislative history. Consider simplifying the process by following these three steps:

1. **Obtain a public law number by looking at the end of your statute in U.S.C.A. or U.S.C.S.**
2. **Look up the public law number (or a key word or phrase related to the statute) in THOMAS (http://thomas.loc.gov), Congress.gov (http://beta.congress.gov), or FDsys (http://www.gpo.gov/fdsys). Link to the relevant documents.**
3. **Read and analyze the pertinent documents, linking to other related documents as needed.**

└───┘

• **Web-Based Tutorials.** A number of websites offer guidance and tutorials on conducting legislative history research for federal statutes. View the following sites:

- Boston College Law Library's Federal Legislative Histories: http://www.bc.edu/schools/law/library/research/researchguides .html. Select "Federal Legislative Histories."
- Georgetown Law Library's videos and slides: http://www.law .georgetown.edu/library/research/tutorials/lh/index.cfm.
- Lexis's legislative history research tutorial: http://w3.lexis.com/ lawschoolreg/tutorials/leghis/default.asp.
- The Law Librarians' Society of Washington, D.C.'s Federal Legislative History *Legislative Source Book*: http://www.llsdc.org/ sourcebook.

5. *State Legislative Histories*

a. The Process of Compiling a State Legislative History

The process of compiling a legislative history for a state statute is substantially similar to that for federal statutes. Unfortunately, collecting the actual documents involved can be frustrating because many of them are not published, and some are available only at the state capitol.

Just as is the case with federal statutes, after you read a state statute, carefully examine the historical notes following it to determine the derivation of the statute. For example, you may be presented with information such as the following:

Derivation Stats. 2009, c. 141, p. 621

This would indicate the statute was enacted in 2009 and was initially published at Chapter 141 of the state's session laws and can be found at page 621 of the 2009 session laws.

Consult your law librarian to determine if a legislative service exists for your state. If it does, it will operate similarly to USCCAN or CIS in that it will provide you with a bill number for your statute and information about the committee that considered the bill.

Once you have a bill number or the name of the committee that considered the bill, you can contact the committee staff and ask for copies of the pertinent documents. Although the bill and its versions will likely be available, many states do not maintain transcripts of committee hearings, committee reports, or debates.

To determine what documents are available in your state, consult the following: William H. Manz, *Guide to State Legislation, Legislative History, and Administrative Materials* (7th ed. 2008), which provides a state-by-state outline of the legislative and administrative documents available in all United States jurisdictions.

b. Alternative Methods of Obtaining Legislative History for State Statutes

Because of the difficulties in compiling state legislative histories, you may find that the following alternative methods of legislative history research are the most effective.

• **Commercial Services.** There may be private companies that will perform state legislative history research for you. Because many of the documents are available only at the state capitol, these private companies are often located in a state's capital city. To determine if such a company exists, consult a directory of legal services, contact directory information at the capital city, or contact an attorneys' service. The following fee-based commercial service provides state legislative history information and documents for all 50 states: StateNet, 2101 K Street, Sacramento, CA 95816 (800) 726-4566 (http://www.statenet.com).

• **Web-Based Tutorials.** Several websites will greatly assist you in compiling state legislative histories. Following are some of the best:

- Cornell University Library's site (http://guides.library.cornell .edu/stateleg?hs=a) provides a research guide to finding state legislation.
- Indiana University's website (http://law.indiana.libguides.com/ index.php, select "Legislative History") links to each state's legislative history materials.
- The Law Librarians' Legislative Source Book (http://www.llsdc. org/state-legislation) links to state legislative bodies, laws, and regulations.
- The National Conference of State Legislatures (http://www.ncsl .org) is a gateway to state legislative sites, allowing direct linking to the legislative website in each state.

• **Lexis and Westlaw.** Both Lexis and Westlaw provide bill text and bill tracking for all United States jurisdictions. Westlaw's Graphical Statutes provides links to state reports and bill text for larger United States jurisdictions.

• **Reference Assistance.** Ask your law librarian for assistance or to determine if a worksheet or checklist is available to assist in compiling a legislative history.

• **Law Reviews and Annotations.** Shepardize or KeyCite the statute you are researching to determine if it has been the subject of any law review article, A.L.R. annotation, or attorney general opinion.

6. *Tracking Pending Legislation*

You may need to monitor pending legislation for clients who must keep abreast of emerging laws that could affect their organizations. For example, assume a client wishes to monitor pending campaign finance reform legislation. Following are some sources that will help you track pending legislation (with the fee-based services listed before the free services):

• A conventional print source entitled *CCH Congressional Index* describes action on a bill and provides weekly updates on pending legislation. Your law library will likely have this set.

• ProQuest Congressional (discussed earlier) provides bill tracking. Similarly, its service called "Alerts" will provide you with monthly, weekly, daily, or more frequent updates on legislation you are monitoring.

• Lexis and Westlaw also provide bill tracking. Their alert and clipping services, Alerts and WestClip, respectively, deliver periodic updates to your e-mail account about legislation you are tracking.

• StateNet, the commercial service described earlier, provides bill tracking and e-mail alerts for pending federal and state legislation.

• THOMAS and its beta-stage successor Congress.gov do not provide automatic alerts to you regarding changes in legislative status, but by routinely checking the status and summary of a bill, you can monitor its progress.

• GovTrack (http://www.govtrack.us) is a free service that allows you to track pending federal legislation and will provide you with e-mail updates about the legislation you are monitoring.

• Scout (https://scout.sunlightfoundation.com) is another free service that allows you to track pending federal and state legislation. You may create alerts to be notified by either e-mail or text message of any new action on legislation you are following.

• Many states now automatically provide e-mail updates on pending legislation. For example, California provides a bill status updating service that sends you an e-mail to alert you to actions affecting the legislation you are monitoring. The free tracking service is located at http://leginfo .legislature.ca.gov.

```
┌─────────────────────────────── Ethics Alert ───────────────────────────┐
│                                                                         │
│  *Tracking Legislation*                                                 │
│                                                                         │
│  If a client retains your firm to monitor pending legislation           │
│  that affects the client, you have an ethical duty to monitor the       │
│  legislation on a periodic basis and notify the client of the progress  │
│  of the legislation. Because legislation tracking is so easily          │
│  accomplished, and you can readily arrange to have status updates        │
│  delivered to your e-mail account, it will be legal malpractice to      │
│  "drop the ball" when you are tracking pending legislation.             │
│                                                                         │
└─────────────────────────────────────────────────────────────────────────┘
```

B. Executive Materials

The executive branch issues certain directives and documents that affect all of us, although they are of varying legal effect.

1. *Proclamations*

A *proclamation* is a presidential statement. Proclamations are often issued for ceremonial or public awareness reasons. For example, Presidential Proclamation No. 8321 declared a certain week to be National Family Week. Proclamations often have no legal effect because they do not command or prohibit any action, although some proclamations, such as President Lincoln's Emancipation Proclamation, have legal effect. You can locate proclamations in a variety of sources:

- USCCAN.
- *Federal Register*, the daily newspaper published by the Office of the Federal Register.
- Title 3 of the *Code of Federal Regulations*.
- *Daily Compilation of Presidential Documents* (which replaced the *Weekly Compilation of Presidential Documents*), available at http://www.gpo.gov/fdsys.
- Lexis and Westlaw.

2. *Executive Orders*

Executive orders are declarations issued by the President to direct government officials and agencies. These executive orders have the force of law (unless a court rules otherwise) and require no action by Congress. Thus, they are primary authority. An example of an executive order is Executive Order No. 13354 for the establishment of a National

Counterterrorism Center. Executive orders may be located in the same sources as proclamations.

One of the best sources for materials relating to the executive branch is the *Daily Compilation of Presidential Documents*. This publication includes a wide variety of presidential materials, including addresses and remarks, appointments and nominations, interviews with news media, and executive orders and proclamations.

The online *Daily Compilation* replaced the earlier printed *Weekly Compilation* in 2009. They are available together online with coverage since 1993 at FDsys at http://www.gpo.gov/fdsys. You may search by date, proclamation or executive order number, or by key words.

C. Administrative Law

1. Introduction

To keep up with the demands of modern society, Congress has delegated certain tasks to agencies, each created to administer a body of law. For example, the use of airwaves to communicate information by radio led to the creation of the Federal Communications Commission. Note that agencies have different titles, with some being referred to as "Administrations," some referred to as "Boards," and others as "Agencies," and so forth. Agency heads and staffers are individuals with expertise in the area of law that the agency regulates.

Note that whereas the product of a legislature is a "law" or "statute," the product of an administrative agency is a *rule* or *regulation*, which terms are synonymous. Thus, rules of administrative agencies are primary authorities (as are cases interpreting administrative law issues). Rules or regulations are issued by an agency to carry out its policies. Violation of a rule or regulation may subject one to punishment just as can violation of a statute. Administrative agencies are often referred to as *regulatory bodies* because their function is to regulate a body of law. The statutes that create agencies and set forth their powers are called *enabling statutes*. Some agencies, such as the Department of Labor, issue advisory opinions, which opinions generally state whether they are legally binding.

2. Publication of Federal Administrative Law

For any rule or regulation to be effective, it must be published in the *Federal Register*, a pamphlet that is published weekdays and distributed by the United States Government Printing Office. The *Federal Register* includes proposed, interim, and final rules, as well as presidential documents, and various notices. It does more than merely recite the language of the agency rules. It provides a summary of the regulation, its effective date, a person to contact for further information, and background material relating to the regulation. See Figure 7-1 for a sample page from the *Federal Register*.

The *Federal Register* includes about 80,000 pages each year, making research a difficult task. Thus, just as our federal statutes that are originally published in *United States Statutes at Large* are better organized or codified into the 51 titles of the *United States Code*, so also has the *Federal Register* been codified to enable researchers to access administrative materials. In fact, the *Federal Register* has been codified in 50 titles in a set called *Code of Federal Regulations* (C.F.R.). These 50 titles represent the areas subject to federal regulation and roughly correspond to the titles of U.S.C. For example, Title 29 of both U.S.C. and C.F.R. is "Labor." Each of the 50 titles in C.F.R. is divided into chapters, which chapters are further subdivided into "parts" and sections covering specific regulatory areas. For example, 14 C.F.R. § 252.3 prohibits smoking on passenger flights.

C.F.R. is a softcover set revised annually with one fourth of the volumes in the set issued on a quarterly basis. Thus, revision of the set is staggered throughout the calendar year. Each year the softcover volumes of C.F.R. are issued in a color different from the previous year (although Title 3, containing various presidential materials, is always white or black). See Figure 7-2 for a sample page from C.F.R.

3. Research Techniques for Administrative Law

a. C.F.R. Indexes

C.F.R. contains an Index volume entitled *C.F.R. Index and Finding Aids*. This one-volume Index is revised annually and can be accessed by subject matter (pesticides, shellfish) or by the name of the agency (Nuclear Regulatory Commission). The Index will direct you to the pertinent title and part of C.F.R. There is also a separate Index for each of the 50 titles of C.F.R. located immediately after the last part of each of the 50 titles. See Figure 7-3 for a sample page from the C.F.R. Index.

The C.F.R. Index and Finding Aids volume also contains a table entitled "Parallel Table of Authorities and Rules" (Table I). If you know the citation to the enabling statute that created the agency or by which authority the agency issues its regulations, you can look up this citation in Table I to be directed to the appropriate C.F.R. provision.

West also publishes a separate Index to C.F.R. called *West's Code of Federal Regulations, General Index*, which is designed to provide easy access to C.F.R. by subject matter (for example, port safety) or by geographic location (for example, Appalachia or Boston). You will be directed to a title and part of C.F.R.

The National Archives and Records Administration also provides indexes to the *Federal Register* and C.F.R. at http://www.archives.gov.

b. *Code of Federal Regulations Annotated*

West publishes sets entitled *Code of Federal Regulations Annotated* (for select C.F.R. titles), which are arranged identically to C.F.R. and includes C.F.R. regulations. In addition, however, the sets include references to law reviews and other authorities and annotations to cases interpreting C.F.R. provisions so that you may easily find authorities interpreting and construing C.F.R. provisions that you are researching.

c. *Federal Register Index*

Because C.F.R. is issued annually and has no pocket parts, it will not contain newly promulgated rules and regulations, which are published in the *Federal Register*. To access the *Federal Register*, use the *Federal Register Index*, which is issued monthly in cumulative form. Thus, the *Federal Register Index* for May contains all of the information for the previous months. Entries in this Index are arranged alphabetically by agency (Agriculture Department, Air Force Department, and so forth). The back of each issue of each daily *Federal Register* includes a section called "Reader Aids," which lists any C.F.R. parts affected during the month that issue was published.

4. *Updating C.F.R. Regulations*

Because agency rules and regulations are revised so frequently, you must always check the status of any regulation you have found. Updating C.F.R. regulations is a two-step process.

a. Step One: Review the *List of C.F.R. Sections Affected*

To update any regulation, consult the publication *List of C.F.R. Sections Affected* ("LSA"). LSA is a monthly softcover cumulative publication designed to notify researchers of changes to any C.F.R. regulation. It also publishes new and proposed regulations. By looking up the C.F.R. title and section you are researching, you will be provided a short explanation, such as "revised," and then directed to the appropriate page of the *Federal Register* where the amendatory language is found.

b. Step Two: Review C.F.R. Parts Affected

After you have used LSA (which will update the regulation only through the end of last month), you must further check a regulation by determining its status as of today's date. This is accomplished by reviewing the section titled "Reader Aids" at the back of the most recent issue of the *Federal Register*. Each issue of the *Federal Register* includes a section within "Reader Aids" titled "C.F.R. Parts Affected," which will inform you

Figure 7-1
Sample Page from *Federal Register*

19986   Federal Register / Vol. 78, No. 64 / Wednesday, April 3, 2013 / Rules and Regulations

certified that this rule, when promulgated, will not have a significant economic impact on a substantial number of small entities under the criteria of the Regulatory Flexibility Act.

The FAA's authority to issue rules regarding aviation safety is found in Title 49 of the United States Code. Subtitle I, Section 106 describes the authority of the FAA Administrator. Subtitle VII, Aviation Programs, describes in more detail the scope of the agency's authority.

This rulemaking is promulgated under the authority described in Subtitle VII, Part A, Subpart I, Section 40103. Under that section, the FAA is charged with prescribing regulations to assign the use of the airspace necessary to ensure the safety of aircraft and the efficient use of airspace. This regulation is within the scope of that authority as it amends existing VOR Federal airways in the NAS.

Environmental Review

The FAA has determined that this action qualifies for categorical exclusion under the National Environmental Policy Act in accordance with 311a, FAA Order 1050.1E, "Environmental Impacts: Policies and Procedures." This airspace action is not expected to cause any potentially significant environmental impacts, and no extraordinary circumstances exist that warrant preparation of an environmental assessment.

List of Subjects in 14 CFR Part 71

Airspace, Incorporation by reference, Navigation (air).

Adoption of the Amendment

In consideration of the foregoing, the Federal Aviation Administration amends 14 CFR part 71 as follows:

PART 71—DESIGNATION OF CLASS A, B, C, D, AND E AIRSPACE AREAS; AIR TRAFFIC SERVICE ROUTES; AND REPORTING POINTS

■ 1. The authority citation for part 71 continues to read as follows:

Authority: 49 U.S.C. 106(g), 40103, 40113, 40120; E.O. 10854, 24 FR 9565, 3 CFR, 1959–1963 Comp., p. 389.

§ 71.1 [Amended]

■ 2. The incorporation by reference in 14 CFR 71.1 of FAA Order 7400.9W, Airspace Designations and Reporting Points, signed August 8, 2012, and effective September 15, 2012, is amended as follows:

Paragraph 6010   VOR Federal airways.

*   *   *   *   *

V–68

From Montrose, CO; Cones, CO; Dove Creek, CO; Cortez, CO; Rattlesnake, NM; INT Rattlesnake 128° and Albuquerque, NM, 345° radials; Albuquerque; INT Albuquerque 120° and Corona, NM, 311° radials; Corona; 41 miles 85 MSL, Chisum, NM; Hobbs, NM; Midland, TX; San Angelo, TX; Junction, TX; Center Point, TX; San Antonio, TX; INT San Antonio 064° and Industry, TX, 267° radials; Industry; INT Industry 101° and Hobby, TX, 289° radials; to Hobby.

*   *   *   *   *

V–76

From Lubbock, TX; INT Lubbock 188° and Big Spring, TX, 286° radials; Big Spring; San Angelo, TX; Llano, TX; Centex, TX; Industry, TX; INT Industry 101° and Hobby, TX, 289° radials; to Hobby.

*   *   *   *   *

V–194

From Cedar Creek, TX; College Station, TX; INT College Station 151° and Hobby, TX, 289° radials; Hobby; Sabine Pass, TX; Lafayette, LA; Baton Rouge, LA; McComb, MS; INT McComb 055° and Meridian, MS; 221° radials; Meridian. From Liberty, NC; Raleigh-Durham, NC; Tar River, NC; Cofield, NC; to INT Cofield 077° and Norfolk, VA, 209° radials.

*   *   *   *   *

V–548

From Hobby, TX; INT Hobby 289° and College Station, TX, 151° radials; College Station; INT College Station 307° and Waco, TX, 173° radials; to Waco.

Issued in Washington, DC, March 26, 2013.

Gary A. Norek,

Manager, Airspace Policy and ATC Procedures Group.

[FR Doc. 2013–07472 Filed 4–2–13; 8:45 am]

BILLING CODE 4910–13–P

DEPARTMENT OF HEALTH AND HUMAN SERVICES

Food and Drug Administration

21 CFR Parts 510, 522, and 558

[Docket No. FDA–2013–N–0002]

New Animal Drugs; Enrofloxacin; Tilmicosin; Tylosin

AGENCY: Food and Drug Administration, HHS.

ACTION: Final rule, technical amendment.

SUMMARY: The Food and Drug Administration (FDA) is amending the animal drug regulations to reflect approval actions for new animal drug applications and abbreviated new animal drug applications during February 2013. FDA is also informing the public of the availability of summaries of the basis of approval and of environmental review documents, where applicable.

DATES: This rule is effective April 3, 2013.

FOR FURTHER INFORMATION CONTACT: George K. Haibel, Center for Veterinary Medicine (HFV–6), Food and Drug Administration, 7519 Standish Pl., Rockville, MD 20855, 240–276–9019, *george.haibel@fda.hhs.gov.*

SUPPLEMENTARY INFORMATION: FDA is amending the animal drug regulations to reflect approval actions for new animal drug applications (NADAs) and abbreviated new animal drug applications (ANADAs) during February 2013, as listed in table 1. In addition, FDA is informing the public of the availability, where applicable, of documentation of environmental review required under the National Environmental Policy Act (NEPA) and, for actions requiring review of safety or effectiveness data, summaries of the basis of approval (FOI Summaries) under the Freedom of Information Act (FOIA). These public documents may be seen in the Division of Dockets Management (HFA–305), Food and Drug Administration, 5630 Fishers Lane, rm. 1061, Rockville, MD 20852, between 9 a.m. and 4 p.m., Monday through Friday. Persons with access to the Internet may obtain these documents at the Center for Veterinary Medicine (CVM) FOIA Electronic Reading Room: *http://www.fda.gov/AboutFDA/ CentersOffices/OfficeofFoods/CVM/ CVMFOIAElectronicReadingRoom/ default.htm.*

In addition, the animal drug regulations are being amended at 21 CFR 510.600 to correct the spelling of a street name in the sponsor's address, and at 21 CFR 558.618 to clarify the dosage of tilmicosin phosphate in medicated feeds for beef and non-lactating dairy cattle.

This rule does not meet the definition of "rule" in 5 U.S.C. 804(3)(A) because it is a rule of "particular applicability." Therefore, it is not subject to the congressional review requirements in 5 U.S.C. 801–808.

Figure 7-2
Sample Page from C.F.R.

applicable sections of parts 101 and 130 of this chapter.

[42 FR 14475, Mar. 15, 1977, as amended at 47 FR 11834, Mar. 19, 1982; 49 FR 10103, Mar. 19, 1984; 54 FR 24896, June 12, 1989; 58 FR 2886, Jan. 6, 1993; 61 FR 9325, Mar. 8, 1996; 63 FR 14035, Mar. 24, 1998]

PART 165—BEVERAGES

Subpart A—General Provisions

Sec.
165.3 Definitions.

Subpart B—Requirements for Specific Standardized Beverages

165.110 Bottled water.

AUTHORITY: 21 U.S.C. 321, 341, 343, 343–1, 348, 349, 371, 379e.

SOURCE: 60 FR 57124, Nov. 13, 1995, unless otherwise noted.

Subpart A—General Provisions

§ 165.3 Definitions.

(a) A *lot* is:

(1) For purposes of determining quality factors related to manufacture, processing, or packing, a collection of primary containers or units of the same size, type, and style produced under conditions as nearly uniform as possible and usually designated by a common container code or marking, or in the absence of any common container code or marking, a day's production.

(2) For purposes of determining quality factors related to distribution and storage, a collection of primary containers or units transported, stored, or held under conditions as nearly uniform as possible.

(b) A *sample* consists of 10 subsamples (consumer units), one taken from each of 10 different randomly chosen shipping cases to be representative of a given lot, unless otherwise specified in a specific standard in this part.

(c) An *analytical unit* is the portion(s) of food taken from a subsample of a sample for the purpose of analysis.

Subpart B—Requirements for Specific Standardized Beverages

§ 165.110 Bottled water.

(a) *Identity*—(1) *Description.* Bottled water is water that is intended for human consumption and that is sealed in bottles or other containers with no added ingredients except that it may optionally contain safe and suitable antimicrobial agents. Fluoride may be optionally added within the limitations established in §165.110(b)(4)(ii). Bottled water may be used as an ingredient in beverages (e.g., diluted juices, flavored bottled waters). It does not include those food ingredients that are declared in ingredient labeling as "water," "carbonated water," "disinfected water," "filtered water," "seltzer water," "soda water," "sparkling water," and "tonic water." The processing and bottling of bottled water shall comply with applicable regulations in part 129 of this chapter.

(2) *Nomenclature.* The name of the food is "bottled water," "drinking water," or alternatively one or more of the following terms as appropriate:

(i) The name of water from a well tapping a confined aquifer in which the water level stands at some height above the top of the aquifer is "artesian water" or "artesian well water." Artesian water may be collected with the assistance of external force to enhance the natural underground pressure. On request, plants shall demonstrate to appropriate regulatory officials that the water level stands at some height above the top of the aquifer.

(ii) The name of water from a subsurface saturated zone that is under a pressure equal to or greater than atmospheric pressure is "ground water." Ground water must not be under the direct influence of surface water as defined in 40 CFR 141.2.

(iii) The name of water containing not less than 250 parts per million (ppm) total dissolved solids (TDS), coming from a source tapped at one or more bore holes or springs, originating from a geologically and physically protected underground water source, may be "mineral water." Mineral water shall be distinguished from other types

Figure 7-3
Sample Page from C.F.R. Index

Tobacco products, cigarette papers and tubes, exportation without payment of tax or with drawback of tax, 27 CFR 290

Turbine engine powered airplanes, fuel venting and exhaust emission requirements, 14 CFR 34

Ultralight vehicles, 14 CFR 103

Water resource development projects administered by Chief of Army Engineers, seaplane operations, 36 CFR 328

Aircraft pilots

See Airmen

Airlines

See Air carriers

Airmen

Air safety proceedings, practice rules, 49 CFR 821

Air taxi operators and commercial operators of small aircraft, 14 CFR 135

Airplane operator security, 14 CFR 108

Alien airmen

　Arrival manifests, lists, and supporting documents for immigration, 8 CFR 251

　Landing, 8 CFR 252

　Parole, 8 CFR 253

Aviation maintenance technician schools, 14 CFR 147

Certification

　Airmen other than flight crewmembers, 14 CFR 65

　Flight crew members other than pilots, 14 CFR 63

　Pilots and flight instructors, 14 CFR 61

Certification and operations

　Airplanes having a seating capacity of 20 or more passengers or a maximum payload capacity of 6,000 pounds or more, 14 CFR 125

　Domestic, flag, and supplemental air carriers and commercial operators of large aircraft, 14 CFR 121

　Scheduled air carriers with helicopters, 14 CFR 127

Customs declarations and exemptions, 19 CFR 148

(Margin note: Reference to C.F.R. title and part)

Federal Aviation Administration, representatives of Administrator, 14 CFR 183

Foreign air carrier or other foreign person, lease of aircraft with crew, 14 CFR 218

General aircraft operating and flight rules, 14 CFR 91

Ground instructors, 14 CFR 143

Medical standards and certification for airmen, 14 CFR 67

Pilot schools, 14 CFR 141

Airplanes

See Aircraft

Airports

Air Force Department, aircraft arresting systems, 32 CFR 856

Air traffic control services and navigational facilities, establishment and discontinuance criteria, 14 CFR 170

Airplane operator security, 14 CFR 108

Airport aid program, 14 CFR 152

Airport noise and access restrictions, notice and approval, 14 CFR 161

Airport security, 14 CFR 107

Certification of airmen other than flight crewmembers, 14 CFR 65

Construction, alteration, activation, and deactivation of airports, notice, 14 CFR 157

Customs Service, air commerce regulations, 19 CFR 122

Defense Department, air installations compatible use zones, 32 CFR 256

Environmental criteria and standards, HUD assisted projects in runway clear zones at civil airports and clear and accident potential zones at military airports, 24 CFR 51

Expenditures of Federal funds for nonmilitary airports or air navigation facilities, 14 CFR 169

Federal aid, 14 CFR 151

Foreign quarantine, 42 CFR 71

General aircraft operating and flight rules, 14 CFR 91

Highway engineering, 23 CFR 620

Land airports serving certain air carriers, certification and operations, 14 CFR 139 of any changes to any C.F.R. regulations for the period after the most recent issue of LSA by directing you to the appropriate page in the *Federal Register*. If you do not locate any entries for your C.F.R. title and part in either LSA or C.F.R. Parts Affected, this means there are no revisions to your regulation during the periods covered.

5. *Electronic and Online Methods of Administrative Law Research*

Lexis and Westlaw, the fee-based computer research services, both include the full text of the *Federal Register* and C.F.R. in their easy-to-use and search databases. Updating is accomplished by a click of the keystroke to access Shepard's or KeyCite, respectively.

Free access to both the *Federal Register* and C.F.R. are now provided by the Government Printing Office at its Federal Digital System website (access http://www.gpo.gov/fdsys). Searching can be easily done by key words, agency names, citation, or by browsing tables of contents or volumes.

The versions of C.F.R. and the *Federal Register* available on FDsys are official pdf versions, meaning that they are the same as the print versions of those sources, and they should thus be updated the same as their print versions, namely, by using LSA and then C.F.R. Parts Affected (found in the Reader Aids section of the most recent issue of the online *Federal Register*). Look for your C.F.R. Title (for example, Title 21), and then point and click to review any changes to the section in which you are interested.

Alternatively, you may elect to use e-CFR, the unofficial electronic version of C.F.R., located at http://www.ecfr.gov. Material on this easy-to-use site is updated on a daily basis. Simply select your C.F.R. title (again, Title 21) from the drop-down menu and point and click to review changes to your C.F.R. provision.

Proposed and final rules are also available on another new government website, "Regulations.gov," available at http://www.regulations.gov. This site allows searching by key word, name of agency, and more, allowing quick access to United States government regulations from nearly 300 federal agencies. Regulations.gov includes reminders of rules going into effect and comment due dates (which reminders were previously published in the *Federal Register* until 2009). You may post comments and sign up for regular e-mail alerts about a specific regulation.

6. *Agency Decisions*

In addition to issuing rules and regulations, administrative agencies interpret and enforce their rules and regulations by issuing decisions. For example, if the Federal Communications Commission alleges that a broadcaster has violated one of its rules, it will hold a hearing and issue a decision relating to this matter. The agency hearing is somewhat less formal than a trial conducted in a courtroom, but its purpose is the same: to determine facts and render a decision. There is no jury, and the individual who conducts the proceeding (called an *adjudication*) is an *administrative law judge* ("ALJ") who is an expert in this field. Alternatively, the agency can prosecute violators in court, often by referring the matter to the Department of Justice for prosecution.

The decisions rendered by the agencies will be published so you may access and review them. There is no one set of books containing the decisions of all of the agencies; however, the Government Printing Office publishes sets containing decisions for many agencies. Table T.1.2 of *The Bluebook* and Appendix 8 of *ALWD* identify more than 30 official administrative publications, such as *Agriculture Decisions*. Although these publications are official, they lack a uniform approach. The indexes are often difficult to use, and updating can be sporadic. Thus, private publishers such as CCH, Bloomberg BNA, and Matthew Bender have published easy-to-use sets that report agency decisions. Typically, these sets are in looseleaf format (see Chapter 6), and decisions are located through alphabetically arranged Tables of Cases or through the subject matter index for the set, which will direct you to a narrative discussion followed by annotations to cases. To locate the actual case, use the citation given in the annotation. These cases are often published in separate bound volumes that contain both agency and court decisions. Table T.15 of *The Bluebook* identifies more than 100 of these services, from *Aviation Cases* to *Environmental Law Reporter*.

Additionally, many agencies post their decisions on their own websites. The following site will link you to administrative decisions and actions for many agencies: http://guides.lib.virginia.edu/administrative_decisions.

7. *Federal Cases Reviewing Agency Decisions*

A party who is dissatisfied with an ALJ's decision may appeal the matter to the federal courts. Because a "trial" has already occurred at the agency itself, the aggrieved party typically appeals the agency decision to the appropriate United States Court of Appeals, usually the Court of Appeals for the District of Columbia, bypassing the United States District Courts, which function as federal trial courts. Further appeal may be made to the United States Supreme Court, assuming certiorari is granted. See Figure 7-4 for a chart showing the appeal process for most federal agency decisions. In some cases (for example, those heard by the Social Security Administration), a party who is dissatisfied with an ALJ's decision may file a civil suit in a federal district court. Statutes governing the agency will specify a forum for review.

To locate federal cases that have reviewed agency decisions, use the standard sources you would use to locate federal cases on any topic: digests and annotations. For federal court cases, use West's *Federal*

Figure 7-4
Appeal of Typical Agency Decision

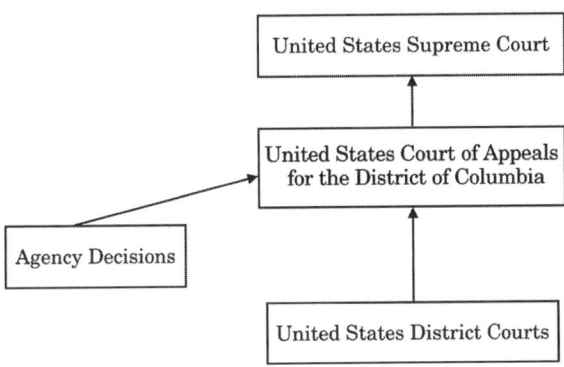

Practice Digests; to locate annotations, use A.L.R. Fed. Don't forget to review West's *Code of Federal Regulations Annotated* (for select titles), which includes references to law reviews and other authorities and annotations to cases interpreting C.F.R. provisions.

If using Lexis or Westlaw, you can also Shepardize or KeyCite the agency decision to be referred to other cases that affect or mention the agency decision.

Finally, many agencies post their decisions on their websites. For example, when you access the site of the National Labor Relations Board (http://www.nlrb.gov), you can immediately link to decisions and search by key word.

─────────── **Help Line** ───────────

FDsys

Users needing assistance with FDsys may access its Contact Center for access to highly trained specialists. Call toll free at (866) 512-1800 or send an e-mail to ContactCenter@gpo.gov. Additionally, FDsys offers webinars on using its collections. To take a tutorial, access http://www.gpo.gov/fdsysinfo/instructional_video.htm.

8.   *State Administrative Law*

There are agencies in most states, the activities of which often parallel federal agencies, although a state agency may impose standards in addition to those imposed by a federal agency. Similarly, many state agencies issue regulations for the practice of certain occupations in the state, such as standards for cosmetologists and real estate agents. Some states, usually the more populous ones, publish their agency's rules and regulations similarly to the publication of administrative law at the federal level, that is, in separate sets of books devoted solely to agency regulations and titled "Administrative Codes." These sets are generally accessed through their alphabetically arranged indexes.

You may also find that after you read a statute in a state code, you are referred to an administrative regulation in the cross-references or library references that follow the statute. In other instances, in the course of reading a case or a local encyclopedia, you may come across a reference to an administrative regulation. In any of these events, carefully review the administrative regulation, because it is typically subject to strict compliance.

Some state agencies issue decisions. With the exception of tax and unemployment compensation decisions, these are rarely published. Some agencies, however, publish newsletters or other publications that briefly review and summarize their decisions and other activities. These newsletters may be available by subscription, at your law library, or through the agency's website.

Practice Tip

Administrative Law Research

- For a tutorial on conducting administrative law research, access the following site: http://www.law.georgetown.edu/library/research/tutorials/admin/index.cfm.
- For a complete overview of all federal administrative agencies, consult *The United States Government Manual*, which identifies principal officials of each agency and gives a brief history of each agency, organization charts, and other pertinent information. The *Manual* is now provided free online by the Government Printing Office at FDsys's website at http://www.gpo.gov/fdsys.

Both Lexis and Westlaw offer state agency rules and some state agency decisions. Agency rules and decisions may also be available for free on the Internet. Access either of the following sites:

- Washburn University School of Law: http://www.washlaw.edu. Select your state's name from the list provided.
- Findlaw: http://www.findlaw.com/casecode. Select your state's name from the list provided.

D. International Law

1. Introduction

International law is broadly defined as the law pertaining to relations among sovereign nations. One often hears that there are two branches of international law: public and private. *Public international law* is what we typically view as international law: the conduct and regulation of nations. *Private international law* is an older and more archaic term, used primarily in Europe to describe an area of law more properly classified as "conflict of laws," pertaining to which jurisdiction's law would apply to a given transaction or event. Many contracts include a choice of law clause that specifies what country's law applies in a dispute and where venue will lie.

Although it is true that international law is a specialized field of law and that most legal professionals will not be involved in this practice area, with the Internet allowing worldwide communication and commerce, you should become sufficiently familiar with international law sources and research procedures so that, if needed, you can adequately perform a basic research task in this field.

2. Sources of International Law

International law is derived from four sources:

- International conventions (for example, treaties), which set forth rules for conduct expressly recognized and voluntarily agreed to by signatory nations;
- International custom, namely, some general practice accepted as law or believed to be obligatory;
- General principles of law accepted by civilized nations; and
- Judicial decisions and the teachings of international law experts.

Note that both treaties and judicial decisions interpreting international law are primary law, whereas any commentary about international law is a secondary authority.

3. Overview of International Law Research Procedure

If you are presented with an international law research task, you should use the following procedure unless you know the exact source for the answer to your problem.

- "Get your feet wet" by reading some background information relating to your issue and familiarizing yourself with the area of law;
- Determine whether a treaty covers your issue and provides a definitive answer to your question (if so, read the treaty and then determine if it is still in force); and
- Read analytical commentary and cases interpreting any treaty.

To follow this research process, you need to know which sources to consult. The following sections of the chapter introduce you to the sources you should consult to perform your research.

4. *Basic Texts and Sources*

Law libraries usually collect all international law materials together. Browse the shelves and become familiar with the library's collection. Some of the better known general texts and guides relating to international law are as follows:

- James Crawford, *Brownlie's Principles of Public International Law* (8th ed. 2012)
- Claire M. Germain, *Germain's Transnational Law Research: A Guide for Attorneys* (1991)
- Green H. Hackworth, *Digest of International Law* (1940-1944)
- Marjorie M. Whiteman, *Digest of International Law* (1963)

These texts provide excellent information on international law. In many ways, they resemble special subject encyclopedias in that most are multi-volume sets that contain articulate narrative statements of the law and citations to cases and other authorities that are located in footnotes. There may also be specialized treatises for your topic. (For example, a multi-volume set exists that covers only issues relating to the North American Free Trade Agreement.)

Also, consult Restatement (Third) Foreign Relations Law of the United States. This Restatement focuses on international law and is an excellent starting place for international law research because it provides general information on international law, international agreements, international jurisdiction, judgments, and remedies. The Restatement will also provide you with citations to cases that have interpreted treaties.

Finally, consult the *American Journal of International Law*, a quarterly periodical that contains analytical articles relating to various international law topics. Use the index for the set or use any of the indexes to periodicals discussed in Chapter 6.

5. *Treaties*

a. Introduction

Treaties, which are formal agreements, may be *bilateral* (between two parties) or *multilateral* (among several parties). Some treaties have ended wars, others have resolved boundary disputes, and still others deal with trade or economic issues. One type of treaty is referred to as a *convention* and usually relates to a formal multilateral agreement with numerous parties.

Although treaties may have been signed and agreed to by representatives of the countries involved, they are not effective until they are ratified or officially approved by each government. In the United States, treaties are entered into by the President with the "advice and consent" of the Senate, namely, by two-thirds approval by the Senate (although one type of international agreement, an *executive agreement*, is entered into with a foreign nation by the President acting without Senate approval).

Because treaties are expressly stated by the United States Constitution to be the "supreme law of the land," they are primary law.

b. Sources for Treaties

- **Pre-Ratification.** During the time between the signing of a treaty and approval by the Senate, treaties can be located in a series entitled *Senate Treaty Documents*, which are available in conventional print form (through *Congressional Information Service* (CIS) *Index* or through the Senate's Treaty Page online at http://www.senate.gov/pagelayout/legislative/d_three_sections_with_teasers/treaties.htm). Access FDsys at http://www.gpo.gov/fdsys and select "Congressional Documents" to obtain treaties submitted to previous Congresses by the President.

- **Post-Ratification.** Since 1945, all treaties and executive agreements to which the United States is a party are published as pamphlets in a set titled *Treaties and Other International Acts Series* ("TIAS"). Since 1950, these pamphlets are then published in hardbound volumes titled *United States Treaties and Other International Agreements* ("UST"), although the last volume of UST was produced in 1984. To locate treaties in either of these sets, use the index *United States Treaties and Other International Agreements Cumulative Index*. You may locate a treaty by country name or by its topic. TIAS treaties and international agreements since 1996 are available online through the United States Department of State's website at http://www.state.gov/s/l/treaty/tias/index.htm.

  Another collection of treaties is the *United Nations Treaty Series* ("UNTS"), which publishes treaties filed with the United Nations. Thus, this set collects numerous treaties to which the United States is not a party. A cumulative index to UNTS provides easy access by country name or treaty topic.

• **Lexis and Westlaw.** Treaties are available on both Lexis and Westlaw. Searching is easily accomplished by treaty citation, country name, or key words and phrases.

Help Line

Treaty Assistance

The Department of State offers excellent information about United States Treaties. If help is needed, call the Treaty Desk at (202) 647-1345 or send an e-mail asking for assistance to treatyoffice@state.gov.

• **Internet Access.** Many treaties are now available on the Internet. Use the following sources:

- United States Senate Treaty Page. Access the Senate site http://www.senate.gov/pagelayout/legislative/d_three_sections_with_teasers/treaties.htm for the text of treaties received or approved by the Senate and information on action taken by the Senate.
- THOMAS provides treaty information since approximately 1967 (although the full text of treaties is not provided). You may search by treaty number, key word or phrase, or the type of treaty. Access the site http://thomas.loc.gov/home/treaties/treaties.html. Eventually, the treaty information available on THOMAS will migrate to Congress.gov.
- The United Nations Treaty Collection offers access to more than 180,000 treaties and international agreements and complete access to U.N.T.S. Access http://treaties.un.org. All multilateral treaties deposited with the United Nations are available. You may search by subject, participant, key word, popular name, and more, including searching the online U.N.T.S. Cumulative Index.
- The United States State Department offers T.I.A.S. treaties and international agreements since 1996 at http://www.state.gov/s/l/treaty/tias/index.htm.
- The Electronic Information System for International Law provided by the American Society of International Law at http://www.eisil.org provides "one-stop shopping" for primary materials, helpful websites, and research guides to international law on the Internet.

c. Determining the Current Status of Treaties

In many instances, treaties themselves specify the date until when they will be in force. For example, a treaty might state, "The treaty enters into force 30 days after ratification and remains in force for a period of 10 years and continues in force thereafter unless terminated by either party by giving one year's written notice to the other."

Perhaps the easiest way to determine whether a treaty involving the United States is still in force is to access the Office of the Legal Adviser of the State Department at http://www.state.gov/s/l/treaty/tif/index.htm, which provides access to *Treaties in Force*, an annual publication that identifies all of the treaties and executive agreements still in force. *Treaties in Force* is easy to use because it is organized by country and topic.

d. Interpreting Treaties

To assist you in interpreting treaties, use both secondary and primary sources. For secondary sources that have construed treaties, review the texts and the *American Journal of International Law* described previously. To locate primary sources, for example, cases that have interpreted treaties, check the following sources:

- *Shepard's Federal Statute Citations.* Look up the volume and page of your treaty citation in the print volumes of this Shepard's set, and you will be directed to cases and A.L.R. annotations that have mentioned or interpreted your treaty.
- **U.S.C.S.** U.S.C.S. contains a separate volume titled "Notes to Uncodified Laws and Treaties," which will provide you with annotations to judicial decisions interpreting treaties.

Once you have located cases construing your treaty, be sure to Shepardize or KeyCite these cases to ensure they are still good law and to help you locate additional pertinent materials.

> ────────── **Practice Tip** ──────────
>
> *International Law Research*
> **For tutorials on conducting international law research, access either of the following sites:**
>
> - **http://www.law.georgetown.edu/library/research/tutorials/intl/ index.cfm**
> - **http://www.law.umich.edu/library/students/research/Documents/ transnational.pdf**

---

6. *International Tribunals*

There are a variety of methods available to nations to resolve disputes. One country may agree to act as an informal mediator in a dispute between two countries. Additionally, the Permanent Court of Arbitration was established in 1899 at The Hague, Holland's royal city, to offer mediation, arbitration, and fact-finding to disputant countries. The International Court of Justice (often called the World Court) is also located at The Hague and is one of the six major organs of the United Nations. Any United Nations member may bring a dispute before the Court, which renders its decision by majority vote of its 15 judges. Its decisions are reported on its website and in a set of books titled *Reports of Judgments, Advisory Opinions and Orders*. In many instances, its decisions are ignored by an offending nation. There is no uniform method of enforcing the World Court's decision. The United Nations itself has no permanent police force to resolve international conflicts and will send peacekeepers when 9 of 15 Security Council members decide and the affected countries agree (although a peacekeeping proposal will fail if any one of the five permanent members of the United Nations, including the United States, votes against it).

Practice Tip

What Does the FDsys Eagle Logo Mean?

As noted in this chapter, the website FDsys (http://www.gpo.gov/fdsys) provides authenticated (meaning complete and unaltered) documents for nearly every research task described in this chapter: legislative history, executive, administrative, and international law research. The site includes more than 50 different collections of documents. The advantage of using FDsys to locate the documents you need for your research tasks is that because the documents have been verified as authentic, they may be cited as if to the original print source without any URL information included in the citation (*Bluebook* R. 18). All documents on FDsys include a digital signature and a graphic of an eagle, verifying their authenticity.

E. Municipal Law

1. Introduction and Terminology

A client's question about whether horses may be kept on his or her property or the height and type of fence required around the perimeter of a swimming pool is answered by conducting municipal or local legal research.

Most municipalities operate under a document called a *charter*, which functions as the municipality's constitution, setting forth the powers and activities in which the municipality may engage. Local laws are usually called *ordinances* rather than statutes. The local governing body may be a city council, board of supervisors, a county executive, aldermen, or other legislative body.

After municipal ordinances are enacted, they are typically organized or "codified" so that all of the zoning ordinances are brought together, all of the animal control ordinances are brought together, and so forth, into the city's or county's code.

2. Municipal Research Materials and Procedure

One of the most difficult tasks in performing municipal research is finding a current version of a city or county code. The law library in your area will usually maintain the codes for the surrounding municipalities. You can also check your public library or the appropriate government office (for example, the city clerk's office, county counsel's office, and so on).

Once you have found the code for your municipality, the research techniques used to locate ordinances are identical to the research techniques used to locate federal or state statutes, namely, the descriptive word or topic approaches.

Municipal codes are usually maintained in looseleaf binders that contain all of the municipality's ordinances organized by topic, such as business regulations, elections, and fire procedures. Use the index at the end of the binder just as you would any other index. Think of words that describe your research issue, look them up in the alphabetically arranged index, and you will be directed to the appropriate ordinance. Alternatively, you can examine the code's table of contents, usually placed at the front of the binder, and browse the list of topics.

3. Interpretation of Municipal Ordinances

Few municipal codes are annotated. Thus, after you read the pertinent ordinance, you are seldom directed to cases interpreting this ordinance. In fact, ordinances are rarely interpreted by court cases. Thus, conducting research on municipal law can be difficult. Perhaps the best way to locate cases interpreting ordinances is through Lexis or Westlaw, although coverage is quite limited. Additionally, West publishes a multi-volume set titled *Ordinance Law Annotations* (available both in conventional print form and on Westlaw), which directs you to cases that interpret or apply ordinances. The set is arranged by topic (demonstrations and parades, street vendors, and so forth) and provides digests or brief summaries of cases that have interpreted ordinances relating to these topics.

4. Municipal Research on the Internet

Hundreds of city and county municipal codes are now available on the Internet. Following are three of the best sites and techniques to locate municipal codes on the Internet:

- Municipal Code Corporation (http://www.municode.com) provides codes for more than 2,700 local governments. Select a state and locality, and then search by key words or by reviewing an index or chapter.
- American Legal Publishing Corp. (http://www.amlegal.com/library/) provides links to numerous city and county codes.
- Locate your municipality's website and look for a link to its code.

F. Citation Form

Legal Materials	Bluebook (for practitioners)	ALWD
Legislative Materials	• H.R. 104, 109th Cong. § 2 (2005). • H.R. Rep. No. 108-796, pt. 1, at 7 (2004), *reprinted in* 2004 U.S.C.C.A.N. 1390, 1395. • *The Methamphetamine Remediation Research Act of 2005: Hearing on H.R. 042 Before the H. Comm. on Sci.*, 109th Cong. 7 (2005) (statement of Gary Howard, Sheriff, Tioga County, New York). • 151 Cong. Rec. H11,462-63 (daily ed. May 25, 2006) (statement of Rep. Sherwood Boehlert).	• H.R. 104, 109th Cong. § 2 (Jan. 4, 2005). • H.R. Rpt. 108-796 at 7 (Dec. 7, 2004). • H.R. Comm. on Sci., *The Methamphetamine Remediation Research Act of 2005: Hearing on H.R. 042*, 109th Cong. 7 (Mar. 3, 2005) (statement of Gary Howard, Sheriff, Tioga County, New York). • 151 Cong. Rec. H11462-11463 (daily ed. May 25, 2006) (statement of Rep. Sherwood Boehlert).
Presidential Materials	• Proclamation No. 8733, 3 C.F.R. 82 (2012), *reprinted in* 3 U.S.C. § 469 (Supp. V 2012). • Exec. Order No. 13,597, 3 C.F.R. 477 (2012), *reprinted in* 3 U.S.C. § 297 (Supp. V 2012).	• Exec. Procl. 8733, 3 C.F.R. 82 (2012) (reprinted in 3 U.S.C. § 469 (Supp. V 2012)). • Exec. Or. 13597, 3 C.F.R. 477 (2012) (reprinted in 3 U.S.C. § 297 (Supp. V 2012)).

Legal Materials	Bluebook (for practitioners)	ALWD
Administrative Materials	• DNA-Sample Collection and Biological Evidence Preservation in the Federal Jurisdiction, 73 Fed. Reg. 74,932, 74,935 (Dec. 10, 2009) (to be codified at 28 C.F.R. pt. 28). • Homeland Security, 6 C.F.R. § 5.1 (2006).	• DNA-Sample Collection and Biological Evidence Preservation in the Federal Jurisdiction, 73 Fed. Reg. 74932, 74935 (Dec. 10, 2009) (to be codified at 28 C.F.R. pt. 28). • Homeland Security, 6 C.F.R. § 5.1 (2006).
International Materials	Agreement for the Promotion of Aviation Safety, U.S.—Ir., art. II, Feb. 5, 1997, T.I.A.S. No. 12,831.	Agreement for the Promotion of Aviation Safety, art. II (Feb. 5, 1997), T.I.A.S. No. 12831.
Municipal Materials	Balt., Md., Code § 7-10 (2006).	Balt. City Code (Md.) § 7-10 (2006).

Internet Resources

http://www.gpo.gov/fdsys	FDsys offers access to the *Federal Register*, C.F.R., public laws, executive materials, and a wide variety of legislative materials and treaties.
http://thomas.loc.gov; http://www.congress.gov	THOMAS offers the text of bills, public laws, committee information, the *Congressional Record*, and treaties (all of which information is migrating to Congress.gov).
http://www.llsdc.org/federal-legislative-history-guide	Consult this excellent guide for information on compiling a federal legislative history.
http://law.indiana.libguides.com/content.php?pid=383443&sid=3145243	Access this website to link to state legislative history information.
http://www.un.org	The website of the United Nations offers the text of many treaties and a glossary of treaty terms.
http://www2.lib.uchicago.edu/~llou/forintlaw.html	Access this site for an excellent primer on conducting international law research on the Internet with links to treaties and websites of major international organizations.
http://www.state.gov/s/l/treaty/index.htm	The State Department provides links to treaty actions and the current edition of *Treaties in Force*.
http://www.municode.com	Municipal Code Corporation provides the text of numerous municipal codes.

Research Assignment

LEGISLATIVE HISTORY

1. Use the CIS Index for 2008.
   a. What public law relates to the Worker, Retiree, and Employer Recovery Act?
   b. Locate the CIS "Legislative History" volume for this public law.
      i. When was it approved?
      ii. What was its designation in the House as an enacted bill?
      iii. On which days did debate occur in the House and the Senate on this version of the bill?
2. Use *United States Code Congressional and Administrative News*.
   a. To which topic or act does Public Law 112-269 relate?
   b. Use Table 4 for the 112th Congress. Locate the following information relating to this Act.
      i. When was this Act approved?
      ii. What was its number in the Senate?
      iii. Give the date on which the Act was passed by the Senate.
      iv. Give the date on which the Act was passed by the House.
      v. Give the House Report Number.
3. Review the legislative history in *United States Code Congressional and Administrative News* for the Public Law identified in Question 2 above.
   a. According to the House Report, page 1, what is the purpose of the Act?
   b. Review page 6 of the Report. Would enactment of the bill have any effect on tax expenditures?
   c. Review page 8 of the Report. Does the legislation contain any earmarks?
   d. Which volume of the *Congressional Record* includes debates and information relating to this legislation?

ADMINISTRATIVE LAW

4. Use the most recent C.F.R. Index.
   a. Which C.F.R. title and part deal with the smallpox compensation program?
   b. Which C.F.R. title and part deal with food grades and standards for milk?

i. Review this provision and its subparts and subsections. How much milk fat must eggnog contain?
ii. Briefly, what is yogurt?

5. Use the Topical Index (Wages-Hours) for the CCH *Labor Law Reporter*.
    a. Which paragraph provides exemptions for the child labor laws?
    b. Review this paragraph (in this same volume).
        i. Is employment of children under age 16 permitted during school hours?
        ii. Do the child labor restrictions apply to children employed as actors or performers?

6. Use the Table of Cases in the CCH *Labor Law Reporter*. Give the citation for the case *Dando v. Stonhard Co.*

7. Use the Master Index to the looseleaf set *Communications Regulation* by Pike and Fischer.
    a. What section relates to children's television, namely, educational and informational programming for children (on commercial stations)?
    b. Review the Digest volume in the set for this section. Can a short segment or vignette fulfill the requirement for license renewal that broadcasting provide educational and informational programming? Answer the question and cite a case that supports your answer.

INTERNATIONAL LAW

8. Use the Cumulative Index, Volume 44, for volumes 2351–2400 of the *United Nations Treaty Series* and find the agreement between Turkey and the United States relating to air transport.
    a. Give the citation to this agreement.
    b. When and where was the agreement signed?
    c. Who signed the agreement for each party?
    d. Briefly, how may the agreement be terminated?
    e. When was the agreement registered with the United Nations?

9. Use Moore's *A Digest of International Law*.
    a. Use the Index. What is the definition of "war"?
    b. Use the "List of Cases Cited" in the Index to the Digest. Generally, to which topic does the case *The Sally* (1902) relate?

10. Use *U.S. Treaties and Other International Agreements*.
    a. What is the general subject matter of 35 U.S.T. 6029 (T.I.A.S. 11035)?
    b. Where was this agreement signed?
    c. Who signed this agreement for the United States?

188

Internet Assignment

1. Access the website for THOMAS. Locate Senate Bill 564 introduced in the 103rd Congress, Review "Bill Summary and Status."
   a. Briefly, what is the purpose of this legislation?
   b. What is its Public Law Number?
2. Access FDsys. What is the subject matter of Presidential Proclamation 8937 issued on March 1, 2013?
3. Access FDsys. Locate 21 C.F.R. Pt. 102.
   a. Briefly, what components must a frozen "heat and serve" dinner include?
   b. What section of C.F.R. governs your answer?
4. Access FDsys. Locate the *Federal Register* issue for April 2, 2013, and locate "C.F.R. Parts Affected" in the "Reader Aids" section. Update 21 C.F.R. 73. What result are you given?
5. Access FDsys. Use the "Find by Citation" feature. Locate Senate Report 112-2. What is its title?
6. Access FDsys. Review the *U.S. Government Manual*. Briefly, what is the role of the Department of Homeland Security?
7. Access FDsys. Review the *Compilation of Presidential Documents*. Locate Proclamation No. 8978 issued on May 10, 2013. What did this proclaim?
8. Access the website of the United Nations. Use the United Nations Treaty Series database and locate "The Law of the Sea Convention."
   a. What type of treaty is this?
   b. Is the United States a participant in this treaty?
9. Access the website of the State Department's Treaty Affairs Office at http://www.state.gov/s/l/treaty/index.htm. Select "Treaties in Force" for the most recent year. Locate a multilateral convention to which the United States is a party relating to physical protection of nuclear material.
   a. When did this agreement enter into force?
   b. What is its citation in T.I.A.S.?
10. Locate the City Code for Seattle, Washington. Is it lawful in Seattle to give a newborn chick to another as a pet? Answer the question and give the section that governs your answer.

Legal Research

Using Electronic and Computer Resources

The Digital Library: Lexis, Westlaw, and Non-Print Research Tools

Chapter Overview

Legal research can be accomplished by means other than using conventional print sources. There are several new technologies that allow you to conduct research efficiently and accurately. This chapter introduces you to the digital library, primarily computer-assisted fee-based legal research. Legal research using the Internet's free resources is discussed in Chapter 9.

A. Introduction to Computer-Assisted Legal Research

1. *LexisNexis and Westlaw*

There are two major competing computer-assisted research services: *LexisNexis* (for simplicity, referred to as "Lexis" in this text and chapter and also commonly known as Lexis in practice) and *Westlaw*. These research systems provide access to a tremendous variety of cases, statutes, administrative regulations, and numerous other authorities that a law firm or other employer may not otherwise be able to afford. Lexis and Westlaw operate in essentially the same manner; most users, however, eventually develop a preference for one or the other. Because both services contain substantially the same materials, it is impossible to declare that one service is superior to the other. The one that is "best" is the one that is best for you.

Each service consists of thousands of databases. The databases include cases, statutes, administrative regulations, hundreds of secondary sources, and other materials for you to access. In general, research using Lexis and Westlaw is highly similar. Both allow easy retrieval of cases, statutes, and other materials when you already have a citation. You merely type the citation into an open field and click on "Go" or a similar button. When you do not have a citation, you will usually access the appropriate database (such as selecting federal cases or Ohio cases) and then formulate a search question by using *Boolean searching* (a search method using symbols, word fragments, and numbers rather than plain English) or by using plain English, usually called "natural language."

Both Lexis and Westlaw have recently upgraded their traditional systems and now allow "Google"-type searching. Thus, Lexis Advance and WestlawNext allow you to type in a question without first selecting a database and will retrieve all documents responsive to your query.

It is important to have a basic understanding of the two computerized legal research systems; however, the best way to learn how to perform computerized legal research is to do it. There is no substitute for "hands-on" experience. Lexis and Westlaw both offer tutorials, training videos, and written materials describing their systems. Contact:

LexisNexis	*West, A Thomson Reuters Business*
9443 Springboro Pike Miamisburg, OH 45342	610 Opperman Drive Eagan, MN 55123
24-hour toll-free customer service: 1 (800) 543-6862 http://web.lexis.com/help/ research/globalhelp_rf_ frameset.asp	24-hour toll-free customer service: 1 (800) WESTLAW http://thomsonreuters.com/ products_services/legal/ legal_products/a-z/westlaw

Ethics Alert

Computer Literacy

Legal professionals are ethically bound to provide competent representation to clients. This duty is broad enough to require that you be sufficiently familiar with conventional *and* electronic research techniques such that you can make an accurate determination as to which sources will yield the best results at the lowest cost for the client. Neither conventional research nor computer-assisted legal research should be used exclusively. Effective researchers use a combination of the two methods and employ selectivity to determine which method is best for a given task.

2. *Getting Started Using Lexis or Westlaw*

Getting started usually requires you to sign on to Lexis or Westlaw with your identification number and password assigned to you by your school or employer. When performing research on the job, you will usually enter a client name or number so that the client can be billed for the time spent conducting the research. In most firms, legal professionals have desktop computer access to Lexis, Westlaw, or both. The first screen presented to you after sign on usually allows you to retrieve a document or case (if you know the citation), check a citation (either through *Shepard's Citations* or KeyCite), or construct a search if you do not have a citation.

3. *Boolean Searching*

You likely know that computers are extremely literal. They will not search for cases containing the word "collision" if you search for "collide." Thus, a method called *Boolean searching* allows you to use words, symbols, numbers, and connectors (collectively, often called *Terms and Connectors*) to overcome the literalness of the computer. For example, Lexis and Westlaw both use an exclamation point (!) to substitute for any number of additional letters at the end of a word. Thus "colli!" will locate "collide," "collision," "colliding," and so forth. Of course, words such as "collie" will also be located, so use the symbols carefully. Both Lexis and Westlaw also offer publications that explain the use of their search symbols, numbers, and connectors. See Figure 8-1 for a chart of Lexis and Westlaw Terms and Connectors.

These symbols and connectors help you narrow your search and make it more manageable. If you merely entered "first amendment," Lexis and Westlaw would retrieve thousands of documents containing this phrase. A more effective search would be as follows: "first amendment" /50 free! and press. This instructs Lexis and Westlaw to locate only those documents that contain the phrase "first amendment" within 50 words of the words "freedom" or "free" and "press." (Of course, documents including terms such as "freely" may also be located.)

Figure 8-1
Comparison of Selected Lexis and Westlaw Terms and Connectors

Lexis Term, Connector, or Symbol	Westlaw Term, Connector, or Symbol	Function	Example	Retrieves documents
!	!	Retrieves words with variant endings	*lend!*	with the words "lender," "lending," etc.

Figure 8-1 *(Continued)*

Lexis Term, Connector, or Symbol	Westlaw Term, Connector, or Symbol	Function	Example	Retrieves documents
*	*	Replaces one or more characters	*m*n*	with the word "man" or "men"
and	&	Locates two search terms in a document	*Probate and damages* (Lexis); *probate & damages* (Westlaw)	containing both "probate" and "damages"
or	Either "or" or a space between two words	Locates documents with either or both words	*Teacher or professor* (Lexis); *teacher professor* (Westlaw)	containing either "teacher" or "professor" or both
/n	/n	Locates documents with one word within a number of words of the other	*patent /10 infringement*	containing the word "patent" within ten words of the word "infringement"
/p	/p	Locates documents with two terms in the same paragraph	*Wrongful /p death*	containing the words "wrongful" and "death" in the same paragraph
/s	/s	Locates documents with two terms in the same sentence	*Wrongful /s death*	containing the words "wrongful" and "death" in the same sentence
and not	but not or %	Excludes documents with certain terms	*Patent and not accounting* (Lexis); *patent % accounting* (Westlaw)	containing the term "patent" but not the word "accounting"

Figure 8-1 *(Continued)*

Lexis Term, Connector, or Symbol	Westlaw Term, Connector, or Symbol	Function	Example	Retrieves documents
" "	" "	Locates documents in the same order as they appear in quotation marks	*"all elements rule"*	containing the phrase "all elements rule"
at least		Term must appear a certain number of times	atleast4RICO	containing the term "RICO" at least four times

4. *Plain English Searching*

Recognizing that many individuals find working with Boolean connectors awkward, both Lexis and Westlaw offer "Natural Language" searching to allow you to enter your issue in plain English and eliminate the need for symbols, numbers, and connectors. Thus, you could enter in a search question such as "May a city prohibit smoking in restaurants in the city?" Construct your searches before you sign on so that you work efficiently and do not incur excessive costs. Draft some sample queries and search terms.

Practice Tip

Boolean or Plain English Searching? Westlaw's Suggestions

Use Boolean searching when:

- **You are searching for particular terms;**
- **You are searching for a particular document; or**
- **You are searching for all documents containing specific information, such as all cases classified under a particular topic name and key number.**

Use plain English or natural language searching when:

- **You are researching broad concepts; or**
- **You are a new or infrequent computer user, or you are unfamiliar with Boolean terms and connectors.**

B. Lexis

1. Getting Started

Lexis's database consists of a series of *sources* (sometimes called *libraries*)—materials relating to particular areas of law, such as the source titled "GENFED," which contains cases, statutes, and materials relating to federal legal topics. Within each source are "files." For example, the GENFED source contains separate "files" for cases from the U.S. Supreme Court, cases from the Courts of Appeal, and other federal materials. In fact, Lexis provides more than 40,000 sources, including cases, statutes, forms, treatises, the Restatements, encyclopedias, dictionaries, jury instructions, and much more. For a searchable directory of Lexis's sources, access the following site: http://w3.nexis.com/sources.

After you log on at http://www.lexis.com, the first screen provides various research options at the top of your screen, including the following:

- **My Lexis.** By selecting the "My Lexis" tab at the top of the screen, you will be able to do a quick search by entering terms into a search box and then selecting specific sources, such as selecting all treatises dealing with patent law or federal statutes relating to immigration.
- **Search.** The "Search" tab at the top of your screen is divided into several subtabs. You may also add your own subtabs so that the practice areas and jurisdictions you research most often are the first sources you view. The preset subtabs (shown in drop-down menu form) are as follows:
  - "Search All" allows you to view a list of the most frequently used Lexis sources, such as "Secondary Sources." You will then be presented with a list of secondary sources, allowing you to pick and choose the source you desire. This tab is a frequently used starting point and allows you to select a source you want to search (for example, federal cases or state cases) before you enter your search terms. The "All" screen also includes several helpful tools on the right side of the screen page, including a box with your recently used sources (so you may readily return to them), the ability to use Quick Tools to find documents, links to helpful litigation documents, and a search button to find forms. (See Figure 8-2.)
  - "Search by Topic or Headnote" allows you to select the topic you wish to research (for example, Education Law) and then customize the sources and jurisdictions in which to conduct your research or elect to view all headnotes relating to a particular topic.

- "Search by Guided Search Form" lists several broad categories (for example, "States Legal" and "Law Reviews"). When you select a category, you will then be given a search box and a guided form with drop-down menus that has several recommended sources already identified for you.
- "Search by Dot Command" should be used when you know the Lexis library and file name of the source you wish to research (for example, "GENFED;8Cir").
- "Search by Find a Source" allows you to enter a source by its name in a search box or to browse alphabetical lists of sources.
- "Search by Quick Search" allows you to select a jurisdiction or practice area. Quick Search then compiles a list of relevant sources; you then enter your search terms into a search box. (See Figure 8-3.)

- **Get a Document.** Use the "Get a Document" tab when you know the citation to a case, statute, law review, or other authority. Type your citation in the open field (for example, 14 p3d 890) and click "Get." You need not use correct citation form, and Lexis will suggest citation formats for you.
- ***Shepard's.*** Use this feature to Shepardize your authorities (primarily, to ensure your primary authorities are still good law).

Figure 8-2
Lexis "All" Screen

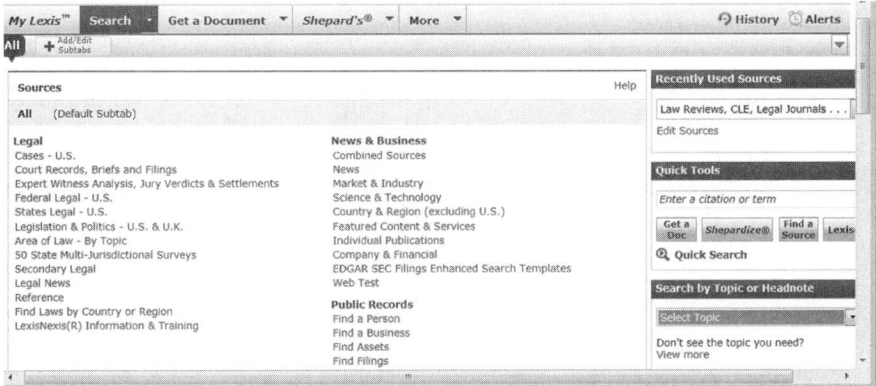

2. *Constructing a Search*

There are three ways to search for materials on Lexis if you do not have a citation: the traditional search using Boolean connectors; the plain English search method; or Lexis's Easy Search, a search method similar to popular Internet searching.

a. Boolean Searching

Most experts agree that Boolean searching provides more targeted results than plain English searching. Following are some tips for constructing a search query using Terms and Connectors on Lexis:

- **Lowercase Letters.** Lexis is not sensitive to capital letters (unless you specify such in your search request). Thus, for basic searching, use lowercase letters.
- **Singulars, Possessives, and Plurals.** Forms of singular, possessives, and plurals are automatically found if they are regular forms. Thus, a search for "tenant" will produce results for "tenants" and "tenant's" but a search for "foot" will not find "feet."
- **Universal Symbols.** Lexis offers some *universal symbols* or "wildcards" to help you expand your search:

  - An *asterisk* (*) replaces single letters within words. Thus, "m*n" will find "man" or "men" and "anders*n" will find "andersen" or "anderson."
  - An *exclamation point* (!) replaces any ending to a word. Thus, "sec!" finds "security," "securities," "secure," and so forth.

- **Connectors.** *Connectors* help you locate needed documents and narrow your search. Following are the most commonly used connectors:

  - **Or.** A search for "teacher or student" will locate documents containing either or both of these words.
  - **And.** A search for "negligence and doctor" will locate documents only if they contain both these terms.
  - **/n.** The connector "/n" instructs Lexis to find documents that contain words appearing within a specified number(n) of words of each other. Thus, a search for "tenant /50 evict" locates documents in which the words "tenant" and "evict" appear within 50 words of each other.
  - **/s and /p.** The connector "/s" finds words in the same sentence and "/p" finds words in the same paragraph. Thus, a search for "alter /s ego" (or "alter /p ego") locates documents in which the words "alter" and "ego" appear in the same sentence or paragraph, respectively

Lexis offers other connectors as well; they are described in any of Lexis's marketing materials and on its website at http://web.lexis.com/help/research/gh_search.asp#TermsConnectors. (See Figure 8-1.)

If your search does not produce sufficient results (or perhaps produces too many documents), you may modify your search. Simply select "Edit Search" to be given a list of additional terms to add to your search query.

b. Plain English Searching

Because many individuals find working with terms and connectors awkward, Lexis allows you to use plain English through its Natural Language feature. First, you must select a source (such as federal cases). Type your words or phrases into the open field. For example, you could type, "What is the term of a design patent" and select the open circle or tab marked "Natural Language." Click "Search" and modify as needed. Use the "Suggest terms for my search" tab to see a list of words that can be included in your search.

c. Easy Search

Lexis's new service, *Easy Search*, is a quick search method, which is used somewhat similarly to Internet search engines such as Google. To use this service, choose a legal source (for example, federal cases) from the menu, and then select "Easy Search." Type in your search terms in the open field and click "Search." Just as you search using Google or another Internet search engine, you may search by phrase ("business judgment rule,"), citation (520 us 10), or other relevant terms. (See Figure 8-3.)

Figure 8-3
Lexis "Quick Search" Screen

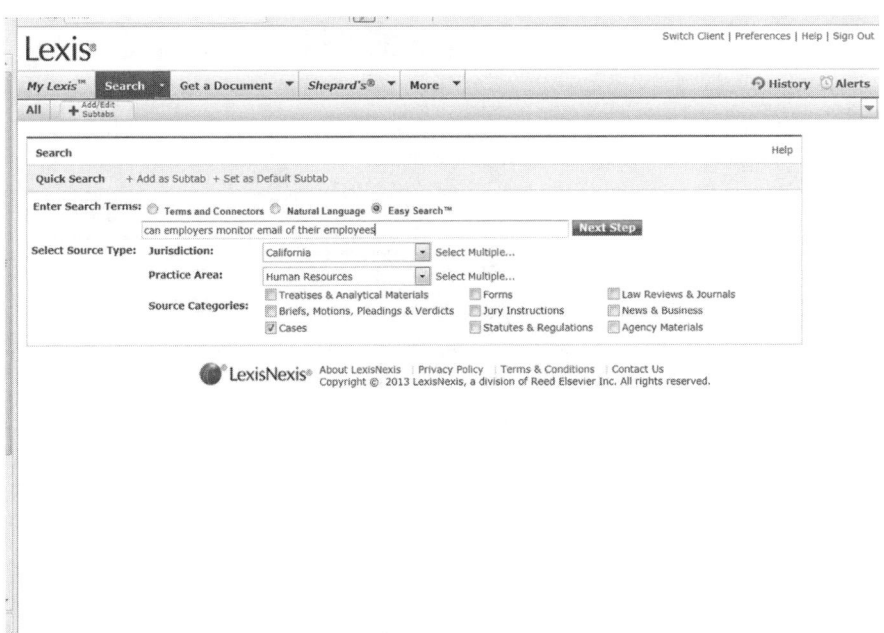

d. Display of Search Results

If your search produces numerous documents, you can weed out irrelevant ones by using the following techniques when reviewing your search results:

• **KWIC.** Use the command "KWIC" to highlight your search terms and the 25 words on either side of your search terms so you can review at a glance the portion of the case or document of most interest to you.

• **FULL.** Select "Full" to display the full text of the document containing your search terms.

Once the search results are on screen, you may move back and forth between documents. You may print or download your results or e-mail them to yourself or others. (See Figure 8-4.)

3. *Specialized Searches*

a. Searching for Statutes and Constitutions

• **By Citation.** If you know the precise citation for a federal or state statute or constitution, click the "Get a Document" tab. Type your citation (such as 35 uscs 101) in the open field and click "Get." You can also review the case annotations following your citation, just as you would in the print version of U.S.C.S.

• **By Topic.** When you do not know a statute or constitutional citation, you must select a library or source (such as "States—Legal" and then "Ohio Statutes"). You may browse various titles within the Ohio code or you may construct a search using terms and connectors, Natural Language, or Easy Search.

Figure 8-4
Viewing Lexis Results

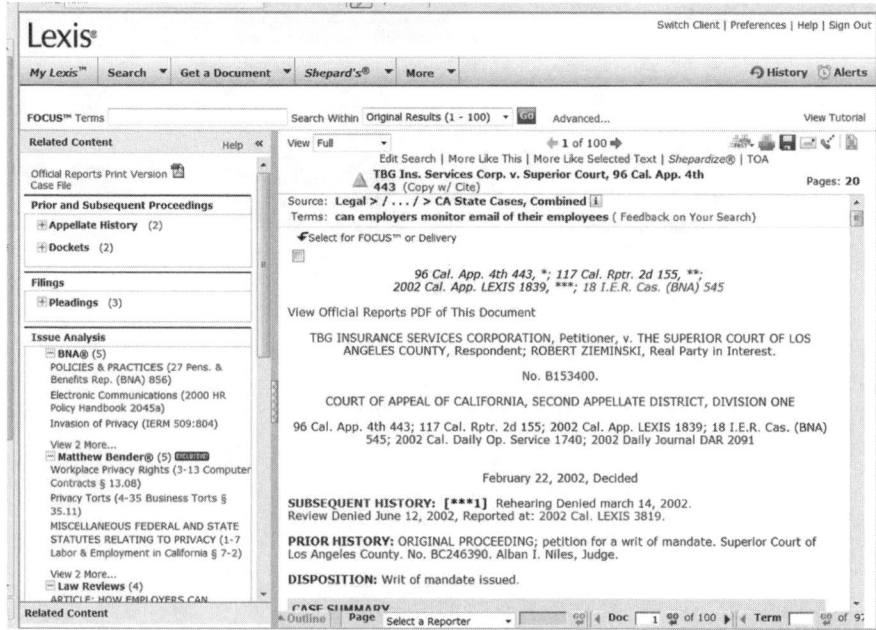

b. Searching for Cases

• **By Citation.** If you know a case citation, use the "Get a Document" feature and type your citation (such as 430 us 128 or 222 s ct 1) in the open field. Lexis includes star paging to inform you of the page number you would be on if you were reading the case in the other parallel sets. Also, a "Related Content" pane is displayed along the left side of the screen (see Figure 8-4), allowing you to access pleadings filed in the case, pertinent law review articles, and other resources related to the topics discussed in the case.

• **By Party Name or Docket Number.** If you know a plaintiff's or defendant's name, click the "Get a Document" tab and then the "Party Name" tab. Type the party's name in the open field and select "Search." If you know a case docket number, you may use "Get by Docket Number" to retrieve it.

• **By Topic.** When you do not have a citation, use one of the Search tabs discussed previously.

c. Searching for Administrative and Legislative Materials

• **By Citation.** If you know the citation to a C.F.R. provision, the *Federal Register*, or a public law number, use the "Get a Document" feature and type your citation.

• **By Topic.** If you do not have a citation, select "Search" and then "Find a Source" at the top of your screen and then type the source you desire (for example, "CFR") in the open field. Type your terms or connectors, use Natural Language or Easy Search in the open field, and select "Search."

• **Legislative History.** Lexis offers several compiled legislative histories. Select "Legal," then "Federal Legal—U.S.," and then "Legislative History Materials."

d. Searching for Law Reviews and Journals

• **By Citation.** Use the "Get a Document" feature if you know the citation to a law review or journal article.

• **By Topic.** When you do not have a citation, use the "Search" and then "Guided Search Form" tabs. Select "Law Reviews" and enter your search terms.

• **By Law Reviews.** Select the "Search" and then "All" tabs at the top of the toolbar and then select "Secondary Legal" and "Law Reviews, CLE, Legal Journals & Periodicals, Combined." Type in your key terms in the open field. Click "Search." Alternatively, you may select specific journals in which to conduct your research.

e. Searching for Secondary Authorities

You may search for secondary authorities by selecting the tab "Search" and then the subtab "All" from the toolbar and then clicking on "Secondary Legal," and then selecting the specific secondary source desired, such as "A.L.R." or "Area of Law Treatises." Alternatively, you may select the tabs "Search" and then "by Topic or Headnote" at the top of the toolbar, and then select a desired area of law (for example, Bankruptcy Law or Torts) to be directed to a list of selected sources.

4. Shepardizing

As will be discussed in Chapter 11, Lexis makes it easy to verify that your cases, statutes, and other primary authorities are still valid. To do so, you may click the Shepard's tab, type your citation in the open field, and click "Check." Alternatively, when you are viewing a case or statute on the screen, watch for the "signal indicators" on the screen. For example, a red stop sign is a warning that your case has been subject to some negative treatment (such as being reversed).

5. Other Lexis Features

Lexis offers numerous features to make your research efficient and accurate.

• **Hyperlinking.** As you read a case, statute, or other authority on the screen, references to other cases or authorities are hyperlinked, allowing you to jump to these other documents by merely placing your cursor on the item displayed.

• **Additional Resources.** Select the "More" tab from the top of your toolbar for access to related products and services, such as "Lexis Transactional Advisor," which allows you to review numerous practice guides and resources related to transactional or business practice as well as a variety of litigation-related tools.

• **Alerts.** By selecting the Alerts tab, you can save a search and schedule it to run again in the future so you can receive updates by e-mail for issues you are monitoring.

• **Practitioner's Toolbox.** When federal statutes or statutes from selected states are displayed on the screen, a Practitioner's Toolbox will appear on the right side of the screen, directing you to the history of the statute and related helpful research resources.

• **Segment Searching.** Lexis allows you to restrict your search using segments. For example, you can select "dissent" or "court" to narrow your research. You can also use date restrictions to locate cases before or after a certain date. A menu allows you to select your desired time period.

• **More Like This.** This feature allows you to find other cases or authorities similar to the one you have identified as relevant to your research. You may also highlight the desired text and click "More Like Selected Text" and then "Search" to locate documents with similar content.

• **Briefs and Records.** As you view a case on your screen, look in the Related Content section for "Case File" so you can review the briefs and arguments filed by the attorneys involved in the displayed case. These briefs may give you ideas for drafting your own briefs and memoranda. Briefs are not offered for all cases.

• **Help.** Lexis offers researchers two different types of assistance: A "Help" button displayed on the screen allows researchers to access drop-down menus with explanations of Lexis features; researchers may also e-mail questions asking for help from Lexis's customer support. This real-time chat support provides immediate assistance.

• **Lexis Web.** The Lexis Web button (found on the "All" screen) allows you to search for legal resources on the Internet and on Lexis itself. All materials are validated by Lexis editors. Enter your search term (such as "corporate governance") in the open field, select "Search," and you will be provided with a list of government and commercial resources as well as links to legal blogs mentioning your term.

• **Lexis Communities.** You may elect to join Lexis's "Communities," which will give you free access to blogs, podcasts, and more. You may select a "community" or practice area, such as Litigation or Bankruptcy, and you will receive daily alerts of new issues and have access to more than 1,000 podcasts, videocasts, and other legal resources. Access http://www.lexisnexis.com/community/portal.

• **Affiliated Services.** Lexis offers numerous complementary services. For example, "Company Dossier" provides business information on more than 80 million companies worldwide, including company overviews, financial reports, and more. The "Academic" service offers documents from nearly 15,000 legal, news, and business publications.

6. *Lexis Advance*

In late 2011, Lexis launched a new research platform called Lexis Advance. Recall that the standard Lexis service usually requires you to select sets of books, a jurisdiction, or a source before you search. Lexis Advance mimics the ease of Google-type searches. A red all-in-one search box allows you to enter any search terms (or a citation or popular name) you like. (See Figure 8-5.) Lexis Advance then searches across all of its content as well as the Web and displays results for you. Alternatively, rather than using the single search box, you may elect to browse a list of topics or view a list of sources to find a specific source, such as a treatise. About 95 percent of Lexis customers automatically have access to Lexis Advance. Lexis Advance provides the following helpful features:

Figure 8-5
Lexis Advance Home Page Screen

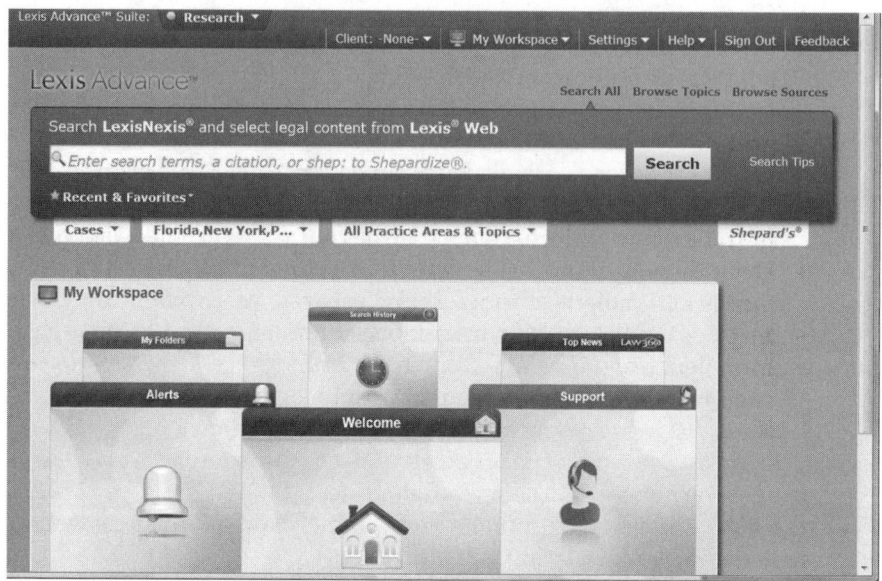

- **My Workspace.** Your "My Workspace" page provides a colorful and visual "carousel" allowing you to review your prior search history, your work folders, and more. (See Figure 8-5.)
- **Viewing Results.** When you view the results of your search on the screen, you will have access to related briefs and motions and Topic Summary Reports (which provide basic information about an area of law, including definitions, links to landmark cases, and more). Select "Snapshot" to view an overview of the top search results from each content type (for example, the top cases, statutes, and secondary authorities that respond to your search).
- **Filters.** You may filter your search before you run it or afterwards, by selecting particular jurisdictions, specific practice areas, or content. These filters allow you to refine the results you are given, by date, jurisdiction, and other fields.
- **Legal Issue Trail.** Lexis Advance will place a "box" around each issue in a case. By clicking on any boxed issue, you will be given links to other cases that deal with the same point of law.
- **Work Folders.** You may create folders and move your search results, documents (which you may annotate with your own comments), links, and notes into these folders.
- **Research History.** Your research history is automatically saved for 90 days, so if you are interrupted, you may avoid having to

re-do a search. A "Research Map" gives you a graphical depiction of your research steps so you may resume your research if you are interrupted.

- **Sheparding.** As you view a result, look for the Shepard's indicator at the top of your page, which will show you at a glance the subsequent history of your authority. Appellate history of a case is shown in a flowchart map and in a graphical grid format. The grid allows you to quickly comprehend how many cases treated your authority positively, questioned it, or merely cited it.
- **Alerts.** You may set up alerts to be notified of changes that occur in the areas of interest to you or in your Shepardizing results.
- **Delivery Options.** You may print, download, or e-mail documents and folders to yourself and others.
- **Support.** Click the "Live Support" tab to access real-time help.
- **Mobile Apps.** Lexis Advance is available for mobile devices such as iPhones and iPads. You may thus find authorities and Shepardize them on the go.

7. *Quick Review of Lexis*

a. To use Lexis:
b. Establish your Internet connection and access http://www.lexis.com.
c. Sign on by typing in your Lexis user number, identification number, or password.
d. Type in the client or billing number.
e. If you know a citation to a case, statute, or other authority, select "Get a Document" at the top of your screen, enter the citation, and click "Get."
f. Use one of the Search tabs when you are unsure where to start your legal research. Click on topics until you reach the most relevant topic, select a jurisdiction, type key words into the search boxes (using Terms and Connectors, Natural Language, or Easy Search), and click "Search" to access relevant cases, treatises, and other materials. Examine your results and Shepardize all primary authorities.

C. Westlaw

1. *Getting Started*

The information in Westlaw is contained in *databases* (analogous to Lexis's "sources") and *files*. Westlaw includes more than 16,000 databases, more than 6,800 news and business publications, and more than 700 law reviews.

Within each database there may be several files. For example, within the database called "Federal Materials" are files for federal cases and federal statutes. You can access Westlaw through the Internet at http://www.westlaw.com. As discussed previously, Westlaw offers its original computer-assisted legal research service, called "Westlaw Classic," and WestlawNext, its enhanced service. This section of the chapter will first discuss Westlaw Classic and then WestlawNext. After you enter your password and client identification, the first screen of Westlaw Classic (see Figure 8-6) will provide you with several shortcut choices, including the following:

- **Find by Citation.** "Find by citation" allows you to find a case, statute, or other document by its citation. Type your citation (such as 11 p3d 105) and click "Go." You need not use correct citation form. Moreover, Westlaw provides citation templates to help you enter your citation.
- **KeyCite.** KeyCite allows you to enter a citation and ensure your authority is still valid (analogous to Shepardizing on Lexis).
- **Search for a Database.** This feature allows you to enter a database identifier (such as "ALLFEDS" for all federal cases) and access that database for searching.
- **Resources.** Westlaw's first screen allows you to select a number of resources, including cases, statutes, the Restatements, C.F.R., Am. Jur. 2d, and so on, and then begin your search by entering words into the search box displayed (using Terms and Connectors or Natural Language).
- **Directory.** If you do not know where to begin, select "Directory" at the top of the screen toolbar for access to Westlaw's list of resources. You can then click and select your desired resource.

Figure 8-6
Westlaw Classic Resources Screen

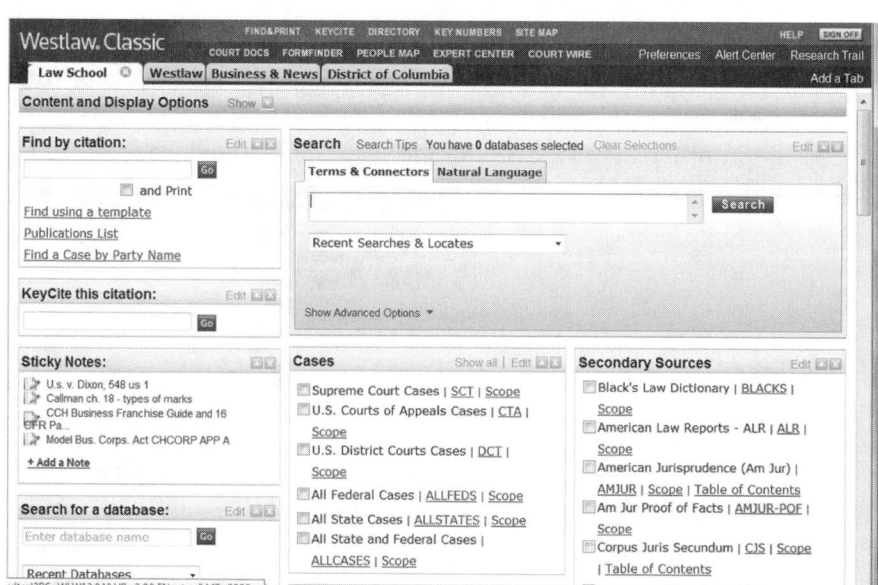

2. *Constructing a Search*

If you do not have a citation, you must construct a search or formulate a *query*. As soon as you access a database, Westlaw will prompt you to enter your query. You may search by Terms and Connectors or Natural Language.

a. Boolean Searching

Following are some tips for constructing a search query using Terms and Connectors on Westlaw. Note that many of these are either similar or identical to the Lexis terms and connectors. (See Figure 8-1.)

- **Lowercase Letters.** Like Lexis, Westlaw is not sensitive to capital letters (unless you specify such). Thus, for basic searching, use lowercase letters.
- **Singulars, Possessives, and Plurals.** Forms of singular, possessives, and plurals are automatically found if they are regular forms. Thus, a search for "deed" will produce results for "deeds" and "deed's."
- **Universal Symbols.** Westlaw offers some universal symbols to help you expand your search:

    - An *asterisk* (*) replaces single letters within words. Thus, "advis*r" will retrieve advisor and adviser.
    - An *exclamation point* (!) replaces any ending to a word. Thus, "valu!" will retrieve value, valued, valuation, and so forth.

- **Connectors.** Connectors help you locate needed documents and narrow your search. Following are the most commonly used connectors:

    - **Or.** In Westlaw, the "or" connector is represented by a single space. Thus, a search for "landlord lessor" will locate documents containing either or both of these words.
    - **And (&).** A search for "landlord & covenant" will locate documents only if they contain both these terms.
    - **/n.** The connector "/n" instructs Westlaw to find documents that contain words appearing within a specified number(n) of words of each other. Thus, a search for "fraud /25 contract agreement" locates documents in which the word "fraud" appears within 25 words of the term "contract" or "agreement."
    - **/s and /p.** The connector "/s" finds words in the same sentence, and "/p" finds words in the same paragraph. Thus, a search for "patent /s infringement" (or "patent /p infringement") locates documents in which the words "patent" and "infringement" appear in the same sentence or paragraph, respectively.

Westlaw offers other connectors as well; they are described in Westlaw's User Guide "Westlaw Quick Reference Guide: Getting Started on Westlaw," available at http://legalsolutions.thomsonreuters.com/law-products (select "User Guides"). The most commonly used Terms and Connectors are also displayed on the screen on which you construct your query, allowing you to pick and choose the connectors desired.

Constructing a proper search is the most important part of computerized legal research because a poorly constructed search query will produce too few or too many documents. Remember to draft your search query before you sign on and costs are assessed. If your search does not produce sufficient results (or else produces too many documents), you may edit your search. Select "Edit Search" at the top of the screen, and modify your search by adding additional terms and connectors.

b. Plain English Searching

Just as Lexis allows searching by plain English, so does Westlaw. When you select a database and the search box is displayed, simply click on "Natural Language." A new search box is given, into which you type your query in plain English. You will be given prompts to add related terms or to restrict by date. (See Figure 8-7.)

c. Database Wizard

Just as Lexis's Search tabs help you find the right sources, Westlaw's *Database Wizard* walks you through the process of picking the right

Figure 8-7
Westlaw Classic Sample Search Screen

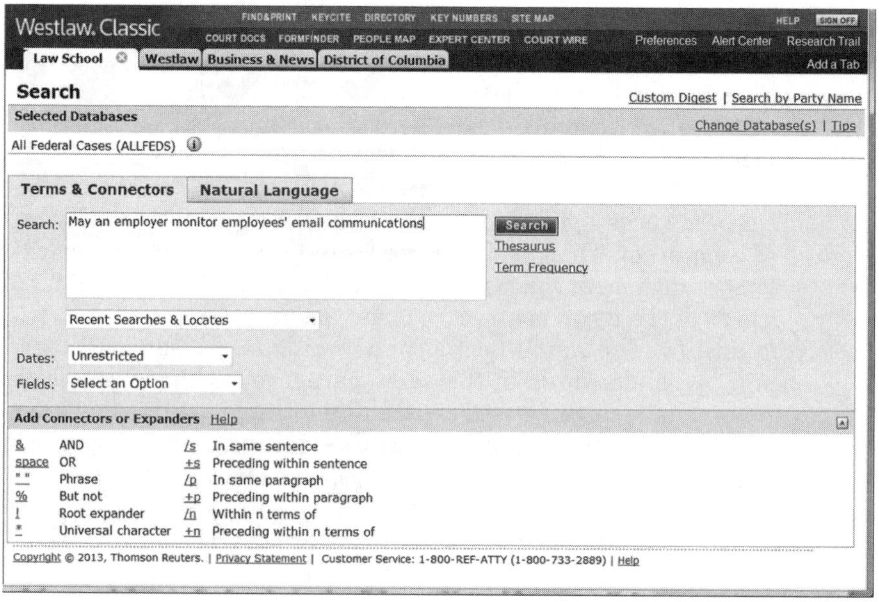

database to meet your research needs. After you select the tab "Directory," select "Find a Database Wizard." You will be asked a series of questions about what you are trying to find, and the "Wizard" will help you select the right database by continually narrowing your options.

d. Display of Search Results

Once your search results are shown on your Westlaw screen, there are several methods you can use to browse the materials to determine if they are on point. Citations to cases that respond to your query will be listed with your search terms (for example, "patent infringement") banded in yellow. Select as desired. After you select your desired case or result, the "ResultsPlus" feature on the left side of your screen displays additional sources that may be of help, such as references to A.L.R. annotations or articles in *Am. Jur. Proof of Facts*. (See Figure 8-8.)

When you select the full text of a case, you can select "Locate in Result" from the menu on the screen and type in terms you wish to find in the document. Thus, you can type in "damages" and Westlaw will locate any use of that word in the document being displayed. Cases include the same features as in West's conventional print volumes, meaning that headnotes and topic names and Key Numbers are given (although Key Numbers are shown in a different format from those used in conventional print volumes).

Figure 8-8
<u>Viewing Westlaw Classic Results</u>

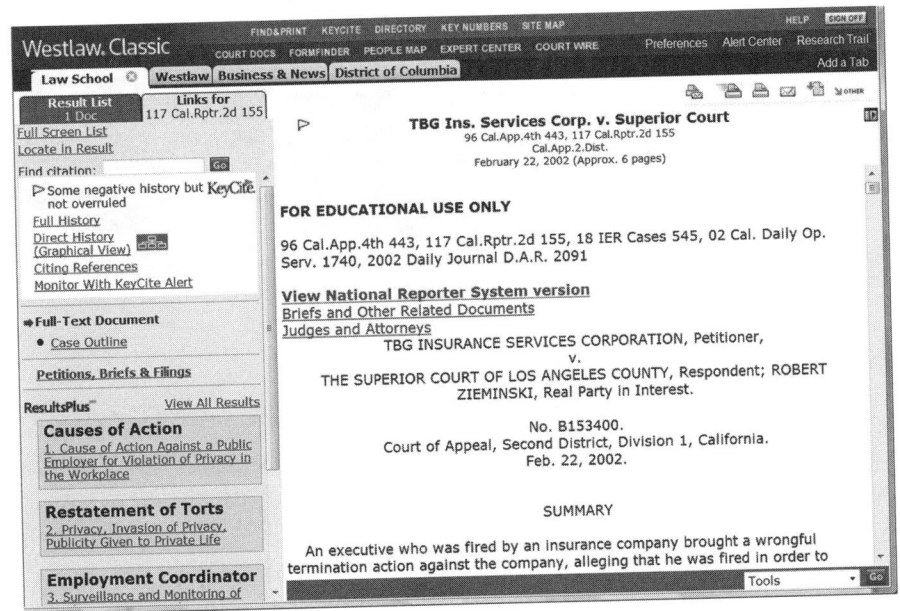

3. *Specialized Searches*

a. Searching for Statutes and Constitutions

• **By Citation.** If you know the citation to a statute or a constitution, select the tab "Find by citation," type the citation in the search box (for example, 17 usca 109), and click "Go." You will be given the statute, library references, and annotations.

• **By Topic.** If you do not have a citation, select a database. For example, for federal statutes, select the database "USCA" from your home screen. You will then need to decide whether you will search by Terms and Connectors or Natural Language (or you may browse the index to U.S.C.A.). Type your search in the search box and click "Search." Westlaw's recently added feature "Statutes Results Plus" provides links to other sources (cases, other statutes, administrative code references, and legislative history documents) that discuss your statute. You will also be informed if pending legislation might affect your statute.

b. Searching for Cases

• **By Citation.** If you know a case citation, use the "Find by citation" tab, enter your citation in the search box (for example, 520 us 788), and click "Go."

• **By Topic.** If you do not have a citation, select "Directory" and then an appropriate database, such as all federal cases or cases from Texas, and then formulate your query by using Terms and Connectors or Natural Language.

- Remember to use "ResultsPlus" to expand your research efforts. References to additional sources such as A.L.R. annotations are automatically displayed on the screen with your search results when you conduct case law research on Westlaw.
- Westlaw includes star paging to inform you of the page number you would be on if you were reading the case in parallel sets for the case.
- If the note "West Reporter Image PDF" is shown on the screen, you may select this to view your case same easy-to-read format you're used to seeing in print reporters.

c. Searching for Administrative and Legislative Materials

• **By Citation.** If you know the citation to a provision in either C.F.R. or the *Federal Register*, you may enter it in the "Find by citation" search box.

• **By Topic.** You can search through the C.F.R., the *Federal Register*, and other sources by accessing the pertinent database from your first search screen and then entering your search query in the search box, using either Terms and Connectors or Natural Language. Alternatively, by selecting "Directory" from the top toolbar, you can select "Topical Practice Areas" and then select the field in which you are interested, such as "Energy."

 • **Legislative History.** Westlaw also includes numerous legislative history documents, including bills, the *Congressional Record*, and compiled legislative histories for certain statutes. Select "Directory" from the toolbar and then "U.S. Federal Materials" and then "Legislative History" (or "Arnold & Porter Collection—Legislative Histories" for numerous compiled legislative histories).

d. Searching for Law Reviews and Journals

When you sign onto Westlaw, the first screen displays the entry "Journals and Law Reviews." Once you select that database, you then enter your search query using Terms and Connectors or Natural Language. Alternatively, you may enter an author's name or title of article, or you may enter a citation to a law review article in the "Find by citation" box. You may also select "Directory" from the top toolbar and then select "Law Reviews," allowing you to search within specifically named law reviews and journals.

e. Searching for Secondary Authorities

When you sign onto Westlaw, a category titled "Secondary Sources" allows you to search through a number of secondary sources, including the Restatements, A.L.R., and other secondary sources. Alternatively, select "Directory" from the top toolbar, and then review the various sources listed, including "Treatises," "Directories, Reference," and others. Select the database you wish to search and proceed to enter your query.

4. *KeyCiting*

To update and validate your primary authorities when using Westlaw, use its service called "KeyCite." The service and process is highly similar to Shepardizing using Lexis. Westlaw's first screen provides a search box titled "KeyCite this citation." Enter your citation into the search box, click "Go," and view your results. Alternatively, when you are viewing a case or statute on the screen, watch for the "signal indicators" on the screen. For example, a yellow flag signals caution. KeyCiting is discussed in detail in Chapter 11.

5. *Other Westlaw Features*

Like Lexis, Westlaw offers a number of added features to make legal research easy and efficient, including the following:

- **Hyperlinking.** As you read through various authorities, references to other authorities will appear in a bright blue color as hyperlinks, which allow you to click and be immediately transported to them.
- **Clipping Service.** WestClip and Alert are electronic clipping services that allow you to monitor topics of interest to you and to update your KeyCiting, respectively; you will receive automatic e-mail notices when there are changes affecting the cases or statutes in which you are interested.
- **Database Wizard.** To help you select the right database for your search, Westlaw's Database Wizard provides questions and prompts and then suggests the best database for you.
- **Key Numbers.** Select "Key Numbers" at the top of the Westlaw toolbar and you can enter descriptive terms into the open search box or you may browse various topics and subtopics to locate topic names and key numbers so you can find numerous cases dealing with the same area of the law.
- **Field Searching.** Like Lexis, Westlaw allows you to retrieve only part of a document or to view documents by name or date. After you select a database, you can restrict your search to search by court, date, judge, topic, or other fields. Drop-down menus help you select fields and dates.
- **Graphical Display of Direct History for Cases.** A recently added Westlaw feature shows you the direct history of your case in an easy-to-understand flowchart format. For example, you would be shown in graphical format, using arrows, how your case progressed from trial, through its initial appeal, when certiorari was granted, and then what the U.S. Supreme Court held. You may easily link to the court briefs and motions filed at each level of the case's history.
- **Graphical Display of Timelines for Statutes.** West now displays timelines for federal statutes and some state statutes, allowing you to link to prior versions of your statute and relevant legislative history. You will also be informed of any pending legislation affecting your statute.
- **Briefs and Records.** Like Lexis, Westlaw also provides access to briefs and petitions filed in many cases. As you view your case on the screen, look for a link to "Briefs and Other Related Documents."
- **Live Help.** Like Lexis, Westlaw offers researchers the opportunity to initiate real-time chat to ask for help and assistance. Simply click the "Help" tab, type in your question, and customer support will respond to your question in moments.
- **Affiliated Services.** Westlaw offers several affiliated services, including the following: "Westlaw Business," a comprehensive collection of materials exclusively for business professionals; FormFinder, which helps you draft forms; and Westlaw Litigator, a complete service for legal professionals engaged in litigation, affording access to jury instructions, court briefs and records, motions, experts, and more.

6. *WestlawNext*

In Spring 2010, West introduced a new electronic research system called WestlawNext. Generally, WestlawNext mimics the ease of use of Google's search engine. Researchers who use WestlawNext will no longer have to choose a specific database before conducting a search (which often presents problems to researchers who may not know where to begin a search). A single search box presented on a clean, uncluttered screen asks WestlawNext researchers to enter "search terms, citations, databases, anything." (See Figure 8-9.) The results presented are ranked in their order of relevance, across multiple databases. For example, when searching on Westlaw Classic, one might select a database of federal cases. A search query is entered, and the results presented are limited, of course, to a list of federal cases. A user of WestlawNext enters search terms in plain English in a search box, and the results presented would include cases, statutes, A.L.R. annotations, and numerous other relevant resources.

Alternatively, rather than using the single search box, you may elect to browse a list of sources to find a specific source, such as federal cases or secondary sources. These content sources are listed on your home page. (See Figure 8-9.) You may also edit your home page so that it displays the sources you most frequently view. Users of WestlawNext pay a subscription fee in addition to the fee they pay for Westlaw. WestlawNext provides the following helpful features:

- **Overview of Results.** After you conduct a search, the center portion of your screen will display the documents that are most responsive to your search query, ranked by their relevance. The left side of your screen will display an overview list of your results, informing you how many cases contain your term, how many secondary sources mention your term, and so forth. When you select one of these content areas (for example, "Cases"), the right side of your screen will direct you to "Related Documents," such as secondary sources that are related to your search.
- **Related Topics.** When you are viewing a certain result (for example, a case), the right side of your screen will direct you to "Related Topics."
- **Filters.** After you select a certain content category, such as "Cases," you may sort and filter your results. For example, you may view cases only after a certain date or from a specific court.
- **Sticky Notes.** When a document is displayed on your screen, you may "annotate" it just as you would a printed document, by adding a "sticky note" to the screen with your comments.
- **Research History.** To view your recent searches, select "History" from the top of your toolbar. You will be given a list of the five most recent documents you viewed. Alternatively, you may elect to "View all" to display all of your searches for the past one year.

Figure 8-9
WestlawNext Home Page Screen

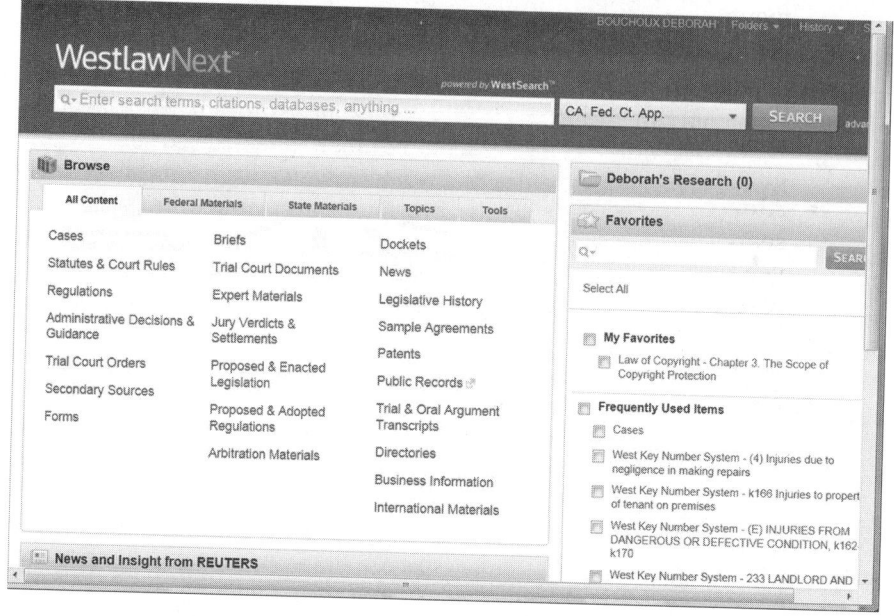

- **Key Number System.** To use West's Key Number System on WestlawNext, select "Tools" from your sign-on page and then select "West Key Number System." Select the topic name you desire (for example, "Landlord and Tenant") and then, using drop-down menus, select the particular issue you wish to research (for example, "Injuries to a tenant's property").

- **Citation Preferences.** WestlawNext provides assistance with citations. For example, you may elect either to italicize or underscore case names, to include parallel citations, or to select *Bluebook* citation form (which is the default approach), *ALWD* citation form, or a jurisdiction-specific citation form, such as California or Texas citation form. Look for the "Preferences" button at the bottom of your screen, and then select "Citations." Set your preferences. Then whenever you highlight text, select "Copy with Preferences." When you drop this text into any document, the citation will be formatted according to your preferences. You may have to tweak the citation a bit, but significant help is given.

- **Research Folders.** You may drag and drop information, citations, text, and more into research folders that you create and name (for example "Moore Litigation") and may share with others.

- **KeyCiting.** You may KeyCite cases, statutes, regulations, and more. You may enter a citation into the all-in-one search box on your home screen and then KeyCite it, or you may KeyCite documents that are being displayed on your screen. If a document you are viewing has a yellow or red status flag, the most negative (and thus, the most important) treatment is displayed next to the flag at the top of your screen. Look for the "History" tabs to be shown a graphical picture of your case's history or a graphical display of your statute.

- **Alerts.** You may elect to receive automatic alerts when your search results have been updated by relevant new material, or you may elect to have KeyCite run an automatic update on your cases, statutes, and more.

- **Delivery Options.** You may e-mail, print, or download any of your results.

- **Help.** Look for the "Help" button at the bottom of your screen to gain access to documentation and online tutorials. A "Live Chat" button provides you immediate help from a skilled editor.

- **Mobile Applications.** WestlawNext is available on smart phones, on iPad tablets, and as an app. Thus, you may find and KeyCite your authorities from any location.

7. *Quick Review of Westlaw Classic*

To use Westlaw:

a. Establish your Internet connection and access http://www.west-law.com.

b. Sign on by typing in your Westlaw user number, identification number, or password.

c. Type in the client or billing number.

d. If you know a citation to a case, statute, or other authority, select "Find by citation" at the top of your screen, enter the citation, and click "Go."

e. If you do not know where to start, you must select an appropriate database. Select "Directory" from your toolbar and browse the databases. Select the desired database (or allow the Database Wizard to help you). Enter your query into the search box, using Terms and Connectors or Natural Language. Review the materials presented, and KeyCite all primary authorities.

Help Line

Lexis and Westlaw Interactive Tutorials

Lexis and Westlaw both offer free online interactive training and tutorials (as well as useful print products) to help you learn to use their services.

* **Lexis.** For interactive training, access http://www.lexisnexis.com/ infopro/training. Take a tour of Lexis at http://web.lexis.com/help/ multimedia/detect.asp?sPage=mom2010. Print materials may be viewed and downloaded at http://www.lexisnexis.com/literature.
* **Lexis Advance.** For tips, webinars, literature, and training videos, access http://www.lexisnexis.com/en-us/support/lexis-advance/ default.page.
* **Westlaw.** For interactive training, access http://legalsolutions .thomsonreuters.com/law-products/product-support/training. For user guides and reference materials, access http://legalsolutions .thomsonreuters.com/law-products/product-support/user-guides.
* **WestlawNext.** For training materials, user guides, and videos, access http://info.legalsolutions.thomsonreuters.com/ westlawnext/learning-support/default.aspx.

D.　Final Pointers on Computer-Assisted Legal Research

1.　When to Use Lexis or Westlaw

Some tasks are best performed by using conventional print research tools, whereas others are best performed by using computer-assisted research services such as Lexis or Westlaw. Still other tasks might call for you to blend both methods of research. Knowing which method to use requires an analysis of many factors, including the complexity of your task, the costs involved, and time constraints. Many instructors urge students to first become familiar with the conventional print tools before becoming too wedded to computer-assisted legal research. Strong skills in manual legal research provide a good foundation for using Lexis and Westlaw more effectively.

Use conventional print sources when:

* You need to "get your feet wet" and get some background about an area of the law.
* You need a thorough and comprehensive analysis of an area of the law, such as that provided by a treatise.
* It would be more cost-effective and easier to use traditional print sources to get a quick answer to a question than to incur costs by using Lexis or Westlaw.

Use computer-assisted legal research when:

- You already have a citation to a known case or other authority.
- The area of law is new or evolving.
- You are looking for the most current information available.
- You are validating your primary authorities (by Shepardizing or KeyCiting).

Computer-assisted legal research is a valuable tool. The services provide rapid access to a wide range of materials that no law firm could afford to purchase or shelve. Nevertheless, computer-assisted legal research may be expensive and will produce useful results only if you understand how to make the systems work effectively for you. This takes practice and experience. Legal research is not as easy as merely inserting some words into a search box. Effective researchers use a combination of computer-assisted legal research and conventional research techniques to obtain the best results for clients.

2. *Limitations of Computer-Assisted Legal Research*

Following are some limitations of computer-assisted legal research:

- **Literalness.** Computers are extremely literal. Thus, a search for "teacher" will not produce results including "instructor." Construct your search query carefully before you sign on and begin incurring costs.
- **Cost.** There are numerous pricing variations for Lexis and Westlaw. Large law firms pay flat rates, allowing unlimited use of Lexis and Westlaw by their legal professionals. Hourly pricing can range from $10 to $800 per hour, depending on the files accessed and the time of day the service is used.
- **Database Limitations.** There are some limitations to the Lexis and Westlaw databases. To determine the date limitations of publications and materials, consult Lexis's and Westlaw's database lists at the following sites, respectively: http://w3.nexis.com/sources and http://directory .westlaw.com/?tf=90&tc=11.

E. Other Competitors in Electronic Research

Although Lexis and Westlaw are the acknowledged giants in the field of computer-assisted legal research, a number of other companies offer access to legal materials through the Internet. Most charge moderate fees and appeal to small firms and sole practitioners. Some cater to government users.

- **Bloomberg Law** (http://about.bloomberglaw.com). The most significant competitor to Lexis and Westlaw is Bloomberg Law, launched in 2009 by Bloomberg Finance L.P., the global business and financial news provider. Bloomberg Law offers a comprehensive collection of federal and state materials, secondary sources such as treatises and practice materials, and in-depth company information, all of which are provided for a flat fee. A number of experts expect Bloomberg Law to pose a serious threat to Lexis and Westlaw. Some of Bloomberg Law's features include the following: a universal "GO" bar for searching by key word, Boolean connectors, or citation; "Practice Areas" that integrate primary and secondary materials for topics such as Intellectual Property and Corporate/M&A; user-friendly tools such as alerts, workspace folders, and research history trails; and BCite, Bloomberg's citation service that informs you if cases are still good law.

- **LoislawConnect** (http://www.loislaw.com). LoislawConnect, a service of Wolters Kluwer, offers case law, statutes, constitutions, administrative law, court rules, and more for all states and the federal courts. LoislawConnect offers a more comprehensive database than many of the other services described in this section, including all federal and state primary materials as well as treatise and forms libraries for a wide variety of secondary sources, such as estate planning and family law. Moreover, LoislawConnect offers *GlobalCite*, a service similar to Shepardizing, which refers you to cases that mention or discuss the case you are researching. Low monthly flat fees are charged.

- **VersusLaw** (http://www.versuslaw.com). VersusLaw provides access to federal and state cases, statutes, and other legal sources for as low as $14 per month.

- **PACER** (http://www.pacer.gov). Public Access to Court Electronic Records or PACER, a service of the U.S. Judiciary, allows users to obtain case and docket information from all federal courts (for modest fees). The PACER system offers electronic access to a listing of all parties and participants in cases, documents filed for certain cases, case status, and other useful information. For example, if you wish to review the bankruptcy filings for American Airlines, you may access the court files and review all documents filed in the matter.

- **Fastcase** (http://www.fastcase.com). Fastcase is a fee-based legal research system that allows its subscribers access to a vast array of federal and state cases and statutes. Secondary authorities are being added. Its libraries are searchable in a variety of ways, from "Google"-type searches, to citation lookup, to natural language and Boolean searching. A number of state bar associations have purchased Fastcase subscriptions for all of their members. Although Fastcase does not verify or update authorities like Shepard's or KeyCite do, its product Authority Check will inform you the number of times a case has been cited. Most impressive, Fastcase offers affordable pricing and a free iPhone app so busy professionals can readily conduct legal research while commuting, in the courtroom, or before an important meeting. Fastcase also provides a free app

for iPhones, allowing access to cases, statutes, and more (access http://www.fastcase.com/iphone to download the app).
   • **Casemaker** (http://www.casemaker.us). Casemaker provides access to federal and state primary materials as well as practice guides at low cost. In addition, more than 25 state and local bar associations have partnered with Casemaker to provide their members free access to these materials. Casemaker offers a Google-like universal search bar, search history features so users can save and reuse their research results, and the ability to store research in folders. Casemaker's citation service, CaseCheck+, provides a green "thumbs up" to indicate your authority is still good law and a red "thumbs down" to indicate negative treatment.

F.   Non-Print Research Tools

In addition to computer-assisted legal research, there are some other non-print tools that legal researchers should know how to use: microforms, sound recordings, CD-ROMs and DVDs, and eBooks.

1.   *Microforms*

a.   Types of Microforms

Microforms are based on the principle of microphotography: Images are reduced and placed on rolls or sheets of film. A microfilm reader is then used to review the images recorded on the film. The readers resemble a television screen and are usually equipped with printers so you may obtain copies of the material being viewed. There are three main types of microforms:

   • **Microfilm.** *Microfilm* is a reel of film that is threaded into a reader. Although microfilm saves storage space, it has not been widely used for legal materials. It is, however, often used for government records, land records, newspapers, and other materials. The image shown on the screen is often fuzzy, and the prints reproduced may be difficult to read.
   • **Microfiche.** *Microfiche* is a microform displayed on a thin transparent celluloid flat sheet rather than on a roll of film. Each sheet of microfiche may contain images of up to 400 pages. Probably the best known use of microfiche for legal research is ProQuest's *CIS Congressional Bills, Resolutions, & Laws on Microfiche*, used to compile legislative histories. Many law libraries maintain their legislative history materials on microfiche.
   • **Ultrafiche.** *Ultrafiche* is a type of microfiche with a high reduction ratio. As many as 1,800 pages of text can be held on a single sheet

of ultrafiche. West has reproduced many older volumes of its National Reporter System in ultrafiche, with each sheet replacing one hardbound volume.

b. Summary of Microforms

All microforms save storage space. Although their use for non-legal purposes has been broad, their role in legal research has never really taken hold. A notable exception is that microfiche may be used for the materials making up a legislative history. Ask your law librarian what materials are available in microform at your law library.

2. Sound Recordings

Many continuing legal education programs are offered for those in the legal profession. Professionals may attend the seminars or programs in person or may usually purchase a sound recording, or CD-ROM or DVD of the program. Law firms often use video for mock trials, helping to sharpen attorneys' skills as well as point out certain characteristics of client witnesses that may bear on credibility. Some firms use videotape presentations to introduce clients to certain routine matters, such as providing clients with basic information about having a deposition taken. Videotapes are often used at trials to show the jury an accident scene or in criminal prosecutions to show occurrence of the crime itself (such as bank robbery or shoplifting).

3. CD-ROMs, DVDs, and eBooks

CD-ROMs and DVDs are highly efficient storage media; they may contain more than 200,000 pages of text. CD-ROMs and DVDs have replaced the earlier technology of floppy disks. Many legal materials are available in CD-ROM form, such as the *Martindale-Hubbell Law Directory*. Lexis and Westlaw both make cases, statutes, and practice guides available on CD-ROM and DVD. One disk can take the place of several bound volumes. For example, West's *Federal Supplement* (since 1980) is available on five disks. Searching is easy, making it efficient to locate cases by citation, party name, key words, or other elements. The CD or DVD can be used with a portable laptop computer and small printer, enabling legal professionals to perform valuable research at home or while traveling. Their use at trial can be extremely valuable. If adverse counsel cites an unfamiliar case, you can insert a CD or DVD and locate the case. Because disks containing new cases and statutes must be purchased, most publishers issue new disks (for a fee) and take back old ones at periodic intervals. The cost for CD-ROM and DVD products is about the same as for their print counterparts.

A newer trend is the offering of eBooks, which are books available in digital form and readable on computers or other electronic devices.

Law-related eBooks are available for downloading onto devices such as iPads, NOOK and Kindle readers, and more. Lexis, West, and Wolters Kluwer offer hundreds of books (including court rules, treatises, student textbooks, and practice guides) on the mobile device of your choice. Advantages of eBooks include their portability, the ability to add notes to the text, and the ability to easily search content. Lexis's eBooks link to Lexis Advance and West's eBooks link to WestlawNext, so you can gain easy access to authorities cited in your eBook. The home pages of each publisher will provide links to the titles and publications available as eBooks.

G. Citation Form

	Bluebook (for practitioners)	*ALWD*
Lexis Case	*Smith v. Jones*, No. 05-233, 2006 U.S. App. LEXIS 19334, at *3 (1st Cir. May 15, 2006).	*Smith v. Jones*, 2006 U.S. App. LEXIS 19334 at *3 (1st Cir. May 15, 2006).
Westlaw Case	*Allen v. Bailey*, No. 05-CV-310, 2006 WL 12656, at *2 (S.D.N.Y. June 10, 2006).	*Allen v. Bailey*, 2005 WL 12656 at *2 (S.D.N.Y. June 10, 2006).

Internet Resources

http://www.lexisnexis.com	Lexis's home page; select "Training and Support" to learn more about Lexis's features and offerings or "Communities" to receive access to free, validated legal resources for various practice areas. Numerous tips and resources are provided.
https://web2.westlaw.com/signon	Westlaw Classic's home page allows you to point and click to review its databases, learn about training options, and view its helpful User Guides, including those for WestlawNext.
http://www.law.georgetown.edu/library/research/tutorials/index.cfm	Georgetown Law Center offers tutorials on performing research using Lexis and Westlaw.

Research Assignment for Lexis

Unless directed otherwise, use Lexis rather than Lexis Advance.

1. Select "Get a Document" and "Get by Citation." Retrieve the case located at 99 S. Ct. 2282.
    a. What is the Lexis database number or citation for this case?
    b. How does page 261 of the official *United States Reports* begin?
    c. Select the yellow triangle shown for this case.
        i. Why was the yellow triangle assigned to this case?
        ii. Select "FOCUS–Restrict by" and then select to retrieve only cases from the Seventh Circuit that explain headnote one of your case. To which 1986 case are you directed? Give the case name only.
    d. Return to your original case. Review "Related Content." To which law review article are you directed (give only the citation)?
    e. Return to your original case. Select "TOA." How many cases were cited in your case?
2. Select "Search" at the top of your toolbar and then select "Search By Topic or Headnote." Select "Business & Corporate Law" and then select "Joint Ventures." Select to review only California cases. Using Natural Language, locate cases addressing the personal liability of joint venturers.
    a. To which 1963 California Court of Appeals case are you directed?
    b. Select the case and review its Case Summary. What was the outcome of this case?
3. At the top of the toolbar, select "More" and then "Research Tasks." Select "Trademarks and Copyrights." Use Natural Language to locate cases dealing with joint authorship of copyrights within the past five years. To which 2012 case from the Second Circuit are you directed?
4. Select "Get a Document" and "Get by Citation." Retrieve the case located at 413 F.3d 3.
    a. What is the name of the case?
    b. Select "More Like This" and then select to review U.S. Supreme Court cases within the past five years. To which case are you directed that was decided on January 10, 2012?

c. Select this case. Elect to view available briefs and other documents. Review the Petition for Writ of Certiorari. From which circuit did this case originate? Which law firm submitted the Petition?

5. Select "Get a Document" and "Get by Docket Number." What is the name of the Wisconsin Court of Appeals Case assigned Docket or Appeal Number 02-2192?

6. Select "Get a Document" and "By Party Name." Locate the 2012 U.S. Supreme Court case in which the defendant's name is *Prometheus*.
   a. Give the name of the case and its citation.
   b. Retrieve the case. Select "TOA." How many decisions were cited by your case?

7. Use Lexis Advance. Using the red search box, search for the case published at 557 U.S. 557. Select the "Topic Summaries–View Report" and select the second report listed. To which statutes are you directed?

8. Use Lexis Advance. Using the red search box, search for information on the discharge of a debtor by a court unless the debtor has concealed information.
   a. How many results are identified by your search?
   b. Select "Legis" at the top of the toolbar. What is the first statute to which you are directed?

9. Use Lexis Advance. Using the red search box, search for the "Kelly/Frye test." Generally, what does this test relate to?

Research Assignment for Westlaw

Unless directed otherwise, use Westlaw Classic rather than WestlawNext.

1. At the initial Westlaw screen, use the "Find by Citation" box and retrieve the case located at 530 U.S. 120.
   a. What is the name of this case?
   b. Select "ResultsPlus." To which C.J.S. reference are you directed?
   c. Retrieve the C.J.S. reference. To which Illinois case are you directed? Give the case name only.

2. At the initial Westlaw screen, select *Black's Law Dictionary* and locate the definition for "fiduciary."
   a. Briefly, what is the definition?
   b. To which topic and key number are you referred?

3. Select "Directory" and continue selecting the appropriate databases to search all California cases. Use Natural Language and develop a query to locate cases from California dealing with

state university disciplinary proceedings (and the requirement that these involve a fair hearing).

    a. To which 1972 California Appeals Court case are you directed?

    b. Retrieve this case. Select "Table of Authorities." How many cases are cited in the 1972 case?

    c. Return to the case. Select "ResultsPlus" and "View All Results." Select the first A.L.R. annotation. What section in the annotation discusses the due process clause as a basis of a right to a hearing prior to suspension or expulsion?

4. At the initial Westlaw screen, select "Find by Party Name" and locate a 2010 case in which the plaintiff's name is *Bilski*.

    a. What is the citation for the case?

    b. Select "Citing References." How many authorities cite your case?

5. Select "Key Numbers" from the top of the toolbar. Browse the Key Number Digest Outlines

    a. What number is assigned to obscenity?

    b. To which topic does Obscenity k253 relate?

6. Select the appropriate database for federal statutes.

    a. What statute deals with FISA (the Foreign Intelligence Surveillance Court)?

    b. Retrieve the statute. Give the citation to the 2001 Notre Dame Law Review Note that discusses this statute.

    c. Retrieve the law review Note and review the "Citing references" for this Note. How many secondary authorities cite this law review?

7. Locate a 2013 UCLA law review article relating to private equity and executive compensation.

    a. Who is the author of the article?

    b. Review page 646. What is one way to link CEO pay to shareholder value?

8. Use WestlawNext. Use the search box and search for the case published at 550 U.S. 81.

    a. What is the name of this case?

    b. What related topics are listed in the pane on the right side?

    c. Select "Filings" and review the Petition for Certiorari filed in this case. Briefly summarize the Question Presented.

9. Use WestlawNext. Select "Federal Materials" and then "C.F.R." Select Title 9. In the search box at the top of the screen, search for regulations relating to the procurement of dogs, cats, and other animals.

a. Which is the first section to which you are directed?
b. Review that section. If a dealer obtains a live dog or cat from a private pound or shelter, how long must the dog or cat be held?
c. Review the "Notes of Decisions." Which 1996 case has interpreted this provision?

10. Use WestlawNext. Select "Statutes and Court Rules" and then select Michigan statutes. In the search box, search for articles of organization for limited liability companies.
    a. What statute relates to the contents for articles of organization for limited liability companies?
    b. Review the statute. Select the treatise that cites your statute. Where is your statute cited in this treatise?

Research Assignment for LoislawConnect

1. Access the Popular Name Table for the U.S. Code. Give the citation to the USA Patriot Act.
2. Access Wisconsin statutes.
   a. To what topic does section 253.12 relate?
   b. Select "GlobalCite." What is the name of the most recent Wisconsin case that cites this statute?
3. At the Start Page, select "Court Rules" and then select the Federal Rules of Appellate Procedure. When must an appellant order the transcript of the record on appeal from the court reporter?
4. What is the status of 35 U.S.C. § 204?
5. At the Start Page, select "Power Search." In the search box, type in the case name *Diamond v. Diehr.* What was its citation at the U.S. Supreme Court?
6. At the Start Page, select "Power Search." Use the drop-down menu and select "Citations." What is the name of the case located at 684 F.2d 902?

Internet Assignment

1. Access Lexis's "Communities" at http://www.lexisnexis.com /community/portal. Select "Helpful Tips." What do Lexis's Podcasts offer researchers?

2. Access the site for Lexis Advance at http://www.lexisnexis .com/en-us/products/lexis-advance.page. Select "Literature" and review page 12 of the Lexis Advance Quick Reference Guide relating to using *Shepard's* Graphical for Citing References. What information does the Citing References Grid provide?

3. Access West's site at http://legalsolutions.thomsonreuters.com/ law-products. Select "User Guides" (see bottom of screen). Select "Searching WestlawNext" and then select the User Guide relating to Retrieving Secondary Sources. What are the two methods you can use to locate secondary sources such as treatises?

E-Research: Legal Research Using the Internet

Chapter Overview

The best legal researchers know how to use a combination of conventional and electronic research methods to achieve results. Although one need not be a computer guru to satisfy the duty to perform legal research competently, legal professionals should be sufficiently proficient in using the Internet that they can quickly find a case or statute. This chapter provides some strategies on conducting legal research on the Internet as well as some cautionary notes about over-relying on the Internet.

A. Introduction

Today's legal professionals have at their fingertips vast amounts of information that is free and available 24 hours each day. Until recently, a researcher wanting to review a newly issued Supreme Court decision had only two options: drive to a law library or subscribe to a fee-based service such as Lexis or Westlaw. The advent of the Internet has dramatically changed legal research, allowing professionals immediate access to cases, statutes, regulations, forms, and much more. In many instances, cases are posted by courts to the Internet within hours after their release. The good news is that there is a vast array of legal materials available for your use; the bad news is that the information is so voluminous that making sense of the materials offered can seem overwhelming.

Legal professionals typically use the Internet for the following purposes:

- **Communication.** Legal professionals use the Internet to communicate with each other and with clients.

- **Court Filings.** Many courts require or permit documents and motions to be filed electronically. In fact, all federal courts permit e-filing. Electronic filing allows courts to verify immediately word count requirements.
- **Marketing.** The American Bar Association reports that all law firms with 50 or more attorneys have a website, which is a marketing brochure about the firm that is published electronically rather than in print form. The site typically describes the firm, its professionals, its locations, and may provide articles on legal topics.
- **Commerce.** Legal professionals can order books, publications, and other materials from publishers and other vendors.
- **Education.** Legal professionals can take continuing education classes online and subscribe to educational newsletters and other informative materials.
- **Research.** Legal professionals can use the Internet to conduct research, including legal research. One can quickly determine an adversary's address, a client's exact corporate name, find a case, and track legislation. This chapter focuses on use of the Internet to conduct legal research.

The general duty of competence imposed on legal professionals to have a sufficient level of competence to represent their clients is broad enough to require competence in new and emerging technologies such as the Internet. Moreover, employers and clients are increasingly technologically proficient and will justifiably expect their legal team to be equally proficient, so that clients can be kept informed of the status of their matters by e-mail, documents can be filed electronically with courts, and others in the firm can access a client's files.

In addition, 2012 amendments to the American Bar Association's Model Rules of Professional Conduct make clear that an attorney's duty to understand technology is not optional. The comment to Rule 1.1, entitled "Competence," states that to maintain the requisite knowledge and skill, "a lawyer should keep abreast of changes in the law and its practice, including the benefits and risks associated with relevant technology . . . ."

Not only is there a nearly overwhelming amount of information available on the Internet, the technology continues to develop rapidly. For example, attorneys can now retrieve and Shepardize or KeyCite cases and statutes on their handheld mobile devices and access authorities on their iPhones (see Chapter 8).

Why use the Internet rather than Lexis or Westlaw? The primary answer is that the Internet offers free legal research 24/7; however, Lexis and Westlaw offer far more complete databases and allow you to ensure the validity of your primary authorities by Shepardizing or KeyCiting, respectively. Nevertheless, the Internet can be extremely helpful in allowing you to check the accuracy of a quotation or citation or to obtain background information on a legal topic. Opinions posted by the courts themselves, of course, are highly reliable.

There is, of course, some danger in relying too much on the Internet, primarily because not all legal materials are available online. Nevertheless, learning good Internet research techniques will save you a great deal of time. Internet legal research should complement your other research techniques, namely, conventional book research and research using Lexis and Westlaw.

B. Conducting Legal Research Online

1. *Getting Started*

To begin searching on the Internet, open your browser (for example, Internet Explorer) or double-click on the icon that identifies your Internet service provider (for example, AOL). Type a URL (such as www.sec.gov) into the address box at the top of your browser window or enter a word or phrase in the search box that appears when you access your Internet service provider or a search engine.

Many researchers begin with a general-purpose search engine. Some of the better known ones are as follows:

- Bing (http://www.bing.com)
- Google (http://www.google.com)
- Yahoo! (http://www.yahoo.com)

Consider using one of these sites as your home page so that when you access the Internet, you see the same page layout every time. With its references to more than 8 billion websites and its ranking of results by relevance, Google is the most popular of all search engines. In fact, its search engine is so intuitive that you can enter a statute citation such as "17 usc 106" into its search box and be referred directly to 17 U.S.C. § 106.

2. *Using a Good Start Page*

There is probably no better tip for conducting legal research on the Internet than to always begin your project with one good *start page*. Your start page should be reliable and easy to use, and it should be formatted in a user-friendly manner without confusing graphics or distracting scrolling advertisements or pop-ups. The advantage of always beginning at the same start page is that you will quickly become familiar with the page, and it will serve as an excellent jumping-off place for your research tasks. Although there are many start pages from which you can begin your research, following are five well-known legal favorites:

• **Cornell Law School's Legal Information Institute** (http:// www.law.cornell.edu). The Legal Information Institute is one of the best known and well-respected legal sites. It offers overviews of legal topics such as bankruptcy and corporations and allows direct linking to federal and state cases, statutes, court rules, and administrative regulations. Use its dictionary and encyclopedia "Wex" at http://www.law.cornell.edu/wex for information about hundreds of legal topics.

• **Washburn University School of Law** (http://www.washlaw.edu). This site alphabetically lists legal materials, courts, and states, making it very easy to locate material of interest. Because it is a site offered by an educational institution, it is highly regarded.

• **FindLaw** (http://lp.findlaw.com). FindLaw is an extremely well-known legal site (now owned by West/Thomson Reuters). It directs users to a vast array of legal materials, including cases, statutes, forms, and legal articles. Links to many sources of interest to legal professionals are provided, including links for law students, links to help locate attorneys, and numerous other helpful sources. See Figure 9-1.

• **Justia** (http://www.justia.com). Like FindLaw, Justia is a commercial site offering links to thousands of useful law-related sites. The site is easy to navigate and offers access to federal and state cases, statutes, court rules, legal forms, and more. See Figure 9-2.

• **PLoL** (http://www.plol.org). One of the newest competitors in free online legal research is the Public Library of Law ("PLoL") provided by Fastcase. PLoL provides access to a wide variety of materials, including all Supreme Court cases, lower federal cases since 1950, the United States Code, C.F.R., federal court rules, state cases since 1997, and statutes, constitutions, and court rules from all states. You may search by citation or key words or by using terms and connectors. Searching is easy and results are presented in an easy-to-read format.

Figure 9-1
Home Page for FindLaw

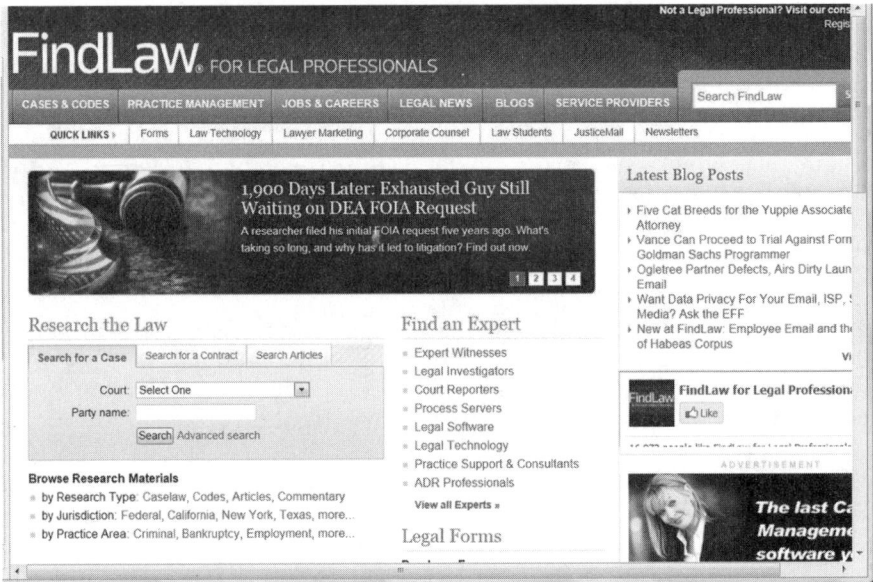

Figure 9-2
Home Page for Justia

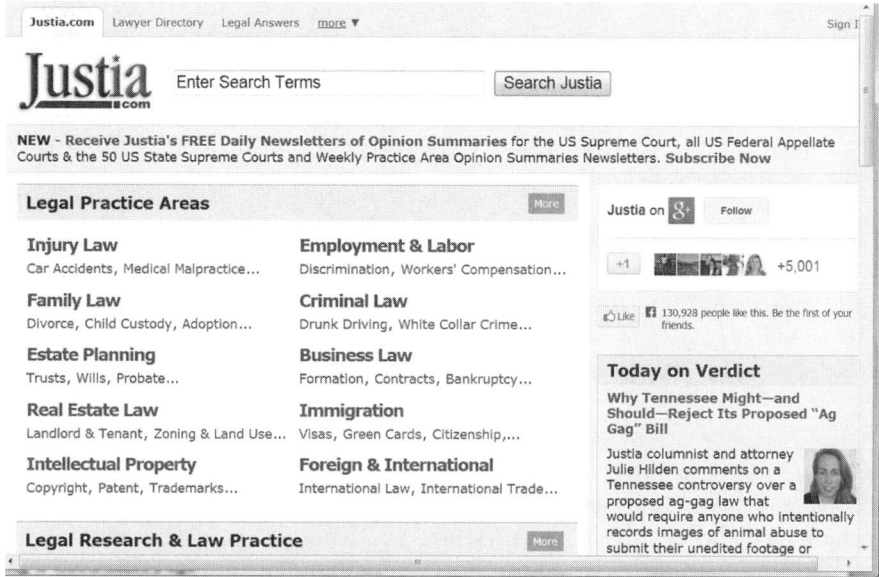

Practice Tip

Using Google Scholar

One newcomer to free Internet legal research is Google Scholar, located at http://scholar.google.com. The searching of federal and state cases is easily accomplished; you may search by case name, citation, or key words. Results are provided in Google's typical fashion in that they are ranked in order of "importance" (at least, according to Google's determination of the cases' order of importance). You may also easily determine which other cases have cited your case.

Once you choose a start page that you are comfortable with, begin your research task with this page and progress from there. After some time, you may encounter other sites that are of more use to you. If you are a beginner in Internet legal research, however, this method of consistently beginning any Internet legal research task with your "one good start page" is the best way to gain expertise on the Internet.

Practice Tip

Using the Internet to Impress Clients

Use the Internet as a tool to track clients' stock prices, determine the weather at the client's headquarters, and obtain basic information about a client's business. Read the press releases issued by clients, and then comment on them when you next speak with the client. Clients will be flattered that you made the effort to learn about their business.

---

3. Strategies and Tips for Internet Legal Research

It is far easier to get distracted when researching on the Internet than when researching using conventional print volumes. A site piques your interest, so you click on it. When you access that site, another link looks promising, and you click on it. Before you know it, you have drifted far afield from your original topic. The vast amount of information on the Internet is a constant source of diversion and distraction. Staying focused is a continuing campaign.

Following are some tips and strategies to help ensure that your Internet research is as efficient and effective as possible:

• **Understand Ranking.** When you enter a term in a search box and a list of relevant sites is given, the sites may be listed or ranked in order of how many times your term (for example, "insider trading") appears on the site, even in coded or hidden form. Thus, the first site listed is not necessarily the best; it may be merely the one that uses or displays the term "insider trading" most often. Some sites, however, most notably Google, list the most relevant and useful sites first, making research easy and productive.

• **Take Notes.** Rather than jumping from site to site, jot down the sites that look promising and visit them later. Stay focused on the task at hand. Use a computer gadget such as a desktop notepad for these notes.

• **Use Bookmarks.** If there are certain sites that you continually visit, "bookmark" them or add them to your "favorites" list so that you can readily link to them.

• **Avoid Reading the Screen.** Do not spend too much time reading screens. Reading material on a computer screen causes eye strain. If material appears promising, print it and read it in hard copy form.

• **Never Rely Exclusively on the Internet.** Although the Internet provides some excellent information and is often the easiest and cheapest way to find a case or statute, it is not a substitute for a law library. Relying solely on the Internet for legal research will result in a research project that lacks in-depth analysis. Many unpublished cases find their way onto the Internet. No one edits out the "dog" cases. Some state courts prohibit citations to unpublished decisions. Thus, exercise care.

• **Be Aware of Gaps in Coverage.** Whereas a law library and Lexis and Westlaw offer all federal court cases, some sites offer only more recent lower federal court opinions.

• **Review Materials.** Retrieving a case is not the same as analyzing it. Locating a case or statute is just the beginning of a research task. Cases and secondary authorities that interpret the statute must be analyzed.

• **Subscribe to a Newsletter.** Consider signing up to receive news bulletins from a law-related website or listserv. You will be e-mailed periodic updates on topics of interest to you.

• **Consider Disclaimers.** Review the disclaimer section of a website. It will tell you the limitations of the site and indicate if you may reproduce the material on the site. Unless otherwise indicated, material on a private, educational, or commercial website is protected by copyright law, and you cannot reproduce it without permission. The "gov" sites, however, publish materials in the public domain, and material on these sites is freely available for use.

4. *Assessing the Credibility of Websites*

Much of the material that appears on the Internet appears authoritative and reliable; however, many sites are not subject to the rigorous fact checking and editing of their print counterparts. Authors who publish in print form are often the acknowledged experts in their field. On the Internet, it is nearly impossible to judge credibility. Articles often fail to identify an author or date. Contributors to blogs or newsgroups are anonymous. Consider the following factors in evaluating the credibility of websites:

• **Domain Name.** Examine the domain name of the website (specifically, examine the ending, such as "com" or "org"). Some sites are considered more reliable than others. For example, the "gov" (government) sites are probably most authoritative, followed by the "edu" (educational) sites. If the domain name shows it is a commercial site (through the use of "com" or sometimes "org"), its content may be influenced by its owner or publisher. Review advertising on commercial sites to determine if there is bias. Consider whether the purpose of the site is to generate revenue. On the other hand, many law firm websites end in "com," and articles posted on the firm website are highly reliable and authoritative.

• **Currency.** Articles posted on the Internet may quickly become stale. Examine the site to determine if material has been recently updated. If hyperlinks connect you to "cancelled" or "unavailable" websites, this is another sign that the site is not current.

• **Author.** A tilde (~) in a Web address indicates that the author is an individual rather than an institution. Well-known experts usually like to be paid for their work; thus, "free" articles on the Internet may not be authored by the best known experts in the field. Check the author's qualifications. Does the author include contact information? Reliable authors often encourage readers to contact them.

- **Appearance.** Review the overall look and feel of the site. If the site is amateurish or accompanied by cartoons and quirky graphics, this may signal that its content is not serious.
- **Errors.** If you locate even one error in content (such as incorrect citation form or out-of-date fee schedules), it may well signal that other errors exist. Similarly, errors in grammar, spelling, and punctuation are signs that the material was not subject to thorough editing and review.
- **Attribution and References.** Quotations and statistics should be attributed to their source (and, ideally, there should be hyperlinks to the original source). Most reliable sites include references and hyperlinks to other resources to allow their users to obtain additional information.
- **Richness of Content.** Review a few other websites to compare their content and to serve as a double-check of the accuracy and depth of analysis of your site. Reputable sites should include an "About Us" section, a thorough site map, and easy search capability.

Although the Internet provides excellent information and is often the easiest and cheapest way to find a case or statute, because of its gaps in coverage, it can never be a substitute for a law library. For example, whereas law libraries, Lexis, and Westlaw offer all lower federal court cases, the free Internet sites do not. Moreover, cases on the Internet do not include useful editorial enhancements, such as headnotes or key numbers. The Internet, however, is an excellent tool for locating a parallel citation or quickly answering a question such as "What is the statute of limitations for negligence actions in Iowa?" To complete a research project, you will need to supplement your Internet legal research efforts with conventional research methods, with computerized legal research services, or both.

Ethics Alert

Avoiding Copyright Infringement

Be careful not to fall into the trap of thinking that everything on the Internet is in the public domain and can be used without permission. Whereas all federal and nearly all state materials are in the public domain and can be freely used, an article posted on the Internet is generally given the same protection against copyright infringement as its print counterpart. Thus, avoid excessive quoting from Internet sources unless attribution is given or permission is received. In many instances, you can directly e-mail the author of an article and ask for permission to reproduce the material. Look at the site to see if the author has granted permission to reprint and use.

C. Best Internet Legal Research Sites

At the end of each chapter in this text, pertinent websites have been given to assist you in your research efforts. There are hundreds of websites available, so many that research using the Internet can seem overwhelming. For example, federal cases can be located through at least ten different websites. This section of this chapter gives you brief descriptions of some of the best sites for legal research.

1. Top Sites for Locating Cases

http://www.supremecourt.gov	The U.S. Supreme Court site allows searching by party name or citation and provides the text of its cases, its rules, and access to briefs filed with the Court.
http://www.uscourts.gov	This is the U.S. federal courts home page and gateway to federal courts and their opinions, briefs, and rules.
http://scholar.google.com	Google Scholar allows free and easy access to federal and state cases. Searching is done by case name or topic.
http://www.justia.com	Justia offers free and easy access to federal cases. You may browse by year, circuit, or volume. Access to state cases is more limited.
http://www.law.cornell.edu	Cornell's site offers access to federal and state cases (availability of state cases varies from state to state).

2. Top Three Sites for Locating Statutes

http://www.gpo.gov/fdsys	FDsys offers the authenticated United States Code.
http://www.law.cornell.edu	Cornell's site offers access to all federal and state statutes.
http://www.findlaw.com/casecode	FindLaw's site offers access to all federal and state statutes.

3.   *Top Three Sites for Government Materials*

Generally, whenever you have a question relating to a government agency, the best place to start is with the agency's website. Most federal and state agencies offer excellent information, forms, and links to other resources. You can usually "guess" the website address for government agencies. For example, the website of the Department of Labor is http://www.dol.gov. Don't forget to use PACER (see Chapter 8) to obtain case and docket information from all federal courts. Following are some useful sites for locating government materials.

http://www.usa.gov	The U.S. government's official Web portal (formerly called "FirstGov") is a gateway to all government information, including federal executive, legislative, and judicial materials, information about agencies, and links to state government home pages.
http://thomas.loc.gov and http://beta.congress.gov	THOMAS and its beta-stage successor, Congress.gov, provide United States legislative information, bills, voting records, public laws, and other legislative information. See Figure 9-3.
http://www.gpo.gov/fdsys	FDsys offers access to the authenticated United States Code, the Code of Federal Regulations, the *Federal Register*, presidential materials, and more.

4.   *Top Three Sites for Locating Forms*

http://www.washlaw.edu	Select "Legal Forms."
http://www.justia.com	Select "Legal Forms."
http://www.allaboutforms.com	All About Forms provides more than 2,000 free legal forms.

5.   *Best Specialty Sites*

Note that two sites provide extensive and reliable coverage of numerous law topics:

  • Cornell Law School's site entitled "Legal Information Institute" (http://www.law.cornell.edu/wex) offers information on more than 100 topics, including bankruptcy, criminal law, and employment law. Select "Browse" and then review the list of topics provided.

Figure 9-3
Home Page of Congress.gov

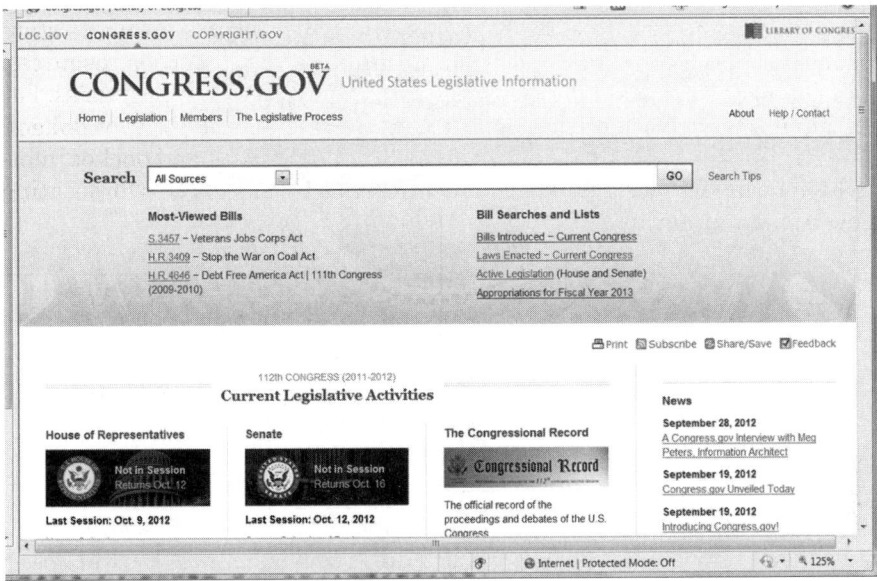

• Washlaw's site (http://www.washlaw.edu) offers information on many legal topics. Select "Reference Resources" for hundreds of links to law-related sites.

Following are some sites for specialized legal topics:

Attorney and Ethics Sites	
http://www.abanet.org/cpr	The ABA's Center for Professional Responsibility offers ethics resources.
http://www.martindale .com	Martindale-Hubbell offers a directory of lawyers.
http://www.legalethics.com	This comprehensive site provides ethics information relating to the use of technology by legal professionals.
Corporate, Business, and Securities Sites	
http://www.sec.gov	The Securities and Exchange Commission's website offers the full text of filings made by public companies, links to securities laws, and more.
http://www.hoovers.com	Basic profiles of more than 25 million companies are provided by Hoover's.

http://www.nass.org	The website of the National Association of Secretaries of State offers direct links to each state's corporations or business division for access to state forms, filing fees, and more. Select "Members."
Intellectual Property Sites	
http://www.uspto.gov	The United States Patent and Trademark Office's site offers the text of statutes, general overviews of patent and trademark procedure and law, and a fully searchable database, allowing one to search for patents and trademarks.
http://www.copyright.gov	The Copyright Office site offers forms, detailed information on copyright law, and links to other valuable resources.
http://www.ipmall.info	The University of New Hampshire's "IP Mall" provides in-depth coverage of intellectual property law and numerous links to other sites and resources.
International Law Sites	
http://www.un.org	The United Nations website offers a variety of international materials and information.
http://www.wipo.int	The World Intellectual Property Organization site offers the text of various treaties and other valuable information.
Legal Research and Writing Sites	
http://www.law.georgetown .edu/library/?85	Georgetown Law Center's guides and tutorials describe legal research methods.
http://www.gpoaccess.gov/ stylemanual/index.html	The U.S. Government Printing Office Style Manual is the authoritative guide to writing, grammar, spelling, and so forth.
http://press-pubs.uchicago.edu/ garner	This site offers exercises and information on writing from expert Bryan A. Garner.

Legal Reference Materials Sites	
http://www.usa.gov	USA.gov (previously called FirstGov) is the government's portal to a wide variety of materials, including both federal and state materials.
http://law.lexisnexis.com/infopro/zimmermans	Zimmerman's Research Guide offers an A to Z list of legal topics with concise and articulate explanations.
http://dictionary.law.com	Use this site for a legal dictionary, searchable by word or phrase.
Tax Sites	
http://www.irs.gov	Website of the Internal Revenue Service, providing information, forms, and links to other resources.
http://www.taxprophet.com	Valuable information and links to other tax sites are provided.

6. *Top Three Non-Legal Sites*

Although it is critical to have a repertory of law-related sites at your fingertips, you also need to be familiar with some basic information sites, so you can determine the weather in the city where tomorrow's deposition will be taken, directions to the client's office, or the last price at which the client's stock was sold. Following are some basic information and reference sites.

http://www.merriam-webster.com	A dictionary and thesaurus are offered at this site.
http://www.refdesk.com	This excellent all-purpose site offers links for news, encyclopedia information, weather around the world, stock ticker symbols, and much more.
http://www.bartleby.com	Bartleby features dictionaries, *Bartlett's Familiar Quotations,* and many reference materials, including portions of *The Elements of Style.*

7. *Tech Trends: Blogs, Apps, and More*

Listservs, newsgroups, and law-related weblogs (sometimes called *blawgs*) help legal professionals share information and keep current on cutting-edge legal issues. Technically, *listservs* are different from newsgroups in that listservs operate through e-mail. For example, a listserv system automatically sends everyone on the mailing list a message at the same time. In a *newsgroup*, anyone with an Internet connection may view the messages, post their own, or reply to other messages. A blog or blawg is an online journal or weblog related to legal topics. Following are some excellent websites:

http://newsletters.findlaw.com	FindLaw allows you to subscribe to daily or weekly newsletters so you will be notified by e-mail of breaking legal news and recently released cases.
http://www.abajournal.com/blawgs	The ABA website will link you to well-known legal blawgs, including Above the Law, a weblog of legal news, information about law firms, and more.
http://blawgsearch.justia.com/blogs	Justia lists more than 4,000 blogs on hundreds of legal topics.
http://www.lexisnexis.com/community/portal	Lexis Communities provides free access to numerous blogs and more than 1,000 legal podcasts and allows you to sign up to receive a daily newsletter with updates in areas of interest to you.
http://www.iphonejd.com	iPhone JD is a blog for legal professionals who use iPhones and iPads and provides reviews and information on law-related apps and accessories for those devices.

Help Line

Maintaining Your Calendar

Most legal professionals routinely calendar dates for responding to pleadings or motions, filing clients' reports with the SEC, and other time-sensitive matters. Use the website Time and Date (http://www .timeanddate.com) to calculate due dates, the duration between two dates, and more. Thus, if a report must be filed with the SEC within 45 days after a certain event, this site will provide mistake-free calculations.

One of the newest tech-related developments is the creation of various applications or "apps" that can be used with iPhones, BlackBerrys, and other similar devices. Some of these apps include databases for the Federal Rules of Civil Procedure, U.S. Constitution, tax and other federal laws, federal regulations, *Black's Law Dictionary*, and various state statutes, all accessible anytime and anywhere. Other apps available to legal professionals include those that calculate court deadlines, apps for time and billing entries, and case management tools. Many are free or offered at reasonable cost. For example, an abridged version of *Wolters Kluwer Bouvier Law Dictionary* is available as a free app from the iTunes store. As noted in Chapter 8, Fastcase provides a free app for iPhones, allowing access to cases, statutes, and more (access http://www.fastcase.com/ iphone to download the app). Finally, an app by this author, entitled *Cite-Checker: Your Guide to Using* The Bluebook, which provides information on and examples of citation form, is available from iTunes.

Lists of popular law-related apps can be found at http://libguides .law.ucla.edu/mobilelegalapps and at http://www.informedlibrarian.com/ MobileAppsforLaw. You may also search for apps at sites such as Apple's iTunes store or the Amazon App Store.

Among other trends are the use of social media sites such as Facebook, LinkedIn, and Twitter. Law firms and practitioners tend to use these tools for client development, networking, and career development.

Law firms and practitioners are increasingly using cloud computing, meaning storing data on a server owned by someone else and then accessing the data or files from any computer or device. A popular online storage service is Dropbox (http://www.dropbox.com), which allows users to store and synchronize their files, giving access to files no matter what computer or device one uses. During an emergency such as a power outage or Hurricane Sandy, the use of Dropbox allows users to access their files from home or their mobile phones, even if they cannot get to their offices.

D. Cautionary Notes on Internet Legal Research

Many beginning researchers confuse locating information on the Internet with researching. Retrieving a case is not the same as analyzing it. Locating a statute or a case is just the beginning of a research task: Cases that interpret the statute must be analyzed; treatises and Restatements should be reviewed; and periodicals and other materials should be consulted.

Moreover, because much of the material that appears on the Internet is anonymous, you cannot assess the credibility or expertise of the author. Just as you would not take medical advice from a stranger on a street corner, you should not take legal advice from strangers on an Internet corner. Similarly, much material is undated; thus, you cannot tell if it is current.

There are obviously tremendously valuable research materials on the Internet, particularly the U.S.C., the C.F.R., state statutes, and federal and state court cases. Note that all of these materials share one thing in common: They are all materials in the public domain. The well-known legal publishers, such as West and Lexis, have not posted their valuable databases on the Internet, and you should not expect that these materials will be made available for free. Moreover, although cases and other materials can be found easily on the Internet, they lack helpful editorial enhancements, such as the headnotes and case summaries that are found in the print sources and on Lexis and Westlaw.

Finally, always consider that even the most reputable-seeming sites can be subject to abuse. The CIA and Department of Justice's websites have both been hacked. Thus, at any given moment, the materials you review on the Internet may be false (or stale).

As long as you remember these cautionary notes, the Internet remains a valuable and efficient tool for beginning many research projects; however, it can never be a substitute for a full in-depth analysis of legal materials, such as those you would find in a law library or through the computer research services such as Lexis and Westlaw. See Figure 9-4 for a chart comparing the pros and cons of Internet research.

Figure 9-4
Internet Research Pros and Cons

Pro	*Con*
Access to Internet sources is available 24/7, from anywhere in the world. Immediate access to breaking legal news is provided through newsgroup subscriptions.	The glut of materials on the Internet can make finding the right source like finding a needle in a haystack. Some websites disappear without a trace.
The Internet provides free access to a wide array of legal materials.	Many unpublished cases find their way onto the Internet. Some state courts prohibit citations to unpublished decisions. Thus, look for the words "published" or "unpublished" at the beginning of a case.

Figure 9-4 *(Continued)*

Pro	*Con*
E-mail, chat rooms, and news-group postings allow you to ask colleagues for assistance and information.	The responders to your requests for information are usually anonymous; thus, you cannot assess their reliability or expertise.
The Internet provides access to many private materials. For example, many law students have posted case briefs and research memos on the Internet and invited others to use them. Similarly, law firms often publish informative articles on legal topics.	Accessing the law is far different from understanding and analyzing it. Once again, whereas law firm authors are generally reliable, other authors are unknown and unproved.
Office space for library books and binders is expensive. The Internet stores incredible amounts of information at no cost.	Reading materials in print form is far easier than reading it on a screen. Internet materials are seldom professionally proofread and edited as are their print counterparts.

E. Citation Form

As discussed in the next chapter, *The Bluebook* and *ALWD* generally require the use and citation of traditional printed sources unless there is a digital copy that is authenticated, official, or an exact copy of the printed source. Rule 18 of *The Bluebook* and *ALWD* Rules 38-42 provide numerous rules for citing to the Internet, some of which are quite complicated.

	Bluebook *(for practitioners)*	*ALWD*
Article Available in Print and on the Internet	Clarisa Long, *Dilution*, 106 Colum. L. Rev. 1029 (2006), *available at* http://www.columbialawreview.org/articles/index.cfm?article_id==817.	No suggested format.
Article Available Solely on the Internet	William Hunter, *Patent Reform Déjà Vu*, Fish News (Nov. 9, 2009), http://www.fr.com/Patent-Reform-Deja-Vu-11-05-2009.	William Hunter, *Fish News, Patent Reform Déjà Vu*, http://www.fr.com/Patent-Reform-Deja-Vu-11-05-2009 (Nov. 9, 2009).

Internet Assignment

1. Access the website USA.gov. Select "Government Agencies" and locate information on the Equal Employment Opportunity Commission. How many employees must a company have to be covered by the Equal Employment Opportunity Commission?

2. Access Cornell's Legal Information Institute.
   a. Select "Wex legal encyclopedia." Briefly, what is a latent defect?
   b. Review the Federal Rules of Appellate Procedure. In a civil case in which judgment was entered on May 1, 2013, the U.S. government is a party. When must it file a notice of appeal as of a matter of right?

3. Access Google Scholar. What is the citation for the 2000 case *Apprendi v. New Jersey*?

4. Access the Hoover's website and locate information about Starbucks Corporation. Identify the company's top three competitors.

5. Access the Justia website. Assume that ABC Inc. is a Pennsylvania corporation with nine directors, seven of whom are present at a meeting of directors. How many directors constitute a quorum? How many directors of ABC Inc. must be present and vote at a meeting to take action if seven are present at a meeting?

6. Access the website for the Public Library of Law. What is the citation for the 2003 case *Eldred v. Ashcroft*?

7. Access the website All About Forms. Select "Wills" and select "Last Will and Testament." What topic does Article VI cover?

Legal Research

Citing and Validating the Authorities

Legal Citation Form

Chapter Overview

All legal professionals must know how to cite legal authorities. This chapter discusses *The Bluebook* and *ALWD*, the best known guides to citation form, and provides examples of citation form for many primary and secondary authorities. Note that although numerous examples of citations are provided in this chapter, most are fictitious and are provided solely for the purpose of illustrating citation rules. Moreover, not all citation rules will be addressed in this chapter. References to *Bluebook* and *ALWD* rules are given in parentheses.

A. Introduction to Citation Form

A critical part of the writing process in many legal documents is citing authorities. Every legal assertion made in a document must be supported by legal authority. These supporting authorities appear as *citations* in your document. Citations must appear in a standard and consistent format so that any reader will be able to retrieve the legal authority you cite and verify that you have accurately represented the status of the law. Because these citations communicate information to readers, legal professionals must use the same "language" or citation form. When you present a persuasive argument, you do not want to distract the reader by using incorrect citation form.

Newcomers to the legal field often inquire what will happen if citations are incorrect in a brief or other document. Citation errors have an effect similar to an egregious spelling error: They cause a loss of respect for the author and make readers question the integrity and analysis of an argument.

B. Citation Manuals

Citation manuals provide the rules for citing legal authorities. There are two primary guides to citation form in the United States:

> • ***The Bluebook***. The oldest and best known citation manual is *The Bluebook: A Uniform System of Citation* (Columbia Law Review Ass'n et al. eds., 19th ed. 2010) ("*The Bluebook*"). *The Bluebook* is complex, and its rules are often poorly worded. It provides few examples for practitioners. Nevertheless, because most judges and practicing professionals were taught to use *The Bluebook* for citation form, at present it is the most commonly used citation manual. Generally, unless you are specifically directed to use some other citation system, follow *The Bluebook*.
>
> • ***ALWD***. In 2000, the Association of Legal Writing Directors and Professor Darby Dickerson introduced an alternative to *The Bluebook*: ALWD & Darby Dickerson, *ALWD Citation Manual* (4th ed., Aspen Publishers 2010). Called *ALWD* (pronounced "all wood"), this citation manual was intended to provide an easy-to-learn and user-friendly alternative to *The Bluebook*, and its presentation and numerous examples do make it easier to use. At the same time, in many instances, the *ALWD* format is identical to *Bluebook* format. There are, however, several differences.

Although there are other guides to citation form, the most notable of which is the *University of Chicago Manual of Legal Citation* (4th ed. 2013), usually referred to as the *Maroonbook*, and used primarily in the Chicago metropolitan area, *The Bluebook* is probably the best known system at this time, although *ALWD* continues to attract a great deal of interest because of its sensible rules and approach. Follow your school or office practice. Note, however, that if local citation rules exist for a court, they must be followed and will supersede any citation system. See Figure 10-1 for a chart showing some differences between *The Bluebook* and *ALWD* rules.

C. *The Bluebook*

1. *Introduction*

It would be unnecessarily time consuming to read *The Bluebook*; however, you should still become familiar with its overall arrangement and read at least the Bluepages section in the front of the book. Also, review the tables at the back of *The Bluebook* and glance at its alphabetically arranged index. Flag the pages and tables you will refer to most frequently.

Figure 10-1
Some Differences Between _The Bluebook_ and _ALWD_

	Bluebook	_ALWD_
Typeface	Large and small capitals are used in law review footnotes; practitioners never use large and small capitals.	Large and small capitals are never used.
U.S. Supreme Court Cases	_Bluebook_ does not allow parallel citations.	_ALWD_ allows (but does not prefer) parallel citations.
Abbreviations in Case Names	Some abbreviations in case names given in Table T.6 differ from _ALWD_ abbreviations. For example, _Bluebook_ uses "Cont'l" for "Continental."	Some abbreviations in case names given in Appendix 3 differ from _Bluebook_ abbreviations. For example, _ALWD_ uses "Contl."
United States as a Party	Present plaintiff or defendant as _United States_.	Present plaintiff or defendant as _U.S._ or _United States_.
Lexis or Westlaw Cases	Include docket number.	Docket number need not be included.
Pinpoints for Page Spans	Always retain last two digits, but omit repetitious digits as in "937-39."	Option is given to drop repetitious digits or retain them, as in "937-39" or "937-939."
Treatises and Dictionaries	• The publisher name is not included. • The volume number is given as the first element for a treatise.	• The publisher name is given in the parenthetical. • The volume number is given after the title of a treatise.
A.L.R. Annotations	The word "Annotation" is included in the citation.	The word "Annotation" is not included.

Figure 10-1 *(Continued)*

	Bluebook	*ALWD*
String Citing	Treat all federal courts of appeal as one court and all district courts as one court and list in reverse chronological order.	Order cases from the federal courts of appeal by ordinal and then in reverse chronological order; order cases from the district courts alphabetically and then in reverse chronological order.
Use of *Supra*	*Supra* may be used in documents with or without footnotes.	*Supra* may be used only in documents with footnotes.
Superscripts	Superscripts (4th) are prohibited.	Superscripts (4th) are not prohibited.
Quotations	Block indent any quotation of 50 or more words.	Block indent quotations of 50 or more words or any quotation that exceeds 4 lines of text.

2. *Typeface Conventions*

The Bluebook uses two different citation formats. The citation form used by those writing law review journal articles is different from that used by practitioners in that LARGE AND SMALL CAPITAL LETTERS are used for many forms. Practitioners do not use large and small caps. Thus, perhaps the single most important fact you should know about *The Bluebook* is that almost all of the examples given in its white pages show how to cite authorities as if you were writing an academic journal article or law review article; the Bluepages, however, show a different format for practitioners. Thus, law students must learn a different format when they enter law firm practice.

The three most significant differences in the way citations are presented in law reviews and by practitioners are as follows:

• **Typeface.** Many authorities (such as periodical titles, authors and titles of books, and state statutes) are presented in LARGE AND SMALL CAPS. Practitioners never use large and small caps.

Example for citing a treatise in a law review or journal article:
2 J. THOMAS MCCARTHY, RIGHTS OF PUBLICITY AND PRIVACY § 5:1 (4th ed. 2004).

Example for citing a treatise in a practitioner's court brief or other document:

2 J. Thomas McCarthy, *Rights of Publicity and Privacy* § 5:1 (4th ed. 2004).

Do not become confused and assume that because an example appears in the body of *The Bluebook* that it is correct. It may well be correct—but only for law review footnotes or academic writing. Practitioners must always check the Bluepages and the inside back cover of *The Bluebook*, and adapt the typeface for use in a court document or legal memorandum (by using ordinary type and not large and small caps). A nice advantage of *ALWD* is that it eliminates this distinction between large and small capitals and ordinary type and uses only ordinary typeface.

- **Location of Citations.** *The Bluebook* states that citations in journal articles appear in footnotes and that practitioners place their citations in the text of a document rather than in footnotes (Bluepages ("B") 2). This rule may be an oversimplification; many practitioners place citations in footnotes in their court briefs.
- **Presentation of Case Names.** Practitioners always underscore or italicize case names. There are no exceptions to this rule for practitioners. However, when full case names appear in journal articles, they are neither underscored nor italicized (although short-form case names are italicized in journal articles).

━━━━━━━━━━━ Practice Tip ━━━━━━━━━━━

Citation Form

In citing legal authorities, do not rely on the way books and cases refer to themselves. For example, many volumes of U.S.C.A. include an instruction similar to the following: "Cite This Book Thus: 42 U.S.C.A. §1220." This form is incorrect according to *The Bluebook* and *ALWD*, which require a space after the section symbol and a year, as in 42 U.S.C.A. § 1220 (West 2009).

You should, therefore, always rely on the appropriate *Bluebook* or *ALWD* rules rather than the citation forms you may observe in books or case reports or on Lexis or Westlaw, which are often more intent on saving space than on complying with *The Bluebook* or *ALWD*.

D. *Bluebook* Citation Rules and Examples for Primary Authorities

Unless otherwise noted, all *Bluebook* citation examples in this chapter are in the form used by practitioners rather than in the form used for law review articles. Thus, large and small capital letters are not used.

1. Cases

a. Introduction

A typical case citation includes the following elements:

- Case name;
- References to set(s) of reports that publishes the case and the page on which the case begins;
- A parenthetical that includes the court and jurisdiction (if not apparent from the name of the set) and the year of decision; and
- Other parenthetical information and subsequent history of the case, if any. (B4.1)

Thus, a typical citation to a Florida Supreme Court case is as follows:

Smith v. Gregory, 675 So. 2d 119 (Fla. 2001).

b. Case Names (B4.1.1; R.10.2.1, R.10.2.2)

(1) General Principles

The Bluebook provides numerous rules regarding case names in citations. Carefully review Bluepages B4.1.1 and Rule 10.2 in *The Bluebook* for a full discussion of these rules. Some of the more common guidelines you should be aware of are as follows:

- Case names may be <u>underscored</u> or *italicized*. Follow your office practice. Select one method and be consistent. When underscoring, use a solid unbroken line, as in <u>Jones v. Smith</u>. The use of italics is far more common than underscoring.
- If there are several plaintiffs and defendants, list only the first one on each side. Do not use *et al.* to signal that other parties exist.

Correct:	*Smith v. Martinez*
Incorrect:	*Smith and Jacobsen v. Martinez, Klein, and O'Brien*
Incorrect:	*Smith v. Martinez, et al.*

- Omit first names or initials for parties (although retain full corporate or business names). Use surnames only.

Correct:	*Smith v. Martinez*
Incorrect:	*Ellen Smith v. T.J. Martinez*
Correct:	*Smith v. Ralph Lauren Ltd.*

- Underscore or italicize the period in words such as "Inc.," "Co.," or "Corp." when such a word ends a case name.

Correct:	*Bailey v. Nike Inc.*
Incorrect:	*Bailey v. McDonald's Corp.*

• The comma that follows a case name is neither underscored nor italicized.

• Omit words describing a party's status, such as "plaintiff" or "trustee."

Correct: *Harrison v. Kendall*
Incorrect: *Harrison, Plaintiff, v. Kendall, Executor*

•If a party is known by a widely known acronym (WHO) or initialism (FDA), you may use it without periods.

Preferred: *Willis v. FBI* *Simmons v. SEC*
Disfavored: *Willis v. F.B.I.* *Simmons v. S.E.C.*

• Do not abbreviate "United States" in a case name if it is the entire name of a party.

Correct: *United States v. Reynolds*
Correct: *Lee v. U.S. Dep't of Justice*
Incorrect: *U.S. v. Reynolds* *U.S.A. v. Reynolds*

• The abbreviation for "versus" in a citation is a lowercase "v" followed by a period. Note, however, that "vs." is often used in pleadings and court documents.

(2) Abbreviations in Case Names (B4.1.1(vi); R.10.2.1(c); Table T.6)

Because case names can be long, learning when you can abbreviate words in case names will save you time and effort. Unfortunately, the rules regarding abbreviating words in case names are awkwardly phrased and located in *The Bluebook*. Which words may be abbreviated in a citation depends on the location and use of the citation.

• If your citation appears as part of a textual sentence (meaning that the citation is needed to make sense of the sentence), then you may abbreviate only widely known acronyms (such as AARP) and initialisms (such as FBI) and the following commonly known and widely recognized words:

& Ass'n Bros. Co. Corp. Inc. Ltd. No.

If one of these eight words begins a party's name, do not abbreviate it.

• If your citation "stands alone" (rather than appearing as part of a textual sentence), you may abbreviate any of the nearly 180 words in Table T.6 of *The Bluebook* even if it is the first word of a party's name.

Examples:

• According to *Harrison Manufacturing & Equipment Inc. v. Southern Mutual Co.*, 430 U.S. 655 (1995), trademarks can be abandoned through nonuse.

Explanation: Because the citation appears as part of a textual sentence, abbreviate only "&," "Inc.," and "Co."

- Trademarks can be abandoned through nonuse. *Harrison Mfg. & Equip. Inc. v. S. Mut. Co.*, 430 U.S. 655 (1995).

  Explanation: Because the citation "stands alone," you may abbreviate any of the words in Table T.6.

Until 2000, *The Bluebook* strictly prohibited abbreviation of the first word in a party's name. This rule changed in 2000. Some law firms and practitioners dislike this rule and continue to follow the prior rule by never abbreviating the first word in a party's name.

c. Citation Form for State Court Cases (B4.1.3; R.10.3, R.10.4, R.10.5)

Prior to 1996, *The Bluebook* required that when citing state court cases, in every instance, all parallel citations should be given, with the official citation given first, followed by the unofficial citation(s). The current Nineteenth Edition of *The Bluebook* rule is as follows:

- If court rules require parallel citations, you must give them (typically giving the official citation first, followed by the unofficial citation(s)).
- Unless court rules require parallel citations, cite solely to the regional reporter (for example, P.2d or N.W.2d) and give a reference to the state and to the deciding court parenthetically, using Table T.1.3 of *The Bluebook* to construct your abbreviation.

Examples:
- *Samson Corp. v. Bailey*, 302 N.C. 118, 671 S.E.2d 909 (1990). This form is used when a court rule requires parallel citations.
- *Samson Corp. v. Bailey*, 671 S.E.2d 909 (N.C. 1990). This form is used in any instance other than when a court rule requires parallel citations.

You do not need to include the name of the court in the parenthetical if the court that decided the case is the highest court of the state. For example, *Bluebook* Table T.1.3 tells us that "N.C." indicates a case from the North Carolina Supreme Court. Thus, no further information is needed in the date parenthetical in the previous example. However, for cases from the lower courts, the rule is different. Examine the following example:

- *Taylor v. Fletcher*, 804 S.E.2d 18 (N.C. Ct. App. 2002).

Because we cannot tell which court decided the case from the reference to "S.E.2d," we must include the deciding court in the parenthetical with the date (as shown in Table T.1.3 of *The Bluebook*).

Remember that more than 20 states no longer publish their cases officially. For cases from these states (decided after the date the official set was discontinued), the correct citation form will refer the reader only to the regional reporter and will include information about the court that decided the case in the date parenthetical, as follows: *Lee v. Lee*, 704 A.2d 119 (R.I. 2001). To determine which states no longer publish officially, see Figure 4-2 of this text, or review Table T.1.3 of *The Bluebook* or Appendix 1 of *ALWD*.

d. Citation Form for Federal Cases (B4.1.3; Table T.1.1)

• United States Supreme Court Cases.

Cite to U.S. If the case has not yet been published in U.S., cite to S. Ct., L. Ed., or U.S.L.W., in that order of preference. Do not give a parallel citation.

Example: *Johnson v. Ruiz*, 514 U.S. 118 (1995).

• Cases from the United States Courts of Appeal.
Cite to F., F.2d, or F.3d. You *must* include a reference to the circuit that decided the case in the parenthetical with the date.

Example: *Garrison v. Monroe*, 145 F.3d 901 (4th Cir. 1999).

• Cases from the United States District Courts.
Cite to F. Supp. or F. Supp. 2d. You *must* include a reference to the particular district court that decided the case in the parenthetical with the date. See Figure 2-2 for abbreviations for our 94 district courts.

Example: *Ryan v. Arne*, 32 F. Supp. 2d 18 (E.D. Va. 1998).

e. Subsequent and Prior History (B4.1.6; R.10.7)

• **Subsequent History.** When a decision is cited in full, give the entire subsequent history. You may, however, omit denials of certiorari or other similar discretionary appeals, unless the underlying decision is less than two years old or the denial is particularly relevant. This rule relating to omitting denials of certiorari is new since 1996 and has often been criticized. Some attorneys believe that denial of certiorari is always relevant and, therefore, should always be included. You will be given the subsequent history of your case when you Shepardize or KeyCite it (see Chapter 11). Then, use Table T.8 of *The Bluebook* to find the appropriate abbreviation for the history of your case. Give the subsequent history after your full citation, as follows:

Examples: *Fraley v. Carson*, 890 F. Supp. 114 (S.D.N.Y. 1996), *rev'd*, 13 F.3d 114 (2d Cir. 1998).
Wells v. Daly, 150 F.3d 120 (3d Cir. 2013), *cert. denied*, 551 U.S. 899 (2014).

• **Prior History.** Give the prior history of your case only if it is relevant.

f. Spacing in Citations (R.6.1(a))

Follow these three rules to determine spacing in citations:

- Adjacent single capitals are placed next to each other with no spaces. For purposes of this rule, the abbreviations for 1st, 2d, 3d, and so forth are viewed as single capital letters.

Correct:	P.2d
	S.E.2d
	U.S.
	F.3d
	A.L.R.5th

- Multiple-letter abbreviations are preceded and followed by spaces.

Correct:	Cal. App. 2d
	So. 2d
	F. Supp. 2d
	Fed. R. Civ. P. 56(c)

- Be careful with the names of periodicals. Set initials referring to institutions (such as "Boston College" below) off from other capitals. Consult *Bluebook* Table T.13 and mimic the spacing shown.

Correct:	B.C. L. Rev.
Incorrect:	B.C.L. Rev.

Do not use superscripts (such as 1st or 4th). Set ordinals (such as 1st or 4th) and numerals "on line" (so they will be consistent with the presentations of 2d and 3d). (See R.6.2(b).)

2. *Statutes*

a. Federal Statutes (B5.1.1; R.12)

Recall that our federal statutes are published in three sets: U.S.C. (the official set), and U.S.C.A. and U.S.C.S. (the unofficial sets). Cite to U.S.C. whenever possible, giving the title number, the name of the set, and the section number. *The Bluebook* also requires a parenthetical giving the year of the code and the publisher name, if you cite to an unofficial set.

Examples:	17 U.S.C. § 102(b) (2006).
	17 U.S.C.A. § 102(b) (West 2009).
	17 U.S.C.S. § 102(b) (LexisNexis 2012).

Note that the "year of the code" is not the date the statute was enacted, but the year that appears on the spine of the volume, the year that appears on the title page, or the latest copyright year (in that order of preference).

b. State Statutes

Use Table T.1.3 of *The Bluebook* for instructions on citing each state's statutes. Most states have numbered statutes, with no specifically named titles.

> *Examples:*   Ariz. Rev. Stat. Ann. § 10-120 (2011).
> Fla. Stat. § 607.0101 (2004).

A few states (including California, Maryland, New York, and Texas) have specific names for their statutes.

> *Examples:*   Cal. Fam. Code § 1204 (West 2009).
> N.Y. Educ. Law § 3220 (McKinney 2008).

c. Notes on Citing Statutes

- Practitioners almost always omit the parenthetical following the statute.
- Follow the section symbol (§) with a space (R.6.2(c)).
- When citing more than one section, use two section symbols (§§) and give inclusive numbers. Do not use "*et seq.*," and do not drop any repetitious digits (R.3.3(b)). Thus, the following is correct: §§ 307-309.

3. *Court and Other Rules (B5.1.3; R.12.9.3)*

> *Examples:*   Fed. R. Civ. P. 56(c).
> Fed. R. Evid. 109.
> Sup. Ct. R. 33(a).

4. *Constitutions (B6; R.11)*

Cite constitutional provisions that are currently in force without a date.

> *Examples:*   U.S. Const. art. I, § 8.
> Cal. Const. art. XX.

5. Administrative Regulations (B5.1.4; R.14)

Examples: 15 C.F.R. § 12.203 (2012).
                 Airworthiness Directives, 74 Fed. Reg. 25,399 (May 28, 2013).

E. *Bluebook* Citation Form for Secondary Authorities

Examples for citations for secondary authorities will be discussed in the order in which those authorities were discussed in Chapters 5 and 6.

1. A.L.R. Annotations (R.16.7.6)

Example: Deborah F. Buckman, Annotation, *Intellectual Property Rights in Video, Electronic, and Computer Games*, 7 A.L.R. Fed. 2d 269 (2005).

2. Encyclopedias (B8.1; R.15.8)

Examples: 23 C.J.S. *Indemnity* § 24 (1998).
                 7 Am. Jur. 2d *Agency* § 14 (1994).

3. Periodicals (B9; R.16)

Following are some notes on citing periodicals and journal articles:

- Note that the form for citing periodical articles differs when the author is a student.
- Give the author's name as he or she does in the publication.
- If there are two authors, list both in the order in which they appear on the title page, and separate the names with an ampersand (&).
- If there are more than two authors, either identify the first author's name followed by the signal "et al." or list all of the authors.
- Italicize or underscore the title of the article and follow it with a comma.
- Use Table T.13 to determine the abbreviations for periodical titles, remembering that the format for citing journal articles in academic writing and law review footnotes uses large and small capitals whereas practitioners use italics for the names of the journals.

Example: Sharon Dolovich, *State Punishment and Private Prisons*, 55 Duke L.J. 437 (2005).

4. Texts and Treatises (B8.1; R.15)

Following are some notes on citing books, texts, and treatises:

- Follow the rules for author names given above for periodical articles.
- Do not place a comma after the title of the book or text.
- If citing to anything other than the first edition of the text, indicate as such in the parenthetical with the date.

Example: 2 Melvin F. Jager, *Trade Secrets Law* § 104 (2d ed. 2005).

5. Restatements (B5.1.3; R.12.9.5)

Example: Restatement (Second) of Contracts § 104 (1995).

6. Attorneys General Opinions (Table T.1.2)

Example: Applicability of the Emoluments Clause to Non-Government Members of ACUS, 17 Op. O.L.C. 114 (1993).

7. Dictionaries (B8.1; R.15.8)

Example: *Black's Law Dictionary* 891 (9th ed. 2009).

8. Uniform Laws (B5.1.3; R.12.9.4)

Examples: U.C.C. § 2-316 (1977).
Unif. P'ship Act § 402 (amended 1997), 8 U.L.A. 18 (2001).

9. Looseleaf Services (R.19)

Example: *SEC v. Edwards*, 5 Fed. Sec. L. Rep. (CCH) ¶ 92,656 (Fed. Cir. July 10, 2004).

━━━━━━━━━━ Help Line ━━━━━━━━━━

The Online Bluebook

The Bluebook is now available online at http://www.legalbluebook
.com. The fee-based online version of *The Bluebook* and its website
offer a video tour and many convenient features including the
following:

- You can search by key word or phrase to find sections of *The
  Bluebook* of interest to you when using the online *Bluebook*.
- Just as you can mark up your print copy of your *Bluebook,* you
  can add notes and bookmarks to your online *Bluebook*.
- The website provides "Blue Tips," which is similar to a FAQ
  section and answers questions frequently asked about *The
  Bluebook*.
- The site provides an "Updates" section, which identifies minor
  corrections made to *The Bluebook*.

━━━━━━━━━━ Practice Tip ━━━━━━━━━━

There's an App for That!

The Bluebook is now available as an iPad and iPhone app. You may
download the Rulebook app for free at http://readyreferenceapps
.com/rulebook.php and then purchase *The Bluebook* content
separately. In addition, an app on citation form by this author,
entitled *Cite-Checker: Your Guide to Using* The Bluebook, is
available from the iTunes Store. This inexpensive app provides
explanations of *Bluebook* rules, examples, and a citation form quiz
and answer key.

F.   *ALWD* Citation Rules and Examples for Primary Authorities

Remember that *ALWD* makes no distinction between the typeface used
by practitioners and that used in law review or article journals, so all of
its examples are acceptable for those writing law review articles and for
practitioners.

1.   *Cases (R.12)*

a.   Introduction

ALWD rules for citing cases are nearly identical to those of *The Bluebook*.
In fact, there are only three major differences for cases published in print
form:

• **Information About Divisions for State Court Cases.** *ALWD* Rule 12.6(b) generally requires that when you cite a state case, you must include available information about departments, districts, or divisions that decided the case. *The Bluebook* generally does not permit this information.

- *ALWD*: *Holt v. Holt*, 14 P.3d 887 (Ariz. App. Div. I 2000).
- *Bluebook*: *Holt v. Holt*, 14 P.3d 887 (Ariz. Ct. App. 2000).

• **Abbreviations in Case Names.** *ALWD* Rule 12.2(e) provides that you may abbreviate any word in a case name when the citation appears as a stand-alone clause or sentence, and that it is "traditional" to spell out all words in a case name when it appears in text. This approach is a bit more permissive than that of *The Bluebook*, which requires that you spell out all words in a case name when it appears in text (except words such as "Inc." and "Corp.") and that you abbreviate words in a case name in a stand-alone citation.

• **General Abbreviations.** The abbreviations used in *ALWD* and *The Bluebook* vary. For example, *The Bluebook* abbreviates the word "County" as "Cnty.," whereas *ALWD* uses "Co." Similarly, *The Bluebook* generally requires that when the United States is a party to a case, the case name must read "United States," while *ALWD* (R.12.2(g)) provides that the case name may read "United States" or "U.S.," as in *U.S. v. Dana*. Finally, abbreviations for names of courts vary. For example, *Bluebook* Table T.1.3 shows "Alaska Ct. App." for the Alaska Court of Appeals, while *ALWD* Appendix 1 shows this as "Alaska App."

b. Federal Cases

ALWD's formats for federal cases are identical to those in *The Bluebook* (although *ALWD* permits, but does not favor, using all parallel cites for U.S. Supreme Court cases).

c. State Cases

ALWD's rules for state cases are identical to those in *The Bluebook*, namely, follow all local rules for citing cases, and in the absence of any rules, cite only to West's regional reporter, and indicate parenthetically the year of decision and the court that decided the case. Thus, give parallel citations only when required by local rules. Use *ALWD*'s Appendix 1 to determine the appropriate abbreviation for state courts.

d. Subsequent and Prior History (R.12.8; R.12.9)

ALWD's rules relating to subsequent and prior history are nearly identical to those of *The Bluebook*. Thus, you must include subsequent history for the cases you cite, although you may omit denials of certiorari unless the cited case is less than two years old or the denial is particularly important. Prior history need not be included.

e. Spacing in Citations (R.2.2)

ALWD's spacing rules are identical to those found in *The Bluebook*:

- Close up all adjacent single capitals, and treat ordinals as single capitals (as in U.S. and N.W.2d). Note that *ALWD* does not prohibit superscripts such as 4th. *The Bluebook* prohibits superscripts.
- Place spaces on either side of multiple letter abbreviations (as in F. Supp. 2d).
- In legal periodicals, set the abbreviations for an institution or geographical entity apart from other capital letters (as in N.M. L. Rev.). Use *ALWD*'s Appendix 5 for examples of periodical names.

2. *Statutes (R.14)*

a. Federal Statutes

The presentation of federal statutes is the same in *ALWD* as it is in *The Bluebook*. The rules requiring you to include a year parenthetical for federal statutes and the name of the publisher for the unofficial sets (U.S.C.A. and U.S.C.S.) are also identical, although *The Bluebook* uses "LexisNexis" and *ALWD* uses "Lexis." Remember that almost all practitioners omit the parenthetical following the section number of the statute.

> *Examples:*   18 U.S.C. § 1889 (2006).
> 18 U.S.C.A. § 1889 (West 2009).
> 18 U.S.C.S. § 1889 (Lexis 2008).

Additionally, whereas *The Bluebook* flatly prohibits the use of "*et seq.*" to indicate a span of statutes, *ALWD* merely discourages it (but does allow it). *ALWD* does not use italics for "et seq." *The Bluebook* does.

b. State Statutes

Appendix 1 of *ALWD* provides the format for each state's statutes. These are highly similar or identical in form to those shown in Table T.1.3 of *The Bluebook*.

> *Examples:*   Cal. Evid. Code Ann. § 5102 (West 2004).
> Fla. Stat. § 607.0101 (2003).

3. *Court and Other Rules (R.17)*

> *Examples:*   Fed. R. Civ. P. 12(b)(6).
> Fed. R. Evid. 501.
> Sup. Ct. R. 17.

4. *Constitutions (R.13)*

Examples: U.S. Const. amend. IX.
Cal. Const. art. XXII.

5. *Administrative Regulations (R.19)*

Examples: 28 C.F.R. § 43.201 (2012).
Suspension of Community Eligibility, 70 Fed. Reg. 16964 (Jan. 10, 2013).

G. *ALWD* Rules and Examples for Secondary Authorities

Most of the *ALWD* rules for citing secondary authorities are identical to those for *The Bluebook*. Following are examples for the most often cited secondary authorities. An asterisk (*) following an example indicates that the format is identical for both *ALWD* and *The Bluebook*.

1. *A.L.R. Annotations (R.24)*

Example: David J. Marchitelli, *Causes of Action Governed by Limitations Period in UCC § 2-725*, 49 A.L.R.5th 1 (1997).

2. *Encyclopedias (R.26)*

Examples: 77A C.J.S. *Sales* § 377 (1996).*
93 Am. Jur. 2d *Trials* § 16 (2004).*

3. *Periodical Materials (R.23)*

Example: Jane S. Schacter, *Sexual Orientation, Social Change, and the Courts*, 54 Drake L. Rev. 303 (2006).*

4. *Texts and Treatises (R.22)*

A key difference in the way citations for treatises are presented under *ALWD* rules is that *ALWD* requires that the publisher of the treatise be identified in the parenthetical with the year. Also, the location of the volume number for a multi-volume set is different in *ALWD* from *The Bluebook*.

Example: Homer H. Clark, *Clark's The Law of Domestic Relations in the United States* vol. 2, § 104 (2d ed., West 1987).

5. *Restatements (R.27)*

Example: Restatement (Second) of Torts § 201 (1997).

6. *Attorneys General Opinion (R.19.7)*

Example: 43 Op. Atty. Gen. 387 (1965).

7. *Dictionaries (R.25)*

Example: Black's Law Dictionary 584 (Bryan A. Garner ed., 9th
ed., West 2009).

8. *Uniform Laws (R.27.4)*

Examples: U.C.C. § 2-316 (1977).*
Unif. P'ship Act § 402 (amended 1997), 8 U.L.A. 18
(2001).*

9. *Looseleaf Services (R.28)*

Example: SEC v. Edwards, 5 Fed. Sec. L. Rep. (CCH)
¶ 92,656 (Fed. Cir. July 10, 2004).*

Ethics Alert

Finding Local Rules

Both *The Bluebook* and *ALWD* provide that any local rules relating
to citation form will supersede their rules. Thus, you have an
ethical obligation to follow these local rules. To find specialized
local citation rules:

- Access the website http://www.uscourts.gov for links to all federal
  court websites, which post their local rules.
- Review each state's judicial website, identified in Table T.1.3 of
  The Bluebook and Appendix 2 of *ALWD*, for state and local rules.
- Review *The Bluebook*'s Bluepages Table BT.2, which identifies
  court rules relating to citation form.
- Review Appendix 2 of *ALWD* for a discussion of local rules
  relating to citation form.
- Call the clerk of the court to which you are submitting a
  document, and inquire whether any local rules dictate the form
  for citations.
- Consult a law librarian.

Practice Tip

WestlawNext's Citation Assistance

WestlawNext (discussed in Chapter 8) provides assistance with citations. For example, you may elect either to italicize or underscore case names, to include parallel citations, or to select *Bluebook* citation form (which is the default approach), *ALWD* citation form, or a jurisdiction-specific citation form, such as California or Texas citation form. Look for the "Preferences" button at the bottom of your screen, and then select "Citations." Set your preferences. Then whenever you highlight text, select "Copy with Preferences." When you drop this text into any document, the citation will be formatted according to your preferences. You may have to tweak the citation a bit, but significant help is given.

H. Special Citation Issues (*Bluebook* and *ALWD*)

1. Introduction

Citations do not exist alone. They appear as part of sentences that must be correctly punctuated, as support for quotations, and together with certain signals that give readers information about the level of support the citation provides for the assertion you have made. This section of the chapter addresses special citation issues such as punctuation, quotations, signals, and short-form citations you may use when you have cited an authority in full and wish to refer to it again later. *Bluebook* examples provided will be shown in the form used by legal practitioners (rather than in the LARGE AND SMALL CAP form used for law review journal articles).

2. Punctuation (Bluebook *B2 and R.1.1; ALWD R.43*)

There are three punctuation marks that may follow a citation: a period, a comma, or a semicolon.

- Use a period to follow a citation when it supports (or contradicts) the entire previous sentence.

> **Example:** An individual may obtain court review after a final decision of the Commissioner of Social Security. *Sims v. Apfel*, 530 U.S. 103, 109 (2000).

- Use commas to surround a citation when it appears as a clause within a sentence, namely, when it supports (or contradicts) only part of the previous sentence.

Example: Although an individual may obtain court review after a final decision of the Commissioner of Social Security, *Sims v. Apfel*, 530 U.S. 103, 109 (2000), review may not be sought unless the individual has exhausted all administrative remedies, *Weinberger v. Salfi*, 422 U.S. 749, 755 (1975).

- Use a semicolon to follow a citation when the citation appears in a *string* of other citations. (*Bluebook* B3.5 and Rule 1.4; *ALWD* Rule 45). Sometimes legal writers cite more than one authority in support of a proposition. When citations appear in a string, however, they must be ordered in a strict hierarchy. *The Bluebook* (but not *ALWD*) allows the reader to place the most helpful citation first. Except in this situation, list citations in the order directed by *The Bluebook* and *ALWD*.

Example: If a claimant fails to request review from the Social Security Appeals Council, there may be no judicial review. 42 U.S.C. § 401 (2006);   *Bowen v. New York*, 476 U.S. 467, 473 (1986); *Weinberger v. Salfi*, 422 U.S. 749, 757 (1975); *Graves v. Lowell*, 433 F.3d 102, 109 (4th Cir. 2005).

3. *Quotations (Bluebook B12 and R.5; ALWD R.5 and R.47)*

a. Introduction to Pinpoints

You must always indicate the exact page a quotation appears on (generally called a *pinpoint* or *pincite*). Moreover, as a courtesy to your reader, you must include a pinpoint even when you paraphrase material. If parallel citations are given, you must indicate the pinpoint for all sources. Per *The Bluebook*, if your quotation spans more than one page, provide the inclusive page numbers but separate them by a hyphen; retain the last two digits, but omit any other repetitious digits.

Bluebook *Example:*   "Divorce ends tenancy by the entirety." *Craft v. Craft*, 535 U.S. 274, 282-83 (2002).

ALWD allows you to either keep all of the digits or drop repetitious digits, so long as two digits are retained. Thus, under *ALWD*, either of the following is correct: 282-83 or 282-283.

b. Indicating Quotations in Text

The rules for showing quotations are nearly identical in *The Bluebook* and *ALWD*: Indent longer quotations (those that are 50 words or more) and do not use quotation marks for such longer quotes. These indented quotations are usually called *block quotes*, and they should be fully justified. Place shorter quotations (those that are fewer than 50 words) in the narrative portion of the text, using quotation marks, and always placing commas and periods inside the quotation marks. *ALWD* allows writers to indent quotations if they are 50 words or more or if they exceed 4 lines of text.

c. Altering Quotations and Using Ellipses (*Bluebook* R.5.2 and 5.3; *ALWD* R.48 and 49)

Use brackets to show a minor addition to or omission from a quotation.

> ***Example:*** "Failure to produce evidence within a party's [exclusive] control raises the presumption that it would operate against him." *Long v. Earle*, 269 N.W. 577, 581 (Mich. 1936).

Use an ellipsis to show an omission from the middle or end of a quotation. Use correct spacing as indicated by *The Bluebook* or *ALWD*.

> ***Examples:*** "The Court of Appeals found that large [political] contributions are intended to . . . gain special treatment." *McConnell v. FEC*, 540 U.S. 93, 119 (2003).
>
> "The appellant's statements permitted the inference that he was prepared to use his weapon . . . ." *Monroe v. Fisher*, 538 U.S. 19, 26 (2002).

4. *Citation Signals (*Bluebook *B3 and R.1.2;* ALWD *R.44)*

Legal writers often use certain *citation signals* as a shorthand method of indicating to the reader the manner in which an authority supports or contradicts an assertion. For example, *The Bluebook* provides that the signal *see* is placed before a citation when the citation clearly supports the proposition.

> ***Example:*** Language in a statute must be read in context. *See Hibbs v. Wynn*, 542 U.S. 88, 101 (2004).

Do not use any signal when your cited authority directly states the proposition, is the source of a quotation, or identifies an authority referred to in the text.

> *Example:*   "An assessment is closely tied to the collection of a tax."
> *Hibbs v. Wynn*, 542 U.S. 88, 101 (2004).

The signals can be very confusing, and often there are only very subtle shadings of difference between one signal and another. Some of the signals have shifted their meanings from one edition of *The Bluebook* to another. Moreover, there are subtle differences in the presentation and meaning of the signals depending on whether you are following *The Bluebook* or *ALWD*. For example, *The Bluebook* follows the signal *e.g.* with a comma, whereas *ALWD* does not. These signals are often used more in academic legal writing, such as law review articles, than in court briefs and legal memoranda. Carefully review *Bluebook* Rule 1.2 and *ALWD* Rule 44 for the use, meaning, and presentation of these signals.

5. *Short-Form Citations*

Once you have cited an authority in full, to save time you may use a short form when you refer to it again later in your writing.

a.   Use of *Id.* (*Bluebook* B4.2 and R.4.1; *ALWD* R.11.3)

The signal *id.* sends your reader to the immediately preceding authority, whether it is a case, statute, or any other legal authority. Underscore or italicize the period in *id.*

> *Example:*   Title X of the Public Health Service Act provides federal funding for family-planning services. *Rust v. Sullivan*, 500 U.S. 173, 179 (1991). When language in a federal statute is ambiguous, courts typically defer to the expertise of the agency charged with administering the statute. *Id.*

Follow these tips when using *id.*:

- Use *id.* alone when directing a reader to the exact source/page/section/paragraph as the preceding citation. Use "*id.* plus" the change to send the reader to a different page or paragraph.

First reference:	*Avco Corp. v. Machinists,* 390 U.S. 557, 560 (1968).
Second reference:	*Id.* at 561.

- *The Bluebook* prohibits the use of the word "at" before a section or paragraph symbol. (Note that *ALWD* includes the word "at" before a symbol.)

First *Bluebook* reference: Susan Gray, *Due Process* § 101 (3d ed. 2001).

Second *Bluebook* reference: *Id.* § 207.

- *Id.* may be used to refer to an immediately preceding authority only if there is one citation in the previous reference.
- If you have given parallel citations for a case, *id.* replaces only the official cite, as follows: *Id.* at 122, 235 A.2d at 574.

b.   Use of *Supra* (*Bluebook* B8.2, B9.2, and R.4.2; *ALWD* R.11.4)

Supra means "above" and is used to direct a reader to a preceding (but not immediately preceding) authority. *The Bluebook* and *ALWD* both prohibit the use of *supra* for primary authorities, such as cases, statutes, and most legislative materials. Thus, *supra* is most frequently used as a short form for books, law review articles, and other materials with an author's name. *ALWD*, however, states that *supra* can only be used in documents that have footnotes. Because many practitioners who submit documents to court do not use footnotes but rather place their citations in the text of the document, *ALWD* would seem to rule out the use of *supra* for these practitioners.

First citation: Stephen Faberman, *Special Relationships, Schools, and the Fifth Circuit*, 35 B.C. L. Rev. 97, 105 (1993).

Intervening citation: 45 U.S.C. § 2442 (2006).

Supra citation: Faberman, *supra*, at 114.

Infra (meaning "below") directs a reader to a later citation and is not commonly used in legal writing, although it is often used in indexes to sets of books such as U.S.C.A.

c.   Short Forms for Cases (*Bluebook* B4.2 and R.10.9; *ALWD* R.12.20)

Assume your full citation is *Hoyme v. Brakken*, 677 N.W.2d 233, 235 (Wis. 1999). Once you have given this full citation, you may use any of the following short forms, so long as the reader will be able to locate readily the earlier full citation:

- *Hoyme*, 677 N.W.2d at 236.
- 677 N.W.2d at 236. (Note that you should use the case name unless it is clear which case you are referencing.)
- *Id.* at 236.

d. Short Forms for Statutes (*Bluebook* B5.2 and R.12.10; *ALWD* R.14.6)

Once you have given a full citation to a statute, generally, you may later use any short form that clearly identifies the statute.

6. *Neutral Citation Format* (Bluebook R.10.3.3; ALWD R.12.16)

Current citation rules mandate citation to conventional print sources, the majority of which are published by West, requiring legal professionals to purchase West sets even though cases and other materials are easy and inexpensive (or free) to access on the Internet. Thus, many legal professionals and consumers advocate the use of what is usually referred to as a neutral, public domain, or universal citation system, meaning that the citation looks the same whether the reader has accessed the case by conventional print format, through Lexis or Westlaw, or on the Internet. Generally, the neutral citation includes the case name, year of decision, the state's two-character postal code, the court abbreviation (unless the court is the state's highest court), the sequential number of the decision, and, if a parallel citation is available, it must be given. A pinpoint paragraph rather than a pinpoint page is given.

> **Example:**   *Renville v. Taylor*, 2007 ND 217, ¶ 14, 607 N.W.2d 109, 114.

The preceding example tells the reader that the case *Renville v. Taylor* was the 217th case decided by the highest court in North Dakota in 2007, and the reader is specifically directed to paragraph 14 in that case. The remaining part of the citation is a parallel citation to West's *Northwestern Reporter, Second Series*.

Only a handful of states have adopted public domain citation formats. In fact, since 2003, only Arkansas and Illinois have done so, and the movement toward universal citation appears to be at a standstill. There is a great deal of discrepancy among the adopting states as to spacing and punctuation in the citations, so carefully follow the examples you are given by local rules, Table T.1.3 of *The Bluebook*, and Appendix 2 of *ALWD*.

Help Line

Online Citation Primer

Professor Peter W. Martin of Cornell University Law School has published an online guide to citation form entitled *Introduction to Basic Legal Citation* (online ed. 2013) for both *The Bluebook* and *ALWD*. The guide provides information on the purpose of legal citations and examples for nearly all citation formats.

The website address is as follows: http://www.law.cornell .edu/citation. Consider "bookmarking" this valuable site as one of your favorite sites. Use it as a "backup" or to confirm the accuracy of your citations.

Caveat: Although this site is excellent and provides great examples, always use *The Bluebook* or *ALWD* as the final authority. Nevertheless, this website will provide you with a wealth of valuable information and numerous examples of citation form.

---

7. *Capitalization Rules (*Bluebook *R.8; ALWD R.3.3)*

The Bluebook and *ALWD* both offer guidance on capitalizing certain words, including the following:

- **Circuit.** Capitalize "circuit" only when used with a circuit number or name, as in "the Fifth Circuit held that . . . ."
- **Court.** Capitalize "court":
  - When naming a court in full, as in "The California Supreme Court held."
  - *ALWD* capitalizes the word "Court" when referring to the highest court in any jurisdiction once it has been identified by full name; *The Bluebook* does not.
  - *The Bluebook* always capitalizes any reference to the United States Supreme Court.
  - When referring to the court to which a document is submitted, as in "Plaintiff respectfully requests this Court grant her motion."
- **Party Designations.** Capitalize "plaintiff," "defendant," and so forth when referring to a party in the pending case, as in "The Defendant in this action moved for a change of venue."
- **Federal.** Capitalize "federal" only when it precedes a capitalized word, as in "the Federal Elections Commission." Do not capitalize "federal" in phrases such as "the federal government."

8. *Electronic Sources* (Bluebook *R.18;* ALWD *R.38-42)*

The Bluebook and *ALWD* both disfavor citing electronic sources, such as Lexis, Westlaw, or the Internet when materials are available in print format. Follow these rules:

- *The Bluebook* requires the use and citation of traditional printed sources when they are available *unless* there is a digital copy that has been authenticated (by the use of a logo showing it has been verified by a government entity as unaltered), it is official (meaning it has been designated as official by some entity), or it is an exact copy of the printed source. When such an authenticated, official, or exact copy of a source is available, it may be cited as if to the original source (without any URL information). For example, because the new Federal Digital System (http://www.gpo.gov /fdsys) offers authenticated federal materials including statutes and regulations, you may cite to these without giving any URL information, as follows: 7 U.S.C. § 1081 (2006).
- *ALWD* provides that if a source is available in both print and electronic formats, cite only to the print source if it is readily available to most readers.
- Under *Bluebook* rules, you may add an electronic source as a parallel citation if it will substantially improve access to the information.

Examples: *Bluebook* example: *Hillside Dairy Inc. v. Lyons*, 539 U.S. 59 (2003), *available at* http://supreme.justia.com/ us/539/59/index.html.

ALWD example: *Kunkle v. Texas*, http://www.supreme-court.gov/opinions/boundvolumes/543bv.pdf (U.S. Nov. 18, 2004).

- If a source does not exist in conventional print format or on Lexis or Westlaw, you may cite solely to the Internet. *The Bluebook* and *ALWD* provide numerous specific formats in Rules 18 and 38-42, respectively. For periodical articles that exist only on the Internet (and not in print form), follow *Bluebook* R. 18 and *ALWD* R. 23.1(i).

Example: *Bluebook* and *ALWD* example for article on the Internet: Vicki L. Gregory, *UCITA: What Does It Mean for Libraries?*, 25 Online 1, ¶ 3 (2001), http://www.info-today.com/online/OL2001/gregory1_01.html.

- You may need to cite to cases that have not been selected for publication, in which instance you will need to cite to either Lexis or Westlaw. Follow *Bluebook* B4.1.4 and Rule 18 and *ALWD* Rule 12.12.

Examples: *Bluebook* examples: *United States v. Carlton*, No. 11-4429, 2012 WL 739246, at *2 (4th Cir. July 2, 2012).

Brown v. Ford Motor Co., No. 12-2513, 2013 U.S. Dist. LEXIS 4539, at *4 (D. Del. Mar. 23, 2013).

ALWD examples: *U.S. v. Carlton*, 2011 WL 739246 at *2 (4th Cir. July 2, 2012).

Brown v. Ford Motor Co., 2013 U.S. Dist. LEXIS 4539 at *4 (D. Del. Mar. 23, 2013).

9. *Lexis and Westlaw Assistance for Citation Form*

Neither Lexis nor Westlaw can perfectly format citations according to all *Bluebook* or *ALWD* rules; however, both services offer resources that provide some citation assistance (see Chapter 11). Lexis offers two automated tools for cite checking: BriefCheck and Brief Suite, both of which help ensure your citations are valid and in proper form. Similarly, Westlaw's KeyCite service (see Chapter 11) also provides citation verification information, such as a correct case name and parallel citations. West also offers CiteAdvisor, which can build a table of authorities and suggest correct citation format in either *Bluebook* or *ALWD* format. In addition, a company called Cite-R-Us.com has introduced Citrus, its fee-based software program that automatically generates citations in correct *Bluebook* form (*see* https://www.correctcite.com). Finally, WestlawNext offers assistance in *Bluebook* and other citation formats (see Chapter 8 and the Practice Tip in this chapter). Although all of these systems are helpful, none can determine when you should use a signal, when you should include a parenthetical, and other similar decisions that require the use of discretion and an understanding of *Bluebook* and *ALWD* principles.

Internet Resources ▬▬▬▬▬▬▬▬▬▬▬▬▬▬▬▬

http://www.legalbluebook .com	*The Bluebook*'s website provides an overview of changes to the Nineteenth Edition, asks for comments and corrections, and provides introductory material about *The Bluebook*.
http://www.alwd.org	The website of the Association of Legal Writing Directors offers information about *ALWD*, updates to *ALWD*, explanations of citation rules, and numerous other resources.
http://www.law.cornell.edu/ citation	Professor Peter W. Martin provides examples and explanations of *Bluebook* and *ALWD* citation forms.
http://lexisnexis.com/icw	Lexis offers an "interactive citation workstation" allowing users to quiz themselves on both *Bluebook* and *ALWD* citation formats.
http://libguides.law.ucla.edu/ citechecking	UCLA School of Law provides a resource guide on citation form.

Citation Form Assignment

There is at least one thing wrong with each fictitious citation below. Correct the citations using the current edition of *The Bluebook* or *ALWD*. You may need to supply missing information such as dates. Punctuation is not needed after the citations. Assume you are preparing a memorandum in your office and, unless otherwise indicated, assume that the citations appear in textual sentences rather than as stand-alone citations. There is no need to include "pinpoints," unless otherwise directed.

1. Adam Anderson versus Sarah Reynolds, a U.S. Supreme Court case from 2009, at volume 545, page 210.
2. Hammond Limited versus Peter Gordon Incorporated, reported at page 761 in volume 335 of the Federal Reporter, Third Series, from the Ninth Circuit and decided in 2012.
3. Show that the U.S. Supreme Court denied certiorari for the above case in 2013.
4. United States of America v. Erica Hanson, reported at volume 303 of the Federal Supplement, Second Series, at page 850, with a quotation from pages 861-863, decided by the Eastern District of Texas in 2009.
5. Show that the Fifth Circuit Court of Appeals reversed the above case in 2010.
6. Michael and Susan Goodman versus Lee Association, a Missouri Court of Appeals case from 2004, at volume 789, page 116.
7. State of Missouri v. Kelly, a Missouri Supreme Court case from 2005, at volume 791, page 322.
8. Cameron Company v. Miller and Harris Incorporated, a Massachusetts case decided by the Supreme Judicial Court in 2009, at volume 406, page 999. Assume that a court requires parallel citations.
9. Shapiro v. Allan and Anna Ross, a 1990 case from the Oregon Court of Appeals at volume 468, page 43. Assume that a court requires parallel citations.
10. Sections 303-309 of Title 11 of the United States Code.
11. Section 409 of Title 35 of the United States Code Annotated.
12. Arizona Revised Statutes Annotated, Section 10-104.
13. California Government Code Section 5062.
14. Federal Rules of Appellate Procedure 32.
15. Restatement of Trusts, Second, Section 406.
16. Volume 3 of Daniel R. Reese's treatise, "Trial Tactics and Strategy," Section 915, third edition (2011).
17. Assume that after your document cites section 915 of the above treatise, you immediately cite section 942 of the treatise (and that there are no intervening citations). How would you present the second citation?

18. A law review article entitled "Shareholder Litigation," written by Samuel A Lawson, Jr. and Lydia Miller, at volume 51 of the Southern University Law Review, page 355.

19. Show how to cite the definition of "merger" on page 780 of the current edition of Black's Law Dictionary.

20. Show that the following 2007 U.S. Supreme Court case was decided by an 8-1 decision: Food and Drug Administration versus Booker, volume 546 of the U.S. Reports, page 390, with a quotation on pages 399-401.

21. Show that Justice Kennedy concurred in the above-referenced case.

22. Show to present the following case name if you were presenting it in a textual sentence and then as a "stand alone" citation: Northern Engineering Enterprises, Inc. versus Philadelphia Unified School District.

23. List the order of the following authorities if you are string citing: A United States Supreme Court case from 2007; a federal statute; a United States Supreme Court case from 2005; a case from the Minnesota Supreme Court from 2012; a case from the California Supreme Court from 2001; a case from the California Court of Appeals from 2008; a case from the Eighth Circuit Court of Appeals from 2010.

24. Show how to cite page 870 of the case United States of America v. Erica Hanson (question 4 above) as a short form (assuming you cannot use *id.*).

25. Show how to cite section 920 of the treatise by Daniel R. Reese (question 16 above) as a short form (assuming you cannot use *id.*).

Memorandum Assignment

There are numerous errors in the fictitious citations in the following brief memorandum. Correct citation errors using the current edition of *The Bluebook* or *ALWD*. You may need to supply missing information.

Under the principle known as the "business judgment rule," corporate directors are generally immunized from liability for decisions made by them so long as they had a reasonable basis for their decision and acted in good faith. *Miller v. Technology Corporation,* 590 F.3rd 109, 116 (8th Circ. 2001). Thus, even if the corporation sustains harm as a result of the board's decision, directors are protected from liability by acting in good faith. See *Harrison v. Parker Manufacturing Company*, 604 F.3d 665, 669-671 (9th Cir. 2004). Thus, if mistakes are made or errors in judgment occur, directors are generally not liable unless they failed to act with reasonable care. US vs. Hamilton Brothers, 540 U. S. 662 (2002). This is the position of California, Calif. Corp. Code sections 404-06, and that of most states, Henry Markham, "Corporate Liability" §109 (Second Ed. 2006) (which noted that states are in remarkable agreement on this principle).

In essence, a presumption exists that the board acted in good faith and with sound business judgment, and so long as some rational business purpose can be found for board action or inaction, the directors will be protected from liability for their decision-making. *Miller*, 590 F. 3d 120. Delaware has taken this approach a step further by providing that the corporation can state in its certificate of incorporation that directors will only be liable for conduct that involves illegality, a breach of the duty of loyalty, personal benefit, intentional misconduct, or payment of an unlawful dividend. Del. Code ann. Tit. 8, section 102.

Courts have stated that the law presumes that in making a business decision, the directors of a corporation acted on an informed basis, in good faith, and in the honest belief that the action taken was in the best interests of the corporation. *Peter O'Brien vs. Reynolds Pharmaceutical Corp.*, 807 S.E. 2d 14, 16 (Ga. S. Ct. 2005). This presumption, however, can be rebutted if a plaintiff shows the directors breached their fiduciary duty of care or loyalty or acted in bad faith. Henry Markham, supra at § 114. In sum, there is a delicate balance between the need for protecting directors' decisions from endless second-guessing and the need for shareholder and investor protection. Id.

Internet Assignment

1. Access the website for *The Bluebook*.
   a. Select "Introduction." What is the best place to begin study of *The Bluebook*?
   b. Select "Blue Tips." What is the function of this page or section?
   c. Select "Bluebook Updates." What is the function of this page or section?
2. Access the website of the Association of Legal Writing directors at http://www.alwd.org. Select "Publications" and then "ALWD Citation Manual Resources." Review the Comparison Chart.
   a. What is the difference in the presentation of capitalization between *The Bluebook* and *ALWD*?
   b. What is the difference in the presentation of page spans between *The Bluebook* and *ALWD*?

3. Locate California Rules of Court. Review Court Rule 1.200. What citation form is used when submitting documents to California courts?
4. Access Professor Peter W. Martin's "Introduction to Basic Legal Citation." Select "Placing Citations in Context" and review the information on Short Form Citations. What are the acceptable short form citations for a federal statute?

Updating and Validating Your Research

Chapter Overview

Before you may cite any primary authority in any document you prepare, you must ensure it is still "good law." This is an inflexible rule of legal research. Updating and validating your authorities can be conducted manually (using a set of books called *Shepard's Citations*) or electronically on Lexis (using *Shepard's Citations*) or Westlaw (using its system called *KeyCite*). Previously, when everyone used the conventional print sources, the process was always called *Sheparding*; this term is often used today to describe the process of ensuring your authorities are still valid, whether one uses *Shepard's* sources or West's KeyCite.

A. Using *Shepard's* in Print Form to Shepardize Cases

1. Introduction

Very few people validate their authorities manually—using print rather than electronic sources—because validating electronically is quicker and provides more current information. In fact, most law firms no longer subscribe to *Shepard's* in print, relying exclusively on electronic updating. Nevertheless, a thorough grounding in the way the conventional print versions of *Shepard's* work will enhance your understanding of the techniques and value of online updating.

There is a set of *Shepard's Citations* for each set of case reports. Thus, for example, there are sets called *Shepard's Arizona Citations* and

Shepard's Atlantic Reporter Citations. A set of *Shepard's* usually consists of two or three hardbound volumes (always a deep maroon color) and one or two softcover supplements or advance sheets. Each advance sheet displays a notice labeled "What Your Library Should Contain," which lists the volumes of *Shepard's* you will need to complete your task.

2. *Locating Shepard's References to Your Case*

Assume the case you are Shepardizing is *People v. Briceno*, 99 P.3d 1007 (Cal. 2004). Because this is a case published in the *Pacific Reporter*, you will need to locate the volumes of *Shepard's Pacific Reporter Citations.* Open the first volume in the set and scan the upper corners of each page looking for a reference to **Vol. 99**, the volume of the *Pacific Reporter, Third Series*, in which *Briceno* is reported. This process is similar to looking at the guide words in the upper corners of each page in a dictionary to determine which page will contain the word you need.

When you have located the page or pages for **Vol. 99**, scan this page looking for the black boldfaced typed reference **–1007–**, because this is the page on which *Briceno* begins (see Figure 11-1). There are three possibilities.

• **No Reference.** It is possible that there is no reference at all to **–1007–**. Lack of a reference to your page is an indication that during the period of time covered by that volume of *Shepard's*, no case or other authority mentioned *Briceno* in any manner. If this occurs, proceed to examine the next *Shepard's* volume, and so forth.

• **References in Parentheses.** Citations or references appearing in parentheses are parallel citations for *Briceno*. The first time a volume of *Shepard's* mentions your case, you will be given parallel citations (assuming they exist). This is an easy and efficient way of locating parallel citations.

• **References Not in Parentheses.** Citations listed below **–1007–** that do not appear in parentheses are references to the history of *Briceno* as it has traveled through the courts and treatment by sources that have mentioned, discussed, or commented on *Briceno*.

3. *Analysis of Shepard's References*

a. **Abbreviations**

You may have already observed that the presentation of citations in *Shepard's* is not in *Bluebook* or *ALWD* format. In fact, the citations given you by *Shepard's* have a uniquely cramped appearance. Because *Shepard's* is tasked with presenting so much information as efficiently as possible, it has developed its own "shorthand" references for cases and other legal authorities. You will quickly learn how to correctly interpret the *Shepard's* references. If you have any difficulty, check the Table of Abbreviations placed in the front of each *Shepard's* volume.

Figure 11-1
Sample Page from *Shepard's Pacific Reporter Citations*

PACIFIC REPORTER, 3d SERIES (California Cases)   Vol. 101

39CaR3d158	f 132P3d247	34CaR3d⁵587	**Vol. 99**	25CaR3d²¹456	106P3d316

39CaR3d158
41CaR3d389
j 114P3d815
  Cir. 2
d 402FS2d440
  Cir. 5
f 2006USApp
  [LX1066
f 163Fed Appx
  [308
39SFR1045
104McL1407

Vol. 96

—30—
People v Coff-
man and
Marlow
2004
cc 17CaR3d825
cc 96P3d126
2006Cal LX
  [5392
2006Cal LX
  [5867
20CaR3d365
22CaR3d24
24CaR3d⁷⁴657
25CaR3d349
25CaR3d713
26CaR3d43
26CaR3d884
29CaR3d599
30CaR3d531
31CaR3d¹⁴⁹
  [147
32CaR3d²⁵48
32CaR3d¹⁴251
32CaR3d²⁶914
33CaR3d527
37CaR3d⁵¹127
37CaR3d⁵²127
37CaR3d⁴⁹131
38CaR3d126
f 38CaR3d130
38CaR3d171
e 39CaR3d451
40CaR3d147
41CaR3d615
f 42CaR3d45
42CaR3d305
101P3d976
106P3d1001
107P3d823
108P3d217
114P3d773
115P3d¹⁴⁹460
116P3d²⁵515
116P3d¹⁴²517
117P3d²⁶608
118P3d560
126P3d962
f 126P3d965
126P3d999
129P3d345
131P3d1014

f 132P3d247
  Cir. 9
2006USDist
  [LX10612
2006USDist
  [LX13546
92VaL327

—126—
People v
Marlow
2004
US cert den
544US953
US cert den
161LẼ532
US cert den
125SC1706
cc 17CaR3d710
cc 96P3d30

—141—
In re Marriage
of Harris
2004
2006CalApp
  [LX471
29CaR3d247
34CaR3d³484
37CaR3d⁵318
37CaR3d⁶318
37CaR3d³458
38CaR3d³21
f 38CaR3d618
e 38CaR3d618
d 38CaR3d902
39CaR3d793
112P3d634
f 121P3d298
f 127P3d34
e 127P3d34
129P3d5
36GGU121
38LoyL1871
78SCL1529

—170—
People v Haley
2004
~ 23CaR3d401
26CaR3d15
41CaR3d614
f 41CaR3d651
108P3d194
131P3d1013
f 131P3d1044

—194—
Sav-On Drug
Stores, Inc. v
Superior Court
2004
26CaR3d339
#f 26CaR3d339
29CaR3d416
32CaR3d487
~ 32CaR3d496
34CaR3d⁵576
34CaR3d²584

34CaR3d⁵587
35CaR3d²100
f 35CaR3d²270
35CaR3d²270
35CaR3d⁷270
35CaR3d¹679
113P3d95
116P3d1166
~ 116P3d1173
  Cir. 9
2006USDist
  [LX9010
2006USDist
  [LX26778

—496—
Claxton v
Waters
2004
j 36CaR3d340
37CaR3d⁴212
j 123P3d614

—507—
People v
Barker
2004
20CaR3d364
#f 20CaR3d365
20CaR3d500
24CaR3d265
f 24CaR3d268
25CaR3d105
26CaR3d372
26CaR3d883
28CaR3d659
34CaR3d656
38CaR3d633
39CaR3d827
111P3d932
120P3d1050
127P3d48
129P3d34

Vol. 98

—876—
People v Wil-
liams
2004
d 28CaR3d10
j 28CaR3d20
d 110P3d1223
j 110P3d1232

Vol. 99

—500—
Stockett v
Association of
Cal. Water
Agencies Joint
Powers Ins.
Authority
2004
2006CalApp
  [LX717
25CaR3d57
  Cir. 9
2005USDist
  [LX26941
2005USDist
  [LX27375
2006USDist
  [LX6838
f 2006USDist
  [LX26651
2006USDist
  [LX28446

—505—
People v
Turner
2004
30CaR3d551
32CaR3d42
32CaR3d¹¹889
33CaR3d¹¹32
33CaR3d433
39CaR3d892
41CaR3d336
114P3d790
116P3d510
117P3d¹¹587
117P3d¹¹649
118P3d481
131P3d414

—1007—
People v Bri-
ceno
2004
22CaR3d277
22CaR3d421
22CaR3d852
f 22CaR3d853
j 30CaR3d579
33CaR3d²635
34CaR3d16
f 34CaR3d¹⁰17
f 34CaR3d18
36CaR3d³454
j 39CaR3d188
i 114P3d813

—1015—
McClung v
Employment
Development
Dept.
2004
j 22CaR3d530

25CaR3d²¹456
25CaR3d⁶508
25CaR3d¹⁸508
26CaR3d535
26CaR3d³633
30CaR3d11
36CaR3d548
d 36CaR3d549
f 37CaR3d¹28
37CaR3d²28
37CaR3d⁸29
37CaR3d¹¹29
37CaR3d¹⁴29
38CaR3d502
f 40CaR3d645
j 102P3d914
32WSR155

Vol. 100

—870—
People v Seel
2004
2006Cal LX
  [6173

Vol. 101

—140—
Graham v
DaimlerChrys-
ler Corp.
2004
2006CalApp
  [LX728
2006CalApp
  [LX789
2006CalApp
  [LX801
19CaR3d322
f 21CaR3d375
j 21CaR3d377
23CaR3d470
24CaR3d820
24CaR3d879
25CaR3d523
30CaR3d206
33CaR3d273
33CaR3d¹281
33CaR3d²281
33CaR3d¹³281
f 33CaR3d283
33CaR3d¹¹284
33CaR3d779
33CaR3d¹822
37CaR3d⁹553
37CaR3d¹¹645
38CaR3d¹¹29
38CaR3d¹965
38CaR3d²¹65
39CaR3d560
39CaR3d793
40CaR3d220
41CaR3d561
d 41CaR3d566
104P3d827

106P3d316
129P3d5
129P3d407
  Cir. 9
f 2005USDist
  [LX36806
2005USDist
  [LX40142
f 373FS2d1032
d 407FS2d1122
q 407FS2d1123
42SDL1295

—174—
Tipton-
Whittingham v
City of Los
Angeles
2004.
2006CalApp
  [LX789
j 21CaR3d362
33CaR3d273
33CaR3d³282
f 33CaR3d283
33CaR3d⁷283
33CaR3d²285
39CaR3d793
41CaR3d566
129P3d5
  Cir. 9
d 2005USDist
  [LX40142
373FS2d1033

—478—
People v
Ramos
2004
US cert den
163LẼ108
US cert den
126SC91
31CaR3d¹⁴506
31CaR3d¹⁵506
32CaR3d²⁶866
33CaR3d544
35CaR3d787
36CaR3d776
f 36CaR3d777
115P3d¹⁴¹162
115P3d¹⁵¹162
117P3d²⁶568
118P3d575
122P3d991
f 124P3d377

—509—
People v San
Nicolas
2004
US cert den
163LẼ79
US cert den
126SC46
29CaR3d849
30CaR3d706
32CaR3d522
Continued

b.   History References

Shepard's will provide you with the subsequent history of your case, meaning you will be informed how your case has been dealt with as it has progressed through the courts. Thus, you will be informed whether your case has been affirmed, whether certiorari was denied, and so forth. *Shepard's* provides you with this information, called *history references*, relating to the later history of your case by means of an identifying letter placed immediately before the citation. Most of the letters are easy to understand. For example, "a" means "affirmed," "r" means "reversed," and "m" means "modified." If you have difficulty understanding the meaning of a history letter, locate the Table of Abbreviations in each *Shepard's* volume.

c.   Treatment References

Shepard's will not only tell you how your case has been dealt with by higher courts, but it will also refer you to every other case as well as selected law reviews, annotations, and other authorities that discuss or even mention your case in passing. These sources, called *treatment references*, have been thoroughly analyzed, and *Shepard's* will inform you specifically how your case has been treated by these other sources, namely, whether it was mentioned in a dissenting opinion or criticized or questioned by a later authority. Some of the most common treatment abbreviations are as follows: "c" (for "criticized"); "d" (for "distinguished"); "e" (for "explained"); "f" (for "followed"); "o" (for "overruled"); and "q" (for "questioned").

Shepard's provides you with this information by means of an identifying letter placed immediately before the reference. Once again, most of the letters are easy to interpret, but if you have difficulty interpreting the letters, check the Table of Abbreviations in each *Shepard's* volume.

Pay careful attention in examining the treatment of your case. If the case you are relying upon is continually being questioned or criticized, you may wish to reevaluate your research strategies and attempt to locate a case that is more authoritative. If there is no identifying letter before a citation reference, the later case likely mentions your case in passing or in a string cite, without significant analysis.

4.   *Arrangement of Later Case References*

Although *Shepard's* does not provide dates for the cases it lists, it arranges the references in chronological order so you are first sent to earlier cases mentioning your case and then to more recent cases, allowing you to easily select more recent cases. Also, *Shepard's* references are precise; they direct you to the very page within a case on which your case is being discussed, rather than directing you to the first page of a case. Finally, *Shepard's* will arrange the cases by jurisdiction, when relevant, grouping together entries by circuit or state so you can readily locate cases from a specific jurisdiction that discuss your case.

Practice Tip

History and Treatment

The difference between the *history* of a case and the *treatment* of it is readily illustrated by comparing *reversed* (relating to the history of a case) with *overruled* (relating to the treatment of a case). A reversal refers to the later treatment of your case by a higher court discussing that very case. An overruling refers to how a case is treated by some entirely different case, perhaps years later. For example, *Brown v. Board of Education*, 347 U.S. 483 (1954) overruled the much earlier case of *Plessy v. Ferguson*, 163 U.S. 539 (1896).

---

5. *References to Headnotes*

Recall that when a case is reviewed by editors at a publishing company, they will assign headnote numbers for each legal issue in a case. It is possible that you are relying on only a portion of a case for a research project. Assume, for example, that you are relying on headnote 1 of *Briceno*. *Shepard's* will not only provide you with information relating to the treatment by later cases of *Briceno*, but will also focus on the cases that have discussed specific headnotes of *Briceno*.

These references are accomplished by small elevated or superscript numbers placed within the case citation given to you by *Shepard's*. For example, when Shepardizing *Briceno*, you observe that one of the *Shepard's* entries is 33CaR3d^2635 (see Figure 11-1). This indicates that page 635 of volume 33 of the *California Reporter, Third Series*, discusses the point of law discussed in headnote 2 of *Briceno*. This feature of *Shepard's* allows you readily to locate later cases discussing the specific points of law discussed in your case.

Thus, if you relied solely on the issue discussed in the first headnote of *Briceno*, you could quickly run your finger down the column of *Shepard's* entries looking for elevated "1s." Similarly, if, when you Shepardize, you discover that only headnote 4 of *Briceno* has been criticized or questioned, and you are relying solely on the point of law discussed in headnote 1 of *Briceno*, you may be able to bypass those references with elevated numbers other than "1." If a case is listed without an elevated number, this indicates that the later case discusses your case only in a general fashion.

6. *References to Sources Other Than Cases*

In addition to validating the case you rely on, *Shepard's* will direct you to a wide variety of other sources that mention or discuss your case. Thus, *Shepard's* functions as a finding tool to expand your research efforts by sending you to a variety of sources, including the following:

attorneys general opinions, law review articles, and A.L.R. annotations. See Figure 11-2 for steps in Shepardizing cases using the print volumes of *Shepard's*.

Figure 11-2
Steps in Shepardizing a Case Using Print Sources

- Locate the volumes of *Shepard's* you need (state *Shepard's*, regional *Shepard's*, or federal case *Shepard's*).
- Examine the front cover of the most recent issue of *Shepard's* and read the box labeled "What Your Library Should Contain." Gather all of the volumes needed.
- Examine the upper right and left corners of the pages in *Shepard's* to locate the volume number of the case you are Shepardizing.
- Scan down the page looking for the bold page number identical to the page on which your case begins.
- Carefully examine the entries listed, paying particular attention to the parallel citation, the history of the case as it progressed through the court system, its treatment by later cases, and any other sources, such as annotations and law review articles that cite your case.
- If desired, verify that you are Shepardizing correctly by checking one or two cites listed by *Shepard's* to ensure your case is, in fact, mentioned by these cites.
- Repeat, as needed, in other volumes of *Shepard's*.
- Examine and analyze troublesome entries, including later cases that criticize or question your case.

7. *FAQs: Using Shepard's and Analyzing Negative Letters*

Following are some of the most frequently asked questions relating to the Shepardizing process:

Question: Must I read every case or source mentioned by *Shepard's*?

Answer: You must certainly read any reference with a "negative" letter, such as "overruled." However, if you are pleased with your research project, you believe the cases you have cited persuasively support the arguments you have made, and Shepardizing reveals no negative treatment, your task is complete. On the other hand, if the issue you are researching is an uncertain area of the law or a newly emerging legal topic, read some of the later authorities identified in *Shepard's* to obtain better insight.

Question: How can I use *Shepard's* to find better or newer cases?

Answer: If you are not entirely pleased with the cases you have located, or the cases are a bit older than you would prefer, use *Shepard's* as a research tool to locate newer cases, cases from higher courts, or cases that more persuasively explain a legal issue. Look for "f" for "followed" or "e" for "explained" and read these cases.

Question: What should I do if my Shepardizing reveals a "negative" letter?

Answer: In all instances, retrieve and read the cases that have been assigned any negative letters; however, understand that it is possible that only a portion of your case has been limited or overruled and that the remainder is still authoritative. Carefully examine the elevated numbers to be sure that the part of the case you rely on (and not some other part or headnote) is, in fact, negatively treated.

Question: My case has two parallel citations—which do I Shepardize?

Answer: For state cases with parallel citations, most legal professionals Shepardize in the companion *Shepard's* for their cases. Thus, if you read a case in the *Kansas Reports*, Shepardize it in *Shepard's Kansas Citations* (rather than *Shepard's Pacific Reporter Citations*). This procedure will enable you to most effectively use the elevated (superscript) numbers given by *Shepard's* to pinpoint later discussion of the headnotes from your case. Few practitioners Shepardize both parallel citations; if your case has received negative treatment, *Shepard's* will inform you of such, no matter what set you use. Nevertheless, *Shepard's* itself recommends that you Shepardize your citation in all sources.

Question: When should I Shepardize?

Answer: When to Shepardize is left to your discretion. Consider Shepardizing fairly early in your research process for two reasons:

- To eliminate the possibility of discovering that a key case has been overruled or reversed, causing a last-minute crisis; and
- To locate other valuable research leads to develop your argument.

Some researchers Shepardize almost concurrently with performing legal research. In any event, you must Shepardize before any document with citations is filed with a court or given to your supervising attorney, a client, or the adverse party.

Question: How many volumes do I use when I Shepardize?

Answer: When you first learn to Shepardize, use all volumes. As you gain familiarity with the process, you will notice that the spines of the *Shepard's* volumes are marked with volume numbers or dates, and you need not Shepardize for any date before your case was decided.

Question: What if I never find any references in *Shepard's* for my case?

Answer: If your case is new, it is possible that no other cases have yet discussed your case; however, it is possible that you have transposed numbers in your citation, so carefully check your citation for accuracy.

B. Using *Shepard's* in Print Form to Shepardize Other Authorities

1. *Sheparding Statutes, Constitutions, and Administrative Regulations*

Just as you must Shepardize a case to determine whether it is still "good law," you must Shepardize the other primary authorities you rely on: statutes, constitutions, and administrative regulations (such as the regulations of the Federal Communications Commission). The process of Shepardizing these authorities is the same as that for cases.

* Locate the volume(s) of *Shepard's* you need, titled *Shepard's [State] Citations [for Statutes]*, *Shepard's Federal Statute Citations*, or *Shepard's Code of Federal Regulations Citations*.
* Examine the upper right and left corners of the pages in *Shepard's* to locate the title or article of the provision you are Shepardizing.
* Scan down the page, looking for a boldfaced entry for the particular section in which you are interested.
* Carefully examine the entries listed, paying particular attention to the history of your statute, constitutional provision, or regulation (for example, whether the statute has been repealed by the legislature) and then to its treatment by later cases (for example, whether a case merely discussed your statute or decided your statute was unconstitutional). Each volume of *Shepard's* will contain a Table of Abbreviations for any abbreviations used. Examine other sources, such as law review articles and annotations, if desired.
* Carefully analyze all troublesome entries. For example, "A2012C37" means that your statute has been amended and that the amending language can be found in Chapter 37 of your state's session laws for 2012.

2. *Shepardizing Other Authorities*

There are several other authorities that you can Sheypardize, including Restatements, court rules, and treaties. You will then be directed to authorities that have discussed your Restatement provision, court rule, or treaty.

Help Line

Shepard's *Daily Update Service*

The print volumes of *Shepard's* are updated approximately every six weeks. To make sure that nothing has happened in the past six weeks that negatively affects your case or statute, use *Shepard's* Daily Update Service. Call (800) 899-6000 to determine treatment of your case since your last print supplement arrived.

C. Electronic Updating of Legal Authorities

1. *Introduction to Electronic Updating*

For nearly 100 years, legal researchers updated their legal authorities through the conventional print versions of *Shepard's*. Electronic updating, however, provides more up-to-date validation of legal authorities and is easily accomplished. There is no need to learn quirky abbreviations. Negative history, such as reversal of a case, appears in plain English. Electronic updating eliminates the worry that you do not have all of the print volumes in a set of *Shepard's*. Checking your adversary's citations is easily accomplished. Finally, references are available online far more quickly than the print versions of *Shepard's* are published, thus giving you the most recent treatment of your authorities. Consequently, updating electronically is the preferred method for nearly all legal professionals. In fact, most law firms and law libraries no longer subscribe to the print volumes of *Shepard's*, and all updating is accomplished electronically, through the use of *Shepard's* online (offered by Lexis) or through West's online product, KeyCite. You may also use mobile devices such as iPhones to Sheypardize or KeyCite, so you may check the validity of your authorities on a moment's notice.

2. *Sheypardizing Online*

a. How to Sheypardize Cases Online Using Lexis

Assume the case you are updating is *United States v. Falstaff Brewing Corp.*, 332 F. Supp. 970 (D.R.I. 1971).

- If you are viewing this case on the Lexis screen, a *Shepard's* signal indicator will be displayed on the screen. If you click it, *Falstaff* will be immediately Shepardized.
- If you are not currently viewing *Falstaff* on your screen but are instead perhaps validating a written brief that mentions *Falstaff*, follow these steps:
  - Sign on to Lexis.
  - Click the *Shepard's* tab at the top of your screen.
  - Type in your citation (332 fs 970) in the open field.
  - By clicking the word "Check" on your screen, select one of the following options: "*Shepard's* for Research" (also called "FULL"), which will list every authority that mentions *Falstaff* or "*Shepard's* for Validation" (also called "KWIC"), which will provide you with negative history only, rather than all authorities that mention *Falstaff*. (See Figure 11-3.)

You are now ready to interpret your results. You will be informed, in plain English, whether *Falstaff* has been distinguished, criticized, followed, and so forth. If you are interested in one of these references, click on it and you will be immediately linked to that reference.

Shepard's uses *Signal Indicators* to inform you at a glance of the status of your case. These signal indicators appear at the top of the authority you are viewing on the screen. The following signal indicator graphics are used:

Figure 11-3
<u>Reviewing Shepard's Results Online</u>

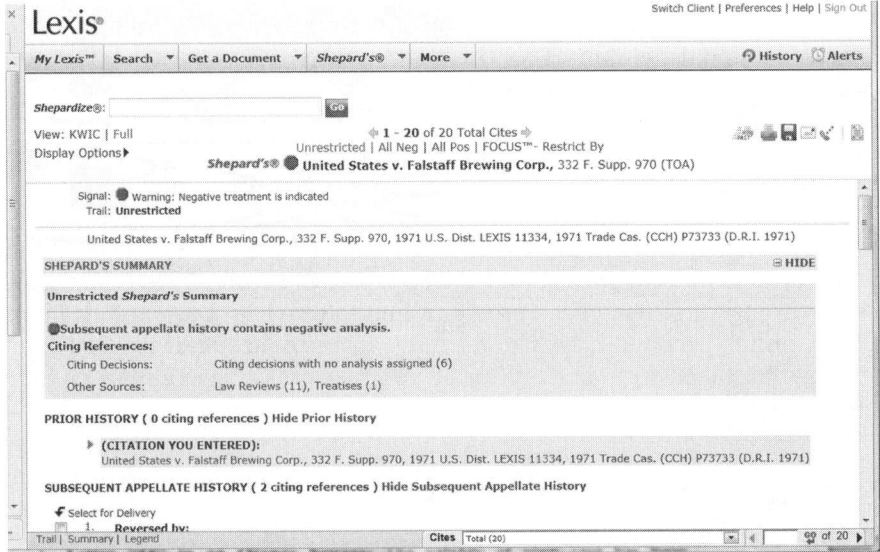

• **Red Stop Sign:** This signal warns that your case has strong negative history or treatment (such as being reversed).

• **Red Exclamation Point in a Red Circle:** A statute is subject to strong negative treatment.

• **Letter "Q" in an Orange Square:** The validity of your case has been questioned by other cases.

• **Yellow Yield Sign/Triangle:** This caution signal indicates that your case may have some negative history or treatment (such as being criticized).

• **Green Plus Sign:** Your case has positive history (such as being affirmed).

• **Letter "A" in a Blue Circle:** Your case has been analyzed in a neutral manner (such as being explained by a later case).

• **Letter "I" in a Blue Circle:** Other citation information is available for your case (such as a law review article that mentions your case).

These signals make Shepardizing online extremely easy because they tell you at a glance whether your citation is in trouble or whether it is cleared for your use. Note, however, that a red stop sign does not necessarily mean that your case is no longer good law; it simply means that your case has received strong negative treatment that you need to analyze.

b. Features of *Shepard's* Online

Shepard's provides a number of tools to maximize your research efforts:

• **FULL.** If you select "FULL," you will be given all prior and subsequent appellate history of your case and every reference from any case, law review, periodical, treatise, and A.L.R. annotation that mentions your case.

• **KWIC.** Selecting the KWIC option provides a quick answer to the question, "Is my case still good law?" You will not be sent to authorities that merely mention your case. Use KWIC when you are satisfied with your research efforts and only want to confirm that your case is still valid.

• **Summary.** Begin your analysis with *Shepard's* "Summary," which presents a readable summary showing why your case received a signal indicator. For example, you might be informed that your case was distinguished two times and followed once.

• **Custom Restrictions.** *Shepard's* "FOCUS" feature allows you to narrow the results you desire by selecting groups of citations to review by date, jurisdiction, and so forth. For example, you can elect to see only those cases that follow *Falstaff* after a certain date. Select "FOCUS."

• **Alert.** Alert is a clipping service that automatically monitors and reports changes in the treatment of *Falstaff*. You can elect to be notified daily, weekly, and so forth, by e-mail.

• **Table of Authorities.** Assume that *Falstaff* relied on and cited four cases. *Shepard's* validation tool called *Table of Authorities* analyzes those four cases cited in *Falstaff*, allowing you to reevaluate the cases on which *Falstaff* relied (because if their authority is weakened, *Falstaff* may also be suspect).

• **Lexis Advance's Graphical Display.** As discussed in Chapter 8, Lexis's new research service, Lexis Advance, provides a graphical view of your results. Select "Map" to see the appellate history of your case in an easy-to-understand flowchart format or select "Grid" to see a colorful grid display of the cases that questioned your case, treated it negatively, and so forth.

c. Sheparding Statutes and Regulations Online

Sheparding statutes or regulations online is nearly identical to Sheparding cases online. To Shepardize 18 U.S.C.S. § 212 (LexisNexis 2009), follow these steps:

- Sign on to Lexis.
- Click the *Shepard's* tab at the top of your screen.
- Type in your citation (18 uscs 212) in the open field.
- Select "FULL" (and you will be given every authority that mentions your statute) or "KWIC" (and you will be given negative history only rather than all authorities that mention your statute).

d. Other *Shepard's* Products

(1) *Automatic Validation Through BriefCheck*

Assume your research project cites 20 cases. Keying in 20 separate entries and then reading the results for these 20 cases can be time consuming. *Shepard's* offers a software program called *BriefCheck* (formerly known as CheckCite), which automatically checks all citations in your brief, without the necessity of your keying in a single citation. After you upload your document, the program "reads" it, locates and extracts your citations, checks them, and then provides the results either on your screen or in a separate printed report. You can elect "FULL" Shepardizing or the "KWIC" option. BriefCheck also checks your quotations for accuracy and locates discrepancies in case names, dates, and page numbers. BriefCheck is also useful for checking your adversary's documents to determine whether authorities cited are still good law.

(2) *Shepard's Link*

A new software application called *Shepard's Link* (formerly known as LEXLink) identifies citations in a word processing document (for example, a brief you are drafting) and creates hyperlinks to Lexis so you and readers of your document can instantly link to the cases you cite.

3. *KeyCite*

a. How to KeyCite Cases Using Westlaw

KeyCite is West's service that electronically updates and validates your legal authorities. KeyCite can be accessed on the Internet through http://web2.westlaw.com. Although there are some differences between online Shepardizing and KeyCiting, the services are probably more alike than different.

Assume you want to KeyCite the *Falstaff* case.

- If you are viewing this case on the Westlaw screen, a KeyCite status flag will be displayed at the top of your case (for example, a red flag, a yellow flag, or a blue "H"). Click the flag or signal to access KeyCite.
- If you are not currently viewing *Falstaff* on your screen but are instead perhaps validating a written brief that mentions *Falstaff*, follow these steps:
  - Sign onto Westlaw.
  - Click the KeyCite tab on the toolbar at the top of your screen.
  - Type in your citation (332 fs 970) in the open field and click "Go."
  - Alternatively, you may type a citation in the "KeyCite this citation" text box that is displayed in the left frame of most screens.

You are now ready to interpret your results. The first thing that appears is any history of the case. Like *Shepard's* online, KeyCite uses signal indicators or graphics to instantly convey information to you about the status of your case:

- **Red Flag.** A red flag warns that your case is no longer good law for at least one of the issues it discusses (such as being reversed or overruled).
- **Yellow Flag.** Your case has some negative history, such as being criticized or limited.
- **Blue "H."** The case has some history, such as being explained or having certiorari granted.
- **Green "C."** This signal indicates that the case has been cited by some references but there is no direct history or negative citing references.

You can easily link to cases that discuss *Falstaff* by clicking on them.

b. Features of KeyCite

KeyCite offers several features (see Figure 11-4) to assist you with your updating and validating:

- **Citation History Options.** You can customize your KeyCite results to display different types of case history for your case. By clicking

Figure 11-4
KeyCite Screen Showing History of Case

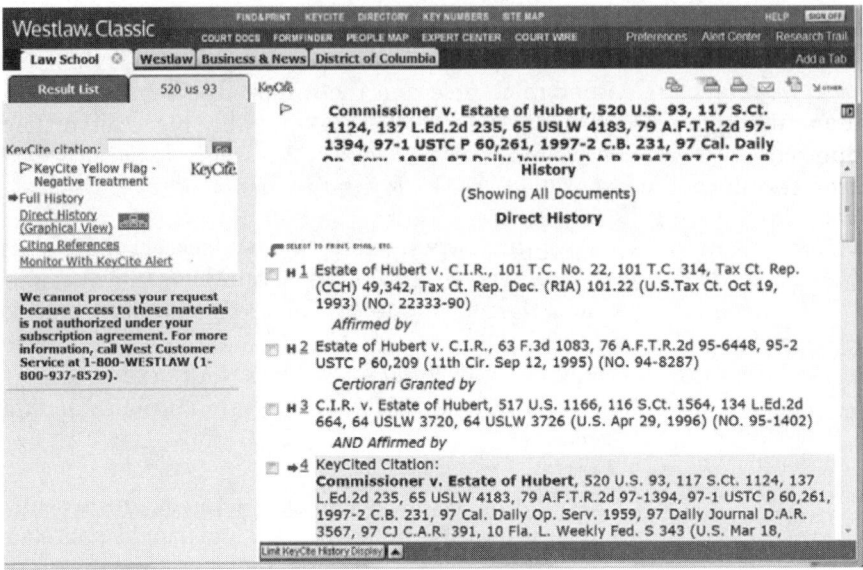

on "Full History," you will be given the complete history of your case; by clicking on "Citing References," you will be directed to numerous other cases and sources that mention or discuss your case, including secondary sources and briefs that cite your case.

• **Graphical Display of Direct History.** A new Westlaw feature shows you the direct history of your case in an easy-to-understand flow-chart format. For example, you would be shown in graphical format, using arrows, how your case progressed from trial, through its initial appeal, when certiorari was granted, and then what the United States Supreme Court held. You may easily link to the case decision and to the court briefs filed at each level of the case's history.

• **Limit KeyCite Display.** If the list of sources that mention your case is lengthy, you can restrict or narrow your list. Select the "Limit KeyCite Display" button at the bottom of the screen to narrow results by date, jurisdiction, headnote, and so forth. For example, you elect to view only cases that discuss headnote 2 of *Falstaff*.

• **Depth of Treatment Stars.** As KeyCite lists the cases that mention *Falstaff*, a number of green stars may be displayed next to each citation. These stars tell you the extent to which a citing case discusses *Falstaff*. Four green stars means that the case examines *Falstaff* in depth; three green stars indicates a substantial discussion of *Falstaff*; two stars means there is some brief discussion of *Falstaff*; and one star indicates that *Falstaff* was mentioned in passing, usually in a string citation.

• **Quotation Marks.** If KeyCite displays quotation marks (") after a case citation, it means that the case quotes from *Falstaff*.

- **Headnote References.** *Falstaff's* headnote references are clearly displayed. Thus, a reference to "**HN:3**" means that the case discusses the point of law discussed in headnote 3 of *Falstaff*.
- **KeyCite Alert.** KeyCite Alert is a clipping service that automatically monitors *Falstaff* and notifies you of any changes in its treatment You can elect to be notified daily, weekly, and so forth, by e-mail.
- **Table of Authorities.** Once again, assume that *Falstaff* relied on and cited four cases. West's validation tool called *Table of Authorities* analyzes those four cases cited in *Falstaff*, allowing you to reevaluate the cases on which *Falstaff* relied (because if their authority is weakened, *Falstaff* may also be suspect). This product is identical to Lexis's product (which shares the same name) and is useful for finding weaknesses in cases relied on by your adversary.
- **Court Documents.** By selecting this button, you will be linked to various court documents and briefs filed by the attorneys for the parties in the *Falstaff* case as well as court documents filed by others that mention *Falstaff*.

c. KeyCiting Statutes and Regulations

KeyCiting statutes or regulations online is nearly identical to KeyCiting cases online. To KeyCite 18 U.S.C.A. § 212 (West 2011), follow these steps:

- Sign on to Westlaw.
- Click the KeyCite tab at the top of your screen.
- Type in your citation (18 usca 212) in the open field and click "Go." Alternatively, you may type a citation in the "KeyCite this Citation" text box that is displayed on the screen and click "Go." If you are viewing the statute on your screen, simply click on its flags or signals displayed at the top of your screen.
- After you enter your statute citation in KeyCite, you may either select "History" (to view the history of a statute, including links to recent session laws that amend or affect your statute, proposed legislation that may affect your statute, and historical and statutory notes describing any legislative changes affecting your statute); "Citing References" (to view cases and other authorities that mention your statute); or "Graphical Statutes" (to view a timeline showing you the enactment history of the statute and allowing you to link to prior versions of the statute and other pertinent legislative materials).

KeyCite provides status flags for statutes as well as cases. For example, a red flag warns you that a statute has been amended, repealed, or held unconstitutional. The process for updating regulations is nearly identical to that of updating statutes. You may also monitor changes to your statute or regulation by selecting KeyCite Alert.

d. Other West Products

(1) *Automatic Citation Validation Through WestCheck*

Similar to Lexis's BriefCheck, West offers a software program called *WestCheck*, which automatically extracts citations from your document, checks their validity, and produces a printed report with the results of the check. WestCheck can also create a table of authorities listing the cases and authorities you have cited in your document. The advantage of using WestCheck rather than KeyCiting each individual case is that WestCheck automatically "reads" your document and validates your citations, thus saving you the time of keying in each citation you wish to check.

The process is easily accomplished. Once the software is "loaded" onto your computer, you merely open your brief or other document that contains the citations you wish to check and then click the WestCheck button on your toolbar.

(2) *BriefTools*

West's new product *BriefTools* is a cutting edge tool that offers the following features (which are helpful for litigators):

- It KeyCites your authorities as you write your document and creates links from the citations in your document to the full-text document in Westlaw.
- It monitors the status of authorities you have cited in your brief or document.
- It retrieves all of your firm's internal documents that contain a particular citation.

(3) *CiteAdvisor*

CiteAdvisor automatically checks the format of the citations in your document (against *Bluebook*, *ALWD*, or state and local rules) and suggests corrections in citation form. CiteAdvisor will also construct a Table of Authorities in your document to show readers where in your document you have discussed the cases and other authorities you have cited.

4. *Comparing Shepardizing Online with KeyCiting*

Most schools and large law firms provide access to both Lexis and Westlaw, realizing their legal professionals develop distinct preferences. Although it is impossible to make absolute statements as to pricing and costs (because most firms have negotiated pricing schedules), nevertheless, fees for Shepardizing online or KeyCiting may be assessed on a per-case basis. Additional fees will be charged by your law firm to the client for your time in performing the updating and reviewing results. Because fees are roughly equivalent, a decision whether to Shepardize online or KeyCite is not usually based on cost. Note that either system allows you to check the validity of your sources without using perfect *Bluebook* or *ALWD* citation form.

Beginning researchers often wonder, "Which service is better?" Both offer many of the same features: rapid and easy citation validating; the use of easy-to-understand, colorful graphics (signs and flags) to tell you at a glance that your citation is in trouble; the ability to limit or narrow your results; and the ability to immediately link to an authority that mentions your case or statute. Both services offer continuous monitoring and automatic citation updating so you need not key in individual citations.

In sum, the use of *Shepard's* online or KeyCite is usually a matter of habit, convenience, or preference. Additionally, because deciphering the reports generated by *Shepard's* online or KeyCite can be somewhat difficult (primarily because so much information is given on each screen), legal researchers tend to stick with one service after they have become familiar with its formatting and layout. Note, however, that at least one expert who has compared *Shepard's* online and KeyCite recommends that citations be checked in both databases because in his samples, between 10 and 37 percent of the references were missed if the citation were checked in only one system. William L. Taylor, *Comparing KeyCite and Shepard's for Completeness, Currency, and Accuracy*, 92 Law Libr. J. 127, 134 (2000), *available at* http://www.aallnet.org (select "Products & Publications"). More recent studies confirm that for the best results, researchers should use both Shepard's and KeyCite (although the realities of law office time and expense constraints will likely dictate the use of one system only).

5. *Other Electronic Citator Services*

Although Lexis and Westlaw are the giants in computer-assisted legal research systems, other systems provide citation updating, including Fastcase, Casemaker, and LoislawConnect. As discussed in Chapter 8, these companies generally aim their services at smaller firms or sole practitioners and charge reasonable fees (or make their services available through state bar associations), and they offer much smaller databases than Lexis or Westlaw. Fastcase's citation updating service is called Authority Check, Casemaker offers CaseCheck+, and LoislawConnect's citator is called GlobalCite. Their use is similar to that of Shepardizing online or KeyCiting, but, in general, they offer fewer enhancements and features for customization. In some instances they merely list other cases that cite your case without analyzing in what manner your case has been cited or treated, requiring you to read these cases to determine their significance. The newest significant entrant into computer-assisted legal research, Bloomberg Law, offers a citator service, BCite, to determine if your case is still good law.

Ethics Alert

Duty to Update and Validate Cases

A number of cases have reminded legal professionals of their
ethical duty to update and validate the cases they cite. In *Gosnell
v. Rentokil, Inc.*, 175 F.R.D. 508, 509 n.1 (N.D. Ill. 1997), the court
sternly admonished the attorneys involved as follows:
    "It is really inexcusable for any lawyer to fail, as a matter of
routine, to Shepardize all cited cases (a process that has been made
much simpler today than it was in the past, given the facility for
doing so under Westlaw or LEXIS)."

---

6.   Summary

Updating and validating your primary authorities is the second component of cite-checking (the first being to place citations in proper *Bluebook*,
ALWD, or local format). Although the primary function of updating is to
check the status of your primary authorities, a related important function is to allow you to tap into additional legal research, because both
Shepard's (in print form or online) and KeyCite will direct you to cases,
periodicals, annotations, and other sources that mention the authority
you are updating. No project is complete until every reference to a case,
statute, constitutional provision, or regulation has been updated and
validated.

The determination of when to perform your updating task is a matter of individual discretion, although updating early in the research process will not only alert you to an invalid or weakened case, statute, or
regulation but also enhance your efforts by directing you to additional
research sources.

Nearly all legal professionals update electronically rather than by
using *Shepard's Citations* in print form. The print forms of *Shepard's
Citations* are nearly relics. *Shepard's* online and KeyCite provide easy
and very recent validation of legal authorities. Moreover, their new software programs (BriefCheck and WestCheck, respectively) offer automatic
updating, eliminating the necessity of keying in any citations. Moreover,
both Lexis and Westlaw are now available on mobile devices such as
iPhones, allowing legal professionals to Shepardize or KeyCite on the go.

Internet Resources ▬▬▬▬▬▬▬▬▬▬▬▬▬

http://www.lexisnexis.com/ infopro/training/reference/ Shepards/Shepardscompgd .pdf	This "How to Shepardize" pamphlet offered by Lexis provides instructions on Shepardizing in print form and electronically.
http://web.lexis.com/help/ multimedia/shepards.htm	Take a tour of various *Shepard's* services.
http://legalsolutions .thomsonreuters.com/ law-products	Select "User Guides" for information about KeyCiting.
http://legalsolutions .thomsonreuters.com/ law-products/solutions/ brief-tools	Information about BriefTools and a tutorial are available at this site.
http://www.law.umich.edu/ library/students/Pages/ LibraryToursandTutorials .aspx	The University of Michigan Law School offers tutorials on Shepardizing and KeyCiting.

Research Assignment Using Print Volumes of *Shepard's*

Your instructor can provide you with some questions requiring you to use print volumes of *Shepard's*.

Research Assignment Using *Shepard's* on Lexis

(Unless otherwise directed, Shepardize using Lexis rather than Lexis Advance and use the "Full" rather than "KWIC" option.)

1. Locate the case published at 347 F.3d 689. Select the Shepard's icon. What negative subsequent appellate history are you given?
2. Shepardize 538 U.S. 216. Review the citing references. What is the oldest Eighth Circuit Court of Appeals case that cites your case in a dissenting opinion?
3. Shepardize 203 F. Supp. 2d 118.
   a. Select "TOA." How many decisions were cited by 203 F. Supp. 2d 118?
   b. Does your case have any positive subsequent history?
4. Shepardize 504 F.3d 106.
   a. Give the citation to the denial of certiorari for this case.
   b. How many briefs have cited this case?
5. Shepardize section 146 of Title 8 of Delaware's Code. What is the oldest case to cite this statute?
6. Shepardize California Corporation Code section 152. What is the history of this statute?
7. Use Lexis Advance. Shepardize 42 Pa. Cons. Stat. § 5524.
   a. Which circuit cases cite this statute most frequently?
   b. Review the "Timeline." Has there been a notable increase in cases and other materials that cite this statute? Describe.
8. Use Lexis Advance. Shepardize 723 F.2d 195.
   a. What is this case's history at the U.S. Supreme Court?
   b. Select "Table of Authorities." How many cases were cited by 723 F.2d 195?

Research Assignment Using KeyCite on Westlaw

(Unless otherwise directed, KeyCite using Westlaw Classic rather than WestlawNext.)

1. KeyCite 200 F.3d 855.
   a. Select "Full History." Which 2006 case distinguished your case?
   b. Select "Citing References." What Southern District of New York case discussed your case positively and quoted from it?
2. KeyCite 668 F.3d 203.
   a. What significant negative history is given for your case?
   b. Select "Table of Authorities." How many cases were cited in your original case?
3. KeyCite 102 F. Supp. 2d 219.
   a. Which 2007 case mentions your case?
   b. What headnote of your original case is mentioned in the 2007 case?
   c. Select the 2007 case that mentions your case. What page of your original case is quoted?
   d. Select "Limit KeyCite Display." Select to review only A.L.R. annotations. How many A.L.R. annotations cited your case?
4. KeyCite 548 U.S. 140. Select "Direct History (Graphical View)."
   a. When was certiorari granted for your case?
   b. What is the citation for your case at the lower U.S. Court of Appeals level?
5. KeyCite 552 U.S. 130. Select "Briefs and Other Related Documents." Review the Brief for the United States. Briefly, what was the question presented?
6. KeyCite 951 N.Y.S.2d 531. What Am. Jur. Proof of Facts article mentions your case?
7. KeyCite Florida Statute § 608.01. What is the status of this statute?
8. Use WestlawNext. KeyCite 15 U.S.C.A. § 1.
   a. Select "Citing References" and then narrow your results by selecting only state court cases. Locate an Ohio Appellate Court case from September 28, 2012, that discusses this statute. Where in this case is 15 U.S.C.A. § 1 discussed?
   b. Return to the KeyCite display. Select "Context and Analysis." How many A.L.R. library references are there to this statute?

9. Use WestlawNext. KeyCite 641 F.2d 619.
   a. What was this case's history at the U.S. Supreme Court?
   b. Select its "Negative Treatment" and then review the "Most negative treatment." What case is identified? Why?
   c. Select the "Citing References" for your case. Locate the 1983 case *Wilkinson v. FBI* that examined your case.
      i. How many depth of treatment "bars" are there for your case?
      ii. Which headnotes in 641 F.2d 619 were discussed in *Wilkinson*?

Research Assignment Comparing Shepardizing Online with KeyCiting (using Lexis and Westlaw Classic)

1. Shepardize and then KeyCite District of Columbia Code § 33.202.01.
   a. What is the status of this statute?
   b. What icons are displayed when you Shepardize this statute and then when you KeyCite it?
2. Shepardize and then KeyCite 28 U.S.C. § 2501.
   a. To how many references does Shepard's direct you?
   b. To how many references does KeyCite direct you?
3. Shepardize and then KeyCite 603 F.3d 112.
   a. To how many cases does Shepard's direct you?
   b. To how many cases does KeyCite direct you?
   c. Do Shepard's and KeyCite cite the same cases?

Internet Assignment

1. Access the website from the University of New Hampshire School of Law at http://library.law.unh.edu/Shepardize. Review step 15. When you Shepardize in the print volumes, for what period of time are you lacking coverage? What should you do to ensure coverage is complete?
2. Access Zimmerman's research guide on Shepardizing at https://law.lexisnexis.com/infopro/zimmermans/disp.aspx?z=1930.

What four reasons are given as to why Sheparding online is preferable to using the print volumes of *Shepard's*?

3. Access West's guide to KeyCiting using WestlawNext at http://info.legalsolutions.thomsonreuters.com/pdf/wln2/L-356347.pdf. What do the "Depth-of-Treatment Bars" provide researchers?

4. Access Lexis's guide to Sheparding using Lexis Advance at http://www.lexisnexis.com/documents/pdf/20120111042317_large.pdf. What features does the Appellate History map provide researchers?

Putting It Together

An Overview of the Research Process

Overview of the Research Process

Chapter Overview

Among the most difficult tasks in performing legal research are beginning and ending the project. It is easy to become so overwhelmed at the task ahead of you that you become paralyzed at the thought of how and where to begin your legal research. Similarly, once you have begun delving into the authorities, it is difficult to know when to stop. This chapter offers some practical guidelines on beginning your research task and knowing when to end it.

A. How to Begin

1. Introduction

There are few inflexible rules in legal research. In legal research, you are asked to provide an answer to a legal question. To reach that answer, there are a number of strategies available to you. The sheer number of authorities to consult offers not only great flexibility, but also produces great uncertainty: Where do I begin? How do I begin? Moreover, researching is rarely a straight line, but often involves backtracking and revisiting sources, requiring patience and flexibility.

This chapter offers you some guidelines and strategies on getting started; however, the best approach is the one that works best for you. If everyone you know prefers to consult an annotated code first, but you like to gain familiarity with a topic by reviewing an encyclopedia, then that is the best approach.

In fact, although the number of sources you can examine may be staggering, this in itself is one of the benefits of our system of legal publishing. If you cannot locate a case or statute using one research technique, there are many alternatives available to you to help you find those authorities.

2.   *Thinking Things Through*

Although it is tempting to go online or to run to the library and start grabbing volumes of books as soon as you are given a research task, the time you spend thinking about a project before you begin is time well spent.

It may be helpful to write down the central question or issue. This will help you "frame" the issue and in and of itself may impose some structure on the project and suggest certain approaches to follow. After you write out the issue, develop a list of descriptive words and phrases. Because almost all legal authorities are accessed by alphabetically arranged indexes, and the descriptive word approach is usually the most efficient method of using an index, jot down the words that initially occur to you in examining the issue. These will be the words you will use in examining the indexes or online sources.

Ethics Alert

The Two Inflexible Rules of Legal Research

There are really only two inflexible "rules" that you must follow when you perform legal research to ensure you comply with your ethical duties of competent representation:

- If the source you review has a supplement or pocket part, you *must* check it; and
- You *must* Shepardize or KeyCite all primary authorities.

As long as you always perform these two tasks, you have tremendous freedom in solving your legal research problems.

---

3. *Narrowing Down the Possibilities*

Once you have given some initial thought to your project and prepared your list of key descriptive words and phrases, narrow the universe of research sources by considering five core issues:

• **Criminal or Civil Law.** You must first determine if the action is a criminal action, brought by the federal government or your state for a wrong done to society, or a civil action, brought by a private party for a wrong done to him or her. The burdens of proof, punishments, and remedies are far different in criminal cases from those in civil cases.

- **Jurisdiction.** You must consider which jurisdiction's authorities you will examine. If the issue is one of Texas law, then you should likely restrict your research strictly to Texas authorities. If the issue is one of federal law, narrow the focus again by considering which circuit is involved.
- **Action.** Consider the legal issues involved. Ask yourself what the plaintiff would allege in a lawsuit based on this issue. Would the plaintiff's action be for fraud? Medical malpractice?
- **Defenses.** Once you have considered the plaintiff's "gripes," put yourself in the place of the defendant and ask what defenses the defendant would assert. Would the defendant allege that the statute of limitations for medical malpractice has expired?
- **Remedies.** After you look at the issue from the perspectives of both parties, consider what remedies the plaintiff is seeking. Is the plaintiff requesting money damages? An injunction?

Figure 12-1 provides an approach that you may wish to follow to help develop your research strategy. This outline will also help you develop words to use in formulating a Lexis or Westlaw query.

Figure 12-1
Research Project Planner

Name: _____

Client Name: _____   Case Name: _____   Assigning Attorney: _____

Client/Billing No.: _____   Date Given: _____

Date Due: _____

Issue/Question/Task:

_____

_____

_____

Law Category	Jurisdiction	Descriptive Words	Synonyms	Antonyms	Plaintiff's Action	Defenses	Remedies
Civil ____ Criminal ____ Administrative ___ International ___ Municipal ____ Other ____	State ____ Federal ____ • District ___ • Circuit ____						Money Damages ____ Compensatory ___ Punitive ____ Equitable Relief ____ Injunction ____ Other ____

B.   Tackling the Project

Once you have formulated the descriptive words and phrases that you will look up in an index, you need to decide with which sources to start. Remember that there are two categories of sources you can consider: primary authorities (cases, constitutions, statutes, and administrative regulations) and secondary authorities (everything else). You can also use digests to help you find cases.

Some research questions will immediately suggest the source to consult. For example, if the question relates to the statute of limitations for a medical malpractice action against a doctor, you should begin with your state's annotated statutes, looking up descriptive words in the index, reading the statute, and then reviewing the cases and authorities that interpret the statute.

If you do not know which source to consult initially, consider the following strategy:

- **Familiarize Yourself.** When you are unsure where or how to start a research project, invest some time in becoming familiar with the area of law involved (contracts, property, wills). The best place to "get your feet wet" may be an encyclopedia, which will offer you introductory information on an area of law. Unless your state has its own local encyclopedia, start with C.J.S. (noting pertinent topic names and Key Numbers) or Am. Jur. 2d (noting pertinent A.L.R. annotations). Additionally, these sources often provide suggestions for search queries for Lexis and Westlaw. Consider reviewing a treatise on your general topic, because it will provide excellent analysis as well as references to supporting case law and other authorities.
- **Consult Primary Sources.** After you have begun to feel comfortable with the subject matter, consult the primary authorities: constitutions, statutes, and cases (and, if applicable, administrative regulations).

  - **Constitutions.** If your issue is a federal one, it may be governed by the U.S. Constitution, included in U.S.C.A. and U.S.C.S., which provide the text of the Constitution and then references to cases and other authorities interpreting it.
  - **Statutes and Regulations.** Always examine an annotated code because it will send you to cases and other authorities interpreting your statutory provision. For federal questions, use U.S.C.A. or U.S.C.S. For state statutes, examine your state's annotated code. Always check the pocket parts or supplements. For federal regulations, use C.F.R. For state regulations, consult your state's administrative code.
  - **Cases.** If reviewing the annotations for a federal or state statutory provision does not produce any cases on point, use digests, which function as case finders. If you can find "one good case," you can use its topics and Key Numbers to locate other cases in

West's Decennial Digest System, and then you can Shepardize or KeyCite those cases to find other authorities.

• **Consult Secondary Sources.** After reviewing the pertinent primary authorities, review the secondary authorities to fill in the gaps. Most secondary authorities will refer you to cases, thus ensuring you find the case law relating to your topic. The most commonly consulted secondary authorities are A.L.R. annotations, encyclopedias, periodicals, Restatements, and texts and treatises.

There are many secondary sources, and you should examine the list of secondary authorities shown in Figure 12-2, and ask yourself if your issue would be addressed by the particular authority in question. You need not examine every secondary authority for every issue you research.

Figure 12-2
Chart of Secondary Authorities

Secondary Authority	Coverage	To Use
Encyclopedias • C.J.S. and Am. Jur. 2d • State-Specific Sets	• All U.S. law • Law of one state	For all sets, consult alphabetically arranged index.
A.L.R. Annotations • A.L.R. Fed. and A.L.R. Fed. 2d	• Federal issues	For all A.L.R. sets, consult *A.L.R. Index*.
A.L.R. • A.L.R.2d, A.L.R.3d, A.L.R.4th, A.L.R.5th, A.L.R.6th	• State and common law topics	
Texts and Treatises	Law related to one topic	Consult alphabetically arranged index or table of contents.
Periodicals	Various topics	Use *Index to Legal Periodicals & Books* or *Current Law Index* (or their online versions).
Restatements	Various topics	Consult alphabetically arranged index to each Restatement.
Attorneys General Opinions • U.S.A.G. Opinions • State A.G. Opinions	 • Federal topics • State topics	For all sets, consult alphabetically arranged index.

Figure 12-2 *(Continued)*

Secondary Authority	Coverage	To Use
Dictionaries	Legal words and phrases	Look up alphabetically arranged words or phrases.
Form Books	Various topics	Consult alphabetically arranged index.
Uniform Laws	Various topics	Consult *Uniform Laws Annotated* and *Uniform Laws Annotated Directory of Acts* (or access http://www .uniformlaws.org).
Looseleaf Services	Various topics	Consult alphabetically arranged index.
Jury Instructions	Federal and state topics	Consult alphabetically arranged index.

• **Review Miscellaneous Research Guides.** In addition to the primary and secondary authorities, be sure to Shepardize or KeyCite not only to tell you whether your primary authorities are still valid, but also to lead you to other sources, such as law review articles. Don't forget to use common sense. If a question can be easily answered by an individual or organization, call or e-mail. Also, browse the library shelves for useful materials. When you come to a dead end, ask the law librarian for help.

Practice Tip

Legal Research in Five Easy Steps

To ensure your research is sufficiently thorough:

• Use encyclopedias to obtain some background on the topic you research.
• Always examine the statutes. Use an annotated code, because it will refer you to cases.
• Use a treatise (or looseleaf service) for more thorough analysis of a topic and to direct you to cases and other authorities.
• If you cannot locate any cases through annotated codes or treatises, use digests.
• Shepardize or KeyCite your cases and statutes to ensure they are still valid and to be directed to A.L.R. annotations, periodical articles, and other relevant sources.

• **Consider the Quality of the Sources.** Once you have collected your authorities, consider their quality, credibility, and reliability. Although primary sources are binding and secondary sources are persuasive only, a project composed solely of nearly ancient cases will not be as authoritative as one composed of a few of those cases that are then supported by credible secondary sources. For cases, remember that, in general, you should read or sort out cases following these guidelines:

- Read newer cases before older ones;
- Read cases from higher courts before those from lower ones;
- Read cases from your forum jurisdiction before expanding your search to foreign jurisdictions.

Similarly, remember that some secondary authorities are considered more authoritative than others. The Restatements have a status nearly equal to that of court decisions; law review articles written by well-known experts, judges, and academics often carry great weight; and many treatises are so highly regarded that a citation to one of them is of significant value to a court. Avoid citing to an encyclopedia; a reference to an encyclopedia is nearly equivalent to screaming, "I couldn't find anything else to support my position!"

C. Working with the Authorities

1. *Note-Taking*

As you begin to read the primary and secondary authorities, you need to develop a focused plan for taking and organizing notes during your research efforts so you can effectively use them to write your project. You may use looseleaf notebooks or binders, index cards, or a laptop. Whichever method works best for you is the best one.

Your notes should contain only the most important and relevant information. Although your notes need not be perfect to be useful, they must be sufficiently complete so that they allow you to write your project. If you need to return to the library or log on again during the writing phase to get a parallel cite or the date of a law review article, your note-taking was ineffective. Be sure that all citations are complete (with pinpoint references) and in proper form. Clearly indicate whether your notes reflect a direct quotation or merely paraphrase the judge's or author's statements. Use a "q" or "p" or some other identifying label.

Don't forget the new features of WestlawNext (which allows you to store your research results in folders, add notes to your research results, and highlight important text) and Lexis Advance's Workspace (which stores your search history, allows you to organize your results in search folders, and more). See Chapter 8.

Similarly, there are a number of research management and citation systems available to help researchers. For example, Zotero (http://www .zotero.com) is a free tool that allows you to save, store, and manage bibliographic references such as books and articles. It helps organize your materials by allowing you to drag articles into folders and capture web pages and screen shots. The program then assists you in citing these materials in *Bluebook* citation form. Additional information on Zotero and similar tools is available at the website of Yale Law School at http://library.law .yale.edu/research-guides.

2. *Staying Focused*

One of the most difficult tasks in performing legal research is staying focused on a specific issue or question. Students commonly report that as they are in the process of researching an issue such as fraud and reading a pertinent case, they come across a reference to what appears to be a promising law review article. Without completing the reading of the case, they locate the law review article, which then refers to two other promising cases. These new cases are then retrieved. At the end of several hours of research, the student is surrounded by a pile of books, none of which has been thoroughly analyzed, and some of which, when later re-read, are a mystery as to their relevance because they discuss topics completely unrelated to the original topic of fraud.

This "hopscotch" approach occurs whether you are reviewing conventional print materials or whether you are online and routinely hyperlink from one authority to the next. The reason it occurs so frequently is that it is incredibly tempting to interrupt your analysis of an issue with the thought that the "perfect" authority is the next one.

Train yourself to stay focused on each specific issue. For example, decide that the first three research hours will be devoted to fraud. If you come across cases or references that relate to other issues during this time, mark them with sticky flags or jot the citations in your notes so you can retrieve them later, but do not interrupt your research on the assigned issue. Use electronic aids, such as Google's "Scratchpad" or "Keep," to take notes, maintain your "to do" list, and record websites of interest on a sidebar displayed on your screen or on your iPhone at all times. Keep notes of your research "trail," so that if you are interrupted, you will know where to resume your work. Use the Lexis and Westlaw features that allow you to maintain and store your research results. With any luck, when it is time to research later issues, you will already have a list of promising leads, eliminating the need to start at the beginning with encyclopedias or digests.

D. When to Stop

One of the most difficult tasks in legal research is knowing when to stop. It seems that some issues can be researched endlessly. If you read a promising case, it may refer to six other cases, which you may also decide to read. When you Shepardize or KeyCite these cases, you discover each of them has been mentioned or discussed in ten other cases, as well as numerous law review articles and other resources. You now have 60 other cases that could be examined and then Shepardized or KeyCited. This process could continue indefinitely. Eventually, you need to call a halt to your research.

1. *Practical Considerations*

In many cases, economics will govern the scope of your research. When the client's budget dictates the amount of research that can be performed, you will have to be as efficient as possible. Keep track of your hours as you go along, and after a few hours, report back to your assigning attorney on your progress. In some instances, when you are assigned a project, you may be instructed to allot a stated number of hours for research.

The balance between the duty to research adequately and the economic realities of a case is a delicate one. At the beginning of your legal career, it is the supervising attorney's task to resolve this issue and give you proper guidance. If you receive no instructions, take the initiative and state that for time-management purposes, you would like to inquire when the project is due (this in and of itself may give you a clue as to how thorough the project is to be) and a range of time the attorney estimates for the research.

Do not be embarrassed to ask for direction or acknowledge that you are having difficulty. Your supervising attorney would much prefer to discover this after six hours of your research than after 30 hours that cannot be billed to the client. If your project is more complex than originally anticipated, stop your research and explain your progress thus far to your supervisor and ask for direction.

2. *Complex Projects*

If the project is complex, you may find yourself in the position described previously, in which there is an ever-expanding list of authorities that could be reviewed. One clue that your research is complete is that you keep bumping into the same authorities. For example, assume that you locate the *Lynch* case, which itself refers to *Adams*, an earlier landmark case. Later cases all refer to *Lynch* and *Adams*, and when you Shepardize or KeyCite *Lynch* and *Adams,* you turn up no new lines of case law.

These references to the same authorities are a signal that your research is complete. You may want to "flesh out" your research by reviewing a current law review article or other secondary authority, but if these confirm the results of your earlier research, you will know you have been sufficiently thorough.

Beginning researchers often lack the confidence to stop researching; they are convinced that there is one perfect case to find, if they can only devote enough time to the effort. This is almost always a fallacy. Seldom, if ever, will you find a "perfect" case; no two cases are exactly alike. You will, however, find cases that are similar to yours, and you will be able to argue that because the cases are similar in reasoning and facts, they should apply to your research problem. It is only when you neglect to review the cases interpreting a statute or fail to update by checking pocket parts and Shepardizing or KeyCiting that your research is incomplete.

3.   Quick Questions

Often, your research issue is specific and well defined. You may be asked to check how many days' notice a landlord must give a tenant before initiating eviction proceedings. Such specific questions are usually easily answered by starting with your state's annotated code. Review the statute and a few cases construing it. Check the pocket parts and Shepardize or KeyCite. This approach is sufficient to answer questions that are straightforward.

4.   Established Issues

If your research relates to an established area of the law, such as a landlord's duty to provide habitable premises to a tenant, you may find a multitude of authorities. Some of them may be decades old, and there may be numerous cases, periodical articles, and discussions in treatises. These authorities, however, may reflect remarkable unanimity. Researching an issue related to an established area of law usually produces numerous authorities in agreement.

Determining when to stop researching will be relatively easy because the authorities will begin referring to each other over and over again. Once you Shepardize or KeyCite to ensure that the primary authorities are still valid, your task is complete.

5.   Newly Emerging Issues

Researching newly emerging areas of law can be frustrating because there may be substantial conflict among courts as judges grapple with a difficult issue and try to establish rules of law. Thus, research relating to the liability of an Internet service provider for defamatory statements posted on a website may produce conflicting results. Often, periodical articles or A.L.R. annotations will be most helpful because they will offer an overview of new topics and attempt to reconcile conflicts. Computer-assisted legal research, with the ability to locate hundreds of documents and sort them by date, is ideal for newly emerging areas of the law.

6. *Issues of First Impression*

Often, the most difficult research task is the one that yields no results whatsoever. Thus, after hours of research, you may not have found any authorities. There are two conclusions to draw from this occurrence: "There are no authorities relating to this issue," or "I must be doing something wrong, because I can't locate any authorities." Beginning researchers will always draw the second conclusion and refuse to stop researching, even though they are retracing their steps over and over again.

It is possible that an issue is one of *first impression*, that is, one not previously considered in your jurisdiction. Although there is no foolproof way to determine this, there are two techniques you can use to assure yourself that it is not your research strategy that has resulted in a lack of authorities.

First, select a populous and varied jurisdiction, such as California or New York, which has a rich body of law. Use the same research techniques and sets of books for one of these states that you used in your home jurisdiction. If you obtain results, you will know that your strategies were sound and that the lack of authorities in your jurisdiction is the result of an issue of first impression, not misguided research efforts.

Second, computer-assisted legal research, with its ability to search for thousands of documents that contain specific terms, will help verify your research techniques. If your search query is sound and yet no authorities are produced, you should feel more confident that your state has simply not considered your issue. To achieve a final comfort level, contact the service representatives for Lexis or Westlaw and ask for assistance.

If your jurisdiction has never before considered your issue, you may search in other states or jurisdictions. Remember, however, that these authorities are not binding in your jurisdiction, although they may be persuasive.

7. *How Many Authorities Are Enough?*

Beginning researchers usually want to know how many cases or authorities should be cited in a brief or project. There is no answer to this question. As a general rule, however, you will need fewer authorities to support a well-established principle and more authorities to discuss an emerging area of law or one in conflict.

Help Line

Research Assistance from Lexis and Westlaw

Both Lexis and Westlaw are extremely helpful in providing research assistance if you encounter difficulties when performing research.

- **Lexis:** Call (800) 543-6862 for 24/7 research help.
- **Westlaw:** Call (800) REF-ATTY for research assistance.

Additionally, both services offer researchers the ability to e-mail questions asking for help from customer support. Real-time chat support provides immediate, personalized assistance.

Is one citation enough? It is possible that a single citation may suffice to answer a quick question, such as the statute of limitations in Oregon for breach of contract actions. More complex questions, such as the test for determining patent infringement, may require careful reading of several cases, statutes, and other authorities.

You should always aim to have at least one primary authority to support each of your arguments. Consider selecting the landmark case in the area and then one recent case from your highest court. This may be sufficient for areas of law that are fairly well established. See Figure 12-3 for a blueprint for conducting legal research.

Cite secondary authorities if they provide useful analysis or if the author is a renowned authority in that field. Consider combining primary authorities with a secondary authority to support your argument. Do not, however, believe that legal research is like a recipe, and that if you always cite two cases and a law review article, your argument will win. Different topics require different levels of analysis, and you will need to exercise your own discretion to determine how many authorities are enough. Although there is no perfect rule for when to stop conducting legal research, consider that it is likely time to stop when:

- You keep bumping into the same authorities and their commentary is much the same;
- You have read the same point in a number of different sources, with nothing new added; and
- Your Shepardizing or KeyCiting reveals no changes in the law.

Figure 12-3
A Blueprint for Legal Research

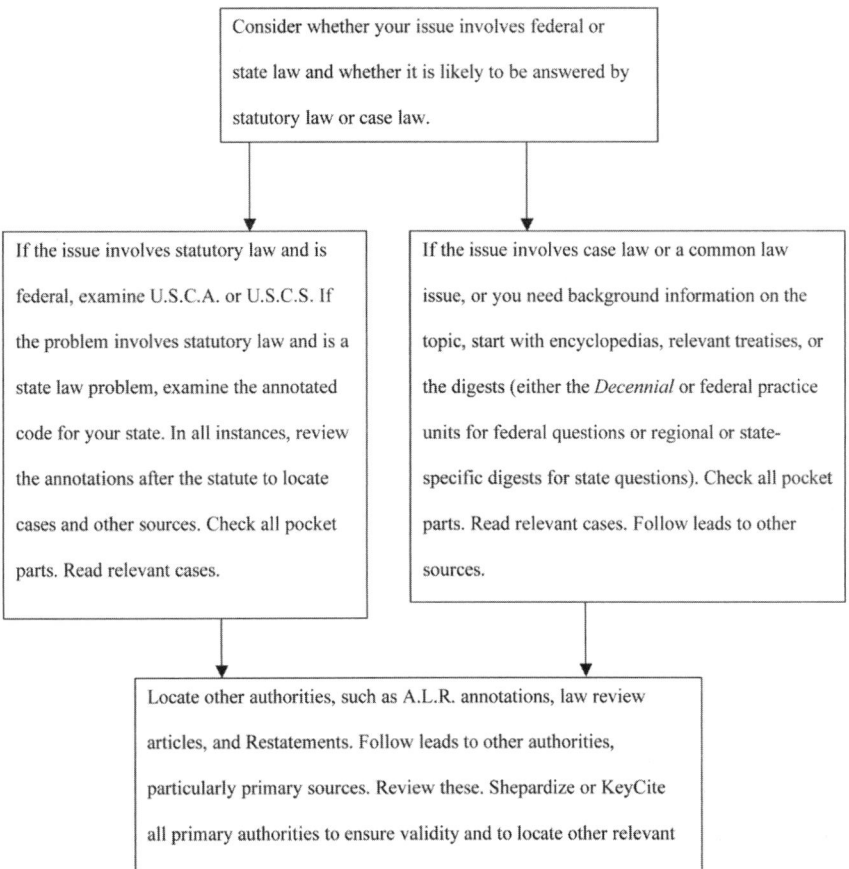

Consider whether your issue involves federal or state law and whether it is likely to be answered by statutory law or case law.

If the issue involves statutory law and is federal, examine U.S.C.A. or U.S.C.S. If the problem involves statutory law and is a state law problem, examine the annotated code for your state. In all instances, review the annotations after the statute to locate cases and other sources. Check all pocket parts. Read relevant cases.

If the issue involves case law or a common law issue, or you need background information on the topic, start with encyclopedias, relevant treatises, or the digests (either the *Decennial* or federal practice units for federal questions or regional or state-specific digests for state questions). Check all pocket parts. Read relevant cases. Follow leads to other sources.

Locate other authorities, such as A.L.R. annotations, law review articles, and Restatements. Follow leads to other authorities, particularly primary sources. Review these. Shepardize or KeyCite all primary authorities to ensure validity and to locate other relevant materials.

---

8. *Ten Tips for Effective Legal Research*

• **Be Prepared.** The time you spend thinking about a project before you begin is time well spent. Give yourself a few minutes to plan your research strategies.

• **Be Flexible.** If the books you need aren't on the shelf or if your efforts are not yielding results, switch to another set of books or source. Consider a variety of research methods (print, computer-assisted legal research, and the Internet) to achieve the best results.

• **Be Thorough.** Check all pocket parts and supplements. Shepardize or KeyCite all primary authorities to make sure they remain valid. Take complete notes.

• **Be Patient.** Research can be a difficult process. Expect some roadblocks.

- **Be Organized.** Tackle one topic at a time. Avoid getting side-tracked on a minor issue.
- **Be Efficient.** Gather together all of the materials you need so you don't waste time wandering around the library.
- **Be Creative.** If all of your colleagues are beginning their research in one set of books, begin in another to avoid the crowd as well as the crowd mentality. Try contacting agencies and individuals and asking for assistance rather than depending exclusively on books.
- **Be Wary.** Approach your problem from all angles. Play devil's advocate. What will the adversary argue?
- **Be Resourceful.** Look for law review articles and A.L.R. annotations on your topic. If someone has already written a thorough analysis of an issue, why reinvent the wheel?
- **Be Calm.** If you get stuck, ask a librarian for help. That's what they're there for.

Internet Resources

http://www.law.georgetown.edu/library/research/tutorials/index.cfm	Georgetown Law Center offers several valuable tutorials relating to legal research.
http://www.bc.edu/schools/law/library/research/researchguides.html	Boston College Law Library offers legal research guides.
http://libguides.law.ucla.edu	UCLA offers legal research guides.

Research Assignment

Answer the following questions, and give the citation to the legal authority that supports your answer.

1. Your firm's client operates a tattoo parlor in Seattle. A young girl requested a tattoo of a heart and told the tattoo artist that she was 18 years of age. Believing this statement, the tattoo artist applied the tattoo. Does the client have any liability for applying the tattoo to the young girl?
2. The firm's client would like to reserve the corporate name "Pupcakes, Inc." with the California Secretary of State while it prepares papers to incorporate its business. What is the fee for the name reservation and how long will it last?
3. What is the citation for the federal Sarbanes-Oxley Act?
4. A Navy admiral has applied to be the Officer in Charge of the United States Navy Band. Is the officer eligible for this position?
5. Your firm's client's son and his wife moved to Minnesota three months ago. May the son begin proceedings in Minnesota for dissolution of his marriage?
6. A client of your firm offered a $200 bribe to a police officer in Florida, asking the police officer not to ticket him for excessive speeding. What is the particular degree of this crime?
7. Your firm's client executed his will in Topeka in 2012, leaving all of his property to his surviving spouse. In 2013, the client purchased a very large parcel of property in Topeka. Is this property covered by the 2012 will, or must the client execute a new will?

Internet Assignment

1. Access the Boston College Law Library website at http://www.bc.edu/schools/law/library.html. Select the Research Guide or "LibGuide" titled "Basic Legal Research Tips." What are the five steps to legal research?
2. Access the Cornell Law Library website at http://www.lawschool.cornell.edu/library/index2.cfm. Select the Research Guide called "Basics of Legal Research" and review the information on how to start.
   a. What are the four methods you can use to develop a list of search terms?
   b. What is the "one good case" legal research strategy?

3. Access the UCLA Law Library website at http://www.law.ucla. edu/library/Pages/default.aspx. Select the Research Guide relating to legal research and writing.
   a. Review the information on the research interview. What four tips are you given?
   b. Review Appendix A, titled "Research Checklist." Where should you begin your research projects?

Legal Writing

*Putting Your
Research to Work*

The Basics of Legal Writing

Chapter Overview

The goal of legal writing is to communicate. Although there are many forms of legal writing (letters, memos, and court briefs), all must comply with standard rules of grammar, spelling, and punctuation so that your final product effectively communicates to its intended audience. This chapter reviews these basics of writing so that you omit any flaws in your communication that distract your reader from your message and make the reader doubt your abilities and reflect on your carelessness.

A. Grammar

1. Introduction

Rules of grammar are used so that we can communicate clearly. Following are some of the most common grammatical errors made by beginning and even experienced writers.

2. Subject-Verb Agreement

A verb must agree in number with the subject of a sentence. That is, if the subject of a sentence is singular, the verb must also be singular. Similarly, if the subject of a sentence is plural, the verb must also be plural. Most problems in subject-verb agreement occur when a subject is used that has more than one word, when the subject is an indefinite pronoun or collective noun, or when several words or a prepositional phrase intervene between the subject and the verb.

a.   Multiple Word Subjects and Indefinite Pronouns

Example:

Incorrect	*Correct*
Compound subject: The transcript and the exhibit was missing.	The transcript and the exhibit were missing.

Because the subject of the sentence in the preceding example consists of two words connected by "and," it is plural, and thus a plural verb (were) is needed.

If the subject is composed of singular words connected by "or" or "nor," use a singular verb.

Incorrect	*Correct*
Neither the plaintiff nor her spouse were present.	Neither the plaintiff nor her spouse was present.

Often, confusion regarding subject and verb agreement arises when a word that ends in -one or -body, such as "someone" or "everybody," or a word such as "each," "either," "neither," or "no one" is used. These indefinite pronouns are considered singular, and a singular verb must be used. Moreover, a singular pronoun (he, she, it) must be used with these words. Although it is common to use plural pronouns in speaking or informal writing, legal writing is more formal and one must be scrupulous in using singular pronouns with such words.

Incorrect	*Correct*
Either of your offers are acceptable.	*Either* of your offers *is* acceptable.
Someone missed their deadline.	*Someone* missed *his or her* deadline.
	Someone missed the deadline.

b.   Collective Nouns

Collective nouns (nouns that stand for a group of people or items) such as committee, court, and jury are usually singular.

Incorrect	*Correct*
The jury have been selected.	The *jury has* been selected.
The board of directors have met.	The *board* of directors *has* met.

c. Intervening Words

Subject-verb agreement problems often occur when words or phrases intervene between a subject and a verb.

Incorrect	_Correct_
The brief, together with all of its exhibits, show the contract was void.	The _brief_, together with all of its exhibits, _shows_ the contract was void.

In the preceding example, the subject is "brief," a singular word that requires the singular verb "shows." Focus on the subject of the sentence and ignore intervening words.

d. Prepositional Phrases

Prepositional phrases that intervene between a subject and a verb often confuse writers who may be tempted to match the verb with the noun in the prepositional phrase rather than with the subject of the sentence.

Incorrect	_Correct_
One of the best judges are resigning.	_One_ of the best judges _is_ resigning.
A small group of city workers were fired.	A small _group_ of city workers _was_ fired.

In summary, always carefully scrutinize your writing to identify the subject. Once you have located the subject, classify it as singular or plural and then select the appropriate verb form, ignoring any intervening words.

3. *Run-on Sentences*

A run-on sentence combines two sentences into one. Run-on sentences can usually be corrected by inserting the proper punctuation or by dividing the run-on into two separate sentences.

Incorrect	_Correct_
The members of the board were in conflict, they could not reach a resolution.	The members of the board were in conflict; they could not reach a resolution.
	or
	The members of the board were in conflict. They could not reach a resolution.

4. *Modifiers*

The incorrect placement of a *modifier* (a word that limits, describes, or qualifies another word or group of words) causes ambiguity. Place modifiers next to or as close as possible to the words they modify. For example, the sentence "Rita agreed only to lend her sister money" is capable of two interpretations. Does it mean that Rita agreed to lend her sister money and no other item? Or does it mean Rita will lend her sister money and will not lend money to anyone else? It may be necessary to add words to a sentence with a modifier in order to achieve clarity. Either of the following two sentences will reduce ambiguity:

> Rita agreed to lend her sister only money and nothing else.
> Rita agreed to lend money only to her sister and not to anyone else.

Modifiers such as "almost," "ultimately," "frequently," "immediately," "eventually," "finally," and "only" are notorious causes of ambiguity. Exercise caution in using these words.

5. *Split Infinitives*

An infinitive is the word "to" with a verb, as in *to run* or *to argue*. An infinitive is said to be "split" when a word (usually an adverb) is inserted between the word *to* and the verb, as in *to quickly run* or *to persuasively argue*.

Nearly all writing experts now recognize that there is no formal rule against splitting an infinitive, and split infinitives are commonly seen in non-legal writing, including newspaper articles; however, legal readers tend to be conservative and may be annoyed or distracted by a split infinitive. Because many split infinitives are so easily corrected (by merely moving the adverb that causes the "split" after the infinitive), correct them when you can, and avoid splitting an infinitive unless you want to place emphasis on the adverb. Thus, rather than writing "The partner asked me to quickly review the transcript," write "The partner asked me to review the transcript quickly."

6. *Dangling Participles*

A present participle is a verb ending in *-ing*, as in *arguing* or *entering*. It is said to "dangle" when it does not modify the subject of a sentence. Also called a dangling modifier, this grammar problem most often occurs when a sentence starts with a word ending in *-ing*, as in *Driving to the meeting, my cell phone rang*. This sentence is incorrect because it lacks an identification of the subject and implies that the cell phone was driving to the meeting. To remedy a dangling modifier, either identify the actor immediately after the introductory modifier, or reword the modifying phrase so that it identifies the actor, as in *As I was driving to the meeting, my cell phone rang*.

7.   *Pronouns*

a.   **Personal Pronouns**

Personal pronouns (I/me, he/him, she/her, we/us, they/them) change forms depending on whether they function as the subject of a sentence or the object of the sentence. When the pronoun functions as or replaces the subject of a sentence, use "I," "he," "she," "we," or "they."

Incorrect	Correct
It was me who prepared the trust.	It was *I* who prepared the trust.
Kyle and her Shepardized the brief.	Kyle and *she* Shepardized the brief.
It was them who informed the police.	It was *they* who informed the police.

When the pronoun functions as or replaces the object of a sentence, use "me," "him," "her," "us," or "them."

Incorrect	Correct
You must give John and I directions.	You must give John and *me* directions.
Between you and I, the defendant is liable.	Between you and *me*, the defendant is liable.

As an aid to determining which form of pronoun to use, omit or cover up the noun and the word "and" accompanying the pronoun, and this will provide a clue as to which pronoun to use. For example, in the sentence "You must give John and *I*/*me* directions," omit "John and" so the sentence reads "You must give _____ directions." This reading makes it clear the correct pronoun is "me." Finally, by custom and usage, the first person pronoun (I/me) is usually placed second, as in "Joe and I went to Rome" (not "I and Joe went to Rome").

b.   **Using the Pronouns That, Which, and It**

The relative pronouns include "that" and "which." "That" is used in a restrictive clause (a clause that is essential to the meaning of a sentence), whereas "which" is used in a non-restrictive clause (a clause that merely adds an idea to a sentence that would be complete without the clause). For example, in the sentence "The books that were outside got wet," the word *that* tells which particular books got wet (namely, the ones outside). Presumably, there are other books that were not outside, and those are fine. On the other hand, review the sentence "The books, which were outside, got wet." This sentence tells us that all of the books were outside, and they all got wet. Many writers have difficulty determining whether to start a clause with "that" or "which." Remember these hints:

- If you can drop the clause and still retain the meaning of the sentence, use "which." If you can't, use "that."
- A clause beginning with "which" is usually set off by commas.
- A clause beginning with "that" is not set off by commas.
- "That" introduces essential information; "which" seldom does.

Use "it" to refer to collective nouns such as jury, court, committee, or association unless you are referring to the members of the group. Also use "it" or "its" to refer to non-human entities or institutions such as corporations.

Incorrect	*Correct*
The corporation held their meeting in May.	The *corporation* held *its* meeting in May.

c. Gender-Linked Pronouns

Avoid the use of gender-linked pronouns. For example, the sentence "A judge must give his instructions to the jury" is objectionable because it presupposes the judge is male.

There are several techniques you can use to avoid offending readers. One technique is to change the singular nouns to plural. This in turn will necessitate a change in the singular pronoun "he" or "she" to a neutral plural pronoun such as "they" or "their." Thus, the example would read "Judges must give their instructions to the jury." A second technique is to rewrite the sentence to avoid using any pronouns, as in "A judge must give instructions to the jury." Avoid the use of "he/she." This construction creates an awkward appearance because slashes are seldom used in legal writing. In sum, correct gender-linked pronouns to avoid offending readers if you can do so without causing an awkward and distracting document.

B. Spelling

One of the most distressing results of misspelling is the effect produced in the mind of a reader. Readers of legal documents, such as employers, clients, attorneys, and judges, tend to be highly critical and perfectionistic. When confronted with spelling errors, they may react by assuming that if you cannot be trusted to spell properly, you cannot be trusted to have found the correct answer to a legal problem.

Following are some tips to becoming a better speller:

- Learn some rules. Many spelling rules are easy to remember and have few exceptions, such as "place *i* before *e*, except after *c*, or except when it sounds like *ay*, as in neighbor and weigh."
- Use a dictionary. Always consult a dictionary to check spelling, and mark and highlight troublesome words. Some dictionaries

contain no definitions; they only list spelled words. These dictionaries are useful and portable. The online dictionary found at http://www.dictionary.com is also helpful. The Wolters Kluwer Bouvier Law Dictionary app (an abridged version of the full dictionary) is available free at the iTunes store.

- Don't over-rely on a spell checker. Studies show that papers written with the help of a spell checker are only marginally better than those that are not.
- Use mnemonic devices to help you remember words, such as "the princi*pal* of your school is your *pal*."
- Pronounce your words carefully. It will be difficult to remember the correct spelling of environment if you pronounce it as *enviroment*.
- Write your misspellings several times. If you catch yourself writing "privelege" rather than "privilege," write it ten times to train yourself.
- Use the "find and replace" feature of your word processor to correct common errors automatically. For example, if you routinely type *Untied States* rather than *United States*, the find and replace feature will locate each occurrence of this error and replace it with the correct spelling.

Ethics Alert

The Duty of Competence

Although errors in spelling, grammar, and punctuation may seem minor or cosmetic, they can and do detract from a polished project. In one case, the court noted with stern disapproval that "the plaintiff's brief is littered with spelling errors, grammatical sloppiness, and incorrect case citations" and condemned this "shoddy professionalism." *Universal Restoration Servs., Inc. v. Paul W. Davis Sys., Inc.*, No. 908-C-2027, 2002 WL 596380, at *7 (N.D. Ill. Apr. 17, 2002). Thus, your duty of competence extends to all aspects of your writing, even the technical aspects such as grammar, spelling, and punctuation.

C. Punctuation

1. Introduction

When you speak, you use pauses and changes in voice inflection as well as gestures to signal meaning to the listener. In writing, these signals are given through the use of punctuation. Punctuation makes writing more understandable to a reader. This portion of the chapter discusses the most common punctuation errors.

2. *Commas*

A comma indicates a brief pause and is considered the most troublesome of punctuation marks due to its numerous uses. In addition to the well-known uses of commas (after an informal letter's salutation, to set off an introductory phrase, and so forth), be sure to use a comma:

(i)   To set off a full date, as in "The deadline of June 19, 2013, is nonnegotiable."

(ii) Before a coordinating conjunction (sometimes called the FANBOYS for "for," "and," "nor," "but," "or," "yet," or "so") introducing an independent clause, namely, one that can function as a complete sentence. You may omit the comma if the clause is short (five words or less). The comma is not needed before the coordinating conjunction if the clause that follows cannot stand on its own. The following examples are correct:

> The plaintiff moved to amend the complaint, but the court refused to grant leave to amend.
> The attorney argued persuasively but the jury convicted.
> He argued the case and was an impressive advocate.

(iii) To set off items in a series. Although the final comma in a series is optional in most writing, in legal writing you must place a comma after each item in the list and before the conjunction. For example, examine the sentence "I leave my property equally to Susan, Bill, Louise, and Tom." Each individual would receive one-fourth of the estate. Note that the omission of the last comma could cause a completely different result, for example, "I leave my property equally to Susan, Bill, Louise and Tom." The omission of the comma after "Louise" arguably indicates the property is to be divided equally into thirds: one-third to Susan, one-third to Bill, and one-third to Louise and Tom together, rather than in equal fourths to each individual. Because the omission of the last comma in a series (the serial comma) can cause ambiguity, always include it.

3. *Apostrophes*

Apostrophes are used to show possession or ownership or to show omission of one or more letters, as in the contraction *don't*. The use of apostrophes to show possession, especially with regard to proper names, is often confusing.

Use an apostrophe:

(i) to show possession or ownership. Follow three basic rules:

- Add an apostrophe and an s ('s) to show possession for all singular nouns, even if the noun ends in s, k, x, or z.

    Correct examples: the first shareholder's ballot
                                        Arkansas's election
                                        Charles's book

- When a plural word ends in s, add only an apostrophe (') to show possession.

    Correct examples: the four girls' coats
                                        the six shareholders' ballots

- When a word is plural and does not already end in s, add an apostrophe and an s ('s) to show possession.

    Correct examples: the children's toys
                                        the women's cars

- To form the plural of most names or to show possession for most names, follow the rules given above.

    Correct examples: Ed Smith's papers were filed today.
                                        The Smiths moved to Memphis.
                                        The Smiths' house is white.

- For names that end in *ch, s, sh, x,* or *z*, however, form the plural by adding es and then form the plural possessive by adding an apostrophe after the es (es'). The singular possessive is formed by following the first rule above (as in *Tim Jones's car is red*).

    Correct examples: The Joneses moved to New York.
                                        The Lynches are Democrats.
                                        The Joneses' car is an Accord.

Practice Tip

Marcus' Pen or Marcus's Pen?

Many grammar books permit the use of an apostrophe alone with a singular word ending in *s* when adding another *s* would make the word difficult to pronounce or look odd. Thus, you may see *Mr. Rogers' sweater* or *Marcus' pen*. Nevertheless, the U.S. Government Printing Office *Style Manual, The Elements of Style*, and most conventional grammar books suggest the *'s*, as in *Mr. Rogers's sweater* and *Marcus's pen*. This form is always correct. Moreover, it is consistent with shorter names, as in *Les's car*. It looks odd to see *Les' car*. Thus, use the form *Les's car*.

       (ii) to indicate omission of letters, as in contractions (such as "can't" for "cannot").

One of the most common errors students and beginning writers make is misusing "it's." "It's" is a contraction for "it is" (or "it has"). The apostrophe is used to indicate that the letter "i" (or the pair of letters "ha") has been omitted. To form the possessive of it, use "its." Only use "it's" when you mean to say "it is" or "it has," not when you mean to indicate possession. The following is a correct example: *It's* a learned court that has the wisdom to reverse *its* decisions.

4. *Quotation Marks*

Use quotation marks to indicate the exact words of a speaker, as in "The motion," said the judge, "is hereby granted."

Use quotation marks only for quotes of 49 words or fewer. For quotes of 50 words or more, block indent the quote, fully justify its margins, and use single spacing. The indentation of these longer quotes itself indicates a quotation. Always place commas and periods inside closing quotation marks. Place colons and semicolons outside closing quotation marks.

5. *Hyphens*

Use a hyphen between the parts of a compound adjective when it modifies the next word, as in "well-known advocate." Remember this example: High-school students attend high school.

Internet Resources

http://www.gpoaccess.gov/stylemanual/index.html	The Government Printing Office *Style Manual* is one of the most widely accepted manuals on English usage.
http://owl.english.purdue.edu	Purdue University's Online Writing Lab offers numerous guides and handouts as well as exercises and answer keys.

Assignment

GRAMMAR

SELECT THE CORRECT WORD.

1. Each of the defendants have/has entered an appearance.
2. Either the judge or the law clerk was/were available.
3. The hospital committee has adjourned their/its meeting.
4. The transcript, along with its attachments, demonstrate/demonstrates that the plaintiff is entitled to relief.
5. Everyone has been given their/his or her memo to edit.
6. The subcommittee of the corporation's board of directors have/has reached its/it's decision.
7. A panel of doctors has/have been convened to review the matter.
8. Dan asked Richard and me/I to cite-check the brief.
9. Him/He and her/she will attend the settlement conference.
10. Give the document to Charles and I/me.

REWRITE THE FOLLOWING TO MAKE THEM CLEARER.

1. Sweating profusely, his jacket was drenched.
2. The judge denied our motion. Although I did not agree with that decision.
3. At the conclusion of a trial, a judge must charge his jury.
4. Drafting the brief, his eyes were strained.
5. I was asked to completely review the deposition transcript.
6. Everyone has been given their brief to review.

SPELLING

SELECT THE CORRECT SPELLING.

1. permissible   permissable
2. license   licence
3. accommodate   acommodate
4. irrelevent   irrelevant
5. decedent   decedant
6. seperate   separate
7. admissible   admissable
8. acknowledgement   acknowledgment
9. maintenance   maintenence
10. apparant   apparent

PUNCTUATION

CORRECTLY PUNCTUATE THE FOLLOWING SENTENCES.

1. All three defendants motions were dismissed.
2. I attended the settlement conference and I also attended the pretrial hearings.
3. Wes deposition was taken yesterday.
4. Judge Higgins chambers were recently renovated.
5. The trial was continued. Even over our objections.
6. The clerk stamped the document with the date of July 12 2012 and filed it.
7. I researched wrote and cite-checked the brief.
8. The judge denied the request, and issued a lengthy opinion giving his reasons therefor.

Internet Assignment

1. Access the website of the U.S. Government Printing Office *Style Manual*.
   a. Review Chapter 3, and either correct the following or indicate if they are correct:
      - The Treasury of the United States has increased its staff.
      - She lives in Northern Virginia.
   b. Review Chapter 6, and either correct the following or indicate if they are correct:
      - She is a law-abiding citizen.
      - ABC Inc. is a wholly-owned subsidiary of XYZ Inc.
   c. Review Chapter 8, and either correct the following or indicate if they are correct:
      - It was another's idea.
      - She was given two weeks pay as severance.
2. Access http://www.bartleby.com, and review *The Elements of Style*.
   a. Review Section II.4, and punctuate the following sentence: The revenues are decreasing and there will be a need for a special tax assessment.
   b. Review Section V. May the phrase "due to" be used as a synonym for "because"? Discuss.

Strategies for Effective Writing

Chapter Overview

Once you have mastered the mechanics of writing, you must focus on making your writing effective. This chapter presents techniques to achieve the four hallmarks of effective legal writing: precision, clarity, readability, and brevity. The chapter concludes with a review of drafting techniques and information on electronic communications.

A. Introduction

One of the recurring criticisms of legal writing is that it is rendered incomprehensible to the average reader by its use of jargon, redundancies, and archaic words and phrases. The increased activism of consumers frustrated with the impossibility of understanding an insurance policy or lease led to the requirement in many states that certain documents be written in "plain English." The trend toward plain language has also gained acceptance in legal writing. Law students and beginning writers are now encouraged to avoid "legalese" whenever possible and to use plain English to enhance readability and comprehension of writings.

Writing in plain English so your reader understands you is not an easy task. Many legal concepts are very complex, and translating them into plain English is difficult. Similarly, some use of "legalese," such as Latin phrases, may be unavoidable in certain instances. Falling into the habit of using archaic phrases such as "the instant case at bar" when you really mean "this case" is easy, and you must make a conscious effort to avoid confusing jargon.

B.   Precision

The most important characteristic of legal writing is precision. Be accurate with regard not only to the "big" issues, such as legal conclusions and arguments, but also as to the "small" elements of a writing, such as names, dates, and dollar amounts. An error in the client's name or address may attract more attention than anything else in the project.

1.   *Word Choice*

The selection of an improper word or the use of vague words causes imprecision in your writing. For example, the use of "will" or "may" for "must" or "shall" causes ambiguity and inaccuracy. One writing professor has estimated that more than 1,000 published cases debate the meaning of "shall." Use "may" for optional action, "will" for future action ("I will appear in court on Thursday"), and "must" for obligatory action. "Shall" is considered by many to be archaic.

Following is a list of words that are commonly misused in legal writing. Just as you use a dictionary to avoid spelling errors, use a dictionary or thesaurus to help you select the precise word you need.

affect/effect

Affect means "to influence," as in "I was greatly affected by the victim's story."

Effect means "to cause or bring about" (as a verb) or "result" (as a noun), as in "He effected a settlement of the case" or "One of the effects of the judgment was impairment of his credit rating."

If you have difficulty remembering the difference between these words, do not use either of them. Use their synonyms (influence, or produce, or result).

among/between

Among is typically used to refer to *three or more objects or persons*, as in "The agreement was entered into among Smith, Jones, and Andersen."

Between is usually used to refer to *two objects or persons*, as in "The settlement was negotiated between Peterson and Powell."

and/or

Many experts criticize the use of *and/or*, which can be confusing and ambiguous. Avoid using *and/or*. Use either "and" or "or."

Unclear You must provide a reference and/or a resume.

Preferred You must provide a reference, or resume, or both.

argue/rule

Courts do not argue cases; lawyers do. Do not write *the court argued . . . .* Similarly, courts do not *contend, believe,* or *feel.* Courts *rule, decide, hold, state, conclude,* and so forth.

compose/comprise

Compose means "to make up," as in "The contract is composed of three sections." *Comprise* means "to include or contain or consist of," as in "Tina's collection comprises rare porcelains." Do not use "of" after *comprise.* Thus, it is as incorrect to write, "The brief is comprised of four sections" as it is to write "The brief is included of four sections." Follow this tip: When using *comprise,* place the "whole" item first and the "parts" item second, as in "America comprises 50 states."

disinterested/uninterested

Disinterested means "neutral" and "impartial," as in "Judges must be disinterested in the proceedings they decide."

Uninterested means "not interested or bored," as in "The jurors appeared uninterested in the statistical evidence presented."

fact/contention

A *fact* is something that has occurred or can be verified. Writers often characterize something as a fact when it is merely an allegation or contention. Use the word "fact" only when you are describing an event or something proven. For example, it is a fact that a defendant has blue eyes. It is not a fact that the defendant is guilty until the jury or court says so.

guilty/liable

The word *guilty* refers to criminal wrongdoing. *Liable* refers to responsibility for a civil wrong. Thus, it is correct to write that "Defendant Smith is guilty of robbery although Defendant Jones is liable for damages in the amount of $50,000 for breach of contract."

judgment/judgement

In legal writing and in most American writings, spell as *judgment.* In Great Britain, the word is spelled *judgement.*

oral/verbal

Oral means something spoken, as in "The plaintiff's oral testimony at trial confirmed her earlier deposition testimony."

Verbal means a communication in words and could refer to a written or a spoken communication. Thus, the statement "We had a verbal agreement" is confusing because it could refer either to a written or nonwritten agreement. To avoid confusion, use *oral* or *written* and avoid the use of *verbal*.

overrule/reverse

A court *overrules* prior decisions in its jurisdiction. For example, "The 1954 case *Brown v. Board of Education* overruled the 1896 case *Plessy v. Ferguson*." A court *reverses* the very case before it on appeal, as in "The defendant appealed the decision rendered against him; the appellate court agreed with the defendant's reasoning and reversed the lower court's holding."

principal/principle

Principal is the supervisor at a school or a dominant item, as in "The principal objective to be gained is the prisoner's freedom." Another meaning of "principal" is a sum of money on which interest is paid, as in "The promissory note required repayment of the principal amount of the debt as well as interest."

Principle is a fundamental rule, as in "The principles of physics are complex." Remember to match the "le" in the word "rule" with the "le" ending of "principle."

2. *Vague Words*

To lend forcefulness to your writing, use concrete and descriptive words. Avoid vague words such as "matter," "development," "system," "situation," "problem," and "process," which provide little, if any, information to the reader. Thus, a sentence beginning "Regarding this matter . . ." offers no guidance to the reader as to what "this matter" might be. A much better approach is to write "Regarding your lease . . . ."

Similarly, avoid using words such as "above," "whereas," or "herein." For example, if in an agreement you state on page 8, "As described above . . . ," the reader does not know where in the previous 7 pages you discussed the issue. Be specific. State, "as described in paragraph 4 . . . ."

Similarly, avoid "made-up" words. While you may have heard of, used, and even written "dialogued" or "liaising," these "words" are not generally found in most dictionaries because they are not yet recognized words in English. Our conversation and writing are often influenced by business and technology terms. Thus, a number of terms, such as "cutting edge," "synergy," and "empower," are overused. Do not write "We need to *interface* to resolve the litigation" when you mean "meet." Do not use "impact" as a verb, as in "His actions will impact our ability to obtain a loan." Use "influence" or "affect" instead. Although English is an evolving language, do not use a word before it has evolved into an entry in a dictionary.

3. *Word Connotation*

When you select a word, consider its connotation or suggested meaning. There is a great difference, for example, in referring to an item as "cheap" rather than "affordable." The word "cheap" connotes shoddy or low quality while "affordable" conveys either a neutral or desirable meaning. Consider the effect of telling someone he or she is "stubborn" rather than "determined," or "blunt" rather than "candid." Certain words carry hostile undertones and will immediately make the reader defensive or angry.

C.   Clarity

The second feature of effective legal writing is clarity—that is, ensuring that your project is easily understood by the reader. Your writing style should be invisible. It is bad writing that is noticeable. Because legal writings are read not for pleasure but for function, readers expect you to make your point clearly and quickly. The three primary legal writing flaws that obscure clarity are elegant variation, the overuse of negatives, and improper word order.

1. *Elegant Variation*

Elegant variation refers to the practice of substituting one term for another in a document to avoid repetition of a term. Writers often hesitate to repeat a term, believing that repetition of a term is boring or unsophisticated. Unfortunately, selecting alternative terms creates the impression that something entirely different is intended.

Elegant variation is deadly in legal writing. For example, if you are drafting a document that continually refers to an individual as a "tenant" and then suddenly you refer to this individual as the "lessee," the reader may believe that the "tenant" is not the same individual as the "lessee." You should, therefore, be cautious about varying words and terms you have used. Although you may believe that selecting alternative terms shows your extensive vocabulary and lends interest to the document, you unwittingly may be creating the impression that there is a reason that different terms have been selected and that there is a legal distinction to be drawn based upon this variation. Use the "find and replace" feature of your word processing program to ensure terms are used consistently.

2. *Negatives*

The overuse of negatives can be confusing to a reader. Using more than two negative words in a sentence usually forces the reader to stop and think through what you have said. The phrase "not unlikely" must thus be converted to "likely" or "probable." Anytime the reader is interrupted from reading the project, your message is weakened. As a writer, your task is to ensure that a reader proceeds smoothly through the document without needing to puzzle over phrases.

In drafting projects, keep in mind that there are many more negative words than the obvious ones: "no," "none," or "never." Many words function in a negative fashion, such as "preclude," "deny," "except," and the like. Although it is impossible to purge your writing of all negative terms, you should carefully scrutinize your writing to ensure that you have not used too many negative words that obscure your meaning.

3. *Word Order*

The most common sentence structure in the English language is the placement of the subject first, the verb second, and the object third. Thus, the sentence "The defendant attacked the victim" is phrased in this standard order. Although the thought can certainly be expressed in another way, such as "The victim was attacked by the defendant," readers typically anticipate that sentences will follow the expected pattern of subject, verb, and object. Although you may not want to structure every single sentence in a project in the same fashion, excessive variation from the expected sentence structure will cause confusion and lack of clarity.

One of the other benefits of using "normal" sentence structure is that you will automatically phrase your thoughts in the active voice. When you vary from the anticipated order of sentences, the result is often conversion to the passive voice, which creates a weaker (and often longer) sentence. (See section D.1.)

Ethics Alert

The Risk of Poor Writing

Courts are becoming more and more impatient with poorly written briefs. In one recent case, the court noted that it could not determine the substance of the defendant's legal argument and therefore denied the defendant's motion for being "incomprehensible." *In re King*, No. 05-56485-C, 2006 WL 581256, at *1 (Bankr. W.D. Tex. Feb. 21, 2006). Thus, poor writing can result in an adverse ruling for a client.

D.   Readability

Because the subject matter discussed in most legal writing is complex, and often rather dry, you need to make your product as readable as possible. Clients will be unfamiliar with legal topics. Judges and other legal professionals will be too busy to struggle through a complex and pompous document. Remember that the more complicated a topic is, the more important is the need for readability. To enhance readability:

1. Prefer the Active Voice

The active voice focuses attention on the subject or actor of the sentence that performs or causes certain action. The active voice is consistent with standard sentence structure of subject, verb, and object.

The passive voice focuses attention on the object of action by placing it first and relegating the subject (actor) of the sentence to an inferior position.

Active Voice	*Passive Voice*
The corporation held its meeting.	A meeting was held by the corporation.
The defendant's attorney argued for acquittal.	An argument for acquittal was made by the defendant's attorney.

The active voice is stronger and more forceful than the passive voice. Readers do not have to search through the sentence looking for the actor or subject. Another advantage of using the active voice is that it usually produces shorter sentences.

There are situations, however, in which the passive voice may be preferable. For example, assume your law office represents a defendant accused of fraud. Instead of stating "The defendant deposited checks in his bank account," you could write "Checks were deposited in the defendant's bank account." This use of the passive voice shifts the focus away from the defendant. The reader is informed of what occurred but not who did it. Consider using the passive voice in the discussion of weaker parts of your argument to deflect attention from them. Conversely, be sure to structure the strongest parts of your writing in the active voice because it lends strength and vitality to your writing. You may also wish to use passive voice when you want to focus on the object of the action or when identifying the actor is not necessary to the meaning of your sentence. In any event, if you decide to use the passive voice, make sure your decision is a conscious one.

2. Use Lists

Another way to enhance readability is to use lists when discussing complex matters. Lists not only enable readers to comprehend information quickly but also create visual impact and interest because they are usually numbered or bulleted and set apart from the rest of the text. When setting forth items such as the elements of a cause of action or the components of a definition, use a list.

Lists (sometimes called *tabulation*) can be structured in several ways, but to increase interest:

- Set the list off from the rest of your narrative by spaces above and below your list;
- Indent your list;
- Identify the items in your list with numbers, letters, or "bullets"; and
- Punctuate correctly by putting a semicolon after each item (except the last item) and include "or" or "and" before the last item.

Not all lists need to be indented. If the list is short, you may separate each item from the other by a comma and include the list as part of your narrative text.

The grammatical structure of all of the items in any list must be identical or parallel. Thus, if the first word in a list is a verb, all of the following items must also start with verbs, as shown in the above bulleted list. Similarly, if the first word in the first item ends in "ing," all subsequent items must also begin with words ending in "ing."

Lack of parallel structure is often seen in resumes in which job applicants will describe their experience as follows: "Drafted documents. Prepared pleadings. Assisting in trial preparation." The last item should be "assisted" to retain parallel structure.

3. Avoid Nominalizations

A nominalization occurs when you take an adjective, verb, or adverb and turn it into a noun. Although nominalizations are technically correct, overuse of nominalizations drains your writing of forcefulness and makes it read as if written by a bureaucrat.

	Nominalizations
The contract was enforced.	Enforcement of the contract was accomplished.
We applied for an extension.	An application for an extension was made.

As you can see, nominalizations not only take strong action words such as verbs and convert them into dull nouns, they also tend to make your writing overlong. To avoid nominalizations, watch for words that end in *-ion, -ent*, and *-ant.*

4. Avoid Legal Jargon

The use of "legalese" frustrates readers and produces stodgy writing. Legalese or jargon includes not only archaic and stuffy words and phrases such as "whereas," "opine," and "hereinafter referred to," but words and phrases that are unfamiliar to a reader, such as Latin phrases or legal terms (res judicata, collateral estoppel). The omission or replacement of archaic words and phrases with familiar ones not only enhances readability but also produces a more concise writing.

You may not be able to omit all of the legalese you would like, particularly when drafting wills, deeds, contracts, litigation pleadings, and other legal documents that have more rigid structures. These documents are often drafted in accordance with standard forms and conventions of many years ago, and people are reluctant to change such commonly used forms. In any case, simply try to eliminate as much of the jargon as possible.

If you are using legal terms or Latin phrases, be sure to give a brief definition for your reader. A client may be completely bewildered by a letter informing him or her that "the doctrine of laches precludes your claim." Rewrite as follows: "The doctrine of laches (an unreasonable and prejudicial delay in bringing an action) precludes your claim." Although the insertion of a definition or explanatory phrase produces a longer document, the effect of enhanced readability is well worth the extra words.

5. *Keep Subjects and Verbs in Proximity*

Because the two most critical parts of a sentence are the subject and the verb, readers typically look for these first to make sense of a sentence. Legal writing is known for creating huge gaps between the subject of a sentence and the verb. When too many words intervene between the subject and the verb, readers no longer remember what the sentence is about by the time they locate the verb. They are then forced to re-read the sentence and hunt for the subject.

Although you need not immediately follow every subject in every sentence with a verb, avoid large gaps between these two parts of a sentence. You can make the words intervening between the subject and verb into their own sentence.

Example

The *partnership*, an entity organized and existing under Ohio law and formed after the passage of the Ohio General Partnership Act, *is composed of* Carr, Lee, and Daly.

Rewrite as:

The *partnership is composed of* Carr, Lee, and Daly. It is an entity organized and existing under Ohio law and was formed after the passage of the Ohio General Partnership Act.

E.   Brevity

The length of a project does not necessarily translate into quality. Some of the most compelling and well-known writings are the briefest. For example, the Lord's Prayer has only 66 words. Yet just one federal statute relating to expenses paid under Medicare has more than 700 words.

Although almost all writers agree in principle that brevity is an admirable goal in legal writing, brevity is not easily accomplished. A contributing factor to the length of legal documents is that the topics discussed are often complex, requiring thoughtful analysis. Finally, over-review of a writing causes increased length. Each legal professional who works on a project will feel a need to improve a writing, generally by adding to it, changing "now" to "at the present time" or "if" to "in the event that." Thus, being concise is difficult.

You must be merciless. Your reader's time is at a premium, and you cannot afford to frustrate the reader by redundancy and long-winded phrases. In addition, many courts impose page limits and word-count limits for submissions. Documents that exceed the stated requirements are rejected. Thus, failure to be brief may be legal malpractice.

To achieve brevity:

1.   Omit Needless Words

There are numerous phrases that we use simply by habit. Many of these can be eliminated or reduced to a more concise word or phrase.

Long-Winded Phrases	Substitutions
Due to the fact that	Because
As a result of	Consequently, therefore
Despite the fact that	Although
During the time that	While
At such time as	When
In the event that	If
In order to	To

Careful writing and revising will help you eliminate extra words. Ask yourself if you absolutely need a phrase and whether there is an effective substitute for it. Many commonly used phrases can be replaced by single words with no loss of meaning. In particular, avoid constructions that include more than one preposition, such as "in regard to." Use "regarding."

2.   Avoid Redundancy

Those in the legal profession are wedded to redundancy. They cannot resist writing "null and void and of no legal effect." Is all this needed? If something is null, isn't it void? If it is void, can it have legal effect? The use of these redundant expressions is often the result of pure habit.

If you find yourself using these "stock" redundancies, stop and ask whether one word is sufficient.

Common Legal Redundancies

> acknowledge and agree
> alter or change or modify
> consented and agreed
> covenant, warrant, and represent
> due and owing
> force or effect
> full and complete
> made and entered into
> null and void and of no legal effect
> refuse and fail
> unless and until

F. Drafting Techniques

1. Getting Started

For most writers, the most difficult task is getting started. The research is completed, the deadline is looming, and yet the writer cannot begin. The best cure for this common disease is to write something. Write anything. Just get started. If the idea of beginning an argument paralyzes you, don't begin there. Start writing the section of the document you are most comfortable with, even if this is not the correct order. If you are familiar with the facts, begin with a statement of facts. If you know how you want to conclude a letter, memo, or brief, begin with the conclusion. The mere act of writing any section of a document will relieve some of your anxiety about being able to write. Set a goal for yourself. Challenge yourself to complete a task within an hour. These techniques may help you get started.

2. Finishing on Time

You will often be given deadlines for finishing projects. Similarly, documents prepared for courts may need to be filed by a specified date. If you have a deadline date, you may find it helpful to work backward from this date and establish a schedule for yourself. Set a date by which all of the research will be done, another date for completing the first draft, another for cite-checking, and another for revising.

If you are a habitual last-minute worker, always finding yourself operating in crisis mode, it may help to go public. By telling your supervisor, "The first draft will be on your desk by Friday morning," you will commit yourself to meet this self-imposed deadline. Without some deadline date, the project will languish on your desk and continually be relegated to the back burner while you work on other projects.

Once the deadline is established, allow yourself some time for emergencies. The copier may break down, you may get sick, or someone else's project may have a higher priority. If you don't allow room for these last-minute crises, you may miss the deadline.

3.   Using a Word Processor

The most popular method of writing today is composing using a word processor. Although this method may be very speedy and allows much flexibility in changing the placement of sections, individuals tend to spend excessive time revising as they go along. Your initial draft should be focused on including the major issues and arguments needed to be addressed. Try to fight the temptation to engage in micro-editing as you draft on a word processor. Allow your first draft to flow smoothly and then devote effort to revision later.

If you use a word processor, consider the following:

- Save your versions frequently. Use the functions on your computer that allow you to select how frequently the document will be saved.
- To ensure that you don't lose important information, back up your versions on disks, print paper copies of the document frequently in case the disk is corrupted, and e-mail your documents to your personal e-mail account or to a friend for safekeeping. Use a cloud computing service such as Dropbox or iCloud to store your data and make it accessible from any device, whether a computer, iPad, or iPhone.
- Use the features of your word processor to help you. Consider using the "track changes" feature to show changes between drafts. With a single keystroke you can then accept (or reject) all changes. This technique, called "redlining," is used when legal professionals negotiate the form and content of a document, because it allows each to see the changes made by the other.
- Understand that viewing the project one screen at a time allows you to see only a small slice of the document. Thus, headings and other items may become inconsistent. Carefully review a hard copy to check for consistency in the presentation of such items.

G.   Electronic Communications

New forms of communication, namely, electronic communications, have arisen in the past several years, changing the way people communicate in the workplace. Although many of them are great timesavers, others are traps for the unwary. Follow your reader's preferences for communications. If you know your recipient checks e-mail only sporadically, use the telephone instead. To be meaningful, any communication must be received and read.

1. Phones and Voice Mail

Although conference calls and voice mail both can reduce the time you spend on communications, there are some guidelines that will assist you:

- When participating in a conference call or webinar, treat it as you would a meeting and be prompt in dialing in or logging on.
- Make sure that introductions are made for all participants and that all participants can hear each other. Don't assume that someone is not on a call merely because you did not hear his or her voice or introduction.
- Always ask for permission before placing someone on a speakerphone.
- Always disclose that another is listening with you if you are on a speakerphone.
- Do not leave overly long or rambling voice mail messages.
- Clearly and slowly state your name and phone number in voice mail messages. Repeat at the end of your message for those unfamiliar with you so they do not have to replay the message to obtain your name and number.
- Avoid using voice mail to "dodge" callers and to evade bad news.
- Avoid disclosing confidential information over a cell phone. Messages may be easily intercepted or overheard.

2. Communication by Facsimile

Communicating by facsimile is not nearly as commonplace as it was just a few years ago because documents can now be easily scanned and sent by e-mail to others Nearly all facsimile cover sheets include a confidentiality notice indicating that if someone receives the communication in error, he or she should return it to the sender. Such notices are used to maintain attorney-client confidentiality and privilege. Pre-program frequently called numbers. Always double-check the facsimile number before pressing "Send." Once the document is sent, it cannot be recalled.

3. E-mail

E-mail may well be the most common method of communication, both within the workplace and to clients. E-mail creates an air of informality, and the ease with which a message can be composed and sent causes countless errors. We have all heard stories of people who, much to their chagrin, have mistakenly replied to an entire "list" rather than solely to the sender of a message. Many firms and offices have policies as to the types of communications that can be sent via e-mail and typically include confidentiality notices at the conclusion of each e-mail message. Follow these ten tips for using e-mail in a business setting:

- Spell-check all e-mail and proof for accuracy. If necessary, print a hard copy of the message, proof it, correct it, and then send it. It is far better to be overly cautious than to be perceived as sloppy.
- Because e-mail is generally "dashed off" without a great deal of thought, it often results in brusque and abrupt communications. The reader will not be able to see your expression, gauge your body language, or hear any intonation. Thus, attempts at sarcasm and humor may be misperceived.
- Never pass along inappropriate e-mail at your workplace. Politely inform the sender that you do not care to receive such information.
- Do not assume e-mail is confidential. Many employers monitor e-mail communications. Moreover, e-mail can be discovered in litigation, so be cautious in corresponding by e-mail.
- Be brief and to the point. Many people receive a great number of e-mail messages each day and won't bother to read a long, rambling message.
- Make the subject line specific. Let the recipient know at a glance what the message discusses. A good subject line is *Taylor v. Reid*. A better one is "Hearing Set in *Taylor v. Reid* for 6.20.13."
- Be a charitable reader. Resist overreacting to an e-mail communication that may seem abrupt. The writer may have been trying to be brief.
- When sending an attachment, double-check to be sure you really did attach it (and that it is the correct version).
- Follow the same rules of courtesy and tone used in traditional communications. Ask yourself, *Would I say this in person?*
- Avoid using e-mail to resolve disputes or for delicate matters in which tone of voice is important.

4. Text Messaging

Text messaging (or texting) is the term used for sending short messages (usually fewer than 160 characters) from cell phones or personal digital assistants. Many law firms distribute mobile devices to their legal professionals on the first day of work so that everyone can stay in touch at all times. If you text message anyone about a business-related matter, remember that although you may understand certain abbreviations, the recipient may not. Be sure your message is clear. When in doubt, write it out. Follow these six basic rules for texting in the workplace:

- Texting in front of other people is rude. If your boss is speaking at a firm-wide meeting, and you are texting, it will be noticed. If you are awaiting critical news and must be "on call," alert the people you are with that you may need to answer your phone or send a text.
- Do not assume that people will read your texts immediately. If you are conveying urgent or time-sensitive information (such as a change in meeting time), follow your text with an e-mail or telephone call.
- Double-check both the recipient's number and the content of your message to ensure that your Auto Correct or Auto Complete feature did not select an unintended recipient or word.
- Avoid informal abbreviations such as *?* for *I have a question.* Do not include emoticons. Remember the difference between personal texting and texting for business purposes.
- If you are texting to someone who may not recognize your number, start with an introduction, such as "I am Lindsey Young, the new associate working with Bill Moss."
- Be considerate of others' schedules and time zones. Sending a text from New York to someone in your firm's Los Angeles office could disturb sleep if sent too early.

Internet Resources

http://www.sec.gov/pdf/handbook.pdf	The website of the Securities and Exchange Commission offers excellent guidance on writing in "plain English," with numerous samples, explanations, and tips.
http://law.lclark.edu/programs/legal_analysis_and_writing/resources.php	Lewis & Clark Law School offers links to numerous websites that provide useful and practical information on legal writing.
http://www.bartleby.com	This site offers direct linking to numerous writing resources, including dictionaries, thesauri, *Bartlett's Familiar Quotations*, and portions of Strunk and White's classic book, *The Elements of Style* (1918 version).
http://www2.law.ucla.edu/volokh/legalese.htm	Professor Eugene Volokh of UCLA Law School provides a thorough list of archaic and stuffy legal terms and suggested replacements.

Assignment

PRECISION

SELECT THE CORRECT WORD IN THE FOLLOWING SENTENCES.

1. My counselor/councilor gave me good advice/advise about paying the principle/principal amount of the loan.
2. Court requirements as to document length will effect/affect my brief.
3. The principal/principle goal of the marketing division is to increase business.
4. The capitol/capital of the United States is Washington, D.C.
5. The corporation's headquarters is composed of/comprised of/comprises four main buildings.

CLARITY

REPHRASE EACH OF THE FOLLOWING TO PRODUCE A CLEARER SENTENCE.

1. It is not unreasonable to think that he will be unable to pay the rent on time.
2. The owner of the trademark registration is Nike Inc. The registrant must thus maintain the mark by filing the appropriate documents with the U.S. Patent and Trademark office.
3. Thursday, the judge said, would be the day of the hearing.
4. Persons other than the landlord are not allowed to receive rent payments.
5. Directors of the corporation determine dividend payments. Corporate managers are also responsible for overseeing all compensation matters.

READABILITY

REWRITE THE FOLLOWING SENTENCES TO MAKE THEM MORE READABLE BY USING THE ACTIVE VOICE AND OMITTING NOMINALIZATIONS.

1. A meeting was held by the committee to determine whether the notice had been sent by the corporate secretary.
2. The brief written by Thomas was reviewed by Glenn after it had been cite-checked by Kate.
3. A party was held by the team to celebrate the granting of the motion by the court.
4. New laws were enacted by the legislature.
5. Revision of the contract has been effected by the legal team.
6. Completion of discovery will occur by next Thursday.
7. A determination that the appointment of the corporation's treasurer will be delayed was made by the board of directors.
8. Settlement of the litigation was proposed by the plaintiff.

356

REWRITE THE FOLLOWING SENTENCES TO MAKE THEM MORE READABLE BY USING PARALLEL STRUCTURE.

1. When she first joined the firm, Shelley worked on drafting contracts, meeting with clients, and assisted with proofreading.
2. James wanted to research, write, and to edit the brief.
3. Among her favorite activities were reading, cycling, playing the piano, and she also helped at the local hospice.

REWRITE THE FOLLOWING SENTENCES TO MAKE THEM MORE READABLE BY ELIMINATING JARGON AND REDUNDANT EXPRESSIONS.

1. The purpose of this agreement is to document and memorialize our understanding and agreement with regard to settlement of the instant case at bar.
2. As stated previously, the corporation's conduct, ab initio, caused and created a dangerous condition and situation to exist, including but not limited to noxious and annoying fumes.
3. During the time that the plaintiffs were residents and inhabitants of San Antonio, State of Texas, the landlord failed and refused to provide safe and habitable premises for their habitation.
4. Until such time as the contract shall be modified, amended, or altered, no party hereto may make any additional contributions to the property, income, monies, or funds of the partnership.

Internet Assignment

1. Review the document *Writing User-Friendly Documents* at the Plain Language website at http://www.plainlanguage.gov.
   a. What are "hidden verbs"?
   b. Change the following negative expressions to a positive form: no fewer than; may not . . . until.
2. Review the SEC's guidance document *Plain English Handbook* at http://www.sec.gov. Review Chapter 6. Review the information on omitting superfluous words. Change the following expressions to shorter replacements: in order to; subsequent to; despite the fact that although.
3. Access Professor Eugene Volohk's site at http://www2.law.ucla.edu/volokh/legalese.htm. What substitutions are recommended for the following terms of legalese: has a negative impact; on a number of occasions; was aware?

Legal Correspondence

Chapter Overview

This chapter introduces you to one of the most common forms of legal writings: legal correspondence. Letters are written for several purposes, and thus the style and tone you use will vary according to the purpose of the letter.

A. Letterwriting

1. Introduction

Unlike some other legal writings, such as contracts or wills, there is no rigid list of elements that must be included in a letter. Although letters should, of course, contain the basics (date, salutation, body, and closing), you will be able to exercise great creativity in letterwriting based upon the goal you seek to achieve in your letter. The tone you adopt and the order in which you elect to discuss items are at your discretion. To beginning legal writers, this flexibility can be intimidating. Without a rigid format to follow, some writers become paralyzed.

The two most important questions to ask yourself before you begin a letter are "Who will be reading this letter?" and "What will this letter say?" The answer to the first question will set the tone for your letter, and the answer to the second question will tell you what type of letter you should write.

a. Who Will Be Reading This Letter?

The tone or style of your letter must be appropriate for the reader. If the letter is directed to an individual who is relatively inexperienced with the topic of the letter, you will need to explain the information you present in the most clear and complete fashion possible. If the letter is directed to another legal professional, you will know that your discussion of some matters need not be as detailed or elementary as for a layperson.

If you find your letters are becoming stuffy and legalistic in style, there are a few techniques you can use to warm up the tone. One is to use personal pronouns, especially "you." Therefore, rather than writing "tenants have a right to withhold rent . . ." try writing "as a tenant you have the right to withhold rent because . . . ." Similarly, contractions such as "can't" rather than "cannot" tend to make a letter slightly less formal because contractions are not commonly used in legal or business writing.

b. What Will This Letter Say?

Before you begin drafting any letter, focus on the central purpose of your letter. Try to distill this to one or two sentences. For example, some purposes may be as follows:

- The client needs to know a deposition has been scheduled for next month.
- The debtor needs to understand that failure to repay the client will result in litigation.
- The client needs to be provided advice regarding discharging an employee.

These examples represent the most basic types of legal correspondence: *general correspondence* or *informative, demand*, and *opinion* letters. Once you decide what type of letter you need to write, a style will come almost naturally.

Before discussing techniques for writing these varieties of letters, we will examine the format and elements of legal letters in general.

2. *The Elements of Letters*

Although there are different types of letters you will write, there are certain "basics" that are common to all legal correspondence. Following is a list of the elements of most legal and business letters:

- **Letterhead:** The sender's name, address, and other pertinent information, usually centered
- **Date:** Centered two or three lines below letterhead with no abbreviations
- **Inside Address:** Recipient's name and address, at left margin, two lines below date

- **Special Notations:** Indications of method of sending, privileges claimed, and so forth, at left margin, two lines below inside address
- **Reference Notation:** Reference to case name, topic of letter, and so forth, at left margin, or indented five spaces, two lines below special notations (usually shown as "Re:")
- **Salutation:** Opening greeting, addressing all individuals as *Mr.* or *Ms.* unless directed otherwise and followed by a colon, placed two lines below reference notation
- **Body of Letter:** Begins two lines below salutation, single-spaced, with double spacing between paragraphs, which may be indented five spaces or not indented
- **Complimentary Closing:** A closing phrase or word such as *Sincerely*, centered, appearing two lines below last line of body of letter
- **Signature Block:** Writer's name and title, aligned with complimentary close, four lines below complimentary close
- **Final Notations:** References to writer's and typist's initials, enclosures, and indications of those who will receive copies of letter, all appearing at left margin, beginning two lines below signature block, each appearing one line below the other

---

Practice Tip

Unknown Addressees

If you do not know the name of the recipient of a letter, for example, the Commissioner of the Internal Revenue Service, consider the following:

- **Use a title, such as *Dear Commissioner*; or**
- **Do some research on the Internet to find out the name of the Commissioner. In other situations, use the salutation *Dear Colleague*.**

---

3. Format Considerations for Letters

Letters are written on standard 8½" × 11" paper and are usually single-spaced and then double-spaced between component parts (for example, between the date and inside address and between the inside address and reference notation) and between paragraphs.

Some letters show no indentations for paragraphs because new paragraphs are clearly indicated by the double-spacing between paragraphs. This style is referred to as "block form" or "left justified." In full block form, all elements of the letter, including the date and complimentary closing, begin at the left margin. Some firms and authors prefer to indent five spaces for new paragraphs even though they are set apart by double-spacing. This style is called "modified block form." Here, the date, complimentary closing, writer's identification, and signature are all centered.

When the right-hand margin is even and every line ends at the right at the same space (as in this text), this is referred to as "right justification" or "full justification." Such letters present a very crisp appearance. One drawback to right justified margins is that the spacing in some words may be cramped while others may be slightly spread out. Continuing improvements in word processors are eliminating these spacing problems. Nevertheless, some writers prefer a "ragged edge" at the right margin, believing it is more readable and has less of a "computer" look and more of a "personally typed" look.

Never allow a page to begin or end with one line by itself or one heading by itself. Referred to as "widows and orphans," these single lines or headings present an unprofessional appearance. Use 12-point typeface for readability. Use a common typeface such as Times New Roman or Courier New.

4. Types of Letters

a. General Correspondence

General correspondence or informative letters may include letters requesting or responding to requests for information, cover letters that accompany some document or other enclosure, confirmation letters that confirm some agreement reached with another party, or status or report letters providing a report to a client or insurance company of the progress of a case. Except for status letters, these letters are often brief and may be only one or two paragraphs in length.

These letters should contain the components of all letters (date, inside address, reference notation). They also should conform to the elements of good legal writing set forth in Chapter 14, namely, precision, clarity, readability, and brevity. If you misspell the client's name or send the letter to the wrong address, this will attract far more attention than the content of the letter. See Figure 15-1 for sample general correspondence letters.

Ethics Alert

Corresponding with Parties

One of the most basic rules of ethics is that lawyers and those they supervise may not have any contact with parties once those parties are represented by counsel. Thus, never call or write a party without checking whether that party is represented by counsel. If you are unsure, when you make a telephone call, your first question should be "Are you represented by counsel?" If the person answers "yes," politely end the call, and contact that attorney.

b. Demand Letters

Demand letters set forth a client's demands. The most common type of demand letter is a collection letter, which outlines the basis for a debt due to a client and sets forth a demand that it be paid. Other demand letters, however, demand that certain action be taken, such as a demand that a landlord repair a leaking roof. Your tone should be firm and business-like, not strident or nasty. To eliminate any disputes whether and when the letter was received, send the letter by some verifiable type of delivery, such as registered mail. The only portion of a demand letter that will differ from a general correspondence letter is the content of the body. Include these elements:

- *Introduction of your firm.* Identify your firm and specify your role. A simple sentence stating "We represent Joel K. Chase regarding the automobile accident that occurred on January 8, 2013" is sufficient.
- *Recitation of facts.* You must include the facts upon which the client's claim is based. Because your aim is to motivate the reader to pay your client or take some action, phrase the factual statement as persuasively as possible.
- *Demand.* Set forth your client's demand as clearly as possible. If this is a collection letter, specify the exact amount due. If you are demanding that the reader take some specific action, such as assigning a contract, say so.
- *Consequences of non-compliance.* Because your aim in a demand letter is to persuade the reader to pay your client or take some action, you should include a statement telling the reader of the consequences of not complying with the demand letter. These consequences may include the institution of litigation, the cessation of work on a project, or some other adverse action. Although nearly all readers will be offended by heavy-handed threats, there is nothing wrong in clearly and concisely explaining to a reader what will occur if the client's demands are not met.
- *Date of compliance.* You must set forth in explicit terms the deadline for compliance. Do not write "You must pay the sum of $10,000 immediately." When is immediately? Two days? Ten days? Set forth a specific date so the reader will know exactly when compliance is expected.

Figure 15-1
Sample General Correspondence Letters

LAW OFFICES
OF
MICHELLE L. MONACO, P.C.
2300 BIRCH DRIVE
PHOENIX, ARIZONA 60234
(602) 788-4000

November 8, 2013

Stephen L. James, Esq.
6200 Tenth Street
Phoenix, AZ 60244

Re: *Brownell v. Kaplan*

Dear Mr. James:

This letter will confirm that you have granted us an extension to respond to the plaintiff's complaint in the above-referenced action until December 6, 2013. As I explained, the additional time is needed due to my client's recent hospitalization. Thank you for your courtesy and cooperation.

Please feel free to call me if you have any comments or questions.

Sincerely,

Michelle L. Monaco

MLM/pmr
cc: Sharon J. Kaplan

Figure 15-1 *(Continued)*

SMITH, CHURCH, AND UPSHAW, L.L.P.
1414 SOUTH ADAMS STREET
SUITE 1000
BOSTON, MASSACHUSETTS
(617) 649-1200

January 14, 2013

Ms. Ann B. Milstead
2001 Elysian Fields Avenue
New Orleans, LA 70015

Re: *Sanderson v. Milstead*

Dear Ann:

I am enclosing a copy of the transcript of the plaintiff's deposition in the above-referenced action. Please review this carefully and call me with any comments you may have. As you know, we are particularly interested in the plaintiff's version of the events in the two hours preceding the accident. Any inconsistencies that you may find in the plaintiff's testimony would be extremely helpful. We look forward to hearing from you.

Very truly yours,

William B. Church

WBC/swa
Encl.

Follow these guidelines in drafting demand letters:

(i)   *Know the facts.* Be sure you have all of the relevant facts. A mistake in reciting the facts will immediately call forth a response by the recipient pointing out your error, and any momentum you may have had, along with your credibility, will be lost. To be sure your recitation of the facts is correct, send a copy of your demand letter in draft to the client asking that the client review the letter and approve it before it is sent to the other party.

(ii) *Know the law.* You must perform some minimum amount of research to ensure that the client's claim is valid and enforceable. Similarly, review the code of ethics for your state. It is unethical to correspond with a person who is represented by counsel. Therefore, once you know an individual has retained counsel, all correspondence must be directed to counsel. Most codes of ethics set forth other rules you should be familiar with, such as that it is unethical to threaten criminal prosecution if a demand is not met.

(iii) *Don't argue the case.* A demand letter should set forth the facts underlying the demand, state the demand, and outline the consequences of non-compliance. You need not, and should not, present all the evidence you would need to prevail at a trial of this matter. If the problem cannot be resolved by direct negotiation, your firm will have ample opportunity to argue the case at trial. Although a few legal authorities may be cited in some instances, routine collection letters rarely include legal analysis.

(iv) *Do what you say.* If you have told the recipient of the letter legal action will be instituted by May 5 unless the amount of $10,000 is paid to the client, you must be prepared to follow through. Nothing jeopardizes credibility more than empty threats. If May 5 comes and goes and you send another demand letter setting forth a new deadline date, the reader will know you do not mean what you say and that there is no need to comply with the second demand. Note, however, that if you write "We look forward to a counter proposal from you," you have made a serious concession and have invited the recipient to play "let's make a deal."

c.   Opinion Letters

Letters offering legal advice or opinions can be signed only by properly licensed attorneys. In fact, opinion letters are often signed by senior partners on behalf of the firm itself. Nevertheless, you may find that you are given the task of researching the law and writing drafts of the letter. These opinion letters are usually requested by clients seeking advice on a particular matter. In addition to the standard components of a letter (reference line, salutation, and so forth), there are eight key elements to an opinion letter.

(1) Date

Although all letters include dates, the date of an opinion letter is especially important because the opinion will relate to the status of the law on that date. Changes in the law after that date may well affect the correctness of the opinion.

(2) Introductory Language

It may be a good idea to remind the client why he or she is receiving an opinion letter. An opinion letter may take several hours to research and prepare and may well be costly. Reminding a client that he or she specifically requested the opinion may protect you from a client's refusal to pay the bill on the ground that this work was never requested. Consider the following introductions:

- We enjoyed meeting you last week. As you requested, we have researched . . . .
- You have asked for our opinion whether . . . .

This introductory language not only protects you from a client's faulty memory, but also sets forth the scope of the letter by stating the issue that is addressed by the letter.

(3) Review of Facts

An opinion letter should always set forth the facts upon which it is based. Including the facts gives the client the opportunity to correct you if any of the facts are wrong. Thus, include the facts so the reader understands that the accuracy of the opinion depends upon these facts and that changes in the facts may cause changes in the legal conclusions reached. Consider introducing the facts as follows: "As we understand them, the facts are as follows: On June 24, 2013, you suffered an injury at your workplace and . . . ."

(4) Conclusions

The essence of an opinion letter is the advice given to the client. Clients are particularly eager to get to the "bottom line," and many writers immediately give their opinion or conclusion after a recitation of the facts, and then follow the conclusion with an explanation. This is an effective technique if the opinion you give is one the client wants to hear. If, on the other hand, you will be giving the client bad news, such as informing him or her that a lawsuit cannot be initiated because the statute of limitations has expired, you may want to lead the reader to this unfavorable news gradually. By explaining the law first, you will be preparing the reader for the unfavorable outcome, so by the time you actually give the bad news, the reader understands exactly why the outcome is unfavorable. Consider introducing the conclusion as follows: "Based upon the facts you have provided us and the applicable law in this state, it is our opinion that you may initiate an action for negligence against James Diaz."

You may have observed that many opinion letters use "we" and "our" rather than "I" and "my." For example, an opinion is often introduced as follows: "Based on our interpretation of the contract, our advice is . . . ." This use of "we/I" is a matter of preference by attorneys. Some attorneys believe it is cowardly to hide behind the royal "we" and insist on using the first person "I/me," as in "It is therefore my opinion . . . ." Other attorneys believe the opinion is actually issued by the firm itself rather than by any one particular attorney, and thus the "we/our" form is appropriate. You must learn the preference and policy of your supervisor and firm to determine which form to use.

(5) Explanation of Conclusion

This portion of the letter explains and summarizes the law upon which your conclusions are based. Because most opinion letters are received by laypersons who may not be familiar with the law, avoid detailed discussions of statutes and cases. It is sufficient to summarize the legal authorities in a general fashion. Generally, avoid giving citations unless your reader is sufficiently sophisticated to understand the citations. Similarly, do not merely set out the text of a statute or case; rather, explain what the case or statute means. Refer to the legal authorities as follows:

- Applicable case law provides . . . .
- The legal authorities in this state are in agreement that . . . .

You may use headings and subheadings (such as "Fraud") if this portion of the letter is long, and you can divide your explanation into easily understood separate sections.

(6) Recommendation

After you have explained the law that governs the conclusion you have reached, provide a recommendation to the client. Be sure that your recommendation is not unduly optimistic. Do not include any language that could be viewed by a client as a guarantee of success. Phrase your advice as a probability rather than a certainty. Thus, write "A court may hold that" rather than "Your claim is undoubtedly valid." Similarly, if you need to give the client bad news, try to soften your approach by saying "The chances of a favorable outcome are remote" rather than a blunt "Taking your case would be a waste of time and money." Be sure, however, that you clearly deliver the bad news. Readers often perceive what they want to, and there is no room for ambiguity in delivering unfavorable news to a client. If you must give bad news, try to find an alternative avenue for the client, as follows:

> Because the statute of limitations has expired, you will not be able to bring an action against your neighbor for trespass. We would suggest, however, that you attempt to negotiate directly with your neighbor. If this approach is unsuccessful, contact the company that issued your homeowners insurance because it may offer coverage for the damage to your property.

Use wording such as "we regret" or "unfortunately" when delivering bad news.

(7) Instructions

The last portion of an opinion letter should be a clear direction to the client to contact the office or take some other action. Consider the following:

> Because the governing statutes require that a claim be submitted to the city within 100 days of the wrongful act, please contact us immediately and provide us with your instructions. Unless the claim is filed by May 8, 2013, it will be barred.

(8) Protection Clauses

On occasion, you may not have all of the information you need to provide a complete opinion. For example, the client may have informed you that he is a tenant under a written lease and yet has not provided the lease to your office for your review. In such cases, protect yourself by explaining that you lack certain information and that the opinion may change depending upon the information you receive. Finally, think ahead and consider what defenses or arguments the other party may assert. Prepare your client to meet these arguments.

Consider the following example:

> Although your employer may argue his business is not subject to the provisions of the Family and Medical Leave Act, we believe such an argument is without merit because . . . .

B. Conclusion

Always write your letter with its intended audience in mind and clearly understand your goals in sending the letter. Do you want to inform? Convince? Settle? This will help you achieve the correct style and tone.

After you have finished the letter, re-read it, putting yourself in the recipient's place. This will allow you to focus on whether the letter conveys the information it needs to, whether it will be readily understood by the reader, and whether the tone is appropriate.

Because you will have the opportunity to review correspondence from others, keep copies of those letters that you feel are well written and adopt the techniques you believe make the letters effective. Notice the way others order their paragraphs or conclude their letters. Learn from others.

Internet Resources

http://owl.english.purdue.edu/owl/ resource/653/01	This site provides information on writing business letters and gives sample letters.
http://writing.colostate.edu/guides/ documents/ business_writing/ business_letter	Colorado State University provides numerous writing resources, including tips on writing business letters.
http://www.michbar.org/journal/ pdf/pdf4article449.pdf	Attorney Wayne Schiess, writing for the *Michigan Bar Journal*, offers advice on writing client letters.

Assignment

You have been given the following fact pattern by Judith Harris, one of the senior partners in your law firm.

The firm represents Stephen Miller who is one of four members of a limited liability company organized in our state. When the limited liability company was organized last year, Mr. Miller contributed 70 percent of its capital. The other three members each contributed 10 percent of the company's capital. Although the company has a written operating agreement that governs many of its procedures and operations, the agreement is silent on distributions of profits. The company has $100,000 of profits that it intends to distribute. The managing member of the company, Joshua Adams, has stated that each member will receive $25,000. Because Mr. Miller contributed 70 percent of the company's capital, he believes he is entitled to a distribution of $70,000.

Ms. Harris would like you to prepare an opinion letter (for her signature) to Mr. Miller explaining how the company's profits will be distributed.

By way of background, the Uniform Limited Liability Company Act (Revised) includes provisions relating to distributions of profits. Our state has adopted the Act in its entirety. The Act is available on the website of the National Conference of Commissioners on Uniform State Laws at http://www.uniformlaws.org. Assume there are no cases interpreting the applicable provisions of the Act.

Internet Assignment

1. Access the site http://www.michbar.org/journal/pdf/pdf4article449 .pdf and read the article about writing client letters.
   a. What three options are given for legal citations in letters to clients?
   b. What tone should be used in client letters?
2. Access the site http://www.irmi.com/expert/articles/2004/blake01 .aspx and read the article by Gary Blake on writing letters to opposing attorneys. What five tips are given to help you avoid an adversarial tone?

Legal Memoranda

Chapter Overview

An office or research or legal memorandum is a well-known document in legal writing. It calls for you to research an area of law thoroughly and set forth your findings, both positive and negative, in a specific format.

It is only by being completely knowledgeable about the strengths and weaknesses of a case that a law firm can make a fully informed decision whether and how best to represent the client. Thus, office memoranda or "memos" are used to guide those representing the client in every aspect of a case—from the initial decision whether to accept a case to a final appeal. If the law firm knows in advance the weaknesses of a case, it can adopt certain strategies to overcome these weaknesses and prepare the client for a possible negative outcome. If the memo shows the weaknesses are fatal, the memo saves the client time and money that would be expended in a trial and assists in making a decision to settle the case. A well-written memo can form the basis for motions to be made later in the case or even a trial or appellate brief. Thus, skillful research and careful written analysis at this early stage of a case will contribute to the successful management of a case throughout its progress in your office.

A. Objectivity of Legal Memoranda

An office memorandum is a research document designed to provide information about a case or matter. It is an internal document, meaning it is prepared for use within a law firm, company, or agency. Although a copy of the memo may be provided to a client, it is generally protected by the "work product" privilege and thus is not discoverable by an adverse party. Because the office memo is not usually discoverable and will only be read by those representing the client (and possibly the client as well), its distinguishing feature is its objectivity. It should set forth not only the strong points of a case but the weak points as well.

The most difficult part of writing a memo is remaining neutral and objective. Once we hear the words "our client," we immediately tend to ally ourselves with the client's position and ignore the negative aspects of a case while focusing only on the positive.

If you are not objective in pointing out weaknesses and flaws in the client's case, you do the client a disservice. It is much better (and far less costly) to determine early in the representation that the other party has a complete defense to your client's action than to find this out at trial. Force yourself to play devil's advocate. Approach the project as your adversary might and closely examine the cases that appear unfavorable to your position. Your adversary will certainly do so, and you should be as prepared as possible to overcome weaknesses in your case.

On occasion, attorneys request more persuasive memoranda, which then avoid objectivity and argue persuasively for a certain position. These memoranda are often prepared in advance of some hearing or motion in court and are thus more similar to trial court briefs (discussed in Chapter 17) than the traditional memoranda discussed in this chapter.

B. Format of Legal Memoranda

Unlike documents filed in court, there is no one rigid format for an internal office memorandum. The format suggested below is a very common and standard format. There are usually seven components to an office memorandum, each of which should be set forth as a heading and capitalized and centered, or in some other way set off from the narrative portion of the memo. To some degree, the elements of a memorandum are similar to those of a case brief, discussed in Chapter 4. See Appendix A for a sample memo.

1. Heading

The heading identifies the document, the person for whom the memo is prepared, the author and his or her position, the subject matter of the memo, and the date it is prepared. The subject matter notation (found in the "Re:" line) should include some descriptive content, such as "Standards for Injunctive Relief" as well as a file name and number to help facilitate indexing and later retrieval of the memo.

2. Issue(s) or Question(s) Presented

This section of the memo sets forth the issues that will be addressed by the memo. If your memo will discuss more than one issue, number each one. Do not number a single issue. Drafting the issues can be very difficult. In fact, you may not be able to formulate the issues until you are almost finished researching the law to be discussed in the memo. If you have trouble drafting your issues, wait until your memo is complete and then convert the conclusion you reached into a question.

> ***Example of conclusion:*** The copyright in works created by employees during the scope of their employment is presumptively owned by their employers.

> ***Example of issue:*** Does the employer or the employee own the copyright in works created by the employee while he or she is employed?

The issues are normally set forth in a question format. They are usually one sentence, although they may include subparts. Be careful that a one-sentence issue is not so long as to be confusing. The issues should be phrased so that they relate to the particular fact the problem presented. For example, questions such as "What is a sublease?" or "What is burglary?" are far too broad. Incorporate a few facts from your case. Consider the following:

- Under West Virginia law, may a tenant sublease rented property when a written lease fails to address this issue?
- In California, has a burglary occurred when an intruder enters a residence through an open door?

Some writers prefer the issues or questions to start with the word "whether," as in "whether a battery occurred when parties involved in a fistfight agreed to fight." Because questions that begin with the word "whether" produce incomplete sentences, many attorneys disfavor this form. Whichever format you choose, be consistent and use the same format for all questions.

The questions presented should be phrased in a neutral manner so that an answer is not suggested by the question itself. If you have more than one issue, consider listing the most critical issue first. It is possible that by addressing the threshold issue first, later issues may be rendered moot. For example, if you first determine there is no breach of contract, any later discussion of damages for breach of contract is unnecessary.

3. *Brief Answer(s)*

This section of the memo briefly answers the questions you set forth. Avoid answers that merely repeat the question. Your answers should incorporate the reasons for your conclusions; thus, a one-word answer, such as "No," is inappropriate. Brief answers for the issues posed above would be as follows:

- Yes. In West Virginia, a tenant may sublease rented property to another unless the landlord and tenant have agreed in writing to restrict the tenant's right to sublease.
- Yes. In California, forcible entry is not required for burglary to exist; an intruder who enters a residence with the intent to commit theft has committed burglary.

Keep your answers brief—no more than one or two sentences. Do not include formal citations in the brief answers. This section of the memo is only a quick preview of what will be discussed in greater detail later in the body of the memo. Maintain symmetry in your brief answers. If you have set forth three issues, you must have three answers, each of which corresponds in order and number to the questions previously asked.

4.   *Statement of Facts*

The statement of facts may precede the issues or follow the brief answers. Either approach is acceptable. Some readers prefer the facts to be given first so they can make sense of the questions the memo will address. Most writers, however, place the statement of facts after the brief answers.

The statement of facts will be based upon what you know about the case, what your supervisor and client have told you, and your review of the file. In brief, you are telling the client's "story." The factual statement must be neutral and objective. Therefore, you will need to include even unfavorable facts. Do not allow your opinions about the case to color your presentation of the facts. For example, the statement "He endured four years of employment by ABC" includes an opinion or judgment. State "He was employed by ABC for four years."

Do not include arguments in your memo or conclusions that are not supported by the file. If you are unsure whether a statement or event is true, refer to it as an "alleged" statement or event. If there is a dispute as to the facts, include both versions. It is perfectly acceptable to state "Although the tenant alleges she provided notice to the landlord of the leaky roof, the landlord disputes this."

Do not omit the facts on the assumption that "surely the attorney who gave me this project knows the facts." It is possible a new legal professional may be assigned to the case, and your memo may be the first source consulted to become familiar with the case. Therefore, the statement of facts should be self-contained and not require reference to other sources, such as pleadings or correspondence. To eliminate unnecessary facts, reread your statement of facts after you have completed your first draft of the memo. If the statement of facts includes facts that are not later mentioned in the analysis or discussion section, those facts can probably be omitted.

The best presentation of a factual statement is narrative, that is, sentence after sentence, paragraph after paragraph, written in the third person. Use the past tense unless facts are developing as you prepare the memo. Finally, although other approaches are acceptable, the most typical approach is to present a statement of facts in chronological order. In other words, relate the facts in the order in which they occurred.

At this point, you probably realize that a legal memorandum is unlike any document you have yet prepared. The presentation of questions, followed by answers, followed by facts, is indeed unusual. Remember, however, that your final project will include these critical elements within the first page or two, allowing your reader to review only a portion of the memo and yet comprehend a total view of the case. Simply by reading these first three substantive sections, the reader will know the strengths and weaknesses of the client's position.

5. *Applicable Statutes (Optional)*

Some memos include a section describing or setting forth any applicable statutory provisions that will be discussed in the memo. This section is optional and need not be included. If you include applicable statutes, you may either paraphrase the statutes or quote from them. If the statute is long, you may include only the pertinent language and then attach a copy of the full statute to your memo. Use correct citation form.

6. *Analysis or Discussion*

The heart of the memorandum is the analysis, or discussion, section. This portion of the memo provides an in-depth analysis of the issues presented. Cases, statutes, and other authorities will be presented and discussed. Citations typically appear in the body of the memorandum, not as footnotes. Citations should be prepared according to *Bluebook* or *ALWD* form unless local or other form is used. Keep in mind the critical distinction between primary and secondary sources: Primary sources are mandatory and binding authorities, which must be followed, while secondary authorities are persuasive at best. Thus, rely on secondary authorities only when there are no relevant primary authorities.

There are several things to keep in mind as you write the analysis section of your memo.

• **Using Thesis Statements.** Many writing experts suggest that authors use a thesis statement when writing projects. A thesis statement distills the central ideas and arguments in a project into one or two assertive sentences. It usually appears at the beginning of a project or issue to give focus and direction to the analysis to follow. Sometimes, a thesis statement is called an umbrella statement because every part of the discussion to follow must fit beneath it. Thus, later sentences in the paragraph merely elaborate upon the point made by the thesis statement; they do not introduce new material. A thesis statement is not the same as a topic sentence. It is far more assertive than a topic sentence, which merely announces the subject matter or theme of a paragraph to follow; a thesis statement, on the other hand, provides a specific conclusion. Consider the following thesis statement:

- To be enforceable, a noncompetition agreement must be reasonable as to its scope, duration, and geographic area.

You can see that a thesis statement is a strong, conclusory assertion and that it serves to frame the discussion to follow. For example, using the illustration given above, after providing the thesis statement, the writer would then proceed to discuss the scope, duration, and geographic area of the noncompetition agreement in his or her case. The thesis statement thus provides the applicable rule and a preview of the analysis to follow.

• **Using the Cases.** It is not enough to merely locate authorities and summarize them. Almost anyone can read a case and then restate its holding. You will be expected to do more, namely, to analyze the authorities and discuss how and why they relate to your particular problem. This requires you to compare the facts of your case with the authorities you rely upon. If the client's particular situation can be distinguished from the situation in the case law, say so. Explain why cases apply and why they do not. Be sure to give some of the facts of the cases you rely on so readers can see how and why they apply to your issue. One warning sign that you are merely providing case summaries rather than analysis is that each paragraph in your memo discusses a single case. If you find this happening, restructure the memo to ensure the cases you rely upon are being analyzed and compared with the client's fact situation rather than merely being summarized.

This section of the memo will require all your effort to remain objective. Thoroughly discuss not only the authorities that support the client's position, but also those that do not. If you find weaknesses in a client's case, continue researching to determine if there are ways to surmount them. If new issues are disclosed by your research, discuss them. Typically, memo writers discuss the cases and authorities that support the client's position before discussing those that are unsupportive. Once all authorities are discussed for an issue, move on to the next issue.

If a direct quotation is particularly apt, use it. Be careful, however, to ensure that your analysis consists of more than a series of quotations. It is easy to read cases and then retype what the judge has stated. Use quotations, but make sure you explain their relevance to your research problem.

• **Ensuring Readability.** Retain symmetry in your memo. If you have identified three issues and provided three brief answers, divide your discussion into three parts, each of which corresponds in number and order to the issues you formulated. Each section should be labeled with a descriptive heading. Brief headings, such as "Fraud" and "Damages," are acceptable and clearly alert the reader as to the topic to be addressed. If desired, you may repeat your issues as headings, although this will add to the length of your brief. Use subheadings if these would be helpful to a reader.

Be sure your discussion is readable. If every paragraph starts with a phrase such as "In *Smith v. Jones* . . . the court held . . . ," your finished project will have a choppy, stodgy style and appearance. The most

important part of the memorandum is not a dull recitation of facts and
holdings of several cases, but rather your analysis of the effect these cases
and other authorities will have on the client's particular situation.

In many instances, although writing style and techniques should
vary to enhance readability, the analysis can be reduced to the following
basic format for each separate issue:

> According to . . . [citations], the law is . . . [explain and discuss]. In the pres-
> ent case, . . . [compare with authorities]. Therefore, . . . [conclude].

• **Analyzing Using the IRAC Method.** In discussing and analyzing authorities, many writers follow what is referred to as the "IRAC"
method. "IRAC" is an acronym for Issue, Rule, Analysis or Application,
and Conclusion.

First, the issue being considered is presented. Introduce the question or topic you will be analyzing. In a memo, the issue is originally set
forth in the form of a question, such as "Does the Uniform Partnership Act
govern a partnership that has no partnership agreement?" In a discussion
section, the issue is often set forth in the following form: "The key issue is
whether the Uniform Partnership Act governs a partnership that has no
written agreement." This serves to frame the discussion that will follow.

Next, provide the rule or legal authority that you rely upon to respond
to the issue. The authority can be a case, a statute, or some other primary
or secondary authority or authorities. If you rely on a case, give sufficient
facts from the case that the reader will understand why and how it governs your case. If your rule is a statute, set forth the applicable provisions.
Several authorities may be used. In fact, you should have at least one
primary authority for every conclusion you reach. Complex matters will
require citation of more authorities, including secondary authorities.

The most critical part of an IRAC discussion is the analysis or application of the rule to your case. Explain why the rule you have set forth
does or does not apply to your particular case. Do more than merely summarize a case or statute. Summarizing should have taken place when
you set forth the rule. Analyzing requires you to compare and contrast
the facts of your case with those in the cases you rely upon or to review
a statute and show the reader why your client's situation falls within (or
without) the activity described by the case or statute.

Finally, after a thorough analysis, present the reader with a conclusion based upon your analysis of the rule. If the rule has been set forth
clearly and the analysis is complete, the reader will likely be able to draw
a conclusion even in advance of your stating it. Nevertheless, presenting
a conclusion wraps up your analysis and serves as reinforcement of prior
discussion as well as a signal that discussion of a particular topic is complete and that a new topic will likely be presented next, once again using
the IRAC method.

Many beginning researchers are reluctant to draw a conclusion. They
simply summarize applicable cases and then move on to the next topic.
You will need to synthesize the authorities you discuss by comparing and
contrasting them to each other and then applying them to the client's

particular case to reach a conclusion. See Figure 16-1 for an example of an IRAC discussion.

Figure 16-1
Sample IRAC Discussion

Issue
The issue in this case is whether a single remark made in a workplace (namely, Hey, babe—looking good) constitutes sexual harassment.

Rule
The cases interpreting the Civil Rights Act of 1964 are in agreement that although a single utterance can constitute harassment, the remark must be so severe and outrageous that it creates an intolerable and hostile work environment.

Application
[Discuss cases and give citations.] In the present case, the remark, although offensive and inappropriate, is not "severe" and "outrageous" as those terms are used in the cases governing this issue.

Conclusion
Thus, the remark is unlikely to rise to the level of actionable sexual harassment.

Following the IRAC approach to discussing problems helps ensure that you conduct a thorough analysis of an issue and is a commonly accepted writing approach both for law students and legal practitioners.

• **Analyzing Using the CRAC or CRuPAC Methods.** Some experts suggest a variation of IRAC, often called "CRAC" (for Conclusion, Rule, Application, and Conclusion). In this analysis, the conclusion is given first, followed by the principal rule of law that supports the conclusion. The rule is applied and illustrated through analysis of cases and other authorities. The rule is then applied to the client's particular case, and the conclusion is restated. Still another variation of IRAC is "CRuPAC" (for Conclusion, Rule, Proof, Application, and Conclusion). In this analysis, the conclusion is first stated, followed by the pertinent rules that govern the issue. The proof section then analyzes the relevant case precedents. The rules and proof are then applied to the specific facts in the case, and the second conclusion reiterates the introductory conclusion.

Some writing experts dislike IRAC and its variations because they believe these methods encourage a rigid and formulaic approach to writing. Others believe that IRAC is more useful for writing objective projects such as legal memoranda (because it requires the writer to state the issue in a neutral manner) and that CRAC and CRuPAC (with their assertive conclusions given at the beginning) are more useful in persuasive writings, such as court briefs. Still others believe that IRAC and its variations are better suited to school examinations rather than memos and other documents. In any event, IRAC and its variations may be useful tools to help you remember to include critical elements when you analyze a legal problem.

• **Being Concise.** If you are concerned that your memorandum is too long, challenge yourself to write an "e-mail memo," which is an abridgement of a traditional memo to a length that would be acceptable if included in an e-mail message that a recipient could read on an iPhone or similar device without endlessly scrolling down the screen. In fact, attorneys frequently request legal analysis of an issue while they are traveling or in another office. The response to this request must convey the analysis clearly and succinctly and in a format suitable for reading on a small screen.

Practice Tip

Using Quotations and Paraphrasing

Many beginning writers wonder when to use direct quotations and when to paraphrase. Consider the following guidelines:

- **Use a direct quotation when what has been said is so articulate and apt that to paraphrase it would dilute its meaning.**
- **Use a direct quotation when the author of the quotation is so well known that a quotation from this person would provide instant credibility.**
- **Avoid overlong quotations. They may be skipped. Use quotations sparingly so that they grab the reader's attention.**
- **Paraphrase when the original quotation is difficult to understand or would require so much restructuring (for example, with ellipses and brackets) that it would be distracting to the reader.**
- **Always provide a full citation, with a pinpoint cite, for every quotation and paraphrase.**

---

7. *Conclusion*

The conclusion should be brief and should be a highlight of the conclusions you reached earlier in the Discussion or Analysis section of the memo. In many ways, the conclusion will resemble your brief answers, although it tends to provide more information than the brief answers do. Do not include formal citations in your conclusion. Simply sum up your analysis. The conclusion should not present any material that has not previously appeared in the body of the memo.

If, during the course of your research, you determine that certain information is needed or that a certain course of action should be followed, such as propounding interrogatories to the adverse party, include these recommendations as part of your conclusion, or you may create a new section titled "Recommendations." Similarly, if certain issues have not been discussed, identify those excluded issues. See Appendix A for a sample memorandum.

———— Ethics Alert ————

Being Objective

The duty of competent representation owed to clients requires that clients be fully informed of both the strengths and weaknesses of their cases. Counsel may not bring or file frivolous actions and can be sanctioned for doing so. Fed. R. Civ. P. 11. Thus, you are ethically bound to research all matters relating to a client's case, even unfavorable authorities.

C. A Blueprint for Preparing a Memorandum

Although legal professionals will invariably adopt individual approaches in preparing a legal memorandum, there are several steps you can follow to ensure you provide a thoughtful, complete, and objective analysis of a client's case. The process usually begins with an assignment from your supervising attorney. Do not be reluctant to go back to the attorney if you later discover you need additional information. Take the following steps:

1. Consider whether the issue is governed by federal law or state law. Next, consider whether it is a matter more likely to be covered by statutory law or case law.
2. Draft a preliminary issue statement based on the information you have. For example, your initial issue might be written, "In California, are noncompetition agreements entered into by employees valid?"
3. Develop a research plan. If the matter is likely to be covered by statutory law, review the applicable statutes and then examine the case annotations following the text of the statutes. If you are unfamiliar with the topic of law, initially consult a treatise or encyclopedia to "get your feet wet." Prepare a list of key words or search terms to use when examining the indexes to the statutes, encyclopedias, treatises, digests, and other authorities. For example, terms might include "employment," "employer-employee," "noncompetition," and "competition."
4. Conduct research, paying attention to leads to other sources, such as law reviews, A.L.R. annotations, and Restatements.
5. Shepardize or KeyCite the primary authorities to ensure they are still valid and to direct you to other authorities on point.
6. Brief the cases you locate if this is helpful to you.
7. Organize your notes, using index cards, notebooks, sheets of paper, or online tools and resources. Use these to construct a working outline.

8. Begin writing. If you have difficulty getting started, begin with the section that is easiest to write. In many instances, this will be the statement of facts. Proceed to other sections, always checking to make sure your writing is balanced and objective. Consider using the IRAC method in the Discussion section to ensure you are analyzing cases rather than merely summarizing them.

9. Check for content. Make sure each conclusion you have drawn is supported by legal authority. Review to ensure that the cases you discuss include sufficient facts that the reader will immediately be able to discern why they do or do not apply to the client's situation.

10. Edit the memo to eliminate unnecessary material and clarify ambiguous portions. Proofread to omit spelling and typographical errors. Do a final check of citation form.

Tips for Memo Writing

- **Do not use first person pronouns. Avoid statements such as "The next case I found . . ." or "I believe . . . ."**
- **Use complete *Bluebook* or appropriate citation form so that if the memo becomes the basis for a document submitted to court, you will not have to return to the law library or go online to track down cites.**
- **Some law firms maintain files or "banks" of previously prepared memos. Before beginning a new project, check the memo bank to see if a memo on your topic has been prepared previously.**
- **Some attorneys prefer that all cases cited in the memo be printed and attached to the memo for ready reference. Check to see if the individual assigning the memo prefers this practice.**
- **Gather all documents and materials before you begin to write.**
- **After you Shepardize or KeyCite, provide your supervisor with copies of cases that negatively affect any cases cited in the memo so they can be reviewed.**
- **Save memos you have prepared and others you come across in your own mini-memo bank. You may be surprised how often you will need to retrieve previously prepared memos to verify certain legal issues or to use as a starting point for a new project.**

Internet Resources

http://lscontent.westlaw.com/images/content/WritingOpenMemo10.pdf	West offers a guide on using Westlaw to prepare memos.
http://www.lawnerds.com/guide/irac.html	This site provides a thorough discussion of analyzing issues using IRAC.
www.law.wisc.edu/lrw/small_section_guide_-_memo_writing.docx	An excellent guide to writing memos is provided by the University of Wisconsin Law School.

Legal Memorandum Assignment

Our client, Ray Thomson, is currently serving a term of ten years in a federal prison for bank robbery. Thomson has carpal tunnel syndrome in both hands, which is a serious condition in which there is pressure on a nerve in the wrist that causes pain and numbness in the hands.

A team of three prison doctors meets with Thomson every two weeks. These doctors have given Thomson over-the-counter pain medication for relief of his intermittent pain and have treated him with hand and wrist splints. The doctors have stated that if the splints are not successful, they will consider surgery in the future, but they believe surgery is premature at this time. Although many doctors believe surgery should be the first choice for treatment of carpal tunnel syndrome, others believe splints should be tried prior to surgery. Thomson contends that he should be prescribed Vicodin, a prescription drug, for his pain and that he should undergo surgery.

Thomson has asked us whether the denial of his desired medication and surgery constitute cruel and unusual punishment in violation of the Eighth Amendment to the Constitutions.

Please prepare a memorandum for me relating to this matter. The memorandum should be no more than eight pages in length and should be double-spaced. Use *Bluebook* or *ALWD* citation form. Our federal district has no cases or statutes regarding this issue. Therefore, do not restrict your research to the law of any particular federal district or circuit.

Internet Assignment

1. Access the site http://www.lawnerds.com/guide/irac.html.
   a. Review the information on Analysis–the Art of Lawyering. How do you form the analysis?
   b. Review the information on Conclusions. When drafting a conclusion, what is the first question to ask when reading a case?
2. Access the site http://www.tsulaw.edu/centers/facultyTip/tipno5 .pdf. What is the difference in function in thesis statements in legal memos and in legal briefs?
3. Access the article on legal memos at www.law.wisc.edu/lrw/small_ section_guide_-_memo_writing.docx. What are the primary goals of a legal memorandum?

Legal Briefs

Chapter Overview

This chapter introduces you to documents submitted to court. These documents, commonly referred to as "briefs," differ from letters and memoranda in their purpose and audience. Whereas letters and memoranda are intended primarily to inform and explain, briefs are intended to persuade judges. The writing techniques used for briefs are therefore different because each element of a brief must be crafted with its objective in mind: to persuade a court to rule in a client's favor. This chapter discusses both trial court briefs and appellate briefs.

A. Introduction

Briefs are formal written legal arguments submitted to a court and attempt to persuade a court to rule in favor of a party. Be careful not to confuse these court briefs with the internal office memoranda or with the case briefs or case summaries previously discussed.

Trial court briefs are submitted in pending actions and may relate to a variety of issues, such as a motion to dismiss a case, a motion relating to discovery, or a motion for a new trial. Appellate briefs are submitted to reviewing courts to obtain affirmance, reversal, or modification of some lower court action.

If an office memorandum has been prepared in a case, it may be a good starting point for a brief because it will contain an analysis and discussion of the authorities pertinent to the case. Although the memo may thus serve as a source of cases and other authorities, the manner in which these were discussed in the memo and the manner in which these will be discussed in a brief vary greatly. The style of writing used in a memo is informative and objective because your function as a memo writer is to explain the law. The style of writing used in a brief is persuasive because your function as a brief writer is to persuade the court.

One effective way to learn to write better briefs is to review those of others. A number of websites offer free access to briefs, including http://www.legaline.com/freebriefslinks.html, and both Lexis and Westlaw offer briefs, pleadings, and motions for many cases. These collections enable researchers to locate briefs on the precise point of law for their own cases.

B.   Five Tips for Effective Briefs

There are five critical rules to follow when writing court briefs:

1. *Be Persuasive*

In some ways, you may find it easier to prepare a brief than a memo. Most writers find it difficult to maintain the neutral and objective tone required in a memo. It is often easier and more natural to advocate the client's position.

Aim at being persuasive throughout every portion of the brief. Even the Table of Contents and headings provide an opportunity for you to persuade the court. Consider the following two headings:

PUNITIVE DAMAGES

DEFENDANT'S RECKLESSNESS ENTITLES
PLAINTIFF TO PUNITIVE DAMAGES

Although both headings inform the reader that the next topic will deal with punitive damages, the second one is considerably more forceful.

Each heading should be distinguishable from surrounding text. Headings may appear in capital letters (although longer headings presented in all capitals are difficult to read and may be ignored). Headings are usually centered and are assigned a Roman numeral or Arabic number placed above or next to them. Use parallel structure, so if a reader reads only the headings in a brief, the headings provide a clearly written outline of the argument. Headings are usually one sentence. Maintain consistency and do not switch between sentences and phrases. Do not include citations in your headings.

2. *Be Concise*

Judges and law clerks are almost always overworked. Moreover, judges are often unfamiliar with the area of law in a brief; they are likely not experts in immigration law or civil rights as your firm or practice group may be. Similarly, law clerks are often inexperienced. Thus, it is critical for the writer to explain the law clearly and concisely and then specifically apply it to the facts of the case. The reader wants to know only two things: what relief you are requesting and why you deserve it. Use a thesis statement (see below) at the beginning of your brief to answer these questions and set the stage for the analysis to follow.

3. *Use a Thesis Statement*

Recall from Chapter 16 that a thesis statement distills an argument into one or two assertive and conclusory sentences placed at the beginning of a project or issue. Always use a thesis statement in brief writing. It is a preview or roadmap for your reader of the argument and analysis to follow. Remember that legal writing is entirely unlike creative writing: Readers do not want suspense; rather, they need a conclusion up front to lead them through your analysis. A thesis statement provides structure to your project and controls your analysis to follow.

Remember that a thesis statement is far more emphatic than a topic sentence. Consider the following:

> **Topic Sentence:** This brief addresses the business judgment rule.
>
> **Thesis Statement:** The business judgment rule protects the corporate directors in this case because their actions in opposing the takeover were directed to maximizing shareholder value rather than enriching themselves.

If you find it helpful in crafting your thesis statement, in your first draft, use the words *In a nutshell, my client should win because . . .* and then delete these unpolished words in your next draft. Recall that it is possible that you will not be able to finalize your thesis statement until near the end of your writing when you are certain of your conclusions. Refining and modifying a thesis statement throughout the writing process is common.

Remember that the thesis statement is also called an umbrella statement because every point you make thereafter fits under it. Think of your thesis statement as a campaign or ad slogan. It provides the overarching theme of your document. Every part of your brief must remind your reader of and advance this theme.

Using a thesis statement will not only guide your reader but also help you retain focus. As you draft each section of your brief, reread your thesis statement and then test your analysis against it to ensure that your argument is advanced by and is consistent with your thesis statement.

4. *Be Honest*

Although you need not present the adversary's argument, you have an ethical duty to be honest and bring to the court's attention anything that would assist the court in reaching a decision. If, in the course of your research, you discover cases that do not support your position, mention these in a straightforward fashion, and then show the reader why they do not apply to your situation.

Act on the assumption that your adversary will discover these cases and that if you introduce these problem areas yourself, you will decrease the effect of the adversary's "smoking gun." Discussing these authorities does not mean you need to highlight them and make the adversary's case for him or her. Use placement in the brief to assist you, and "bury" the most troublesome parts of your argument in the middle of the discussion. Use passive voice to minimize the impact of these weak spots.

5. *Know the Rules*

Most courts issue rules relating to briefs filed before them. Some of these rules relate to the size, color, and quality of the paper used, whereas others may relate to the elements required in a brief. Many courts establish maximum page or word-count limits and require that briefs exceeding certain page limits include tables of contents and authorities. Make sure you have obtained a copy of the court rules and have thoroughly read them before you prepare your brief because failure to follow the rules may be fatal. Nearly all courts have posted their rules on their websites. Table T.1.3 of *The Bluebook* and Appendix 2 of *ALWD* provide each state's judicial website, and federal court websites can be accessed through http://www.uscourts.gov.

C.   Trial Court Briefs

1. *Introduction*

Briefs submitted to trial courts are aimed at persuading the judge to rule in a certain way. These briefs may be accompanied by other documents, such as deposition transcripts, declarations, or exhibits. They may be written in support of a certain position or in response or opposition to another party's argument.

In some jurisdictions, this brief is referred to as a Memorandum of Law or Memorandum of Points and Authorities. Although many jurisdictions have rules relating to the format, citation form, or length of these trial court briefs, these rules tend to be far less formal than the rules for appellate briefs.

As in all legal writing, remember your audience. The judge or clerk who will read the brief will be busy and will become frustrated with a lengthy and repetitious document. The other reader, opposing counsel, will have a hostile attitude toward your brief and will scrutinize the brief looking for errors and flaws in everything from citation form to Shepardizing and KeyCiting to the conclusions you draw from your research. Although it is a futile effort to believe you can persuade opposing counsel, aim at presenting a brief that at least cannot be attacked by opposing counsel. A sample trial brief is found in Appendix B.

2. *Elements of a Trial Court Brief*

The elements of a brief submitted to a trial court will vary from jurisdiction to jurisdiction. The following elements are found in most briefs, but always review your local court rules to determine if there is a required format.

a. Caption

Because the brief submitted to the court is a pleading, it must display the "caption" of the case. The caption identifies the pertinent information about the case: the court, the parties, the docket number, and the title of the document, such as "Memorandum of Law in Support of Defendant's Motion to Change Venue." Rule 8 of *The Bluebook* and *ALWD* Rule 3.0 provide instructions for abbreviations and capitalization in headings and titles of court documents.

b. Introductory Statement

The party submitting the brief typically begins with a brief introductory statement such as the following: "Defendant Ryan J. Shaw respectfully submits the following Memorandum of Law in support of his Motion to Dismiss."

c. Statement of Facts

To save the judge the time of reviewing all of the pleadings submitted in a case to determine what the case is about, the brief should include a statement of facts. Although these facts must be accurate, you should strive to present these facts in a manner most favorable to the client. Use active voice and descriptive words to emphasize facts supporting your position. Use passive voice and placement of unfavorable facts in less noticeable positions to minimize facts that are troublesome.

Most facts are presented in chronological order, though you may depart from this order and discuss facts by topic if you wish to emphasize certain facts. Present the facts in the third person and in past tense unless they are still unfolding as you write the brief. Be careful not to jump the gun and argue your case. This section of the brief should be devoted solely to facts, namely events that have occurred, not legal theories and analysis.

Do not overlook the importance of the statement of facts. Because most judges have a thorough understanding of the law, they may begin forming impressions and drawing conclusions even as they read the facts.

Moreover, at this stage of the brief, the reader is still enthusiastic and fresh. Use the statement of facts to win over your reader.

d. Argument

The argument section is the heart of the brief. This section contains the analysis of the legal authorities that support the client's position and demonstrates why and how those authorities support the position advocated.

Divide your argument into sections, giving each section a heading and an Arabic or Roman numeral and centering the heading on the page. The headings should be as persuasive as possible. You may need subheadings. These can consist of short phrases or even single words. Subheadings are usually preceded by capital letters (A, B, and C).

Citations should appear in the body of your brief. Although footnotes are popular with some writers, they are distracting to most readers. The use of footnotes in legal documents engenders vigorous debate. Check your firm or office policy or practice, but in any event, avoid "talking" footnotes (those containing argument or discussion) and footnotes that "wrap" from one page to the next, or even beyond. Some readers will leave the narrative discussion, review the footnote that meanders on for several pages, and then simply resume reading where they are, rather than returning to the page on which the footnote began.

As you discuss cases and other authorities, emphasize the extent to which favorable cases are similar to the client's case. In the interest of credibility, point out unfavorable authorities and then distinguish them from the client's position by showing why and how they are different and thus inapplicable. Discuss cases in the past tense because references to "this case states" or "the plaintiff argues" will be interpreted as references to your brief itself rather than published precedents.

Avoid any use of the first person. Do not write "we argue" or "it is my contention." Instead use expressions such as "Defendant will show" or "Plaintiff has contended." This keeps the focus on the parties, not on you as the writer. Also, avoid weak statements such as "it would seem that."

Be sure you have done more than merely summarize a series of cases. Analyze and apply the cases and other authorities to the client's case so the reader can readily see why these cases mandate the result you advocate. Consider using the CRAC approach (discussed in Chapter 16) to ensure you thoroughly analyze and discuss each issue. It is perfectly acceptable to rely upon cases in which a different result was reached than the one you desire. Simply write, "Although the Court denied injunctive relief in *Gray v. Smith*, 508 U.S. 110, 112 (1995), that denial was caused by the plaintiff's failure to take prompt action. In the present case, however . . . . Thus, the decision reached in *Gray* is not applicable to this case." Use an assertive thesis statement (discussed above and in Chapter 16) to give focus to your argument.

Although the aim of your document is to persuade, you need not denigrate the adversary's position. A logical and well-reasoned argument will command respect. A hostile and sarcastic diatribe will destroy your credibility.

```
┌─────────────────────── Practice Tip ───────────────────────┐
│                                                             │
│  Responding to an Adversary's Brief                         │
│                                                             │
│  When you are responding to briefs filed by adversaries,    │
│  review the authorities cited in their briefs. Dissents     │
│  in the cases cited by your adversary often provide good    │
│  ammunition for drafting a reply or response brief.         │
│                                                             │
└─────────────────────────────────────────────────────────────┘
```

e. Conclusion

The conclusion should be a very brief recap of the highlights of the argument. Because it is a summary, no citations should be included. The last sentence of the conclusion should remind the reader of the relief requested, such as the following: "For the foregoing reasons, Defendant Ryan J. Shaw respectfully requests the Court grant his Motion to Dismiss."

f. Signature and Date

The brief is typically "closed" much like a letter. The favored closing is usually "Respectfully submitted." Include a date.

g. Certificates of Service and Compliance

For all pleadings filed in court you must verify that all parties have received copies. A certificate of service is placed at the conclusion of a pleading and states that a copy of the pleading has been served on all parties and identifies the method and date of service. Many courts also require that those submitting briefs acknowledge in a separate Certificate of Compliance that they have complied with all court rules relating to the format, length, and other requirements for submissions to the court.

h. Exhibits

It is possible you may have attached exhibits to the brief for review by the court. These may consist of transcripts of deposition testimony, affidavits, or other documents. Each exhibit should be fully described in the brief itself and then should be appended after the end of the brief and clearly labeled.

i. Order

Many courts require the parties to submit a proposed order with the brief so that if the judge agrees with a party, an order is ready for the judge's signature.

Ethics Alert

Know the Rules

Always check the court's rules to ensure your brief complies
with all requirements as to form, contents, and filing. In a recent
case, an appellate brief was filed six minutes late, and the court
dismissed the appeal as untimely. *Alva v. Teen Help*, 469 F.3d 946
(10th Cir. 2006). Failure to comply with even seemingly minor court
rules and requirements may well be malpractice.

D. Appellate Briefs

An appellate brief seeks reversal, affirmance, or some modification of a
lower court's action. Appellate work is highly complex and is often performed by law firms whose practices are devoted solely to appellate work.
Because appellate work is so specialized and is a field in which few attorneys are actively engaged, this section of the chapter quickly summarizes
appellate briefs.

- **Cover Sheet.** The cover sheet or title page identifies information
  about the case, including the court hearing the appeal, the docket
  number, the title of the document, and the attorneys involved.
- **Identification of Parties.** All parties are identified so reviewing judges can determine if they have a disqualifying conflict of
  interest.
- **Table of Contents.** The table of contents identifies the location
  of each section of the brief, including all headings and subheadings. Phrase these as persuasively as possible.
- **Table of Authorities.** A list of all authorities cited in the brief
  and the page location on which they appear is included. Follow
  appropriate citation form. Group authorities so that all cases
  are together (arranged alphabetically), all statutes are together
  (arranged in ascending order), and so forth. Include subsequent
  history for your cases but omit pinpoints.
- **Jurisdictional Statement.** A concise statement of the statute
  or other legal authority that allows the appeal is included.
- **Constitutional and Statutory Provisions.** If the brief includes
  references to constitutional provisions, statutes, or regulations,
  usually they must be set forth in full.
- **Questions Presented.** Most courts require that the parties
  set forth the questions the court is being asked to address. They
  should be drafted in such a persuasive manner that the desired
  answer is obvious.

- **Statement of the Case.** The statement of the case includes a brief overview of the case's procedural history, namely a review of what happened below and how the case arrived at this reviewing court.
- **Statement of Facts.** The statement of facts includes only the facts proven at trial, with references to the locations in the court record or transcript where such facts were established.
- **Summary of the Argument.** A concise summary of the argument to follow is often presented to aid the reader.
- **Argument.** The argument is the heart of the appellate brief. This section analyzes the authorities and convinces the reviewing court to rule for the client. Use persuasive headings and subheadings that, when read together, provide an outline of the argument. Use strong and assertive thesis statements for each section of the argument.
- **Conclusion.** The conclusion in an appellate brief typically only specifies the relief sought, such as requesting reversal of the lower court's decision.
- **Signature, Date, Certificates of Service and Compliance, and Appendix.** The brief is signed and dated by the attorney submitting it. A certificate of service is attached to verify that all parties were served and the dates and method of service. A certificate of compliance verifies that the brief complies with all court rules. An appendix is often included, which may consist of portions of the trial court transcript or pleadings from the lower court action. See Figure 17-1 for a chart comparing elements of trial and appellate briefs.

Figure 17-1
Elements of Trial Court Briefs and Appellate Court Briefs

Trial Court Briefs	Appellate Court Briefs
Caption	Cover Sheet
Introductory Statement	Identification of Parties
	Table of Contents
	Table of Authorities
	Jurisdictional Statement
	Constitutional and Statutory Provisions
	Questions Presented
	Statement of the Case
Statement of Facts	Statement of Facts
	Summary of the Argument
Argument	Argument
Conclusion	Conclusion
Signature and Date	Signature and Date
Certificates of Service and Compliance	Certificates of Service and Compliance
Exhibits	Appendix
Order	

E. Ten Pointers for Effective Brief Writing

Whether you are submitting a brief to a trial court or to an appellate court, remember the following ten tips:

1. Know the rules of the court to which the brief will be submitted.
2. Do more than summarize cases. By following the IRAC or CRAC methods, show the reader how and why the cases and other authorities apply to the client's situation. Use a strong thesis statement to give direction to the argument to follow.
3. Write from the client's perspective. Omit any references to yourself as the writer, such as "we believe." Use the third person.
4. Avoid a rote or routine method of writing. If each paragraph discusses one case and ends with a citation to that case, the brief will have a rigid appearance and tone. Variety in the method of analysis of the cases will enhance readability.
5. Avoid string-citing unless there is a definite need to do so. Select the best case supporting a contention and use that case.
6. Avoid sarcasm, humor, or irony. Although these techniques may provide drama in oral argument, they are often misinterpreted in written documents. Maintain a respectful tone toward the court and all parties.
7. Avoid the overuse of quotations. It is often the case that a judge has said something so articulately and eloquently that you prefer to use a direct quote. Used sparingly, quotations give force and impact to your writing. Overuse of quotations, however, dilutes their strength. Anyone can retype language found in a case. Do more: Analyze why this language applies to the case at hand.
8. Keep the focus on your argument. If you spend too much time refuting the opponent's position, you will shift the focus of the brief from the client's point of view to that of the opponent. Fully argue the client's position before you respond to the opposition.
9. Do not distort or overstate your position. If any portion of the brief is not supported by valid authority, the entire brief is undermined
10. Use prominent placement to emphasize your strongest arguments. Bury weaker portions of the argument in the middle of the brief, the middle of paragraphs, and the subordinate clauses of sentences.

Internet Resources

http://howappealinglaw.com	This blog is devoted to appellate litigation with interesting articles and more.
http://www.legaline.com/freebriefslinks.html	This site provides direct links to numerous free briefs filed with trial and appellate courts.
http:www.uscourts.gov	This site allows direct linking to all federal courts, which post their rules on their own websites. Most courts also post filed briefs, so you can readily review the formatting and presentation of briefs.
www.ca4.uscourts.gov/pdf/briefchecklist.pdf	The Fourth Circuit Court of Appeals offers an excellent checklist for the content and format of briefs filed with federal courts.

Court Brief Assignment

Our client, Michael Carlsen, was sued one year ago by Lindsey Young for damages arising out of a car accident allegedly caused by Carlsen's negligent and reckless driving. Young has alleged that she has suffered great pain and injury and was unable to work for nine months.

During discovery, we requested that Young produce various documents, including all postings and photos posted by her to her Twitter and Facebook accounts relating to physical activities engaged in by Young that would be inconsistent with her claims concerning the nature and extent of her injuries. Specifically, after another witness testified during a deposition as to the existence of photos, tweets, and posts on social media showing Young after the accident, we requested the production of any materials on Twitter or Facebook showing or discussing Young hiking in Europe, dancing, or riding a motorcycle during the nine months after the accident.

Young refused to produce the documents requested and has claimed that such would be a violation of her right to privacy and is a "fishing expedition" based on Carlsen's mere hope of discovering relevant information.

Please prepare a brief (or memorandum of law) in support of a motion to compel production of documents (under Anywhere Ct. R. Civ. P. 37) that will persuade the Anywhere Circuit Court in the Anywhere State that Young must produce the social media documents requested. Our state has no cases or statutes regarding the issue of production of social media evidence. Therefore, do not restrict your research to the law of any one jurisdiction. By way of background, Anywhere's court rules are identical to those found in the Federal Rules of Civil Procedure.

Court rules impose an eight-page limit on all briefs. In addition, court rules require that the brief be word-processed and double-spaced and that current *Bluebook* or *ALWD* citation form be followed. There are no other court rules relating to citation form.

Table of Authorities Assignment

You have been asked to prepare the table of authorities for an appellate brief to be filed in the United States District Court for your district. There are no special rules for citation form. You should use the rules set forth in the current edition of *The Bluebook* or *ALWD*. Do not worry about the page numbers. The following citations will appear in the brief.

15 U.S.C. section 1051

Arizona Revised Statutes § 10-309

Brady v. DiCosta, 540 U.S. 119, 231 S. Ct. 165, 119 L. Ed. 2d 877 (2004)

Fox Company v. Ellen and David Nelson, 628 Federal Reporter, Third Series, page 220, Second Circuit (2003), reversed, 539 U.S. 990 (2004)

United States v. Booker, 544 U.S. 330, 338 (2005)

Steven Griffin versus Charles Greenwood, 102 Pacific Reporter, Third Series (California Court of Appeals 2006)

Arizona Revised Stat. section 10-212

United States v. Morrison, 548 U.S. 228 (2006)

Hill Engineering Association v. Hartley, 648 Federal Reporter, Third Series, page 522 (Ninth Circuit 2004), cert. denied 540 U.S. 988 (2005)

New York Debtor and Creditor Law section 1099

Grant v. Timkim, 211 Federal Supplement, Second Series, Northern District, New York, 2003.

42 U.S.C. section 2244

Kennedy v. USA, 244 Federal Supplement, Second Series, District Court for the District of Columbia, 2005

McKay v. Middleton, 630 F.3d 430, 444 (Third Circuit 2004)

Internet Assignment

1. Use http://www.uscourts.gov to access the Federal Rules of Appellate Procedure. Review Rule 32.
   a. May a brief be typed on both sides of a page?
   b. What is the appropriate color for an appellee's brief?
   c. Generally, what is the maximum length of a reply brief?
   d. Does the Table of Contents in a brief count when determining the length of a brief? Do headings in a brief count when determining the length of a brief?
2. Use http://www.uscourts.gov. What is the street address for the Fifth Circuit Court of Appeals Clerk?
3. Access the site http://appellate.net/briefs. Review the appellants' brief in *Action Marine, Inc. v. Continental Carbon Inc.* filed in 2007 in the U.S. Court of Appeals for the Eleventh Circuit. What is the argument heading for Argument C.4? Do you think this is a neutral heading or a persuasive one? Why?

Proofreading and Document Design

Chapter Overview

Although proofreading is typically accomplished at the end of a writing project, its importance cannot be overlooked. It is at this stage of the writing process that unclear passages should be revised, redundant phrases should be omitted, and spelling and grammatical errors should be corrected. Even a minor typographical error will impair the professionalism of your project. This chapter focuses on reviewing and revising your writing and polishing the finished product so its appearance enhances readability.

A. Reviewing and Revising: Stage One

When you have the first draft of your project in hand, the difficult tasks of reviewing and revising begin. Your initial review, usually called copyediting, should be to ensure that the writing accurately conveys all the information needed. At this stage, focus on content. Consider the following strategies:

- Keep the purpose of the project in mind. If the project is a brief, its purpose is to persuade. If the project is a memorandum, its purpose is to inform. Ask yourself if the writing meets these goals. Consider whether the tone is appropriate for the reader and whether the project is either too formal or too informal.
- Review your thesis statement. Does it fully encapsulate the discussion to follow?

- Be careful not to engage in micro-revision during the writing process itself. Agonizing over the choice of each word and continually striking out or rephrasing sentences may be a waste of time and energy because you may eventually omit a section you spent considerable time revising during the first effort.
- Do not interpret the previous advice to mean that no revisions should be done during the writing stage. It is both necessary and helpful to revise throughout the process of writing. Do not, however, write your initial draft expecting that the first version will be suitable for submission to court. You may even wish to insert reminders to yourself in the initial draft, such as "revise," to remind you that further work needs to be done for a certain section. When writing, if you cannot decide between two ways of expressing an idea, initially include them both. When you read through your completed first draft, you can then decide which version to retain.
- Try to allow at least a few hours (and, if possible, overnight or longer) to pass between the completion of your first draft and your initial review. It is extremely difficult to review effectively a project with which you are too familiar. If you can come to the review "cold," you will be better able to detect flaws and gaps in the writing.
- Focus 100 percent on the review. Ask someone to hold your calls, and find a quiet space where you can concentrate on your task. If you attempt to review a project and are interrupted by phone calls and meetings, you may unintentionally skip over sections.
- You may find it helpful to read your project aloud. This will enable you to hear repetition or awkward phrasing or to realize something is missing from the project.
- If you have collaborated on the project with another writer, be especially alert to ensure your headings, numberings, and presentations of lists are consistent.
- Read only your headings to ensure that they are consistent and that, taken alone, they provide a mini-view of the project.

Practice Tip

Using a Style Sheet

Most professional editors develop a style sheet that they rely on when editing. The style sheet is their blueprint for the correct spelling of names, how they intend to present headings, how issues will be numbered, and so forth. For example, will the writer use "Section I" or "Section One"? Will the writer use "email" or "e-mail"?

During the process of review, they then have a quick guide they can consult to ensure accuracy and consistency. Develop your own style sheet and include a list of any planned exhibits so you can readily ensure consistency in their names and numbering.

B. Reviewing and Revising: Stage Two

The first review and revision of your project should alert you to major problems in content and organization. Use the second review to focus on three specific areas.

1. *Needless Words and Phrases*

Read through the project looking for unnecessary words. It is easy to become attached to your product. Writers often have difficulty omitting words and phrases because they are reluctant to omit anything after hours of research and writing. Be merciless. Most writers are far better at adding words than at deleting them. Watch carefully for modifiers such as "clearly," "obviously," or "naturally." These should be omitted for two reasons: They add nothing to a sentence, and they often create a patronizing tone. Look for prepositional phrases such as "during the time that" and change them to one-word replacements, such as "when."

2. *Legalese*

Keep alert to the use of jargon and legalese, including the overuse of archaic words and phrases and the overuse of nominalizations such as "discussion" or "exploration" instead of strong words like "discuss" or "explore." You can detect nominalizations by looking for words ending in -ent, -ant, and -ion.

3. *Passive Voice*

The overuse of passive voice will result in a distant and weak project. The active voice, coupled with the selection of forceful words, will lend strength and vigor to your writing. You can detect passive voice by looking at a subject introduced with the phrase *by the* (as in "The report was filed *by the* company").

C. Proofreading

The third and final review of your writing, called proofreading, should focus on technical errors such as grammatical errors, spelling mistakes, and typos. The more familiar you are with a project, the more difficult this task becomes. Your mind will automatically supply the word you intended, and you will not be able to see your errors. Do not proofread on a computer screen. Print a copy of the document and work from that. Reading a hard copy is easier on your eyes. Moreover, it is presented in the way it will be to the ultimate reader, allowing you to see it as it will be seen by its audience. Consider photocopying the document in an increased size, for example, to 120 percent of its original size, to allow you to read the document easily and make notes in the margin.

Although there are a few techniques you can use to assist you in proofreading, the best tip is to allow as much time as possible, preferably two to three days, to elapse before you begin this final step in writing. This break will allow you to come to the project with a fresh approach and will counterbalance the familiarity that hampers a careful scrutiny of your writing. In many instances, and in busy law firms, it is not always possible to allow time to elapse between drafting and proofreading. Energy levels are often higher in the morning, so try to schedule your proofreading as the first thing you do in the day.

Do not underestimate the difficulty of editing and proofreading. All major publishers require that writings be edited by professional editors and proofreaders for the very reason that authors are notoriously unlikely to catch their own errors.

Because a normal reading of your project will naturally focus on content, and you will read groups of words and phrases rather than isolated words, you need to force yourself to slow down and focus on each word. Try the following techniques:

(i) Slide a ruler or piece of paper under each line as you read the document. This will prevent you from jumping ahead to the next sentence or thought and force you to focus on each word.

(ii) Read the project backwards, from the last page to the first page and from right to left. Although this technique is excellent for finding typos and spelling errors, it will not help you pick up a missed word or ensure that you have used a word such as "form" rather than "from."

(iii) Read the document aloud with a partner who has a copy of the document. Each of you will then focus on isolated words, and the listener, in particular, will concentrate on the mechanics of the project rather than the content. Additionally, if your partner stumbles over certain sections, you will know these need to be fixed.

(iv) Read sections of the project out of order. Read Section V first, then the Conclusion, then Section III, then the Statement of Facts, and so on. You will not be able to focus on the flow of ideas, and your concentration will then be aimed at the mechanics of spelling, grammar, and typos.

(v) Devote extra attention to the parts of the project that were prepared last. More errors occur when you are tired.

(vi) To ensure accuracy in complicated passages, such as in patent claims and in descriptions of real property in deeds, read the original description into a tape recorder or iPhone and then play it back, listening and proofreading against your text.

You can also ask someone else to proof the project for you. Having someone else review the project can be extremely helpful because this newcomer will have no familiarity with the writing. He or she will be able to review the writing with a fresh approach and no preconceived ideas or expectations. If you only want the reader to review for mechanical errors, say so, or you may receive a project with substantial corrections and suggestions. It is an intrusion on someone else's time to review your work; therefore, if you have asked for help, you should give the reviewer the courtesy of considering his or her comments or suggestions without becoming defensive. If you have difficulty accepting comments and criticism from others about your writing, do not ask for help. It is a waste of the other person's time if you are not able to keep an open mind about accepting suggestions.

Be alert to the dangers of over-reliance on word processor spell checking programs. Although these programs can be of great assistance and can offer suggestions for word choice, they do not recognize contextual misspellings. Thus, if you mistakenly referred to the complaint as "compliant," the spelling program will not alert you because the word "compliant" is correctly spelled. Although spell checking programs help speed up the editing and proofing process, they also encourage complacency. There is no substitute for human proofreading, as witnessed by the fact that a review of some recently published court decisions disclosed 817 cases referring to the "trail court."

Similarly, the use of templates and forms prepared for an earlier transaction increases the risk of importing incorrect terms into later documents. Thus, a document prepared for a tenant needs to be scrupulously checked when it is later used for a subtenant. Make sure that defined terms are used consistently. For example, if an agreement uses the term "Franchisor," check to make sure the term is defined in the agreement, that it is always capitalized, and that it is consistently spelled and used. Use the "find and replace" feature in your word processing program to check for consistent presentation and use.

Ethics Alert

Competency in All Aspects of the Representation

Remember that the duties imposed on those in the legal profession are the highest duties of competency and that they extend to every aspect of the representation. In one case, a U.S. Magistrate reduced an attorney's fees from $300 per hour to $150 per hour, in part because of numerous typographical errors in pleadings. *Devore v. City of Phila.*, Civ. A. 00-3598, 2004 WL 414085 (E.D. Pa. Feb. 20, 2004). Thus, your duty to represent the client competently is broad enough to encompass even seemingly minor matters such as proofreading, editing, and cite-checking.

D. Proofreading Projects by Others

If you are asked to review someone else's work, obtain clear instructions so you know if you should review for content or review only for mechanics such as typos, spelling mistakes, and grammatical errors. Reviewing for technical errors in someone else's writing is fairly easy. If you are not familiar with the content, the errors will fairly leap off the page at you (just as they will for the ultimate reader, such as the client or the judge). If you are asked to review for content, be judicious. All writers are sensitive about their product, and overcriticizing may result in the writer believing you have a grudge and then discounting everything you suggest.

Recognize that each writer has a unique style. Just because a thought is not expressed in the exact way you would express it does not mean it is inaccurate or vague. Limit your corrections to meaningful items. It is unproductive to change "glad" to "happy" or "concerning" to "regarding." Your credibility as an effective reviewer will be jeopardized if you engage in such meaningless changes.

Comments such as "weak" or "expand" placed beside a paragraph are nearly useless. Specifically explain to the writer why the section is weak and make a suggestion for improving it. Try phrasing suggestions diplomatically, such as "Have you considered . . . ?" or "Let's discuss some alternatives . . . ." These approaches focus on the two of you as colleagues committed to producing a quality product rather than on the writer's perceived inadequacies.

E. Proofreaders' Marks

Although there is some variety in the marks writers use to show errors, most legal writers employ the standard marks, called proofreaders' marks, used by professional editors. Many attorneys learned these marks while writing articles for law reviews. Their use in law firms and among legal professionals is common.

Most dictionaries (and many Internet sites) will provide descriptions and illustrations of proofreaders' marks. These marks are designed to show clerical staff where and how to make corrections in your project. Be sure all of your working drafts are double-spaced with generous margins so you will have sufficient room to note corrections. The most commonly used proofreaders' marks are shown in Figure 18-1.

F. Document Design

Even if your project is well written, clear, and readable, it should be presented in such a manner that it creates a favorable impression on the

Figure 18-1
Commonly Used Proofreaders' Marks

Mark	Explanation	Example
☰	Capital letters	president obama
/	Lowercase letters	the eleventh Juror
∿	Boldface	April 16, 2013
⌒	Close up space	in as much
¶	Begin new paragraph	¶ The plaintiff
℮	Delete	The hearing was was
stet	Let original text stand	Many courts have concluded
∧	Insert item	The plaintiff and his attorney argued
#	Add space	the court.The defendant
∿	Transpose	complaint
⌐	Move left	⌐ any jury
⌐	Move right	⌐ any jury
⋏	Insert comma	the Plaintiff John Brownell argued
⋎	Insert apostrophe	its a fact that
⊙	Insert period	the court The jury also requested
◯ or ⓈⓅ	Spell out	Jan. 10, 2013

reader. Many factors play a part in making a project readable, including quality of paper, typeface, margins, and headings. If your goal in writing is to communicate, you must avoid producing a document so messy in appearance that it frustrates a reader or one that is simply not read because of its physical appearance.

Visually appealing documents are easier to understand. Replace blocks of text with headings, tables, lists, and more white space. Make sure the layout of your project is uncrowded.

1. *Paper*

Use the highest-quality paper possible. Some courts require that the paper used for documents submitted be of a certain quality. Select a paper of sufficient weight so that page two of a document doesn't show through to page one. Although some law firms use cream-colored paper, most use white because black type provides a greater contrast on white paper than on cream-colored paper.

2. *Typeface*

Use ordinary Roman type for most of your writing. Practitioners use italics (or underscoring) for case names, book titles, law review article titles and other publications, citation signals, and foreign words and phrases. Italics (or underscoring) may be used to emphasize certain words or phrases. Use boldface only for headings or special purposes, such as emphasizing a deadline date in a letter to a client.

As to type of font, many experts prefer a "serif" style, which is one that adds small decorative strokes to the edges of letters (as shown in this text). Serif styles are generally viewed as enhancing readability because the "wings" in each word draw the eye from one word to the next. Old-fashioned typewriters always used a serif style. Well-known serif styles include Garamond, Times New Roman, and Century Schoolbook. "Sans serif" styles (those without extra brushstrokes) such as Arial might be acceptable and dramatic for headings. In any case, do not select a font style that is so different as to be distracting to a reader. Do not use all capital letters, except for short headings, because they are difficult to read and might be ignored.

Practice Tip

Typefaces

Consider the following tips to ensure the design of your document enhances its readability:

- Don't mix typefaces in a document. Variations in typeface make a project look too much like an advertisement. Moreover, readers assume that headings in the same size and font style signal information of the same importance.
- Typefaces may be monospaced (meaning that every letter takes up the same amount of room) or proportional (meaning that, for example, a capital M takes up more room than a capital I). Most readers find proportionally spaced typefaces (such as this text) easier to read.

---

3. *Type Size*

Word processors can provide you with numerous choices for type size. Type size is measured in "points," such as 10-point type or 12-point type, with the larger the number showing larger print. Many courts require documents to be printed in a certain size type. If there are no rules you must follow with regard to type size, select 12-point type, which is easily read.

4. *Length of Document*

If court rules require that a document not exceed a specified page or word limit, you will need to be able to calculate and estimate the length of a project. The average typewritten or printed page, measuring 8½ × 11 inches, double-spaced, contains about 250 words. If you are handwriting a document, count the words on any one sheet of your handwritten draft. Multiply this by the number of pages in your draft and divide this figure by 250. This will provide a rough estimate of how many typed pages your handwritten draft will produce. Some courts exclude certain sections, such as tables of contents and tables of authorities, from the limits. Always check your court rules. Word processing programs easily provide statistics on document length and word and character counts.

If your project exceeds a maximum length requirement, you have several alternatives:

- Revise the project, omitting extraneous material.
- Use one space rather than two after sentence-ending periods.
- Alter your margins so that more words fit on each page.
- Use a smaller point type size to include more text on each page.

Although these last two techniques will allow you to squeeze extra material into the document, many court rules mandate margin size and type size. For example, the rules of the United States Courts of Appeal flatly require one-inch margins on all sides. Fed. R. App. P. 32.

It is increasingly common for courts to require that documents comply with word-count limits rather than page limits (otherwise, writers would "cram" extra words and text into footnotes, using smaller typeface than in the body of the text). For example, the U.S. Supreme Court requires that principal briefs not exceed 15,000 words (including footnotes) and that a certificate be attached to all documents verifying that they comply with the word-count limitations. Sup. Ct. R. 33(g) and (h). Additionally, briefs on the merits must now be submitted electronically to the Court (which allows the Clerk of the Court to verify compliance with the word-count limits). *Id.* at R. 25.9.

The chief disadvantage of squeezing material into a document is that it creates a more cramped appearance. Pages filled with text from the upper-left corner to the lower-right corner cause eyestrain and frustration. Using adequate white space will cause headings and quotations to be more easily noticed. Although the technique of leaving ample white space on a page, including adequate or generous margins, may seem like an artificial device, reading studies have demonstrated that it results in a more readable project.

Another formatting device is the use of right justified margins. A right justified (or "fully justified") margin is one in which all of the words end at the exact same location at the right side on the page (as shown in this text). This type of margin creates a clean and crisp-looking document. The only disadvantage is that to ensure the margin is even at the right side, uneven spacing between letters and words may occur. This uneven spacing can reduce ease of reading. Carefully proofread any document with right justified margins to make sure the spacing is acceptable. If it is not, use a ragged right edge.

5. *Headings*

Headings not only provide the reader with an idea as to what will follow, but also create visual drama on a page. Main headings should be centered and single spaced. Although many writers use all capital letters for main headings, such headings are difficult to read and may be ignored. Each heading should be given a Roman numeral or Arabic number. Some writers use boldface print to make sure the headings stand out. Subheadings that occur with a main heading should use capital letters only for the first letter in each major word, such as nouns, verbs, adjectives, and adverbs. Follow *Bluebook* Rule 8 or *ALWD* Rule 3 for instructions on capitalizing words in headings. Label each subheading with a capital letter and underline or use boldface for emphasis. All headings should be separated from the remainder of the narrative by double-spacing above and below. If the heading is a complete sentence, follow it with a period.

Do not use an "I" or an "A" unless a "II" or a "B" follows. On your final proofreading effort, scan through your project examining only the lettering and numbers of the headings to make sure you haven't skipped over or repeated a letter or number.

6. Quotations and Lists

Quotations and lists can serve to provide relief from a long narrative. Select quotations with care and be careful not to overquote. Follow *Bluebook* or *ALWD* rules and keep quotes of 49 or fewer words in text. Indent quotes of 50 words or more.

Lists also create interest and are an effective tool for presenting information. Overuse of lists, however, can make your project have an outline-look to its appearance. Be consistent in presentation of lists. Don't use bullets in some lists and dashes to introduce others. Review lists to make sure the presentation of the material is in parallel structure.

G. The Final Review

Just before your writing is sent to the reader, check these four items:

(i) *"Widows and orphans."* A "widow" or "orphan," respectively, is a heading or isolated line occurring at the top of a page or at the bottom of a page. Omit that awkward and distracting placement. Remember to keep at least two lines of text together.

(ii) *Numbering.* Quickly scan the project to make sure the page and footnote numbering is correct. If the document has a table of contents, review it to make sure all references to pages are correct.

(iii) *Dates, Names, and Amounts.* Do one final check to make sure dates, names, and money amounts are accurate.

(iv) *Exhibits.* Make sure all exhibits or attachments to the project are included and are properly marked.

H. Conclusion

Although the foregoing comments relating to paper quality, type size, and white space may seem inconsequential, remember that if your objective is to inform or persuade your reader, any device that keeps the reader's interest is significant. View these techniques as weapons in your arsenal of writing tools. Your goal is to produce a writing that is accurate and readable. Errors and typos impair the accuracy of a writing, and an unprofessional project impairs the readability of a writing. If you discover errors, don't be afraid to send the document back for correction. Better that you are viewed as a perfectionist than as someone uninterested in quality.

Strive for excellence. Make every project something you and your fellow legal professionals will be proud to sign.

Common Writing Errors

Watch for the following common errors:

- Errors in figures, dates, monetary amounts, and names.
- Substitutions of letters in small words, such as a change of "now" to "not."
- Transpositions of letters such that "trial" becomes "trail."
- Misspellings of compound words such as "can not" for "cannot."

Internet Resources

http://writingcenter.unc .edu/handouts/editing-and-proofreading	The University of North Carolina provides information on proofreading and editing.
http://www.prenhall.com/author _guide/proofing.html	Prentice Hall provides examples of common proofreaders' marks.
http://www.typographyforlawyers .com/?page_id=1405	Attorney Matthew Butterick offers information on document design for legal documents.

Assignment

CAREFULLY PROOFREAD THE FOLLOWING PASSAGE AND MAKE THE NECESSARY CORRECTIONS

DEFENISVE STRATEGIES IN HOSTILE TAKEOVERS

Corproations that are threatened with hostile takeovers may take a number of actions too avoid being taken over. These takeover defenses range form the simple to the complex and may be developed even before at offer is made to the target, in order to discourage a a takeover bid in the the frist place. Alteatively, they may be adopted after an offer has been made, in an attempt by the target to defeat the agressor. In genreal, the response of the target's management to the takeover bid is subject to the duty of due care and the business judgement rule. Directors of the target often set up takeover commitees to evaluate the proposed merits of the takeover to ensure that the baord fulfils its duties. Thus, actions by the target's directors that are directing only to perpetrating their won satus, rewarding themselves, and entrenching their positions, rather than promoting the bset interests of the coproation and it's shareholders might be breeches of fiduciary duty. Once in becomes apparent that a sale or takeover in inevitable, however, directors must cease taking defensive measures and act to get the best price four the sharehodlers.

Internet Assignment

1. Access the site http://writingcenter.unc.edu/handouts and review the handout entitled "Revising Drafts."
   a. What is the difference between "revising" and "proofreading"?
   b. Should one revise first or proofread first?
   c. What is "editing"?
2. Access the site http://writing.colostate.edu/guides and select "Revising & Editing." Review the information on editing strategies. What is the first piece of advice given?
3. Access the site http://www.typographyforlawyers.com.
   a. Why does good typography matter?
   b. Review the information on Type Composition. Does the author recommend the use of "straight" quotes or "curly" quotes? Why?
4. Review the proofreading marks found at http://www.prenhall.com/author_guide/proofing.html.
   a. How would you indicate that you wanted a word displayed in lowercase letters?
   b. How would you indicate that you wanted to insert a hyphen in a word?

Sample Legal Memorandum

MEMORANDUM

To: Adam S. Sawyer

From: Joanna Roache

Re: Reginald Nelson

         Visual Artists Rights Act

Date: January 30, 2013

ISSUE

Under the Visual Artists Rights Act, do destruction and removal of sculptures and destruction of posters violate a freelance artist's rights to prevent destruction or modification of his works of visual art?

BRIEF ANSWER

Under the Visual Artists Rights Act, a freelance artist has the right to prevent destruction of his sculptures but not removal of them to another location. Moreover, an artist has no right to be compensated for destruction of posters because these are not works of "visual art" as defined by the Act.

FACTS

Our client, Reginald Nelson ("Nelson"), is a nationally known freelance artist and sculptor. Nelson works primarily with granite and bronze forms although he has also created lithographs and posters. Four years ago, Nelson signed a written contract with Stonegate Development Company ("Stonegate") by which he agreed to create a variety of sculptures to be placed in a small park owned by Stonegate and located outside of a commercial building Stonegate was developing. Working in his studio, with a few of his long-term assistants, Nelson created six original bronze sculptures for placement in the park, all of which displayed his signature curving motifs. The park included a variety of other elements not designed by Nelson, such as benches and picnic tables. After the sculptures were unveiled, a number of art critics and artists hailed them as having significant artistic merit. Nelson then created posters of the sculptures, which Stonegate placed in the building lobby. Stonegate fully paid for all of Nelson's work.

Two months ago, Stonegate began to redesign its park. It plans to destroy two of the sculptures and move the remainder to another one of its parks. Stonegate also destroyed the posters in the building lobby and replaced them with those by another artist.

DISCUSSION

The Visual Artists Rights Act and Works Made for Hire

In 1990, Congress passed the Visual Artists Rights Act ("VARA" or the "Act") to allow artists to prevent any intentional destruction, mutilation, distortion, or other modification of their works of visual arts. 17 U.S.C. § 106A (2006). These rights are often referred to as "moral rights" and are intended to allow artists to protect their artistic reputations, even after they have sold their works.

The Act provides three specific rights: the right of attribution, which is the author's right to be known as the author of a work; the right of integrity, which ensures that the work not be distorted, mutilated, or misrepresented in a way that would injure the artist's reputation; and in the case of works of visual art of "recognized stature," the right of the author to prevent destruction of the work.

The Act, however, is quite limited and applies only to works of visual arts such as paintings, drawings, and sculptures that exist in a single copy or in limited editions. *Id.* In the present case, the original sculptures are works of visual art covered by the Act. The Act, however, excludes from its protection works made for hire. *Id.*

A work made for hire is one that is presumed to be authored by an employer because it was created by an employee on company time or authored by a party specially commissioned to create the work when the parties have agreed in writing that the commissioning party will own the copyright and the work falls into one of nine statutorily enumerated categories. 17 U.S.C. § 101 (2006).

In the present case, Nelson was a freelance artist and not Stonegate's employee. If Nelson were an employee, Stonegate would be the presumptive owner of all rights in the works. Nelson was an independent contractor who was specially engaged by Stonegate to create the works in question. Although some cases have examined whether freelancers are, in fact, employees rather than independent contractors, the Supreme Court has held that the term "employee" for purposes of determining authorship of works made for hire should be interpreted according to general common law agency principles. *Cmty. for Creative Non-Violence v. Reid*, 490 U.S. 730, 740 (1989). The Court identified certain factors that characterize an employer-employee relationship: control by the employer over the work, control by the employer over the employee, and the status of the employer. *Id.* at 738-39.

If the employer has a voice in how the work is done, has the work done at the employer's location, and provides equipment and tools to the person to create the work, such tends to show an employer-employee relationship. Similarly, if the employer controls the worker's schedule in creating the work, has the right to have the worker perform other assignments, and has the right to hire the worker's assistants, such shows an employer-employee relationship. Finally, if the employer is in business to produce such works, provides the worker with benefits similar to those received by other workers, and withholds taxes from the worker's compensation, such is supportive of an employer-employee relationship. *Id.*

These factors are not exhaustive, but all or most of these factors characterize a regular, salaried employment relationship. In the present case, Nelson created the work at his studio using his own tools and equipment and using his own long-term assistants. Moreover, Stonegate is in the real estate development business, not the art business, and Nelson was not a regular salaried employee of Stonegate. Accordingly, Nelson should be held to be an independent contractor and thus entitled to moral rights under the Act.

A work not prepared by an employee but rather one prepared by an independent contractor can be deemed a work made for hire and thus owned by the commissioning party (in this case, Stonegate) if the parties agree in writing that it is to be a work made for hire and it is specially commissioned for use as a contribution to a collective work, as part of a motion picture or other audiovisual work, as a translation, as a supplementary work, as a compilation, as an instructional text, as a test, as answer material for a test, or as an atlas. 17 U.S.C. § 101. Both statutory conditions (the specially ordered work must fall into one of the nine enumerated categories *and* the parties must agree in writing that it is a work made for hire) must exist. In this case, the works (sculptures and posters) do not fall into any of the nine specially enumerated categories of work, and thus the works are not ones made for hire. Therefore, Nelson has retained any moral rights in the works because they were not "made for hire."

Destruction of Sculptures

The Act allows an author of a work of visual art to prevent any destruction of a work of "recognized stature." 17 U.S.C. § 106A(3)(B). Thus, determining that the sculptures are of "recognized stature" is necessary in order to protect them from destruction. The phrase "recognized stature" is not defined in the Act, and thus, its interpretation has been left to the courts. In *Carter v. Helmsley-Spear Inc.*, 861 F. Supp. 303, 325 (S.D.N.Y. 1994), *aff'd in part, rev'd in part, vacated in part*, 71 F.3d 77 (2d Cir. 1995), the court formulated the following test: A work of visual art has "stature" if it is meritorious and is recognized by art experts, other members of the artistic community, or by some cross-section of society. In the present case, because of the critical acclaim afforded the works by art critics and others, the sculptures are likely to be found to be of "recognized stature" such that Nelson can prevent their destruction.

Removal of Sculptures

In *Phillips v. Pembroke Real Estate Inc.*, 288 F. Supp. 2d 89, 99-100 (D. Mass. 2003), *aff'd on certification*, No. SJC-09181 (Mass. Dec. 21, 2004), Phillips, the creator of 27 sculptures placed in a park, argued that his work was so site-specific that moving it to another location would be an intentional destruction or modification under VARA. He contended that taking his sculptures to another park would be like painting over the background landscape in the Mona Lisa. The court, however, agreed with the defendant's assertion that moving the sculptures to another location was permissible, just as a museum curator could move the Mona Lisa from one wall in the Louvre to another.

The Act permits the modification of a work of visual art that is the result of conservation or of the public presentation and placement of a work, and specifically states that such is not a destruction. 17 U.S.C. § 106A(c)(2). This "public presentation" exception would permit Stonegate to move Nelson's sculptures from one location to another. As one court noted, the focus of VARA "is not . . . to preserve a work of visual art *where* it is, but rather to preserve the work *as* it is." *Bd. of Managers of Soho Int'l Arts Condo. v. City of New York*, No. 01-CIV-1226 DAB, 2003 WL 21403333, at *10 (S.D.N.Y. June 17, 2003). Accordingly, Nelson has no right to control the placement of the sculptures. Stonegate is not obligated to display the works in the park and may remove them to another location because VARA provides no protection for a change in placement or presentation.

Destruction of Posters

The U.S. Copyright Act specifically provides that a work of "visual art" does not include "any poster." 17 U.S.C. § 101. Thus, Stonegate's destruction of the posters in the building lobby was permissible because posters are not works of "visual art" and accordingly are not protected under the Act.

CONCLUSION

Under VARA, Nelson can prevent the planned destruction of the sculptures he created for Stonegate but cannot prevent their removal to another park. Moreover, because posters are not works of "visual art" covered by VARA, Nelson cannot prevent their destruction.

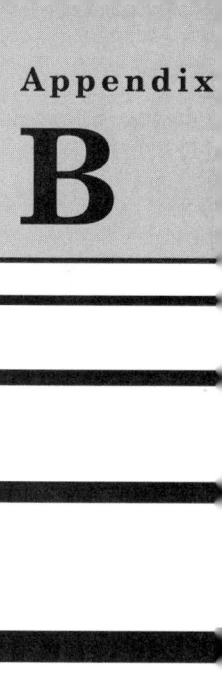

Sample Brief for Court

IN THE ANYWHERE COURT

United States of America	)	
	)	
v.	)	Docket No. Cr-14789
	)	
Bryan E. Taylor	)	
	)	

MEMORANDUM OF LAW IN SUPPORT OF MOTION TO EXCLUDE EVIDENCE

Defendant, Bryan E. Taylor ("Defendant" or "Mr. Taylor") respect-fully submits the following Memorandum of Law in support of his Motion to Exclude Evidence.

STATEMENT OF FACTS

In late 2009 a robbery and assault allegedly occurred at First Bank and Trust located in Anytown, Anywhere. Approximately one week after the charged offense, the only eyewitness, Paul Slattery, an employee at First Bank and Trust, was shown a photo array consisting of nine mug shot photographs of various individuals, including that of Defendant, which photograph was taken in 2005. Upon viewing the photographs, which showed both a front and side view of Mr. Taylor, Mr. Slattery iden-tified Mr. Taylor's photograph, saying, "That's him. This is the guy."

Prior to the identification procedure, Mr. Slattery informed the police that he recognized the assailant as someone he had previously known. It is undisputed that Mr. Slattery has known Mr. Taylor for several years.

The mug shot photograph of Mr. Taylor is particularly unflattering. Mr. Taylor's eyes are shut, his face is contorted into a grimace, his hair is unkempt, and his beard is untrimmed. Police markings or numbers are not evident in the photographs, but only because they have been crudely covered with masking tape. Thus, even a casual observer would recognize the front and side shot photographs (sometimes referred to as "double shot pictures") as mug shots taken upon an arrest. The prosecution seeks to introduce these photographs at the trial of this matter.

MUG SHOT PHOTOS ARE
IMPERMISSIBLY SUGGESTIVE

Courts have long recognized the potential for prejudice in the admission of mug shot photographs that reveal the prior criminal involvement of a defendant. In *United States v. Reid*, 376 F.2d 226, 228 (7th Cir. 1967), the court noted that there was grave risk in the introduction of photographs which carry prejudicial implications, either through police notations or the appearance or pose of the accused in the photograph. In the present case, although police notations have been crudely masked, the photographs of Mr. Taylor show him in the traditional dual pose (front and side view) used nationwide by police. This type of photograph will clearly imply to the jury that Mr. Taylor has either a prior criminal record or a prior arrest record. Consequently, the photographs will raise the issue of his character without his having placed the issue in evidence, thereby prejudicing him.

Moreover, the attempt by the prosecution to cover the police markings and notations does not cure the photographs of their prejudicial taint. In *Barnes v. United States*, 365 F.2d 509, 510 (D.C. Cir. 1966), the court found reversible error in the admission of a mug shot photographs where tape and paper were placed over the prison number in an effort to conceal its origin. The court held, "[i]t is well-settled law that the criminal record of a defendant may not be introduced into evidence at trial unless the defendant takes the stand or otherwise places his character in issue. A photograph which on its surface reveals the existence of such a criminal record is likewise inadmissible." *Id.* The court further found that the rudimentary efforts to disguise the photograph "may well have heightened the importance of the picture and the prejudice in the minds of the jury." *Id.* at 515. Reversal was ordered because the probability that the photograph impressed upon the jury the fact of appellant's prior criminal record was too substantial for the court to ignore. *See also Brown v. United States*, 387 A.2d 728 (D.C. 1978).

In *Williams v. United States*, 382 A.2d 1, 5 (D.C. 1979), the court, recognizing *Barnes* as controlling authority, found reversible error in the admission of mug shot photographs, with numbers blackened out, from which an identification was made. The court followed a three-factor analysis adopted in *United States v. Harrington*, 490 F.2d 487, 494 (2d Cir. 1973) to assist courts in ruling on the admissibility of suggestive photographs. In *Harrington*, the court held that mug shots can be introduced as evidence only if the following tests are satisfied: (i) the government must have a demonstrable need to introduce the photographs; (ii) the photographs themselves, if shown to a jury, must not imply that the defendant has a prior criminal record; and (iii) the manner of introduction of the photographs at trial must be such that it does not draw particular attention to the source or implications of the photographs. *Id*.

Admission of the 2004 photographs of Mr. Taylor would fail the test set forth in *Harrington*. First, there is no demonstrable need for the introduction of the photographs. Mr. Slattery will be able to identify Mr. Taylor at the trial of this matter and his ability to do so will not be contested by Mr. Taylor. There is no need to use photographs to identify Mr. Taylor when an eyewitness will be present at the trial to do so based upon several years of acquaintance with Mr. Taylor.

Second, the photographs themselves imply that Mr. Taylor has a prior criminal record. In *Harrington*, 490 F.2d at 495, the court remarked that "double shot" pictures produce a "natural, almost automatic" inference of prior encounters with the police and that inartful masking of their origins heightens, rather than diminishes, their significance to a jury. *Id*. Accordingly, in the present case, the inartful covering of police numbers and markings with masking tape will only strengthen the impression to the jury that the photos are mug shots, evidencing prior contact with the police, and thereby serving to brand Mr. Taylor as a repeat offender. Moreover, the double shot configuration of the pictures automatically conveys to a viewer that their subject is in policy custody. Thus, the condition of the photographs will prejudice Mr. Taylor's right to a fair trial.

Third, any manner of presentation of the mug shots at trial will inevitably focus the jury's attention on the source of the pictures. The double shot configuration, the crude cover-up of police markings with masking tape, and Mr. Taylor's disheveled appearance will immediately convey to any juror that the photographs were not taken by a beloved family member for inclusion in a family photo album but were rather taken while Mr. Taylor was in law enforcement custody. No reasonable viewer would believe the mug shots in this case are ordinary photographs.

Even in cases in which photographs have probative value in identifying a defendant, such value is outweighed when the photographs on their face imply prior criminal conduct on a defendant's part. *United States v. Torres-Flores*, 827 F.2d 1031, 1037 (8th Cir. 1987). In the present case, the photographs have little, if any, probative value because Mr. Slattery will identify Mr. Taylor at the trial of this matter. Because the photographs of Mr. Taylor imply criminal conduct on their face due to the "classic" double shot pose and the crude attempt to cover up the police markings, these photographs fail the three-part test set forth in *Harrington*, and thus should not be admitted at the trial of this matter.

In some cases, courts have upheld lower court rulings that have admitted suggestive photographs into evidence, primarily because the photographs constituted harmless error in light of other strong evidence against the defendant. *See Torres-Flores*, 827 F.2d at 1038. In the present case, however, there is only one witness who will identify Mr. Taylor. Thus, the introduction of mug shots of Mr. Taylor could not be later deemed to be harmless error.

Additionally, although some cases have allowed judges to issue cautionary instructions directing juries not to consider covered material in mug shots, *id.* at 1037, instructions in the present case would not remove the taint of Mr. Taylor's classic pose in the photographs. In fact, the mug shots, with their police numbers covered by masking tape, leave little room for imagination in the minds of jurors as to what is being concealed. The risk of prejudice to Mr. Taylor far outweighs any government need to introduce the photographs. Therefore, they should not be admitted into evidence.

CONCLUSION

For the foregoing reasons, this Court is respectfully urged to grant Defendant's Motion to Exclude Evidence.

Respectfully submitted,

_____

Dated:_____

Glossary

A.L.R.: *See American Law Reports.*

ALWD: Citation manual issued by the Association of Legal Writing Directors, now in its 4th edition.

ALWD citation system: A system introduced in 2000 by the Association of Legal Writing Directors ("ALWD") to provide an easier, more readily understood citation format.

Act: A series of statutes related to one topic.

Adjudication: An administrative proceeding before an administrative law judge.

Administrative agencies: A governmental body that enacts rules and regulations on a specific topic and settles disputes relating thereto, for example, the FCC, FDA, or NLRB.

Administrative law: The law relating to administrative agencies.

Administrative law judge: An individual who presides over an administrative adjudication.

Advance sheets: Temporary softcover books that include cases prior to their publication in hardbound volumes.

Alerts: Electronic clipping services offered by Lexis and Westlaw that automatically update research results.

Am. Jur. 2d: A general or national encyclopedia published by West covering all United States law.

American Digest System: West's comprehensive set of digests designed to help researchers find cases.

American Law Reports: Sets of books publishing appellate court decisions together with comprehensive essays or annotations relating to the legal issues raised by those cases.

Annotated: Literally, "with notes"; generally, a reference to one-sentence descriptions of cases that follow statutes in codes such as U.S.C.A. or a state code.

Annotated code: A set of statutes organized by subject matter that contains material accompanying the statutes, chiefly references to cases.

Annotated law reports: *See American Law Reports.*

Annotation: A one-sentence description of a case; an article or monograph about a legal topic published in A.L.R.

Appeal: Review by one court of a lower court's decision.

Appellant: A party who initiates an appeal; sometimes called a petitioner.

Appellate brief: A document presented to a reviewing court to obtain affirmance, reversal, or some alteration of a lower court's ruling.

Appellee: A party who responds to an appeal; sometimes called a respondent.

Apps: Law-related databases accessible on iPhones and other similar devices, allowing legal professionals access to federal laws and other materials.

Attorneys general opinions: Opinions by executive officials on various legal topics; opinions by the U.S. Attorney General or individual state attorneys general.

BCite: Bloomberg Law's citation validation service, used to ensure cases are still good law.

Bicameral: A two-chamber legislature.

Bill: A proposed law.

Binding authority: Legal authority that must be followed by a court.

Blawg: An online journal related to legal topics.

Block form: Style of letter writing in which all the elements, including the date and the closing, begin at the left-hand margin.

Block quotation: A quotation from another source of 50 words or more, indented (typically ten spaces) left and right, that appears without opening and closing quotation marks.

Blog: An online journal or diary (short for "weblog").

Bloomberg Law: The computerized legal research system offered by Bloomberg, L.P.

Blue and White books: Books published by West for individual states that include conversion tables for locating parallel cites.

Bluebook: The best known and used guide for citation form; subtitled *A Uniform System of Citation*, now in its 19th edition.

Bluepages: Section of *The Bluebook* printed on light blue paper, providing rules and examples for practitioners (rather than the citation form used for academic or law review articles).

Boolean searching: A method of conducting research online using symbols and characters rather than plain English.

Brief: A summary of a case; or a written argument presented to a court.

BriefCheck: Lexis's software program that extracts citations from a document, checks their validity, and produces a printed report with results.

Brief Suite: Lexis's citation resource that complements its *Shepard's* citation service and conducts automatic citation validation.

CALR: *See* computer-assisted legal research.

CCH Congressional Index: Sets of books used to compile legislative histories.

CD-ROM: Literally, "compact disk, read-only memory"; a hard disk containing thousands of pages of information.

C.J.S.: West's general or national encyclopedia covering all United States law.

CRAC: An acronym for Conclusion, Rule, Application or Analysis, and Conclusion; a method used to analyze legal authorities and issues in an exam, memo, or other document.

Cable modem: A cable line used to connect to the Internet, allowing faster connection than a telephone line.

Case of first impression: An issue not yet decided by a jurisdiction.

"Case on point" approach: System used by a researcher following West's headnotes and Key Numbers to locate other similar cases by inserting a topic name and Key Number into the various units of the Decennial Digest System.

Certificate of Compliance: A verification that a document or pleading complies with court rules as to word count, page count, or other rules.

Certificate of Service: A verification that a document or pleading has been "served on" or presented to a party.

Certification: The process by which a court of appeals refers a question to the United States Supreme Court and asks for instructions and direction.

Certiorari: Writ of certiorari; the most widely used means to gain review of a case by the United States Supreme Court; issuance of the writ (meaning a decision to review a case) is discretionary with the Court.

Cert pool: The group of U.S. Supreme Court law clerks who takes turns evaluating petitions for certiorari and writing memos.

Cert worthy: A case for which certiorari has been granted.

Chamber opinion: An opinion written by a United States Supreme Court Justice in his or her capacity as the Justice assigned to a particular circuit rather than in the capacity of writing for the majority of the Court; also called "in-chambers opinion."

Charter: The governing document for a municipality.

Chief Justice: The presiding Justice of the United States Supreme Court.

Circuit: A geographical area in which courts are located; the United States is divided into 11 numbered circuits and two unnumbered circuits, each with its own court of appeals.

Citators: Online or print sources that direct one to other materials discussing or treating legal authorities.

CiteAdvisor: West's product that creates a table of authorities and suggests correct citation form.

Cite-checking: The process of verifying that citations in a document are accurate and in compliance with rules for citation form and then verifying that the authorities are still "good law."

Civil law: A body of law depending more on legislative enactments than case law, often seen in non-English-speaking countries.

Code: A compilation of statutes or regulations arranged by subject or topic.

Code of Federal Regulations: The codification of administrative rules and regulations, by subject, into 50 titles.

Codification: The process of organizing laws or regulations by subject matter rather than chronologically.

Comment: Shorter piece in a law review authored by a student; also called "Note."

Committee print: A report or study prepared for a congressional committee.

Committee report: Document reflecting decisions reached by legislative committees considering proposed legislation.

Committee transcript: Report of proceedings before committees considering proposed legislation.

Common law: The body of law that develops and derives through judicial decisions rather than from legislative enactments, usually seen in English-speaking countries.

Compiled legislative history: "Prepackaged" legislative history, usually compiled for significant legislation.

Complimentary close: The ending of a letter, such as "Sincerely."

Computer-assisted legal research: The process of conducting legal research through computer rather than conventional print sources.

Concurrent jurisdiction: The sharing of jurisdiction over a case by federal and state court so that a litigant can select which forum in which to bring the action.

Concurring opinion: Opinion written by a member of the majority who agrees with the result reached in a case but disagrees with the reasoning of the majority.

Congress: The lawmaking body of the federal government, composed of the Senate and the House of Representatives.

Congress.gov: Website for legislative information provided by the federal government, in its test or beta stage, that offers text of proposed and enacted legislation since 1993; successor to THOMAS.

Congressional Information Service: Sets of books used to compile legislative histories.

Congressional Record: A publication that publishes the remarks of the speakers debating a bill prepared for each day Congress is in session as well as other remarks and speeches made on the floor of the House or Senate.

Constitution: The document that sets forth the fundamental law for a nation or state.

Constitutional courts: Courts such as the United States Supreme Court that exist under the United States Constitution and whose judges are protected as to tenure and salary reductions.

Convention: A type of treaty, usually relating to a single topic.

Court reports: Sets of books that publish cases.

Courts of Appeal: Intermediate appellate courts; in the federal system, these are sometimes called circuit courts.

Courts of first resort: Trial courts.

Current Law Index: Separately published index designed to direct researchers to periodicals, such as articles in law reviews.

Cyberspace: The electronic or computer world in which vast amounts of information are available; sometimes used as a synonym for the Internet.

Daily Compilation of Presidential Documents: Publication including materials relating to the executive branch; formerly *Weekly Compilation of Presidential Documents.*

Database: Westlaw's groupings of materials offered in its computer-assisted legal research system.

Database Wizard: A service offered by Westlaw designed to help researchers select the right computer database; Database Wizard assists in selecting a database and narrowing research options.

Decennials: Digest books published by West that arrange cases in ten-year (or more frequent) groups; *see American Digest System.*

Decision: Technically, the final action taken by a court in a court case; generally, the term "decision" is used synonymously with "opinion," "judgment," or "case."

Demand letter: A letter setting forth a client's demands or requirements.

Depository library: A library designated by the United States government to receive selected government materials and publications.

Descriptive word approach: A method of locating legal materials by inserting words describing a problem or issue into an index or search engine that then directs the reader to relevant information; sometimes called the "index method."

Dictionary (legal): An alphabetical arrangement of words and phrases providing the meaning or definition of those words and phrases.

Dictum: Technically, "obiter dictum"; a remark in a case said for purposes of illustration or analogy; dictum is persuasive only.

Digests: Books or indexes that arrange one-sentence summaries or "digests" of cases by subject.

Directory: A list of lawyers.

Dissenting opinion: An opinion written by a judge in the minority who disagrees with the result reached by the majority of a court.

District courts: The trial courts in our federal system.

Diversity jurisdiction: A basis upon which federal courts take cases, due to the different or diverse citizenship of the parties in the case.

Docket number: A number assigned to a case by a court to track its progress through the court system.

eBook: Book available in electronic form.

E-mail: Electronic mail or messages sent through the computer rather than in physical form

Ellipsis: Three periods separated by spaces and set off by a space before the first and after the last period, used to indicate omission of a word or words.

Enabling statute: A statute that creates an administrative agency such as the FDA or FCC.

En banc opinion: Literally, "in the bench"; an opinion in which all judges in an appellate court participate.

Encyclopedias: Sets of books that alphabetically arrange topics related to legal issues; treatment of legal issues is somewhat elementary; the best known general sets are C.J.S. and Am. Jur. 2d; some state-specific sets exist.

Exclusive jurisdiction: The basis upon which a court's ability to hear a case is exclusive to the federal court, such as a bankruptcy case, and which cannot be heard by another court.

Executive agreement: An agreement entered into with a foreign nation by a president acting without Senate approval.

Executive branch: The branch of the United States government that enforces laws.

Executive order: Regulations issued by a president to direct government agencies.

Ex rel.: Latin for "upon relation of"; a designation in a title of a case filed on behalf of the government but at the instigation of a private party.

FDsys: Federal Digital System; an advanced digital system that enables the Government Printing Office to provide free and authenticated government documents to the public over the Internet, including federal laws and regulations; formerly GPO Access.

Federal Appendix: West's set of books that prints unpublished federal courts of appeal cases.

Federalism: Sharing of powers by the federal and state governments.

Federal question jurisdiction: The power of a federal court to hear a case based upon the fact the case arises under the United States Constitution or a United States law or treaty.

Federal Register: A pamphlet published every weekday relating to administrative law and publishing proposed and final agency rules and regulations.

Federal Reporter: West's unofficial publication containing cases from the federal courts of appeal.

Federal Supplement: West's unofficial publication containing cases from the federal district courts.

FindLaw: Internet site providing free access to many legal authorities.

Form books: Sets of books including forms for use in the legal profession; may be general or related solely to one area of law.

FULL: A feature of "Shepard's for Research," a software program provided by Lexis that lists every authority that mentions a case.

General encyclopedia: *See* Encyclopedia.

GlobalCite: LoislawConnect's citation validation service, used to ensure cases are still good law.

Google Scholar: A free search service offered by Google allowing one to access federal and state court cases by case name or topic.

GPO Access: *See* FDsys.

Header: Information found on the second and any following pages of letters in the upper left-hand corner listing the addressee, page, and date.

Headnotes: Short paragraphs prepared by editors, given before a case begins to serve as an index to the points of law discussed in a case.

History references: References provided by Shepard's relating to the subsequent history of a primary authority.

Hyperlink: A method of instantaneous transport to another destination; hyperlinks are often underscored or appear in different color on the computer screen; by clicking the colored line, you will be immediately transferred to that particular site or page.

IRAC: An acronym for Issue, Rule, Application or Analysis, and Conclusion; a method used to analyze authorities and legal issues in a memo or brief.

Id.: A citation short form used in citation form to direct a reader to an immediately preceding citation.

Indefinite pronoun: A pronoun that does not refer to a specific person, such as "anyone."

Index: An alphabetical arrangement of words and terms designed to direct researchers to relevant cases, statutes, or legal information; usually contained in the last volume of a set of books or in separate volumes after the last volume.

Index method: *See* Descriptive word approach.

Index to Legal Periodicals & Books: Separately published index (both in print and online) designed to direct researchers to periodicals such as articles in law reviews.

Infra: A citation short form used in books or citation form meaning "below" directing a reader to a later citation.

International Court of Justice: A court under the responsibility of the United Nations, created to hear and decide disputes between and among nations; also called the World Court.

International law: The law relating to relations among nations.

Internet: A collection of worldwide inter-connected computer networks originally developed for defense purposes and which are linked together to exchange information; the Internet is not owned by any one person or company.

Internet Service Provider (ISP): A company that provides Internet access, such as Verizon, for a monthly fee.

Judge: Individual who sits on a lower court.

Judiciary: The branch of the government that interprets laws.

Jump cite: *See* Pinpoint cite.

Jurisdiction: The power of a court to act.

Jurisdictional statement: A statement in a brief explaining the grounds upon which the court's jurisdiction to hear the case rests.

Jury instructions: Sets of books containing proposed instructions to be used to charge a jury in a civil or criminal case.

Justia: Free Internet site providing access to numerous legal authorities.

Justice: Individual who sits on an appellate court, especially the United States Supreme Court or the highest court in a state.

KWIC: A computer program offered by Lexis that provides subsequent appellate history of a case; used primarily to confirm that authority in question is still good law by showing negative history only. Also a method of displaying a band or window of words around a requested search term or phrase.

KeyCite: A citation service offered through Westlaw providing valuable and automatic information relating to the validity of primary authorities cited in a document.

KeyCite Alert: A software clipping service that automatically notifies a researcher of changes in treatment of a legal authority.

Key Number: West's assignment of a number to a particular topic of law, allowing researchers to retrieve numerous cases dealing with the same point of law.

Law: *See* Statute.

Law review: The periodic publication by a law school providing scholarly treatment of a legal topic; sometimes called "law journal."

Legalese: The overuse of legal terms and foreign words and phrases in legal writing.

LegalTrac: An online index to articles published in *Current Law Index*.

Legislative courts: Specialized courts, such as the United States Tax Court, which do not exist under the Constitution and whose judges are appointed for specific terms.

Legislative history: The documents reflecting the intent and activity of a legislature at the time it enacts a law.

Legislature: The branch of the government that makes law.

Letterhead: Information printed on stationery identifying the correspondent.

Lexis: The computerized legal research system offered by Reed Elsevier.

Lexis Advance: Lexis's new research system allowing easy searching across all of Lexis's content without requiring researchers to select a database.

Lexis Communities: Lexis's free service offering podcasts, videocasts, and other resources for certain practice areas.

"Library References": A feature of U.S.C.S. comparable to that of U.S.C.A. in that it provides cross-references as well as directing the researcher to books, encyclopedias, annotations, and a wide variety of law review articles.

Link: *See* Hyperlink.

Listserv: A system that allows groups of people to e-mail each other and participate in group discussions, usually about a topic of common concern; for example, there may be a listserv comprising law students, and when one message is sent by a user, it is automatically sent to all others in the group; sometimes called "newsgroup."

LoislawConnect: The computerized legal research system offered by Wolters Kluwer.

Looseleaf (or looseleaf service): A set of materials collected in ringed binders due to the need for frequent updating and related to a specific area of law such as labor law or tax; includes both primary and secondary authorities.

Majority opinion: Any judicial opinion written by a member of the majority after a court reaches a decision.

Maroonbook: A citation manual published by the University of Chicago and used in the Chicago area.

Martindale-Hubbell   Law Directory: A comprehensive directory of lawyers in the United States and in foreign countries.

Memorandum (legal): A document explaining legal issues involved in a case in a neutral and objective manner.

Memorandum of Law: Document presented to a court to persuade the court to rule in a party's favor; occasionally called Memorandum of Points and Authorities.

Memorandum of Points and Authorities: *See* Memorandum of Law.

Memorandum opinion: An opinion that provides a result but offers little or no reasoning to support that result.

Microfiche: Celluloid strips of film used in cataloging or archiving documents.

Microfilm: Film containing images displayed on screens and often used for efficient storage of voluminous records.

Microform: A type of technology embracing microfilm, microfiche, and ultrafiche, based on photography and that stores material more efficiently than print sources.

Model act: Proposed law intended to be used as a guideline for actual legislation.

Modifier: A word that limits, describes, or qualifies another word.

Moot: Resolved; cases that have been resolved or settled in some manner are said to be moot.

National Reporter System: A set of unofficial court reporters published by West and including federal and state cases; often called "regional reporters."

Natural language: A "plain English" computer method of conducting legal research, in contrast to using Boolean connectors.

Neutral citation: A citation that does not refer to a particular vendor or to a particular type of source; also called *public domain citation* or *universal citation*.

Newsgroup: Electronic communications method allowing its participants to view, post, and reply to messages on the Internet.

Nominalization: The conversion of an adjective, verb, or adverb into a noun, for example, the conversion of the verb "decide" into "render a decision."

Noncritical: Treatment of a legal topic in explanatory rather than analytical or critical manner.

Notes: *See* Comment.

Obiter dictum: *See* Dictum.

Official: Publication of cases, statutes, or other legal materials as directed by a statute.

On all fours: *See* On point.

Online: The process of being connected to the Internet through electronic communication.

Online catalog: An electronic database used by libraries in place of a conventional card catalog to catalog materials owned by the library.

Online journal: A journal that is published exclusively online, not in print form.

On point: A case that is factually similar and legally relevant and that controls another case; sometimes called a case "on all fours."

Opinion: A court's explanation of the law in a particular case; also called "case" or "decision."

Opinion letter: A letter setting forth advice to a client.

Ordinance: A local law.

Original jurisdiction: The ability of a court to act as a trial court.

Overrule: The overturning of a case by a higher court considering a different case on appeal.

PACER: Service of U.S. Judiciary, allowing access to documents filed in federal courts.

Parallel citation: Two or more citations to the same case allowing researchers to read a case in two or more sets of reports.

Parallel structure: The requirement that the grammatical structure of all items in a list be identical or parallel.

Password: The secret code used to gain access to a computer system.

Per curiam: An opinion by the court in which no justice is identified as the author.

Periodical: A publication issued on a periodic, such as monthly or quarterly, basis; for example, the *Computer Law Journal*.

Permanent law: A law that remains in effect until it is expressly repealed.

Personal digital assistant (PDA): A handheld computer device such as the BlackBerry, which provides wireless access for updating and validating through both Shepard's and KeyCite.

Persuasive authority: Legal authorities that a court is not required to follow but might be persuaded to do so; secondary authorities are persuasive.

Pinpoint cite: A reference to the exact page in a source to which a reader is directed; also called a "pincite," "jump cite," or "spot cite."

Plain English movement: A modern approach to legal writing calling for the use of plain English and an end to stuffy, archaic, and jargon-filled writing.

Plain English searching: *See* Natural Language.

Plurality opinion: The result reached when separate opinions are written by members of a majority.

Pocket part: A booklet or pamphlet inserted into the back of a hardbound volume to provide more current information than that found in the volume.

Popular name: The practice of calling certain statutes or cases by a popular name.

Popular name approach: A method of locating cases or statutes by looking up their "popular names"; generally, the names of the sponsoring legislators, the parties to the case, or a name assigned by the media.

Posting: The entering of information or messages into a network, for example, cases are "posted" to the website of the United States Supreme Court and legal professionals "post" messages on a listserv.

Primary authority: Official pronouncements of the law, chiefly cases, constitutions, statutes, administrative regulations, and treaties, all of which are binding authorities.

Private international law: The law relating to which country's law will govern a private contractual transaction or arrangement.

Private law: A law affecting only one person or a small group of persons, giving them some special benefit not afforded to the public at large.

Procedural history: The path a case takes, for example, from trial to appellate court.

Proclamation: A statement issued by a president, which often has no legal effect.

Proofreading: The process of reviewing a writing to correct errors, especially technical errors.

Public domain system: With regard to format- or vendor-neutral citation systems, the citation appears the same whether the reader has accessed the case by conventional print format or by electronic methods, such as CD-ROM, Lexis, Westlaw, or the Internet.

Public international law: The law relating to the conduct of nations.

Public law: A law affecting the public generally.

Query: A search request used to access a computer-assisted legal research system.

Quick Index: An easy-to-use one-volume index published by West that directs the researcher to annotations in A.L.R.3d, A.L.R.4th, A.L.R. 5th, and A.L.R.6th. Note that there is also an A.L.R. Federal Quick Index.

Ratio decidendi: The "reason of the decision"; the holding of a case.

Reference notation ("Re"): An indication of the subject matter of a document.

Regional reporters: *See* National Reporter System.

Regulation: A pronouncement by an administrative agency; sometimes called a rule.

Regulatory body: An administrative agency.

Remand: An order by a higher court that returns a case to a lower court, with directions.

Removal: Sending of a case from one court to another.

Report: Set of books publishing cases, generally official sets.

Reporter: Set of books publishing cases, generally unofficial sets.

Resolution: A proposed local ordinance.

Restatements: Publications of the American Law Institute designed to restate in a clear and simple manner legal doctrine in specific areas, such as contracts, torts, or trusts.

Reverse: The overturning of a lower court decision by a higher court considering that same case on appeal.

Rule: *See* Regulation.

Rules of court: Procedural requirements issued by courts and that must be followed by litigants.

Rules of procedure: Rules governing practice before a court, such as the FRCP, which govern significant matters.

Running head: The printed line across the top of published cases that identifies the parties' names and case citation.

Salutation: The greeting in a letter, such as "Dear Ms. Howard."

Sans serif style: Print style without embellishments of extra lines forming letters, such as the Arial font.

Scope note: A brief paragraph outlining the matters treated in a legal discussion and those to be treated elsewhere.

Search box: A blank box on a computer screen, in which you type or key in the word or terms you are interested in researching.

Search engine: A particular service that helps one locate useful information on the Internet, usually through the use of key words; common search engines are "Bing" and "Google." A search engine is a website that looks for and retrieves other websites. Search engines look for words in the millions of web pages on the Internet and direct you to pages that include the search words or key words you enter in a search box.

Secondary authorities: Legal authorities that are not primary law and which explain, discuss, and help locate primary authorities; persuasive authority; includes encyclopedias, A.L.R.

annotations, law reviews, texts, and treatises.

Selective publication: The process whereby not all cases are published but rather only those that advance legal theory are published.

Series: Newer or more recent editions of cases or other legal materials.

Serif style: A style of print that adds small decorative strokes to the edges of letters, generally viewed as enhancing readability, such as Garamond and Times New Roman fonts.

Session laws: The chronological arrangement of laws prior to their arrangement in a code.

Shepard's: Sets of books or Lexis's online service that allows researchers to verify that primary authorities are still "good law."

Shepardize: The process of ensuring that authorities are still "good law."

Short form citation: An abbreviated form of a citation used after a citation has been given in full.

Signal indicator: A symbol showing on the computer screen that informs the user of the precedential status of a case or other authority by indicating through colors or letters the history and treatment of the case or other authority.

Signals: In citation form, words indicating how a citation supports or contradicts an assertion; references to preceding or later-given citations in a legal writing.

Slip law: A piece (or pieces) of looseleaf paper containing language of a law; the manner in which laws are first published.

Slip opinion: A court decision available on looseleaf sheets of paper; one not yet available in a published reporter.

Sources: Lexis's databases of materials; also called "Libraries."

Stack: Shelf in a library.

Standing: Personal injury or damage sustained by a plaintiff enabling the plaintiff to bring suit.

Stare decisis: The concept whereby courts follow and adhere to previous cases.

Star paging: A technique to convert page numbers in cases published in unofficial sets to page numbers in cases published in official sets.

Statute: An act of a legislature declaring, commanding, or prohibiting something.

String citing: The somewhat disfavored practice of citing more than one authority in support of a proposition.

Style sheet: A guide to presentation of terms and words used by copyeditors to ensure consistent presentation.

Subject matter jurisdiction: *See* Federal question jurisdiction.

Supplement: A softcover pamphlet that updates material found in a hardbound volume.

Supra: A citation short form used in books or citation form meaning "above," directing a reader to a preceding (though not immediately preceding) reference or citation.

Syllabus: A comprehensive but unofficial summary preceding an opinion of a court, prepared by the court's reporter of decisions or the publisher.

Synopsis: A brief summary of a case prepared by editors to provide a quick overview of the case and given before the case begins.

Table of authorities: List of authorities cited in a brief or document and that must be arranged in a certain order.

Tabulation: To arrange in a table or list.

Temporary law: A law that has specific language limiting its duration.

Terms and connectors: A method of searching on a computer, using words, symbols, and characters rather than plain English; often called "Boolean searching."

Text messaging: A style of communication using wireless devices and using abbreviated words and symbols.

Thesaurus: A book providing synonyms and antonyms for words and terms.

Thesis statement: An initial sentence or two at the beginning of a project or issue that encapsulates the central argument to follow; also called *umbrella statement*.

THOMAS: Website for legislative information provided by the federal government that offers text of proposed and enacted legislation, committee information, calendars for hearings scheduled, and House and Senate Directories; THOMAS is being replaced by Congress.gov.

Thomson Reuters: A law book publisher; formerly West Publishing Co.; usually referred to as "West" by legal professionals.

Titles: Categories of statutes or regulations.

Topic approach: A method of locating legal materials by bypassing the general index and going directly to the appropriate title or topic in a source.

Total Client-Service Library: Collectively, the sets of books published by the former Lawyers Co-op and including U.S.C.S., Am. Jur. 2d, A.L.R., Proof of Facts, Am. Jur. Trials, and various form books.

Treatise: A scholarly book (or set of books) devoted to the treatment of a particular legal topic, such as *Treatise on the Law of Contracts*.

Treatment references: References provided by Shepard's relating to the later treatment and discussion of primary authorities by other cases, attorneys general opinions, law review articles, and so forth.

Treaty: An agreement between two or more nations.

Ultrafiche: An enhanced microfiche holding a great many images.

Uniform law: Model legislation prepared by the National Conference of Commissioners on Uniform State Laws on various legal topics, such as the Uniform Commercial Code, and designed to be adopted by the 50 states.

United States Code: The official publication of all federal laws, arranged by topic.

United States Code Annotated: West's annotated version of the United States Code, including all federal statutes arranged by subject.

United States Code Congressional and Administrative News: A monthly publication including public laws, legislative history of selected bills, summaries of pending legislation, presidential proclamations and executive orders, various federal regulations, and court rules.

United States Code Service: Annotated set of federal statutes arranged by subject and published by Lexis.

United States Government Manual: A manual or handbook providing information about the United States government, particularly the administrative agencies.

United States Law Week: A weekly publication that prints U.S. Supreme Court cases and information about the Court.

United States Reports: The official publication containing cases from the United States Supreme Court.

United States Statutes at Large: The set of books containing all federal laws, arranged in chronological order.

Universal symbols: Symbols and characters used in constructing a search on Lexis or Westlaw; sometimes called root expanders.

Unofficial: Publication of cases or statutes not directed by statute.

Unreported case: A case marked "not for publication" by a court; persuasive authority although it may be available from Lexis, Westlaw, or on the Internet.

Versus Law: A commercial legal research system offering cases via the Internet for a moderate fee.

WWW: World Wide Web, commonly used to refer to the entire collection of resources that can be accessed in cyberspace, through the Internet.

Web: *See* WWW.

Website: A collection of web pages; for example, IBM's website (www.ibm.com) will consist of numerous web pages, each of which is devoted to a specific topic. A website always begins with a "home page," which is the first screen viewed when the website is accessed.

West: The common name of the largest law book publisher in the United States; formerly West Publishing Co. and now owned by Thomson Reuters.

WestCheck: A West software program providing automatic validation of all cases cited in a document.

Westlaw: The computerized legal research system offered by West.

WestlawNext: A new user-friendly research platform that allows easy "Google"-type searching of Westlaw, with results ranked in order of importance.

Widows and orphans: A heading or isolated word or line occurring at the bottom or top of a page.

Words and Phrases: A multivolume set of books directing researchers to cases that have construed certain terms.

World Court: The United Nations court, officially named the International Court of Justice, which provides final decisions regarding international disputes.

World Wide Web: *See* WWW.

Writ of certiorari: *See* Certiorari.

Zotero: A free tool that allows the saving, storing, and management of bibliographic references and assists in citing the materials.

Index

AALL (American Association of Law
    Libraries), 5
ABA Journal, 128
Abbreviations
    citation form, 257–258
    history and treatment of case, 284
    practice tip, 6
Active voice, 347, 403
Administrative law and regulations,
    167–176
    citation form, 185, 262, 267
    Code of Federal Regulations (C.F.R.),
        168, 169, 171
    decisions, 173–174
    electronic and online methods, 173
    federal, 167–175
    Federal Register, 167–168, 169, 170
    KeyCiting, 297
    overview, 167
    publication of, 167–168
    research techniques for, 168–169
    review of agency decisions, 174–175
    Shepardizing, 290
    as source of law, 8, 10
    state, 175–176
Advance sheets, 70
affect/effect, 342
A.L.R. *See* American Law Reports
ALWD Citation Manual
    abbreviations, 77
    Bluebook compared, 253–254
    capitalization in court documents and
        other legal memoranda, 275
    citation signals, 271–272
    electronic sources, databases, and
        Internet, 276–277

id., use of in citations, 272–273
infra, use of in citations, 273
    overview, 252, 264
    primary authorities, citation rules and
        examples for, 264–267
    punctuation, 269–270
    quotations, 270–271
    secondary authorities, citation rules
        and examples for, 267–269
    short form citations, 272–274
    string citing, 254
    supra, use of in citations, 273
    Supreme Court cases, citation of, 76
    underlining, 16
    websites, 278
American Association of Law Libraries
    (AALL), 5
American Digest System
    Descriptive Word Index, 98
    Key Numbers, method for assigning, 97
    location of topic and Key Number,
        97–100
    National Reporter System, relationship
        to, 96
    organization of, 96–97
    use of, 100–102
American Journal of International Law,
    178, 181
American Jurisprudence 2d (Am. Jur. 2d)
    Corpus Juris Secundum compared, 121
    Desk Book, 121
    Legal Forms 2d, 124
    New Topic Service, 121
    overview, 120–121
    *Pleading and Practice Forms,
        Annotated*, 124, 146

American Jurisprudence 2d (Am. Jur. 2d)
(*continued*)
Proof of Facts, 123
research strategies, 123
sample pages, 122
Trials, 124
American Law Institute, 137. *See also*
Restatements
American Law Reports (A.L.R.)
Annotation History Table, 112
citation form, 112
features of, 108–109
finding annotations, 109–112
organization of, 107–108
overview, 107
pocket parts, 109
sample pages, 110–111
updating annotations, 112
websites, 113
among / between, 342
and / or, 342
Annotations, 10, 48, 262, 267. *See also*
individual annotated sources
Apostrophes, 334–336
Appellate briefs
appendices, 395
arguments, 395
Certificates of Service and Compliance,
395
conclusions in, 395
constitutional and statutory provisions,
394
cover sheets, 394
elements of, 394–395
identification of parties, 394
jurisdictional statements, 394
overview, 394–395
questions presented, 394
signatures, 395
statement of case, 395
statement of facts, 395
steps in appeal process, 394–395
summary of arguments, 395
Table of Authorities, 394
Table of Contents, 394
Arbitration, Permanent Court of, 181–182
argue / rule, 343
Aspen Publishers, 11
Attorney-client relationship, 4
Attorneys general opinions
citation form, 151, 263, 268
research strategies, 138, 140
websites, 152
Authority Check, 299

Bankruptcy Developments Journal, 128
Bankruptcy Reporter, 78
Bar association publications, 128
Batson v. Kentucky (1986), 74
BCite, 299
Bender's Federal Practice Forms, 143
Bender's Forms of Discovery, 143
Bills. *See also* Legislative history
enactment of legislation, steps in, 39–40
numbering of, 39–40

pending, 165–166
tracking, 165–166
versions of, 158
Black's Law Dictionary
common law defined, 6–7
overview, 140–141
table of abbreviations, 77
Blogs, 241–242
Bloomberg BNA (Bureau of National
Affairs), 174
Bloomberg Law, 220
Blue and White Books, 82–83
*The Bluebook: A Uniform System of
Citation*
ALWD Citation Manual compared,
253–254
capitalization in court documents and
other legal memoranda, 275
citation signals, 271–272
electronic sources, databases, and
Internet, 276–277
id., use of in citations, 272–273
infra, use of in citations, 273
organization of, 252
overview, 252
primary authorities, citation rules and
examples for, 255–262
punctuation, 269–270
quotations, 270–271
secondary authorities, citation rules
and examples for, 262–264
short form citations, 272–274
string citing, 254
supra, use of in citations, 273
Supreme Court cases, citation of, 76
typeface conventions, 254–255
underlining, 16
websites, 278
Books. *See* Looseleaf services; Treatises
Brevity, 350–351
answers, legal memoranda, 375–376
redundancy, avoiding, 350–351
repetition, avoiding, 350–351
unnecessary words, omitting, 350, 403
BriefCheck, 294
Briefing cases. *See* Case briefing
Briefs, legal
appellate, 394–395
being concise, 388–389
case briefs distinguished, 387
honesty in, 389–390
legal memoranda distinguished,
387–388
overview, 387
persuasiveness in, 388
purpose of, 387
rules for, 390
sample, 424–428
thesis statements, 389
tips on writing, 388–390, 396
trial court, 390–394
websites, 397
BriefTools, 298
*Brownlie's Principles of Public
International Law* (Crawford), 178

Brown v. Board of Education (1954),
    12–13, 16, 287
Burton's Legal Thesaurus, 140–141
Business Lawyer, 133

*California Legal Forms: Transaction
    Guide*, 143
Capitalization in court documents and
    other legal memoranda, 275
Case briefing, 83–89
    case reading strategies, 85–86
    definition of, 83
    elements of brief, 85–89
    format for, 83–84
    formulating issues, 90
    legal briefs distinguished, 387
    procedural history, determination of, 85
    purpose of, 83–84
    reading case, importance of, 83
    sample, 88–89
CaseCheck+, 299
Case law, 61–91
    advance sheets, 70
    best websites for locating, 237
    case name, 63
    citation, 256–260, 264–266, 273
    concurring opinions, 68
    deciding courts, 63
    decision date, 67
    decisions, 69
    digests to locate, 95–106. *See also* Digests
    dissenting opinions, 68
    docket numbers, 63
    elements of opinion, 63–69
    federal cases, publication of, 74–76
    Google Scholar, 80
    headnotes, 67
    holding, identification of, 14
    KeyCiting, 295–297
    Lexis search for, 203
    majority opinions, 68
    memorandum opinions, 68
    names of counsel, 67
    non-majority opinions, 68
    opinions, 67–68
    parallel cites, how to find, 82–83
    per curiam opinions, 68
    plurality opinions, 68
    as primary source, 10, 312–313
    publication of, 69–70, 83
    sample of published cases, 64–66
    selective publication, 61–63
    series of cases, publication of, 70
    Shepardizing, 283–291
    slip opinions, 70
    as source of law, 6–7
    standards for publishing, 61–62
    star paging, 76–78
    state cases, publication of, 70–74
    synopsis, 67
    unpublished opinions, 62–63
    websites, 91
    Westlaw search for, 212
Casemaker, 221, 299
Case on Point approach, 100

CCH. *See* Commerce Clearing House Inc.
CCH Congressional Index, 165
CD-ROMs, 222–223
C.F.R. (*Code of Federal Regulations*), 168,
    169, 171
Circuit Courts. *See* Courts of Appeals,
    United States
*CIS Congressional Bills, Resolutions, &
    Laws on Microfiche*, 221
Citation form. *See also specific systems
    and manuals*
    abbreviations in case citations,
        257–258, 265
    administrative law and regulations,
        185, 262, 267
    American Law Reports, 112
    annotations, 262, 267
    attorneys general opinions, 151, 263,
        268
    books, 263, 267
    capitalization in court documents and
        other legal memoranda, 275
    case history, 259, 265
    case names, 256–259
    cases, 256–260, 264–266, 273
    clauses, citations in, 269
    constitutions, 261, 267
    court rules, 32
    Courts of Appeals, United States, 259
    dictionaries, 151, 263, 268
    District Courts, United States, 259
    electronic sources, 276–277
    encyclopedias, 151, 262, 267
    errors in, 251
    executive materials, 184
    federal cases, 16, 35, 90, 259, 265
    federal statutes, 58, 260–261, 266
    id., use of, 272–273
    infra, use of, 51, 273
    international materials, 185
    Internet, 245–246, 276–277
    jury instructions, 151
    legislative materials, 184
    Lexis, 223, 277
    looseleaf services, 151, 263, 268
    multiple sections of statute, 261
    municipal materials, 185
    neutral formats, 274
    non-majority opinions, 68
    overview, 251
    parallel citations, 73, 82–83
    periodicals, 151, 262–263, 267
    presidential materials, 184
    prior history, 259
    punctuation, 269–270
    quotations, 270–271
    Restatements, 151, 263, 268
    rules, 261, 266
    section reference, statutes, 261
    sentences, citations in, 269
    short forms, 272–274
    signals preceding citation, 271–272
    spacing rules, 260, 266
    state cases, 16, 35, 90, 258–259, 265
    state statutes, 58, 261, 266

Citation form. *See also specific systems
        and manuals (continued)*
    statutes, 260–261, 274
    string citation, 254
    subsequent history, 259
    superscripts, 260
    supra, use of, 51, 273
    Supreme Court cases, 259
    treatises, 151, 263, 267
    typeface conventions, 254–255
    uniform laws, 151, 263, 268
    websites, 278
    Westlaw, 223, 277
CiteAdvisor, 298
Cite-checking, 405. *See also* Citation form
Civil law tradition, 8
C.J.S. *See Corpus Juris Secundum*
Clarity in writing
    elegant variation, 345
    negatives, overuse of, 345–346
    poor writing, risk of, 346
    word order, 346
Code of Federal Regulations (C.F.R.), 168,
        169, 171
Collective nouns, 328
Collier on Bankruptcy, 16th Edition, 134
Commas, 334
Commerce Clearing House Inc. (CCH),
        11, 174
Common law tradition, 6–7
compose/comprise, 343
Computer-assisted legal research,
        193–223
    Bloomberg Law, 220
    Boolean searching, 194, 195, 209–210
    Casemaker, 221
    CD-ROMs, 222–223
    DVDs, 222–223
    eBooks, 222–223
    Fastcase, 220–221
    introduction to, 193–194
    Lexis. *See* Lexis
    limitations of, 219
    LoislawConnect, 220
    overview, 12
    PACER, 220
    plain English searching, 197, 210
    U.S. Supreme Court cases, 74
    VersusLaw, 220
    Westlaw. *See* Westlaw
Computer literacy, need for, 194
Concurrent jurisdiction, 21–22
Concurring opinions, 68
Conference calls, 353
Congress, U.S.
    assistance with legislative histories,
        162
    enactment of legislation, steps in,
        39–40
    representatives, requests for
        information from, 41
Congress.gov, 41, 161, 238–239
Congressional Information Service (CIS),
        160
Congressional Record, 158, 160

Constitution, U.S.
    citation form, 261, 267
    enactment of legislation, 39–40
    reserve clause, 19
    as source of law, 7
    Tenth Amendment, 19
    in U.S.C.A., 52
    in U.S.C.S., 52
Constitutions
    citation form, 261, 267
    legal research process, 312
    Lexis search for, 202
    as primary source, 10
    as source of law, 7
    Westlaw search for, 212
Copyright infringement, 236
Cornell University Law School website,
        58, 91, 231–232, 237–238
Corpus Juris Secundum (C.J.S.)
    abbreviations, table of, 77
    American Jurisprudence 2d compared,
        121
    cross-referencing, 105–106
    overview, 120
    research strategies, 123
Court of Appeals for Federal Circuit, 28
Court rules. *See* Rules of procedure and
        court rules
Courts of Appeals, United States
    cases, publication of, 75
    citation form, 259
    District Courts compared, 24–26
    overview, 26–28
CRAC method of analyzing cases, 380
CRuPAC method of analyzing cases, 380
*Cumulative Later Case and Statutory
        Service*, 47
Current Index to Legal Periodicals, 133
Current Law Index (C.L.I.), 130–131, 133

*Daily Compilation of Presidential
        Documents*, 167
Dangling participles, 330
Databases, electronic. *See* Lexis; Westlaw
Deadlines, 351–352
Descriptive word approach, 49, 54, 98,
        109, 123, 136
Dictionaries
    citation form, 151, 263, 268
    overview, 140–141
    use of, 10
    websites, 152
Digest approach, 109
Digest of International Law (Hackworth),
        178
Digest of International Law (Whiteman),
        178
Digests, 95–106
    *American Digest System. See American
        Digest System*
    citation form, 113
    common features of, 104–106
    cross-references, 105–106
    *Decennial Digest System. See American
        Digest System*

descriptive word indexes, 104
Federal Practice Digests, 102
location of topic and Key Number, 97–100
non-West, 106
overview, 95
parallel citation, 83
purpose of, 95
regional, 104
sample page, 99, 101, 103
specialty, 104
states, 83, 104
supplementation, 105
table of cases, 104
uniform classification, 104
United States Supreme Court Digest, 102
use of, 100–102, 106
websites, 113
words and phrases volumes, 105
Directories
Martindale-Hubbell Law Directory, 141, 143
purpose of, 141
websites, 152
Discovery
Bender's Forms of Discovery, 143
disinterested / uninterested, 343
Dissenting opinions, 68
District Courts, United States
Circuit Courts compared, 24–26
citation form, 259
overview, 23, 26
publication of cases, 75
Diversity jurisdiction, 20–21
Dropbox, 243
Duty of competence, 4, 333, 382, 405
DVDs, 222–223

eBooks, 222–223
E-Government Act of 2002, 62
Electronic communications, 352–355
e-mail, 353–354
facsimile, 353
phones and voice mail, 353
text messaging, 354–355
E-mail, 353–354
Encyclopedias, 119–126. *See also American Jurisprudence 2d* (Am. Jur. 2d); *Corpus Juris Secundum* (C.J.S.)
citation form, 151, 262, 267
common features, 124–126
general or national, 120–124
noncritical approach of, 120
reference to cases through footnotes, 119
research strategies for use of, 123, 126
special subject, 126
state or local, 124–126
Total Client-Service Library, 123–124
use of, 126
E-research, 229–246
advantages and disadvantages of, 244–245

best websites, 237–243
blogs, 241–242
bookmarks, 234
cautionary notes regarding, 243–245
citation form, 245–246
copyright infringement, avoiding, 236
credibility of websites, assessing, 235–236
disclaimers, 235
Dropbox, 243
ethical concerns, 236
Facebook, 243
getting started, 231
Google Scholar, 233
information gaps, 235
learning how to conduct, 231–236
LinkedIn, 243
listservs, 241–242
mobile applications, 243
newsgroups, 242
newsletters, 235
notes, 234
overview, 229
reading screen, 234
search boxes, 234
search engines, 242
as sole source, 234–235
strategies and tips for, 234–235
Twitter, 243
Ethics
corresponding with parties, 362
court rules, abiding by, 394
duty of competence, 4, 333, 382, 405
duty to update and validate cases, 300
research accuracy and, 4, 52
Exclusive jurisdiction, 22
Executive branch of federal government
citation form, 184
Daily Compilation of Presidential Documents, 167
executive orders, 8, 10, 166–167
federalism and, 19–20
proclamations, presidential, 166
as source of law, 8
Executive orders, 8, 10, 166–167

Facebook, 243
Facsimile communications, 353
fact / contention, 343
Falstaff Brewing Corp.; United States v. (1971), 291
Fastcase, 220–221, 299
FDsys, 58, 161, 175, 182, 237
Federal agencies, functions of, 8
Federal Appendix, 62, 75
Federal cases
citation form, 16, 35, 90, 259, 265
publication of, 74–76
Federal Cases, 78
Federal Claims Reporter, 78
Federal court system, 22–32
actual cases and controversy requirement, 22
advisory opinions, 22
caseloads, 28

Federal court system *(continued)*
  citation form, 35
  constitutional courts, 32
  Courts of Appeals. *See* Courts of
      Appeals, United States
  District Courts. *See* District Courts,
      United States
  establishment of, 20
  ground rules for cases, 22
  jurisdiction, 20–22
  legislative courts, 32
  moot cases, 22
  specialized courts, 32
  standing, 22
  structure, 22–32
  Supreme Court. *See* Supreme Court, U.S.
  websites, 35
Federal Depository Library, 5
Federal Digital Systems (FDsys), 58, 161,
    175, 182, 237
Federalism, 19–20
Federal judges and justices
  appointment of, 23, 28, 32
  Circuit Courts, 28
  District Courts, 23
  impeachment of, 29
  salaries of, 26, 28
  Supreme Court. *See* Supreme Court,
      U.S.
*Federal Legislative History Research: A
    Practitioner's Guide to Compiling
    the Documents and Sifting for
    Legislative Intent*, 158
Federal Practice Digests, 102
Federal question jurisdiction, 20
Federal Register, 167–168, 169, 170
Federal Reporter
  coverage, 75–76
  federal appellate cases, source of, 75
  Federal Cases compared, 78
  list of judges, 82
  National Reporter System, part of, 96
  series of cases, publication of, 70
Federal Rules Decisions, 76
Federal Rules of Appellate Procedure, 76
Federal Rules of Civil Procedure, 55–56,
    76, 251
Federal Rules of Court, 56
Federal Rules of Criminal Procedure, 76,
    261
Federal Rules of Evidence, 76, 261
Federal statutes, 39–52
  citation form, 58, 260–2619, 266
  classification of, 40–41
  enactment of, 39–40
  enforcement of, 8
  exact wording, sources of, 41
  KeyCiting, 297
  legislative history. *See* Legislative
      history
  Lexis search for, 202
  numbering of, 39–40
  permanent laws, 40
  private laws, 40
  publication of, 41–48
    public laws, 40
    research techniques, 48–51, 57
    Shepardizing, 290, 294
    temporary laws, 41
    websites, 58
    Westlaw search for, 212
Federal Supplement, 75–76
FindLaw website, 11, 232
FirstGov website, 238
Fonts, 408
Footnotes, 119, 392
Forms
  books, 143–144
  metadata and, 144
  overview, 143–144
  sample page, 142
  use of, 144
  websites, 152, 238

Gender-linked pronouns, 332
*Germain's Transnational Law Research:
    A Guide for Attorneys* (Germain),
    178
GlobalCite, 299
Google Scholar
  case law, 80, 91
  e-research, 233
Gosnell v. Rentokil, Inc. (1997), 300
Government Printing Office (GPO), U.S.
  access to, 161
  federal statutes, publication of, 41
  Style Manual, 337
GovTrack, 165
Grammar, 327–332
  dangling participles, 330
  modifiers, 330
  pronouns, 331–332
  run-on sentences, 329
  split infinitives, 330
  subject-verb agreement, 327–329
*Guide to State Legislative and
    Administrative Materials*, 164
*A Guide to the United States Treaties in
    Force*, 181
guilty / liable, 343

Headings, in legal writing, 374, 410–411
Headnotes, 67, 287
HeinOnline, 133
Hyphens, 336

Id., use of in legal citation, 272–273
Impeachment, federal judges, 29
Indexes
  Code of Federal Regulations, 168, 172
  periodicals, 130–131
  state statutes, 53
  United States Code Annotated, 44, 50
  *United States Code Service Lawyers
      Edition*, 44
  United States Statutes at Large, 41
  West's digests, Descriptive Word
      Indexes in, 99
Index to Legal Periodicals & Books
    (I.L.P.), 130, 132, 133

*Index to Periodical Articles Related to
        Law*, 131
Index to the Code of Federal Regulations,
        168, 172
Infra, use of in legal citation, 51, 273
International Court of Justice (World
        Court), 182
International law, 177–182
    basic texts and sources, 178
    definition, 177
    international tribunals, 181–182
    Internet sources, 180
    Internet tutorials on research, 181
    overview, 177–178
    research procedure, 177–178
    sources of, 177
    treaties, 179–181
Internet. *See also* Websites
    advantages and disadvantages,
        244–245
    cases published on, 74
    citation form, 245–246, 276–277
    legal professionals, uses of by, 229–231
    legal research on. *See* E-research
    legislative history, use of, 160–161
    Lexis and Westlaw compared, 235
    municipal research, 183–184
    periodicals available on, 133
    reasons for use, 229–231
    as research tool, 12
    specific resources. *See* Websites
    THOMAS, 41
    Uniform Laws on, 145
    U.S. Supreme Court cases on, 74
Internet Litigation, 130
Interstate Commerce Act of 1887, 30
IRAC method of analyzing cases, 379–380

Jargon, 341, 348–349
judgment / judgement, 343
Judicial branch of federal government, 10
Jurisdiction
    concurrent jurisdiction, 21–22
    Courts of Appeals, 26, 28
    District Courts, 23, 26
    diversity jurisdiction, 20–21
    exclusive jurisdiction, 22
    federal courts, 20–22
    federal question jurisdiction, 20
    state courts, 33
    U.S. Supreme Court, 29–30
Jury instructions, 145–146
    citation form, 151
    websites, 152
Jury Trials and Tribulations, 130
Justia website, 58, 232–233

KeyCite, 295–297
    accessing, 295
    features of, 295–297
    parallel citations, 83
    research strategies, 314
    screen showing history of case, 296
    Shepardizing compared, 298–299
    statutes and regulations, 297
    symbols, 296

websites, 301
Westlaw, use of, 133, 213, 295
WestlawNext, use of, 217

Law, definitions of, 6–7
Law libraries, 4–6
    arrangement of, 5–6
    courtesy, 6
    courthouse law libraries, 5
    law firm libraries, 5
    law school libraries, 4
    local law libraries, 5
    as noncirculating libraries, 6
    online public access catalog (OPAC), 5
    reshelving books, 6
    types of, 4–5
Law reviews
    legislative history and, 162
    overview, 10, 127
    sample cover, 129
Ledesma; People v. (1987), 4
Legal briefs. *See* Briefs, legal
Legal correspondence. *See* Letterwriting
Legalese, 341, 348–349, 403
Legal memoranda. *See* Memoranda, legal
Legal newsletters, 130
Legal newspapers, 74
Legal periodicals. *See* Periodicals, legal
Legal research process, 309–322
    action, 311
    beginning, 309–311
    blueprint for, 321
    complex projects, 317–318
    constitutions, 312
    criminal versus civil law, 310
    defenses, 311
    established and newly emerging issues,
        318
    failure to provide adequate research, 4
    familiarization, 312
    inflexible rules of, 310
    issues of first impression, 319
    jurisdiction, 311
    knowing versus finding law, 4
    Lexis Advance's Workspace, 315
    miscellaneous research guides, 314
    narrowing down possibilities, 310–311
    note-taking, 315–316
    number of authorities to cite, 319–320
    practical considerations, 317
    primary sources, 312–313
    quality of sources, 315
    quick questions, 318
    remedies, 311
    scenarios for, 14–15
    secondary sources, 313–314
    statutes, 312
    staying focused, 316
    strategies for. *See* Research strategies
    thinking things through, 310
    tips for effective, 321–322
    websites, 16–17, 237–243, 322
    WestlawNext, 315
    when to stop, 316–322
    worksheet, 311
    Zotero, 316

Legal Resources Index (LegalTrac), 133
Legal systems
    non-U.S., 8–9
    U.S., 6–8, 9–10, 12–14
Legal thesauri, 140–141
LegalTrac, 133
Legal writing
    active versus passive voice, 347, 403
    audience and writing style, 360
    brevity, 350–351
    common errors, 412
    deadlines, 351–352
    electronic communications, 352–355
    exhibits, attaching, 393
    final review, 411
    getting started, 351
    goals of, 411–412
    grammar rules, 327–332
    headings, use of, 410–411
    jargon, 341, 348–349
    legal briefs, 387–397
    legalese, 341, 403
    letters, 359–370
    lists, use of, 347–348, 411
    memoranda, 373–384
    nominalizations, avoiding, 348
    plain English movement, 341
    polishing, 406–411
    poor writing, risk of, 346
    postwriting activities. *See* Postwriting
        activities
    precision, need for, 342–345
    proofreading, 403–407
    proximity of subject and verb, 349
    punctuation, 333–336
    readability, 346–349
    redundancy, 350–351
    repetition, 350–351
    reviewing and revising, 401–403
    spelling, 332–333
    unnecessary words, eliminating, 350,
        403
    vague words, 344
    websites, 337, 355, 412
    word choice, 342–344
    word connotation, 345
    word order, 346
    on word processors, 352
Legislative branch of federal government,
    10
Legislative history, 157–166
    commercial services, 162, 164
    committee hearings, transcripts of, 158
    committee reports and prints, 158
    compiled histories, 161, 163–164
    congressional assistance, 162
    debates, 158
    electronic sources, 160–161
    federal, 157–158
    GPO access, 161
    law reviews and annotations, 162, 165
    legislative assistance, 165
    on Lexis, 160
    pending legislation, tracking, 165–166
    process of compiling, 159–161

public law numbers, 159–160
    reference assistance, 162, 165
    state, 163–165
    THOMAS, 161
    versions of bill, comparing, 158
    web-based tutorials, 163, 164
    on Westlaw, 160
Legislative Intent Service, 162
Legislative Source Book (Law Librarians'
    Society of Washington, D.C.), 158
Letterwriting, 359–370
    audience, 360
    body, 361
    central purpose of, 360
    closing and signature, 361
    conclusions, 367–368
    corresponding with parties, 362
    date, 360, 367
    demand letters, 363, 366
    explanation of conclusions, 368
    format considerations, 361–362
    general correspondence, 362
    inside address, 360
    instructions, 369
    introductory language, 367
    letterhead, 360
    opinion letters, 366–369
    overview, 359–360, 369–370
    protection clauses, 369
    recommendations, 368–369
    reference or subject notation, 361
    review of facts, 367
    salutations, 361
    sample letters, 364–365
    special mailing notations, 361
    types of, 362–369
    unknown addresses, 361
    websites, 370
Lexis, 198–207. *See also* Shepardizing
    administrative and legislative
        materials, search for, 203
    Affiliated Services, 205
    Alerts, 204
    "all" screen, 199
    Boolean searching, 195, 200–201
    Briefs and Records, 205
    case law, search for, 203
    citation form, 223, 277
    constructing search, 200–202
    contact information, 194
    Dot Command, search by, 199
    Easy Search, 201
    federal statutes, 41
    getting started, 198–199
    Guided Search Form, search by, 199
    hyperlinking, 204
    interactive tutorials, 218
    law reviews and journals, search for,
        203
    legislative history, 160, 165
    Live Help, 205
    More Like This, 205
    My Lexis, 198
    new developments in, 218
    pending legislation, tracking of, 165

periodical articles online, 133
plain English searching, 197, 201
Practitioner's Toolbox, 204
quick review of, 207
Quick Search screen, 201
search results, display of, 202
secondary authorities, search for, 204
Segment Searching, 204–205
Shepardizing with, 204, 291–293
Shepard's, 199
Source, search by, 199
statutes and constitutions, search for,
  202
terms and connectors, 195–197
Topic or Headnote, search by, 198
treaties, 180
uniform laws on, 145
viewing results, 202
websites, 223
Westlaw compared, 223
when to use, 218–219
Lexis Advance, 205–207
  Alerts, 207
  Delivery Options, 207
  filters, 206
  home page screen, 206
  Legal Issue Trail, 206
  Live Support, 207
  mobile applications, 207
  My Workspace, 206
  Research Map, 207
  Shepardizing with, 207
  viewing results, 206
  work folders, 206
  Workspace, 315
LexisNexis Legal & Professional (Lexis),
  11
Libraries, law. *See* Law libraries
LinkedIn, 243
List of C.F.R. Sections Affected (LSA), 169
Lists, use of, 347–348, 411
Listservs, 241–242
LoislawConnect, 11, 220, 299
Looseleaf services. *See also* Treatises
  citation form, 151, 263, 268
  overview, 145
Los Angeles and San Francisco Daily, 130
LSA (*List of C.F.R. Sections Affected*), 169

Majority opinions, 68
*Maroonbook (University of Chicago
  Manual of Legal Citation)*, 252
Martindale-Hubbell, 11
Martindale-Hubbell Law Directory, 141,
  143, 222
Matthew Bender, 11, 174
Memoranda, legal, 373–384
  analysis or discussion, 377–381
  applicable statutes, 377
  being concise, 381
  blueprint for preparing, 382–383
  brief answers, 375–376
  case law, citation to, 378
  completeness, need for, 373
  conclusion, 381–382

CRAC and CRuPAC methods of
  analyzing cases, 380
elements of, 374–382, 382–383
formats, 374–382
headings, 374
IRAC method of analyzing cases,
  379–380
issues or questions presented, 374–375
objectivity in, 373–374, 382
overview, 373
quotations and paraphrasing, 381
readability, 378–379
sample, 416–421
specificity in, 373
statement of facts, 376–377
thesis statements, 377–378
tips for writing, 383
uses for, 373
websites, 384
Memorandum opinions, 68
Michie Co., 11
Microfiche, 221
Microfilm, 221
Microforms, 221–222
Military Justice Reporter, 78
Mobile applications
  Lexis Advance, 207
  overview, 243
Modern Federal Jury Instructions, 146
Modifiers, 330
Moot cases, 22
Municipal research, 182–184
  citation form, 185
  Internet, use of, 183–184
  interpretations of municipal
    ordinances, 183
  overview, 182–183
  procedure for, 183
  research materials, 183
  terminology, 182–183
  websites, 186

National Black Law Journal, 130
National Conference of Commissioners on
  Uniform State Laws, 144
National Reporter Blue Book, 82–83
National Reporter System, 70–73
  advantages of, 73
  American Digest System, relationship
    to, 96
  features of, 80–82
  Key Number System, 82
  lists of judges, 82
  parallel cites, 73
  specialty sets, 78
  tables of cases, 80
  tables of statutes and rules, 80–82
  tables of words and phrases, 82
  units of, 71–72
  as unofficial publication, 70, 82
Newsgroups, 242
Newsletters, legal, 130
Newspapers, legal, 74, 130
New York Law Journal, 130
Nominalizations, avoiding, 348

Non-majority opinions, 68
Nonprint research tools
    CD-ROMs, 222–223
    DVDs, 222–223
    eBooks, 222–223
    microforms, 221–222
    overview, 12
    sound recordings and videocassettes, 222
    use of, 221–223
Note-taking, 315–316

Office of Law Revision Counsel (U.S.), 58
Online legal research. *See* E-research
oral / verbal, 343–344
Ordinance Law Annotations, 183
"Orphans," 411
overrule / reverse, 344

PACER, 220
Pacific Reporter, 70, 80
Page numbers, 411
Parallel citations
    Blue and White books, 82–83
    cross-references, 82
    finding, 82–83
    National Reporter Blue Book, 82–83
    National Reporter System, 73
    state digests, 83
Paraphrasing in legal memoranda, 381
Passive voice, 347, 403
People v. Briceno (Cal. 2004), 284
Periodicals, legal, 127–133
    bar association, 128
    citation form, 151, 262–263, 267
    indexes, 130–131
    law school publications, 127–128
    location of articles in, 130–133
    newsletters, 130
    newspapers, 130
    overview, 127
    specialty, 128, 130
    types of, 127
Permanent Court of Arbitration, 181–182
Personal pronouns, 331
Plain English movement, 341
Plessy v. Ferguson (1896), 12, 287
Plurality opinions, 68
Pocket parts
    American Law Reports, 109
    state statutes, 53
    United States Code Annotated, 44, 47
    *United States Code Service Lawyers
        Edition*, 44, 47
Popular name approach, 49, 51, 54
Postwriting activities, 401–412
    common errors, spotting, 412
    document design and length, 409–410
    final revision, 411
    headings, structure and labeling of,
        410–411
    legalese, eliminating, 403
    lists, use of, 411
    margins, 410
    page numbering, 411
    paper, choice of, 408

passive voice, 403
    proofreader's marks, 406–407
    proofreading, 403–407
    quotations, use of, 411
    reviewing and revising, 401–403
    typeface, selecting, 408–409
    type size, selecting, 409
    unnecessary words, elimination of, 403
    websites, 412
Precedents, legal. *See Stare decisis*
Prepositional phrases, 329
President
    *Daily Compilation of Presidential
        Documents*, 167
    executive orders, 8, 10, 166–167
    judicial appointments, 29
    proclamations, 166
    signing of bills by, 40
    vetoes and veto overrides, 40
Primary authorities. *See specific
    publications*
principal / principle, 344
Prior history, 259
Pronouns, 331–332
    gender-linked, 332
    personal, 331
    relative, 331–332
Proofreading, 403–407
    computer spell checking programs,
        dangers of, 405
    projects by others, 406
    proofreader's marks, 406–407
ProQuest Congressional, 160, 165
Protection clauses, 369
Public law numbers, 159–160
Public Library of Law, 232
Publishing of law books, 10–11
Punctuation, 333–336
    apostrophes, 334–336
    citation form, 269–270
    commas, 334
    hyphens, 336
    overview, 333
    quotation marks, 336

Quotations, 270–271
    alterations of, 271
    ellipses, use of, 271
    in legal memoranda, 381
    length of, 411
    omitted citations, indicating, 271
    pinpoint citation, 270
    quotation marks, 336

Readability, 346–349
    active versus passive voice, 347, 403
    jargon, avoiding, 348–349
    legal memoranda, 378–379
    lists, use of, 347–348
    nominalizations, avoiding, 348
    proximity of subject and verb, 349
Redundancy, avoiding, 350–351
Reed Elsevier, Inc., 11
Regulations. *See* Administrative law and
    regulations

Relative pronouns, 331–332
Repetition, 350–351
Reports of Judgments, Advisory Opinions and Orders, 182
Research process. *See* Legal research process
Research strategies. *See also specific types of materials*
    checklist, 314
    descriptive word approach, 49, 54, 98, 109, 123, 136
    locating state statutes, 54–55
    popular name approach, 49, 51, 54
    table of cases approach, 100, 123, 136
    table of statutes approach, 123, 136
    topic approach, 49, 54, 98, 100, 123, 136
Restatement (Third) of Foreign Relations Law of United States, 178
Restatements, 137–138
    arrangement of, 137–138
    chart of, 137
    citation form, 151, 263, 268
    overview, 137
    purpose of, 137
    research strategies, 138
    sample page, 139
Roman law, civil law tradition based on, 8
Rules of procedure and court rules
    citation form, 58, 261, 266
    failure to follow, 32
    Federal Rules of Civil Procedure (FRCP), 55–56
    Federal Rules of Court, 56
    interpretation of, 55
    legal briefs, 394
    overview, 55–56
    states, 56
Run-on sentences, 329

Scout, 165
Search engines, 242
Secondary authorities
    chart of, 147–150, 313–314
    legal research process and, 313–314
    overview, 10
    starting research projects with, 119
    summary of, 146–150
Session laws, 53
Shepardizing, 283–291. *See also* KeyCite
    abbreviations, 284
    administrative law and regulations, 290
    constitutions, 290
    court rules, 291
    Daily Update Service, 291
    defined, 283
    features, 293–294
    headnotes, references to, 287
    history references, 286
    KeyCiting compared, 298–299
    later case references, arrangement of, 286–287
    with Lexis, 204
    with Lexis Advance, 207

    miscellaneous citators, 299
    negative letters, analysis of, 288–290
    online, 291–294
    references, location of, 284
    regulations, 294
    Restatement provisions, 291
    sample page, 285
    Signal Indicators, 292
    sources other than cases, references to, 287–288
    statutes, 290, 294
    steps in, 288
    treaties, 291
    treatment references, 286
    websites, 301
Shepard's Citations, 10, 83, 290, 300, 314
Shepard's Code of Federal Regulations Citations, 290
Shepard's Federal Statutes Citations, 181, 290
Shepard's Link, 294
Shepard's Pacific Reporter Citations, 284
Slip form, 41, 70
Slip laws, 41
Slip opinions, U.S. Supreme Court, 74
Smith v. Lewis (1975), 4
Sound recordings, 222
Sources of law
    administrative rules and regulations, 8, 10
    case law, 6–7
    common law, 6–7
    constitutions, 7
    executive branch of federal government, 8
    statutes, 7
Spelling, 332–333
    commonly misspelled words, 333
    computer programs for checking, 333, 354, 405
    errors, 251, 333
    tips to better, 332–333
Split infinitives, 330
Standing, 22
Stare decisis
    changes in our legal system and, 13–14
    definition, 7
    judicial hierarchy and, 13–14
    purpose of, 7
    rejection of by lower courts, 13–14
Star paging, 76–78
State cases
    citation form, 16, 35, 90, 265
    publication of, 70–74
State court systems. *See also* Rules of procedure and court rules
    appeals to U.S. Supreme Court from, 30
    appellate courts, 33–34
    citation form, 35
    highest courts, 34
    judges or justices, 34
    jurisdiction, 33
    organization of, 33–34
    structure of, 33–34
    websites, 35

StateNet, 162, 165
State statutes, 53–55
  annotations, 53
  citation form, 58, 261, 266
  codification, 53–549
  conversion tables, 54
  enactment of, 53
  historical notes, 54
  indexes, 53
  KeyCiting, 297
  legislative history. *See* Legislative
      history
  Lexis search for, 202
  locating, 54–55
  numbering systems of state codes, 54
  pocket parts, 53
  publication of, 53–54
  research techniques, 54–55
  sample page, 54
  session laws, 53
  Shepardizing, 290, 294
  websites, 58
  Westlaw search for, 212
Statutes. *See also* Federal statutes; State
      statutes
  best websites for locating, 237
  citation form, 58, 260–261, 266, 274
  definition, 7
  legal research process, 312
  research overview, 57
  session laws, 53
  as sources of law, 10, 72
  state, 53–55
String citing, 254
Subject-verb agreement, 327–329
  achievement, 327
  collective nouns, 328
  intervening words, 329
  multiple word subjects, 328
  prepositional phrases, 329
Subsequent history, 259
Superscripts, use of, 260
Supra, use of in legal citation, 51, 273
Supreme Court, U.S., 28–32
  appeals to, 30
  case load of, 28
  certification, 30
  certiorari, writ of, 30–31
  citation form, 259
  jurisdiction, 29–30
  Justices. *See* Supreme Court Justices
  legal briefs, 394–395
  opinions, 30
  oral arguments before, 30
  publication of opinions of, 68, 74
  rules of, 32
  terms of, 29
  traditions, 32
  websites, 35
Supreme Court Justices
  appointments of, 29
  Chief Justice, 28–29
  "conference handshake," 32

  number of, 28
  salaries of, 28
  special and emergency matters of
      Circuit Courts, 29
  terms of, 29
Supreme Court Reporter, 74, 76, 80
Supreme Court Reports, Lawyer's Edition,
      76, 79
Supreme courts
  state, 34
  U.S. *See* Supreme Court, U.S.

Tax Adviser, 128
Taxation
  United States Tax Court, 32
  websites, 241
Text messaging, 354–355
Texts. *See* Treatises
Thesauri, legal, 140–141
Thesis statements, 377–378, 389
THOMAS database, 41, 161, 165, 238
Thomson Corporation, 11
Thomson Reuters, 11
T.I.A.S. (*Treaties and Other International
      Acts Series*), 179
Title approach, 49, 54
Topic approach, 49, 54, 98, 100, 123, 136
Total Client-Service Library, 123–124
Tracking bills, 165–166
*Tracking Current Federal Legislation
      and Regulations: A Guide to Basic
      Sources* (Davis), 158
Treaties, 179–181
  citation form, 151
  determining current status of, 180–181
  interpreting, 181
  overview, 8
  post-ratification sources, 179
  pre-ratification sources, 179
*Treaties and Other International Acts
      Series* (T.I.A.S.), 179
Treatises, 134–136. *See also* Looseleaf
      services
  as casefinders, 134
  citation form, 263, 267
  features of, 136
  overview, 134
  research strategies for, 136
  sample page, 135
Trial court briefs, 390–394
  adversary's brief, responding to, 393
  argument, 392
  captions, 391
  certificate of service, 393
  conclusions, 393
  elements of, 391–394
  exhibits, 393
  introductory statement, 391
  orders, 393
  overview, 390–391
  rules for, 394
  signatures and dates, 393
  statement of facts, 391–392

Twitter, 243
Typeface, 254–255, 408–409
Type size, 409

Ultrafiche, 221–222
Umbrella statement, 377
Uniform Commercial Code, 145
Uniform Law Annotated, 145
Uniform laws, 144–145
   citation form, 151, 263, 268
   Lexis, 145
   Model Acts compared, 145
   overview, 144–145
   research strategies, 144–145
   state adoption of, 56–57, 144–145
   websites, 152
   Westlaw, 145
Uniform Laws Annotated, 145
   Directory of Acts, 145
Uniform Partnership Act, 56
United Nations, 182
United Nations Treaty Series (*U.N.T.S.*),
   179
United States Code (U.S.C.), 41–43
   annotated versions. *See United States*
      Code Annotated; *United States*
      Code Service Lawyers Edition
   Constitution in, 51
   official code, 43
   titles of, 42
   use of, 48
United States Code Annotated (U.S.C.A.),
   43–48
   arrangement of, 44
   Constitution in, 51
   cross references, 44
   features of, 44
   historical and statutory notes, 44
   indexes, 44, 50
   library references, 44
   notes of decisions, 44
   pocket parts, 44, 47
   Popular Name Table, 51, 52
   sample pages, 45–46, 52
   supplements, 44, 47
   updating statutory research, 47–48
   U.S.C.S. compared, 47–48
   use of, 48
United States Code Congressional and
   Administrative News Service
   (USCCAN), 41, 159
United States Code Service Lawyers
   Edition (U.S.C.S.), 43–48
   arrangement of, 44
   Constitution in, 51
   cross references, 44
   historical and statutory notes, 44
   indexes, 44
   interpretive notes and decisions, 44
   library references, 44
   pocket parts, 44, 47
   Popular Name Table, 51
   research guides, 47–48

supplements, 47
treaties, judicial decisions interpreting,
   181
updating statutory research, 47–48
U.S.C.A. compared, 47–48
use of, 48
United States Court of Appeals for
   Veterans Claims, 32
United States Court of Federal Claims, 32
United States Court of International
   Trade, 32
United States Courts of Appeals. *See*
   Courts of Appeals, United States
United States Government Depository
   Library, 41
United States Law Week, 74
United States Reports, 31, 68, 74, 76–78
United States Statutes at Large, 41–43
   arrangement of, 41–43
   deficiencies of, 41
   indexes, 41
   legislative histories, 159
   state statutes, 53
United States Supreme Court. *See*
   Supreme Court, U.S.
United States Supreme Court Digest, 102
United States Supreme Court Reports,
   Lawyers' Edition, 74
United States Tax Court, 32
United States Treaties and Other
   International Agreements (U.S.T.),
   179
University Law Review Project, 133
University of Chicago Manual of Legal
   Citation, 252
Unpublished opinions, 62–63
U.N.T.S. (*United Nations Treaty Series*),
   179
Updating and validating research,
   283–301
   electronic, 291–300
   with KeyCite, 295–297
   as legal duty, 300
   Shepardizing, 283–291
   summary, 300
   websites, 301
U.S.C.A. *See United States Code*
   Annotated
USCCAN (*United States Code*
   Congressional and Administrative
   News Service), 41, 159
U.S.C.S. *See United States Code Service*
   Lawyers Edition
U.S.C.S. Advance, 47
U.S.T. (*United States Treaties and Other*
   International Agreements), 179

Vague words, 344
Validating research. *See* Updating and
   validating research
VersusLaw, 220
Veterans Appeals Reporter, 78

Veterans Claims, United States Court of
    Appeals for, 32
Vetoes, presidential, 40
Videocassettes, 222

Washburn University School of Law, 232
Websites. *See also* Internet
   ALWD Citation Manual, 278
   American Law Reports, 113
   attorney and ethics, 239
   attorneys general opinions, 152
   best for E-research, 237–243
   Bluebook, 278
   case law, 237
   case law and judicial opinions, 91
   citation form, 278
   corporate, business, and securities,
      239–240
   dictionaries, 152
   digests, 113
   directories, 152
   executive materials, 186
   federal court system, 35
   federal statutes, 58
   forms, 152, 238
   government materials, 238
   intellectual property, 240
   international, 240
   international materials, 186
   jury instructions, 152
   KeyCiting, 301
   legal briefs, 397
   legal memoranda, 384
   legal research and writing, 231–234,
      240
   legal research process, 16–17, 322
   legal writing, 337, 355, 412
   legislative materials, 186
   letterwriting, 370
   Lexis, 223
   municipal research, 186
   non-legal sites, 241
   reference materials, 241
   research process, 322
   research validation, 301
   Shepardizing, 301
   specialty sites, 238–241
   specific resources. *See* Websites
   state court systems, 35
   state statutes, 58
   statutes, 237
   strategies for using, 234–235
   taxes, 241
   treaties, 186
   uniform laws, 152
   U.S. Supreme Court, 35
   Westlaw, 223
WestCheck, 298
Westlaw, 207–218. *See also* KeyCite;
     Westlaw Classic; WestlawNext
   administrative and legislative
     materials, search for, 212–213
   Affiliated Services, 214
   Boolean searching, 195, 209–210

case law, search for, 212
citation form, 223, 277
Clipping Services, 214
constructing search, 209–211
contact information, 194
Database, Search for, 208
Database Wizard, 210–211, 214
Directory, 208
federal statutes, 41
Field Searching, 214
Find by Citation, 208
getting started, 207–208
Graphical Display of Direct History of
   Cases, 214
Graphical Display of Timelines for
   Statutes, 214
Graphical History, 85
Graphical Statutes, 162
hyperlinking, 214
interactive tutorials, 218
Keyciting, 208, 213
Key Numbers, 214
law reviews and journals, search for,
   213
legislative history, 160, 165
Lexis compared, 223
Live Help, 214
new developments in, 218
pending legislation, tracking, 165
periodical articles online, 133
plain English searching, 197, 210
search results, display of, 211
secondary authorities, search for, 213
statutes and constitutions, search for,
   212
Sticky Notes, 215
terms and connectors, 195–197
treaties, 180
Uniform Laws on, 145
websites, 223
WestClip, 165
when to use, 218–219
Westlaw Classic
   directory search screen, 208
   quick review of, 217
   resources screen, 208
   results screen, 211
   sample search screen, 210
WestlawNext
   citation assistance, 269
   home page screen, 216
   KeyCiting, 217
   note-taking in, 315
   overview, 215–217
West Publishing, 11. *See also* Westlaw
West's digests. *See American Digest*
     System
West's *National Reporter System. See*
     National Reporter System
"Widows," 411
Williston on Contracts, 4th, 134
Wolters Kluwer, 11
Wolters Kluwer Bouvier Law Dictionary,
   141

Women's Rights Law Reporter, 130
Word choice, 342–344
Word connotation, 345
Word order, 346
Word processing
    spell checkers, 333, 354, 405
    track changes feature, 352

Words and Phrases, 140
World Court (International Court of
    Justice), 182
Writing. *See* Legal writing;
    Letterwriting

Zotero, 316